£6.95

FRANCE

1814–1940

J. P. T. BURY

METHUEN
LONDON AND NEW YORK

First published in 1949 by
Methuen & Co. Ltd
11 New Fetter Lane, London EC4P 4EE
Second edition 1950
Third edition 1954
Fourth edition 1969
Reprinted with revisions 1976
Fifth edition 1985
Published in the USA by
Methuen & Co.
in association with Methuen, Inc.
733 Third Avenue, New York, NY 10017
© 1969, 1976, 1985 J. P. T. Bury
Typeset in Great Britain by
Scarborough Typesetting Services
and printed by
Richard Clay (The Chaucer Press),
Bungay, Suffolk

British Library Cataloguing in Publication Data

Bury, J. P. T.
France 1814–1940.—5th ed.
1. France—History—19th century
2. France—History—20th century
I. Title
944   DC251

ISBN 0–416–37930–3

Library of Congress Cataloging in Publication Data

Bury, J. P. T. (John Patrick Tuer), 1908–
France, 1814–1940.
Bibliography: p. Includes index.
1. France—History—1789–1900
2. France—History—Third Republic, 1870–1940
I. Title
DC251.B8   1985   944   84–18937

ISBN 0–416–37930–3 (pbk.)

Foreword

This book has no pretensions to originality. It is merely an endeavour to furnish the general reader, and anyone else who may be interested, with a straightforward and continuous survey of the vicissitudes of French history between 1814 and 1940. My excuse for such a work, apart from the courteous invitation of the publishers, must be that, although the period is wholly or partly covered in more general histories of France, there are, I believe, few books easily available in English which are entirely devoted to these momentous years. Furthermore, this century and a quarter of French history has a certain unity: it begins and ends with catastrophe and invasion and it is largely dominated by the working out of two great Revolutions, the political one of 1789 and the vast and still uncompleted process of economic change which goes by the name of the Industrial Revolution. Unhappily for France both of these revolutions brought schism in their train and so the tale is mainly one of a society divided against itself. Yet that society was also one which never ceased to be brilliantly creative in many spheres of human activity beside the purely political and economic. It is my regret that within the space allotted I have not found it possible to do more than hint at the splendour of some of these achievements. For such 'old-fashioned' neglect and for my numerous other sins of omission I take full responsibility.

My debt to many historians of France, some of them English and still more of them French, will be obvious to those who know their works and is to some extent laid bare in the bibliographies and footnotes which I have added in the hope that they may be useful. To them I express my admiration, and to Mr P. E. Charvet, Mr J. P. C. Roach, and the various members of my family who have been so helpful alike with encouragement and criticism my deepest gratitude.

I ought also to express my gratitude to the late Dr Philip Spencer for helping many years ago to improve my references to French literature and to Professor Geoffrey Warner for assisting me to recast the account of the demonstrations of 6 February 1934.

J.P.T.B.

November 1948

Note to fifth edition

Several excellent books have appeared since the last reprint. I have amended the booklists to take account of some of those which are not too specialized. I have also made a number of mainly minor changes in the text, especially on pp.11–12, 15, 18–20, 39, 41–2, 46–8, 62, 64, 71–5, 77, 83, 114, 132, 152, 161–2, 176, 202, 209–14, 221–4, 226, 229, 239, 252, 278. Such changes have been limited by unavoidable constraints of economy and space.

Contents

Belgium, Italy, and the Eastern Question – Algeria – Conservatism of the regime – Growing criticism – Economic crisis – Setbacks in foreign policy – Agitation for extension of the franchise – The Revolution of February 1848 – Material and intellectual achievements during the reign.

Hopes and fears after the February Revolution – The Provisional Republican Government and its reforms – Election of a Constituent Assembly by universal suffrage – The right to work – The June Days – The new Constitution – Election of Louis Napoleon as President of the Republic – Foreign policy – The Loi Falloux – Conflict between the Prince–President and the Legislative Assembly – *Coup d'état* of December 1851.

Louis Napoleon the saviour of society – Authoritarian character of the new regime – Early prosperity and prestige of the Second Empire – Napoleon's character – The Crimean War – The Italian Question – The turning point of 1860: commercial treaties and Liberal reforms – Napoleon and the German question – Overseas ventures – The Mexican expedition – The Parliamentary Empire – Strength and weakness of the regime in 1870 – Outbreak of the Franco-Prussian War – Sedan and the Revolution of September 4 – Economic importance of the reign – Cultural developments.

The Government of National Defence – The siege of Paris and the Delegation at Tours – Gambetta and the war in the provinces – Fall of Paris – Significance of France's resistance – Election of a National Assembly – the Treaty of Frankfurt – The Commune, its origin, repression and consequences.

Changed situation of France in Europe – Reconstruction – Prospects of a restoration of monarchy – M. Thiers – The reign of 'Moral Order' – MacMahon's term of office prolonged – The 'Constitution of 1875' – The constitutional crisis of 1877.

The Republicans' triumph – Their consolidation of victory – Ferry's education laws and the relations of Church and State – The two Frances – Gambetta – Colonial expansion and the fall of Ferry.

Economic and social discontent – Defects of the parliamentary Republic – Boulangism and its consequences – The Ralliement – The Franco-Russian alliance – The Panama Scandal and its effects – The Dreyfus Affair and its significance.

Contents

Maps

General bibliography

(This is a list of books which refer either to the whole period or to periods covered by several chapters. I have also added short lists of books at the end of each chapter; these may sometimes include titles already in this general bibliography.)

Ageron, C. R., *Histoire de L'Algérie contemporaine* (1830–1966), Paris, 1966.

Anderson, R. D., *France 1870–1914*, London, 1977.

Bouju, Paul *et al.*, *Atlas historique de la France contemporaine, 1800–1965*, Paris, 1966.

Brogan, D. W., *The Development of Modern France (1870–1939)*, London, 1967.

Cahen, L. and Mathiez, A., *Les lois françaises de 1815 à 1914*, 4th edn, Paris, 1933.

Cameron, Rondo E., *France and the Economic Development of Europe, 1800–1914*, Princeton, 1961.

Campbell, P. W., *French Electoral Systems and Elections since 1789*, 2nd edn, London, 1965.

Caron, F., *An Economic History of Modern France*, London, 1979.

Charlton, D. G. (ed.), *France: A Companion to French Studies*, 2nd edn, London, 1979.

Charvet, P. E., *A Literary History of France*, vols 4 and 5, London, 1967.

Chevallier, J.-J., *Histoire des institutions et des régimes politiques de la France moderne (1789–1958)*, Paris, 1967.

Clapham, J. H., *The Economic Development of France and Germany, 1815–1914*, 4th edn, Cambridge, 1968.

Cobban, A., *A History of Modern France*, vol. 2, London, 1965.

Collins, Irene, *The Government and the Newspaper Press in France, 1814–1881*, London, 1959.

Dansette, A., *Histoire religieuse de la France contemporaine*, Paris, 1948–51, English trans. Freiburg, 1961.

Duguit, I. and Monnier, H., *Les constitutions et les principales lois politiques de la France depuis 1789*, 7th edn, Paris, 1952.

Dupeux, G., *La société française 1789–1960*, 6th edn, Paris, 1972, English trans. London, 1976.

Girard, Louis, *La garde nationale 1814–1871*, Paris, 1964.

Girardet, R., *La société militaire dans la France contemporaine (1815-1939),* Paris, 1953.

Girardet, R., *Le Nationalisme français 1871-1914,* Paris, 1966.

Goguel, Francois, *La politique des partis sous la Troisième République, 1871-1939,* Paris, 1958.

Halévy, D., *Trois épreuves, 1814, 1871, 1940,* Paris, 1942.

Kindleberger, Charles P., *Economic Growth in France and Britain, 1851-1950,* Cambridge, Mass., 1964.

La Gorce, P. M. de, *The French Army: a Military-Political History,* London, 1963.

Lefranc, G., *Le mouvement socialiste sous la Troisième République,* Paris, 1963.

Lefranc, G., *Les gauches en France 1789-1972,* Paris, 1973.

Lhomme, Jean, *La grande bourgeoisie au pouvoir (1830-1880),* Paris, 1960.

Loubère, Leo, A., *Radicalism in Mediterranean France: its Rise and Decline 1848-1914,* Albany, 1974.

Lough, J. and M., *An Introduction to Nineteenth-Century France,* London, 1978.

McManners, J., *Church and State in France 1870-1914,* London, 1972.

Mayeur, J. M. and Rebérioux, M., *The Third Republic from its Origins to the Great War, 1871-1914,* Cambridge, 1984.

Muret, Charlotte T., *French Royalist Doctrines since the Revolution,* New York, 1933.

O'Brien, P. and Keyder, C., *Economic Growth in Britain and France 1780-1914,* London, 1978.

Prost, A., *L'enseignement en France 1800-1967,* Paris, 1968.

Rémond, R., *La vie politique en France 1789-1879,* Paris, 1965-9.

Rémond, R., *La droite en France de la première restauration à la Ve République,* vol. 1, 1815-1940, 3rd edn, Paris, 1968, English trans. Philadelphia, 1969.

Schuman, F. L., *War and Diplomacy in the French Republic,* New York and London, 1931.

Soltau, Roger, *French Political Thought in the Nineteenth Century,* London, 1931.

Thibaudet, Albert, *Les idées politiques de la France,* Paris, 1932.

Thomson, D., *France: Empire and Republic, 1850-1940: Historical Documents,* New York, 1968.

Thomson, D., *Democracy in France,* 5th edn, London, 1969.

Weber, E., *Peasants into Frenchmen: the Modernization of Rural France, 1870-1914,* London, 1977.

Weill, Georges, *Histoire du parti républicain en France de 1814 à 1870,* Paris, 1928.

Weill, Georges, *Histoire de l'idée laique en France au XIXe siècle,* Paris, 1929.

Wright, Gordon, *France in Modern Times, 1760 to the Present,* London, 1962.

Wright, Gordon, *Rural Revolution in France: the Peasantry in the Twentieth Century,* Stanford, 1964.

Yacono, X., *Histoire de la colonisation française,* Paris, 1969.

Zeldin, T., *France 1848-1945,* Oxford, 1973-7.

1

The First Restoration and the Hundred Days

On 6 April 1814 Napoleon I, Emperor of the French, abdicated at Fontainebleau. Europe rejoiced: men believed that the 'Universal Tyrant' was finally overthrown, and even France thought gladly of relief from the burden of an increasingly onerous administration and hoped for peace at last. For the best part of twenty years France of the Revolution and the Empire had been almost incessantly at war and now by 1814, after the débâcle of the Grande Armée in Russia and the costly campaigns of 1813, she was weary, a 'mutilated and exhausted nation', poorer for the loss of some two million men, eager for peace, for the restoration of some degree of liberty and for the end of conscription, but uncertain where to look for such blessings.

The imminence of peace after nearly a quarter of a century of European upheaval brought its own tremendous problems. For the Allied leaders the main task was to re-establish a harmonious European order, and not the least of the necessary conditions of such an order was the settlement of the government and frontiers of France in such a way as to ensure that she should not again disturb or endanger peace. Already on 30 March Paris had capitulated to the Allied armies and on the following day the Tsar of Russia and the King of Prussia had entered the city. Already a provisional government had assumed authority under the leadership of the most versatile of French statesmen, the wily Talleyrand, who combined a nimble sense of his own advantage with a penetrating awareness of his country's interests and an unrivalled ability as a diplomat. The Allies had already discussed the future government of France; a Republic with its revolutionary associations was out of the question, Great Britain had opposed the establishment of any Bonaparte dynasty and there had been no unanimous agreement about the suggested expedient of calling Bernadotte, most astute of Napoleon's marshals, or the Duke of Orléans, rich and radical scion of the old royal family, to the throne. Accordingly, by the Convention of Châtillon of February, they had agreed that the 'French nation' should itself determine its future government. This was a striking recognition of the new principle of popular sovereignty, but in the first days of April the French nation was for all practical interests and purposes Talleyrand; and Talleyrand it was who persuaded a doubtful Tsar and a French Senate composed of Napoleon's nominees that there could be no more satisfactory guarantee of order and good government for France than the restoration of the hereditary Bourbon monarchy in the person of Louis XVI's next surviving brother, Louis Stanislas Xavier, Count of Provence. On 16 April, the day of Napoleon's abdication, Louis was proclaimed King of France with the style of Louis XVIII, which he had assumed in 1795 on the death of his young nephew, the unhappy Dauphin best known to history as the 'Prisoner of the Temple', whom he regarded as the rightful Louis XVII although he had never reigned.

Thirty-six years later, when the future government of France was once again in doubt, Thiers, one of the leading statesmen of the day, made a famous remark that the Republic was the regime which divided French-men least. In 1814 it could be hoped that the return of the Bourbons would be not only the solution which all the Allies could accept, even if they did so without enthusiasm, but also the solution which would win the widest acceptance in France itself. During these first months after Napoleon's fall French affairs were settled with a decision and rapidity which the twentieth century might well envy. On 1 May 1814, peace was signed between France and the Allies with the first Treaty of Paris; on the 3rd, Louis XVIII entered his capital and on 14 June he endowed his people with a Constitutional Charter. Peace, the restoration of the dynasty, and its apparent reconciliation with the ideas of 1789, these momentous events had all taken place within three months. The peace, harsh though it might seem to those who aspired after 'natural' frontiers, was not ungenerous. France retained her borders of 1789 as well as the former enclaves of Avignon and Montbéliard, part of Savoy and some eastern frontier towns of great strategic importance. Except for part of San Domingo, restored to Spain, and St Lucia, Tobago, and Mauritius, which went to Great Britain, she kept her colonies. There was no war indemnity, no continued Allied occupation of French territory. As Talleyrand later said: 'The Treaties of 1814 were as happy as circumstances would allow, for the enemy left the country at the end of six months. The old France was enlarged, her borders rectified to her advantage.'[1] The return of the King had been welcomed by many, and none, not even the Republicans, had attempted to oppose it. The Charter was a guarantee that his Restoration would not mean a purely reactionary return to the Ancien Régime as it had existed before 1789, an assurance that the most cherished gains of the last twenty-five years would not be swept away by a stroke of the pen. Equality before the law; *la carrière ouverte aux talents*; a general system of taxation according to means; freedom from arbitrary persecution and arrest; freedom of worship; freedom to publish and print opinions 'in conformity with the laws which may repress abuses of this liberty'; inviolability of property, including the so-called 'national' property, which had been confiscated by the Revolutionary Government from the Church and *émigré* aristocrats and then sold by the State to new and often peasant proprietors – all these new benefits were preserved by the Charter which has been described as 'the most liberal instrument of government that existed anywhere on the continent.'[2] Nor was this all. It guaranteed the public debt, abolished one of the most onerous of Napoleon's measures, conscription, and attempted to provide a solution for the problem of political liberty which Napoleon had contemptuously ignored. The Charter marked the triumph of one of the Liberal theories of 1789 and of the partisans of a constitutional settlement which, outwardly at least, resembled the English model: Louis XVIII returned as a constitutional king with a parliament of two houses like that of Great Britain. This parliament itself, moreover, emphasized the continuity of new and old, for the members of the old Legislative Body of Napoleon's day became the new Chamber of Deputies, which was, like the English House of Commons, to be subject to election on the basis of property qualification, while the new upper house or Chamber of Peers, made hereditary in 1815, was largely recruited from the old Imperial Senate.

A rapid and lenient peace, followed by the reassertion of France's influence among the Great Powers of Europe through the diplomacy of Talleyrand at the European Congress of Vienna, the restoration of the ancient dynasty, and its reconciliation with the ideas of 1789 formally proclaimed in a Constitutional Charter – here were solid achievements which might well seem to augur well for the future of France. On paper, the provisions of the Charter might seem admirably devised to conciliate all classes of Frenchmen and to enable the Bourbons to strengthen and enlarge the unity which Napoleon had done something to recreate. On paper, there might seem to be no obstacle to the King's wish that all Frenchmen should live as brothers: but unfortunately for France this harmonious pattern of paper schemes was far removed from the sharp cleavages of reality. In less than ten months from the proclamation of the Charter, the restored Bourbon regime which came as the harbinger of peace and unity had toppled like a house of cards. On 1 March 1815 Napoleon escaped from the island of Elba, to which he had been relegated, and landed with a handful of supporters on the French Riviera near Antibes. Within three weeks the former Emperor of the French was in Paris, the King of France a refugee in Ghent. It was not the people of France, but the armies of the European Allies who ensured that Napoleon's second reign should last but a hundred days. It was not the people of France, but the 'baggage wagons' of these armies that brought Louis XVIII back once more from exile and enabled him to resume his throne.

This dramatic interlude in Louis' reign, this episode of the 'Hundred Days', was a calamity both for the Bourbons and for France. It deepened the cleavages that already existed among Frenchmen. It brought war in its train and retribution from the Allies, whose new terms of peace were much more severe.

In fact, the task with which the Restoration Government had been faced in 1814 was singularly difficult. 'If you knew them,' the Tsar had said of the Bourbons before their return, 'you would be convinced that the burden of a crown is not for men such as they.'[3] The collapse of 1815 might seem to many to justify that statement and yet, as we shall see, it would be hard to maintain it as a final verdict. Louis XVIII and some of his immediate advisers suffered from the initial disadvantage of having lived for the best part of twenty-five years in exile. They had had no part or lot in the glorious achievements of the Revolution and the Empire. They had lived obscurely in foreign lands, unknown to or ignored by the great majority of their fellow countrymen, brooding on their wrongs, hating much of the remarkable work accomplished by the French people, because it had been wrought under the guidance of usurping powers. And so it was that, when they returned to their own country, these men who had so long been out of touch with France were virtual strangers to the people they came to rule. They were the heirs of the 'forty Kings who in a thousand years had created France', and yet, said Chateaubriand: 'When I described the royal family to my countrymen, it was as though I had enumerated the children of the Emperor of China.'[4] This strangeness need not have been and was not an insuperable handicap – the English put up fairly easily with Dutch William and Hanoverian George I, who were not merely un-familiar, but foreigners, speaking a foreign tongue – nevertheless it was a disadvantage. Louis XVIII, a dignified, witty, courteous, cynical, and somewhat indolent widower of fifty-nine, ponderously stout, prematurely aged, and so gouty that he was often obliged to move about in a wheeled chair, was not a person to inspire immediate and enthusiastic devotion in subjects who set eyes on him for the first time and were not already converts to or devotees of the cause of legitimate monarchy. He had neither the personal magnetism nor the military glory of the predecessor whose reign he affected to ignore. He had not waged war, but it was his Government which inherited the legacies of a quarter of a century of upheaval followed by a shattering military defeat: and, though peace had been welcomed for its own sake, there had been many to criticize the terms of the treaty, lenient though it was. The genuine Royalists were far from being a majority among Frenchmen. The Bourbons were reimposed by Talleyrand and the Allies *faute de mieux* and were accepted by most Frenchmen with indifference or resignation rather than enthusiasm.

Such indifference was only too likely to turn into censure from one of the most politically critical and acrimonious of peoples unless there was some positive reason for their conversion to loyal admiration of the new sovereign and his Government. No such reason presented itself. On the contrary, the problems of demobilization were bound to create an army of discontented – the disbanded soldiery, the returned prisoners, the civil service that had administered a French Empire extending over half the Continent, could not all expect to find immediate and lucrative employment. 'For each office there were two claimants, for each grade two holders, for each field two proprietors.'[5] Moreover, in spite of the guarantees of the Charter, there were many who soon began to fear that the change of regime would affect them for the worse. With the King there returned a number of *émigrés*, who in a well-known phrase could be truly said to have forgotten nothing and to have learnt nothing; they had shared the King's misfortunes, proved their loyalty to the dynasty, and heedless of the changes of twenty-five years hoped to be rewarded by the restoration of their former lands, rights and privileges. The presence of such men embarrassed a monarch who was tolerant at heart and did not wish to seem ungrateful, but it did little to reassure the numerous classes of persons whose stake in the country largely depended upon the maintenance of the Revolution settlement. The fact that the King had preferred to grant the Charter as a favour bestowed by his prerogative power instead of accepting it from the representatives of the nation, and that the document itself contained certain ambiguities or omissions, also gave rise to criticism or suspicion. Moreover, the natural tension, the exaggerated hopes and fears attendant upon a complete change of regime in dramatic circumstances were aggravated by certain ill-advised acts of Louis XVIII and his counsellors. There were ceremonial acts which jarred: acts of policy which caused alarm. The King's declaration that after God he owed his throne to the English Prince Regent was scarcely gratifying to the proud French people – nor were Parisians pleased when one of his first acts was to review the Allied troops of occupation or when his niece entered the regicide city clad in deepest mourning. His first Government lacked both coherence and authority and the King himself failed to give it a unity of direction: his chief confidant, the Comte de Blacas, was ill-fitted to advise the King at such a time, and the tactless talk and conduct of many returned *émigrés* caused alarm. The substitution of the white flag of the Bourbons for the tricolour of the armies which had conquered Europe, and the restoration of many of the symbols and much of the etiquette of the Ancien Régime acted as irritants. A bill to restore certain national property to *émigrés* passed in December 1814, the reduction of the tariff barriers with the ending of the Continental Blockade, the reimposition of the censorship, and the maintenance, despite princely promises of abolition, of the financially essential but very unpopular *droits réunis* or indirect tax on alcohol and tobacco, all gave grounds for discontent.

In fact, the circumstances under which Louis XVIII succeeded to his heritage were such as to require all the political wisdom and tact of an Henri IV. Henri IV, for whose memory there was indeed something of a Royalist cult in the first years of the Restoration, had largely succeeded in reconciling the factions which had been so bitterly opposed during the sixteenth-century Wars of Religion; but the stiff, ageing and indolent Louis XVIII, however sensible and sincere his intentions, was not the man to exercise the charm and energetic leadership necessary to bridge the gulf between friends and foes of the Revolution. Nevertheless, in spite of the prevalence of much discontent, there was no conspiracy to overthrow the Government and there is no reason to suppose that Louis would have had to flee to Ghent but for his failure to retain the loyalty of the army. Here, too, he had a singularly difficult situation to meet. The army he inherited was one discouraged by defeat, humiliated by the peace treaty, irritated at the disbandment of some 200,000 men and the retirement of 13,000 officers on half pay, concessions essential both to humour the Allies and meet the exigencies of the national economy. To these men the displacement of the tricolour was a provocation, as was the creation of a large military household and the appointment of several officers from among Royalists who had seen no service with Napoleon's army. Small wonder, then, that, once Napoleon by sheer personality had won over the first troops sent to oppose him after his landing, what had seemed a mad adventure became a triumphal progress, and the army returned to the loyalty to which it had been accustomed, loyalty to the man who had led it across Europe, whose courage and commands were still irresistible.

Napoleon's return thus showed how insecure were the foundations of this restored monarchy. In his brief second reign he did his best to undermine what credit it had had, to play upon its suspected reactionary intentions and to pose as a champion of Liberal enlightenment against Bourbon obscurantism. He induced the Liberal Benjamin Constant, till lately one of his bitterest opponents, to frame a new Constitution, he ordered democratic institutions to be set up and had them confirmed by plebiscite. Thereby he paved the way for the Napoleonic legend and for that alliance of Bonapartists and Liberals which was to be so important during the next forty years. Thereby, too, he deliberately added fuel to the flames of 'that old quarrel which the Empire had smothered and the Charter was designed to extinguish, the quarrel of the old and the new France, of the "emigration" and the "revolution".'[6]

Yet all these acts betrayed a sense of insecurity which hung heavily upon the country during these fateful days. The Emperor had won the army, but the people as a whole were too weary to rally with enthusiasm. Inevitably Napoleon's reappearance was a defiance of Europe which meant war and brought invasion upon France for the second time within eighteen months. The Allies, who had been at loggerheads at Vienna over the terms of the general European settlement, hastily composed their differences and prepared to deal with the offender. Napoleon, well aware of their intentions, took the initiative, marched into Belgium and met his fate at Waterloo on 18 June. The Hundred Days had, however, reopened the whole French question. During his second exile, Louis XVIII continued to hold court and council and to act as King of France, but there were many Allied statesmen and French politicians who played with the idea of providing some other ruler for France. Louis, however, had a firm supporter in the Duke of Wellington, and was induced by him to co-operate with Talleyrand and with Napoleon's notorious Police Minister, Fouché, who held the keys to power in Paris. With the help of these three and by acting promptly, he forestalled any serious attempt by the Allies to undo the arrangements of 1814. On 28 June he re-entered France and on 8 July he was back in a capital which was once again occupied by Allied troops. His welcome was cool, but he had anticipated any attempt to supplant him and possession of the throne was nine-tenths of a reign.

The Allies accepted the *fait accompli*, but this time they imposed sterner measures to secure the Continent against any French disturbance of the peace. In 1814 they had taken the line that they were warring against Napoleon rather than against the French people. Now they considered that the French people had been Napoleon's accomplices in his new aggression and that they must be punished accordingly. From the end of June until September two-thirds of France were occupied by more than a million Allied troops, and when a new peace treaty, the second Treaty of Paris of 20 November 1815, was concluded it was much more severe than the first.[7] At Vienna Talleyrand had made one mistake in opposing the transfer of the King of Saxony to the Rhineland and allowing Prussia to expand there instead. Now, in spite of the personal remonstrances of Louis, France was obliged to surrender to Prussia and Austria the fortresses of Sarrelouis and Landau and to give up Philippeville and Marienbourg. She had to destroy the fortifications of Huningue near the Swiss border and to restore the Department of Mont Blanc to the Kingdom of Sardinia; and in addition to these losses of territory she was obliged to pay an indemnity of 700 million francs within five years, to submit to the occupation of her eastern departments for a period of from three to five years by 150,000 Allied troops, and to return the works of art removed by Napoleon from other countries.[8] Moreover, the Ambassadors of Great Britain, Russia, Austria and Prussia were to meet regularly in Paris as a kind of Control Commission, watching the conduct of the French Government and admonishing it when necessary, and one of them, the Russian representative, Pozzo di Borgo, came in fact to exercise a remarkable influence on French politics for many years to come.[9] Thus, as a result of Napoleon's escapades, the Government of Louis XVIII was placed under a species of tutelage, and for a second time within a few months of their return to power the Bourbons were obliged to conclude an inglorious peace. The circumstances of the Restoration of 1815 were thus by no means propitious for the stability of the regime, and the events of a hundred days had rendered a difficult task doubly difficult. Before, however, we proceed to consider how the Bourbon monarchy fared in the years after Waterloo it will be well to take a brief glance at the country and people under its sway.

Notes

1 Cit. Pallain, G., *Ambassade de Talleyrand à Londres, 1830–1834*, p. iii, n.1. See Map 2.
2 Artz, Frederick B., *France under the Bourbon Restoration*, p. 41. For the text see Appendix 3.
3 Cit. Woodward, E. L., *Three Studies in European Conservatism*, p. 121.
4 *Mémoires d'outre-tombe*, vol. 3, p. 340.
5 Marion, M., *Histoire financière de la France depuis 1715*, vol. 4, p. 376.
6 Guizot: cit. Woodward, op. cit., p. 120.
7 Forty-six departments were entirely and fifteen partly occupied. Ponteil, F., *La Chute de Napoléon I et la crise française de 1814–15*, pp. 286–7.
8 See Map 2, pp. 123–4.
9 Temperley, H. W. V., *The Foreign Policy of Canning, 1822–7*, pp. 61–2.

Bibliography

Bastid, P., *Les institutions politiques de la monarchie parlementaire française (1814–48)*, Paris, 1954.
Bertier de Sauvigny, G. de, *La Restauration*, 2nd edn, Paris, 1963, English trans., Philadelphia, 1966, *Au soir de la monarchie: la Restauration*, revised with amended title 1974.

Beugnot, *Mémoires du Comte 1779–1815*, ed. Comte Albert Beugnot, 2 vols,
  Paris, 1866.
Chateaubriand, *Mémoires d'outre-tombe*, vol. 2, ed. M. Levaillant, Paris, 1948.
Cooper, Duff, *Talleyrand*, London, 1932.
Firmin-Didot, G., *Royauté ou Empire, La France en 1814 d'après les rapports
  inédits du Comte Anglès*, Paris, n.d.
Guedalla, P., *The Hundred Days*, London, 1934.
Houssaye, Henry, *1814*, 64th edn, Paris, 1911.
Lacour-Gayet, G., *Talleyrand*, Paris, 1928–34.
Nicolson, Harold, *The Congress of Vienna, A Study in Allied Unity, 1812–22*,
  London, 1946.
Ponteil, Félix, *La chute de Napoléon Ier et la crise française de 1814–15*, Paris,
  1943.
Thiry, J., *La première abdication de Napoléon Ier*, Paris, 1945–8.
Vitrolles, *Mémoires et relations politiques du Baron de*, Paris, 1884.
Webster, C. K., *The Congress of Vienna, 1814–15*, London, 1963.

2

France in 1815

In 1789 Mirabeau had described France as 'an agglomeration of disunited peoples',[1] observing different customs, subjected to differing laws, using different weights and measures, separated from one another by customs barriers, obedient to local rather than national loyalties. Within a few years the Revolution had swept away many cobwebs and the strong hand of Napoleon had seized upon the central institutions of the country and had reinforced, remoulded, and where necessary supplemented them, with the result that France had emerged as the pattern of a nation state, endowed with a highly centralized administration, subject to uniform laws, using common weights and measures, divided equally into departments centrally administered, her people enrolled in a national army and her élite drilled in a national system of education. Three-quarters of a century after Napoleon's fall an English historian could write that 'the Civil Code, the Penal Code, the Conseil d'État, the Judicial System, the Fiscal System – in fact every institution which a law-abiding Frenchman respects from the Legion of Honour to the Bank of France and the Comédie Française was either formed or reorganized by Napoleon.'[2] Thus when the Bourbons came into power in 1814 they found already in being an efficient civil service; they had ready to hand a working machine of government which immensely facilitated their task of retrenchment and reconstruction. Parts of it might require to be adjusted but in spite of much talk of the need for decentralization neither they nor their successors were ever anxious to weaken so efficient an instrument of social control.

Yet the France of 1815, in spite of its centralized administration was still rich in the diversity of its racial types, its dialects and its customs. Provinces might cease to be administrative units, but they still retained, and retain to this day, their own traditions and strongly marked characteristics. The Alsatian was notably different from the Breton who was as different again from the man of the Midi. Moreover, France, now reduced once more to bounds not widely different from those of 1789, comprised a land still singularly blessed in the rich variety of its soil and climate. 'We have iron, forests and harvests,' wrote Chateaubriand with pride, 'our sun ripens the vines in every region; the coasts of the Mediterranean give us oil and silk and the shores of the Ocean nurture our flocks. Marseilles . . . attracts the commerce of the old world, while our ports on the other sea receive the wealth of the new.' Some districts had indeed been ravaged by the campaigns of 1814 and 1815, the development of industry had been retarded during the war by lack of coal and labour, and France lagged well behind England as an industrial power. None the less, she had suffered less from fighting and economic disruption than most of the countries she had overrun. The balance of trade remained steadily in her favour from 1815–21. Rich in agricultural production, proud of her ancient civilization, she seemed a veritable Land of Cockayne to the soldiers of the Prussian army of occupation and they talked of living 'like God in France'. With some 29,000,000 inhabitants she was the most populous state in Europe apart from Russia. She was still regarded as the centre of European culture and her language was still the language of diplomacy and of polite society, the most common currency for the exchange of thought between the educated people of many lands. Her capital city of well over 600,000 inhabitants was surpassed in size only by London. With its splendid public buildings, many of them erected by Napoleon – some such as the Bourse, the Arc de Triomphe and the Church of the Madeleine still unfinished when he fell – its public gardens, theatres, restaurants and cafés, it ranked as the finest and most animated city in Europe. Socially and artistically it was the most brilliant. Chateaubriand was the glory of French letters, Talma the master of the stage; the paintings of David and his school still won widespread admiration.

In this France the main classes of society were still as they had been under the Ancien Régime, nobles, clergy, bourgeoisie of varying degree, and finally the great mass of peasants, workers, artisans, domestics and others who were collectively known as 'the people'; but their conditions had greatly altered. The nobility had lost their ancient privileges and retained only their pretensions. Their numbers had been reduced by the toll of revolution and war and those who had emigrated had lost their estates. The greatest families, whose fortunes had been most closely identified with the old order, had naturally suffered most from the trials of the last twenty-five years. Beside them there still survived a numerous lesser nobility or *noblesse de province*, who lived on their estates, came seldom to Paris and retained considerable influence, social and political, especially in the west, which was long to remain a stronghold of royalism. In spite, however, of their general impoverishment, many of the older nobility clung to the notion that the exercise of any professions save those of arms and diplomacy was beneath their dignity. Others had, however, rallied to the Empire and served it ably in prefectorial and other posts. The older nobility were often politically and socially out of touch, easy game for a popular poet, Béranger, to criticize in his famous song, the 'Marquis de Carabas'; yet even here there were notable exceptions. For instance at Broglie it was the son of the late Seigneur 'who introduced new ideas and democratic tendencies which astonished and sometimes even scandalized his former vassals'.[3] Nevertheless, their misfortunes during the past quarter of a century had had a sobering effect on the nobility as a whole. No longer tempted to flirt with Voltairean and radical ideas, the majority turned their backs on free-thinking and freemasonry and resumed that practice of the Roman Catholic religion which has ever since been a mark of the French aristocracy. Thus, along with their political belief in the Bourbon monarchy, went a renewed belief in the importance of the Church and of religion as a necessary check upon the evil doctrines of revolutionary free-thinkers and as a necessary safeguard of stability in state and society. In general, then, this nobility of 1815 was imbued with a greater seriousness than its forebears of 1789. As Chateaubriand noted:

> In high society morals are purer and domestic virtues more common.
> . . . We are less frivolous, more simple and natural. . . . Our young
> people, brought up in camps or in solitude have something forceful and
> original in them which they did not possess before. Vast interests have
> preoccupied us; the whole world has passed before us. It is one thing to
> fight for one's life and to see thrones set up and overthrown and another
> to be concerned with nothing more than a court intrigue, a stroll in the
> Bois de Boulogne and a literary novelty.[4]

Men, he claimed, were fuller men than they had been thirty or forty years before.

The clergy had suffered still more than the nobility. Not only had the Revolution deprived them of their wealth; it had also decimated their ranks and disrupted their organization, and in 1815 there were far too few to enable each parish to have its own priest. The numbers of the Bishops had been reduced by more than half and they no longer enjoyed the princely status which had been theirs under the old dispensation. Roman Catholicism was no longer the sole religion recognized by the State, for although the vast majority of the French people were, at least nominally, Roman Catholics, Jews and Protestants[5] were now officially recognized. The Concordat of 1801 by which Napoleon and the Pope had determined the relations of Church and State in France, and the Organic Articles subsequently issued by Napoleon,[6] subjected the Church to a degree of State control as strict as any that had been imposed by the Ancien Régime, and in their endeavours to resist this control the clergy tended to look more and more beyond the Alps to the Pope as the defender of their cause. So already there was beginning that ultramontane movement among French Catholics which was to be so important in the history of the French Church during the nineteenth century and which was to appeal to Bishops and ordinary clergy alike. Within his diocese, however, the Bishop now, as the result of the Concordat, had a more absolute control over his clergy. These were for the most part recruited from the peasantry and little better educated than their flocks, so poor too, that their poverty was more than once to be a subject of sympathetic reference in the Chamber even by speakers who were ordinarily anti-clerical in their outlook. In order to supplement the meagre stipend of 1000 or 1500 francs a year allowed them by the State they depended on Church offerings, gifts from parishioners and grants in aid from their commune or parish. None the less this peasant priesthood, like the priesthood in Ireland today, still retained a great hold over the faithful in many country districts, especially in the west and in the more remote and mountainous regions.

It was the bourgeoisie who had been the chief gainers from the Revolution. They had led the Third Estate to victory and were now on the way to complete political ascendancy. Their social aspirations were no longer blocked by the privileges of the aristocracy and the higher clergy. It was they who had been the largest purchasers of the lands confiscated by the Revolution and who were most suspicious of any Bourbon design to undo the land settlement. Many of those who had thus stepped into the shoes of the nobility and clergy were now content to live on the revenues of these estates, thus forming a new class of landed gentry. Such men, successful in some profession or in government service, were more numerous than the industrialists who derived their wealth from factories, and who were mainly to be found in the great cities and among the iron masters of Lorraine and the textile manufacturers of the north and east. In general the liberal professions, especially medicine and the law, were those in which they aspired to place their sons, while they sought to provide their daughters with dowries sufficient to enable them to marry into their own class. To religion they were often indifferent and sometimes actively hostile, but scepticism or anti-clericalism did not necessarily mean that the influence of religious thought and practice was excluded from their homes, since, for lack of any suitable alternative, their daughters were usually educated in convent schools. More than ever prosperous and politically powerful (in fact under the franchise of the Restoration monarchy the wealthiest of them constituted a new privileged class) the bourgeoisie nevertheless in general lived simply and travelled little. Their outlook was limited. Townsmen, they despised the peasantry as ignorant, wild and wretched. When such amenities as seaside resorts, watering places and English sports and games, except for horse-racing and whist, were virtually unknown, their main distractions were those of the dining-table. Thus they helped to maintain the reputation, won for France in the seventeenth century, as the land where the art of good cooking and the growing of fine wines is unsurpassed. The France of the Restoration was the France of Carême, the celebrated master of Talleyrand's kitchens, and the former magistrate, Brillat-Savarin, whose *Physiologie du Goût*, published in 1825, became the classic of epicurean taste.

The rest of the people, *les gens du peuple*, comprised the artisans, industrial workers, small shopkeepers, petty employees and, last but not least, the peasantry, who accounted for more than 75 per cent of the population and were the main source of recruitment for the army and navy, for domestic servants and, as we have seen, for the lower clergy. All those who tilled the soil were loosely termed 'peasants', but they differed considerably in their relationship to the land. While many owned the land they cultivated, it often happened that their own plot was too poor or too barren or too embarrassed by mortgages to meet their needs, and so there was still a considerable though dwindling class of tenant farmers and *métayers* – these last cultivating the land with means provided by its proprietor and sharing the produce with him. Many were thus dependent on large landowners, and the laws of inheritance which imposed further subdivision of the land served only to increase their dependence. Moreover, in some parts of the country, especially in Burgundy and Normandy, there was still a high proportion of landless labourers. The Revolution had altered the legal status of the peasantry and relieved them of onerous burdens in the way of feudal dues, but it had not affected their methods of cultivation or led to any striking improvement in their material lot. Even after 1850 a great French mediaevalist, Delisle, could write that 'a thirteenth century peasant would visit many of our farms today without much astonishment.'[7] In diet, clothes and housing the French peasant of 1815 was no doubt generally worse off than the British agricultural labourer. The British labourer's diet 'was often meagre enough, but nowhere did he live for six months every year' exclusively on potatoes and chestnuts 'like some poor peasants of the . . . Tarn. Nor did he go either barefoot or in sabots', and 'Only in the Western Highlands could any houses be found so bad as the houses in Nogent-sur-Seine.'[8] It was only gradually, in certain districts, that the French peasant was accustoming himself to grow the new crops of sugar beet, turnips and potatoes which were to make a valuable addition to a diet in which meat was still for the most part a luxury. Only on the large farms in the north and east was he beginning to make some use of artificial manures, to learn how to enrich the soil by changing crops and how to improve his stock by cross-breeding. Around the compact villages of the more level lands he still ploughed vast open fields and used the traditional three-course rotation; elsewhere he still tilled the soil according to the age-long dictates of tradition, geology and climate, using the hoe, long-shafted spade and short scythe. For the most part, he and his fellows lacked the knowledge and the capital to make improvements. Communications in districts away from the few main roads were still very poor; prices therefore varied much from region to region, and the peasant depended wholly upon the local market. Thus in a bad year there was still, as under the Ancien Régime, serious risk of local famine and riots: in 1816–17 the Government was obliged to import corn from overseas and to spend large sums in order to relieve distress caused by the shortage of bread and consequent high prices.

Distress and state aid for the needy were also conditions only too well known in the towns of France. In Paris over 100,000 people, or one-sixth of the population of the city, were in receipt of poor relief, either at home or in hospitals and institutions. Artisans and small shopkeepers were mainly concerned to supply the needs of their local clientèle and were often little better off or better educated than the peasantry, working long hours in cramped conditions. The lot of the industrial worker in a big factory was still harder. France was still essentially a country of small industries: compared with Great Britain the workers in large-scale industry were a small class and industry a backward growth – apart from Paris there were only two towns, Lyons and Marseilles, with over 100,000 inhabitants and only five with between 50 and 100,000, namely Bordeaux, Rouen, Nantes, Lille and Toulouse. Nevertheless industrial development, such as it was, raised the same sort of problems as in Great Britain. The introduction of machinery led to riots like the Luddite disturbances in England, and the growth of urban manufactures accelerated the decline of rural industries, particularly of textiles. Towns became overcrowded, workshops were unhygienic, women and children were employed for long hours to the detriment of their health. The English Combination Laws had their counterpart in the Revolutionary and Napoleonic legislation maintained by the Bourbons, which forbade the workers to strike or combine in their own interests and imposed a strict police control over them by means of a system of passports and *livrets* or work-books.[9] The only kind of workers' unions which were tolerated were mutual aid or benefit societies.

Thus the industrial workers had no effective means of improving their lot, and, while the administrative supervision of industry was often marked by a kindly paternalism, the general attitude of the Government was one of *laissez-faire*. The individual worker was left to make his own arrangements with his employer. While the old traditions of *compagnonnage* still survived in certain industries, all attempts to reintroduce the guilds of the Ancien Régime which had been abolished by the Revolution, were unavailing. The interests of the bourgeoisie were much better served by the combination of industrial freedom and police control instituted by Revolutionary and Napoleonic legislation and they had nothing to gain from a return to the restrictive practices of the guilds. The freedom they sought was, however, by no means the freedom of general free trade. One of the main concerns of the industrialists was to be shielded from foreign competition and in this they were at one with the landed proprietors, who feared the import of cheaper foreign corn. Thus the needs of the French people were to a large extent supplied by the French themselves and France continued to be a highly protectionist country throughout the first half of the nineteenth century.

In this France of 1815, as in all other countries of the time, the benefits of secondary education were naturally accessible only to an élite, and even for them it was often a summary matter.[10] Greek and Latin and Mathematics were the staple subjects taught in the secondary schools, whether they were colleges (or Lycées as they had been known under the Empire) or *petits séminaires*[11] which, designed primarily for the education of priests, took many pupils who eventually adopted a lay career. University education was, as in this country, virtually confined to those who were destined either to be gentlemen of leisure or to enter one of the 'liberal' professions. Elementary education was rudimentary and in 1821 there were still as many as 25,000 communes which lacked any sort of school. In the absence of any compulsory system of schooling the unscrupulous industrialist was tempted to exploit child labour. Thus the majority of the people were illiterate and the sight of a messenger or errand-boy reading might still be a phenomenon to a returned *émigré* – '*Voyez! voyez, ce coquin qui lit!*'[12]

The general picture is one of a relatively rich and populous country endowed with an efficient administration and proud of its military and cultural traditions. The vast majority of the subjects of Louis XVIII are a thrifty and hard-working, but poor and illiterate peasantry. 'We are a tranquil people,' said Laboulaye many years later, 'with agitated legislators,' and this saying is profoundly true of France throughout the nineteenth century. The great mass of the French people was indifferent to the constitutional struggles and the contests of political doctrinaires. The questions they asked were: How can I secure a living wage? Will this mean increased taxation or affect the price of corn? Does this mean conscription or a longer term of service in the army for my son? When the grant of universal suffrage gives the whole adult male population a vote, we shall see that time and time again that vote is cast in favour of order and tranquillity.

Notes

1 Cit. Champion, E., *La France d'après les cahiers de 1789*, p. 44.
2 Bodley, J. E. C., *France*, p. 89.
3 *Mémoires du Duc de Broglie*, vol. 1, p. 11.
4 Cit. Halévy, D., *Trois épreuves*, pp. 19–20.
5 It has been estimated that there were at this time in France about 680,000 Protestants and 60,000 Jews. Artz, Frederick B., *France under the Bourbon Restoration*, p. 103.
6 For the text of the Concordat and the Organic Articles see Appendix 1 and 2 in Bodley, op. cit.
7 Artz, op. cit., p. 174.
8 Clapham, J. H., *Economic History of Modern Britain*, vol. 1, p. 317.
9 The worker was to present this book to his employer upon being engaged. In it the employer kept a record of the worker's conduct.
10 'In 1813 the Empire had thirty-six *lycées*, with 14,492 pupils . . .; in the private schools – if private they can be called, when their teachers had to be members of the University, their studies and discipline to admit University inspection, and their students to pay the University tax – there were 30,000 pupils.' Arnold, Matthew, *A French Eton, and Schools and Universities in France*, pp. 248–9.
11 A law of October 1814 permitted one of these *séminaires* to be set up in each department.
12 Siboutie, Dr Poumiès de la, *Souvenirs d'un médecin de Paris*, p. 153.

Bibliography

Clapham, J. H., *The Economic Development of France and Germany, 1815–1914*, Cambridge, 1921.
Sée, H., *La vie économique de la France sous la monarchie censitaire, 1815–48*, Paris, 1927.
Seignobos, Charles, *Histoire sincère de la nation française*, Paris, 1937, English trans. New York, 1974.

3

The Second Restoration

Before his return to Paris in July 1815, Louis XVIII had been induced to get rid of Blacas and on the day after his return he formed a Ministry headed by Talleyrand, who had represented France so brilliantly at the Congress of Vienna, and in which the regicide Fouché, Duke of Otranto, emerged once again as Minister of Police. Chateaubriand recorded his horror at the 'infernal spectacle' of 'Vice leaning on Crime', when he caught sight of Talleyrand and Fouché 'silently' making their way to the King's study.[1] Fouché had indeed worked his passage and Talleyrand had done all he could to extol his own services to the State; but for the loyal Royalists a Ministry with such men in Bourbon France after the Hundred Days was a shocking combination and one which was certain not to survive once all the adroitness of the Minister of Police had failed to secure a moderate Chamber out of the elections of August.

The elections of August 1815 immediately illustrated the damage wrought by the Hundred Days. The Charter had laid down that the deputies should be elected by electoral colleges; that their numbers should be unchanged and that they should sit for five years, a fifth being renewed annually. After his return from Ghent Louis had, however, been induced to issue an ordinance lowering the age of eligibility from forty to twenty-five and increasing the number of deputies to 402. The electorate, however, was still a plutocracy of some 72,000 to 88,000 people, for only Frenchmen of twenty-one or more who paid at least 300 francs a year in direct taxation had the right to vote. Of these, moreover, fearful or apathetic, a third abstained, while the rest, indignant or burning to be revenged, reacted violently against the dislocation and eventual humiliation caused by Napoleon's last wild fling. The electoral colleges in which the electors assembled were often presided over by fanatical Royalists and the result was to bring into being what Louis XVIII dubbed '*La Chambre introuvable*', a comparatively big and youthful assembly which contained a large majority, by no means all aristocrats or *émigrés*, of ardent or 'Ultra'

Royalists – most of whom were new to politics.[2] Now for the first time for many years the forces of the Revolution and Counter-Revolution openly faced one another. With such a Chamber it was impossible for the King to keep his Ministers. The regicides were proscribed, the peers who had rallied to Napoleon were excluded from the upper house, and Fouché had to accept dismissal not only from office but from France. It was his last appearance on the French political stage, and he was speedily followed into retirement by Talleyrand who had lost his diplomatic usefulness by incurring the enmity of the Tsar. Talleyrand, however, was compensated with the office of Grand Chamberlain and his salon soon became a rallying point for opposition and the birthplace of half the witticisms against the Court and the Ministry of the day. Fifteen years later this extraordinary man was again to play an important part in serving yet another regime.

The fall of Fouché and the resignation of Talleyrand meant the disappearance of the noted men of former regimes who had made the Restoration but were not of it. To pass from the men of the Empire to the men of the Bourbons, was, said Chateaubriand, to pass from a stage of giants to one peopled by pigmies.[3] This was, however, a harsh judgement. The new Ministry chosen by Louis XVIII contained several men of considerable ability who rendered notable services. The Duc de Richelieu, who headed it, did not merely look 'the very personification of nobility',[4] but was remarkable among *émigré* Royalists for having taken service in Russia, where he had become Governor of Odessa and proved himself a notable administrator.[5] Now that peace had again to be negotiated his personal friendship with the Tsar Alexander was likely to be an important asset; the Comte Decazes, of bourgeois origin but a special favourite of the King, who wrote to him daily and called him *mon fils*, was a subtle politician; and Corvetto, a disciple of Baron Louis who insisted that a State which wanted to enjoy credit must pay for everything, did good work in re-establishing French finances. Moreover, all these men were moderate in outlook. It was a factor of great importance not only that the King was not obliged to take his Ministers from the majority in the Chamber, but that even when that majority was Ultra-Royalist, he preferred not to do so. Louis XVIII, for all his shortcomings, was sincerely loyal to the Charter, sincerely anxious to put an end to the dissensions of Frenchmen, firmly determined to steer a middle course and not to be forced to go on his travels again.

The *Chambre Introuvable* was not slow to demand punishment for those who had connived at Napoleon's return and courted his favour, and when Great Britain and Prussia made representations the Government, who wished to be lenient, were under pressure at home and abroad. The passions roused by the Hundred Days inevitably led to a provisional suspension of some of the liberties granted by the Charter. From the general amnesty eighteen prominent men were excepted, including the famous Marshal Ney and the young Comte de Labédoyère, men whose desertion to the Emperor had largely contributed to the success of his venture in March. Since their action had brought upon their country much additional suffering and loss of life it might well be thought that they, if any, were worthy to die; but a milder sentence or a royal reprieve would have been more politic, for their execution[6] at once furnished martyrs to the enemies of the regime. As it was, their deaths helped to slake a thirst for revenge which was also exhibited by the re-establishment of special or provost courts set up in each department to try rebels and seditious people, and in the condonation of a series of outrages perpetrated in the south by Catholic Royalists against wealthy Protestants, Republicans, and Bonapartists. This wave of 'White Terror' claimed some 200–300 victims in all,[7] not a great number, yet its occurrence and the exultation in it by the more fanatical Royalists showed how dangerously the Hundred Days had exacerbated passions as between Frenchmen and Frenchmen.

The problem which now confronted the rulers of France was one that was virtually new. It was the task of founding a stable constitutional monarchy upon the basis of revolutionary and imperial achievement. The experiment of constitutional monarchy had indeed been essayed in 1789, but conditions had soon become chaotic and the experiment had been short-lived, a tragic failure. This time the legislators of France had preferred to follow the model of Great Britain. France in the months after Napoleon's fall was swept by a wave of Anglomania, of which not the least important effect was the adoption of a constitution on the British model. But, though equipped with a constitutional sovereign and a bicameral legislature in which many of the outward forms of English procedure were faithfully copied, the French operated the system very differently. As has been said, there was no obligation on the King to choose his Ministers from the party which had the majority in the Chamber. Nor indeed did nineteenth-century France ever develop disciplined parties, much less a two-party system. There soon, however, emerged three main groups of strenuous partisans, Ultras, Independents, and Doctrinaires or Constitutionalists, and it was they who fought in the legislative battles which were ever and anon dominated by the question how far the great Revolution was to be accepted or rejected, ever and anon embittered by invocations of The Terror or the Hundred Days. In Society and in the press the words Jacobin and reactionary were bandied about with the same irresponsible licence with which men were to call each other Fascists or Communists in the twentieth century.[8]

The Ultras, who had emerged triumphant from the elections of August 1815, were essentially the party of the *émigrés* and most of their leaders had long lived abroad. They accepted the Charter as an evil, but they hoped temporary, necessity and although they did not scruple to make use of its machinery to serve their own interests, they retained a rooted belief in the divine right of Kings, unfettered by constitutions. They had no intention of trying to resurrect the Ancien Régime with all its anomalies, but they did hope to effect the return of property confiscated by the Revolution, to gain preferments for themselves, to reassert their social superiority, to restore the political influence of the clergy, and to obtain a revision of the Concordat. Their two foremost thinkers, the Vicomte de Bonald and the Savoyard, Comte Joseph de Maistre, 'prophets of the past' as Barbey d'Aurévilly called them, vividly illustrated the Romantic reaction, which had now set in against the rationalist philosophy of the French Revolution, and constantly preached that France's only way to salvation lay through the monarchy and close union with Rome. This 'alliance of Throne and Altar' was indeed a fundamental point of Ultra policy and a theme which was to recur more than once in nineteenth-century French history. Recruited mainly from the clergy, the nobility, and country bourgeois, and representing landed interests to a large degree, the party included men of distinction such as Chateaubriand, the chief literary glory of the day, a man whose pen wielded considerable power but whose views were often unorthodox since his character was essentially egotistical, romantic and *Frondeur*, and Villèle, later for some years to be the chief Minister of Louis XVIII and Charles X; but among the mass of its representatives there were many returned *émigrés* of the type satirized by Béranger, and many whose fanatical hatred of the Revolution and all its works warped their political judgement and blinded them to the real temper of the nation. The ardent Royalists who aimed at a veritable counter-revolution were, as Louis XVIII himself said, more Royalist than the King, and all the more embarrassing to him because their acknowledged leader was no less a person than the King's own brother, the Comte d'Artois, the heir to the throne, and because other members of the royal family such as the Duchesse d'Angoulême and the Duc de Berry[9] gave them open support. As a result of their extravagances the King after his second restoration was soon to be at loggerheads with those who, had they been more moderate, should have been his warmest friends.

Very different, and at first very few in the Chamber, were the Independents. For them the Charter was an indispensable guarantee of essential liberties, and if they disliked it, it was because it had been granted by the King of his royal prerogative instead of emanating from the nation. The will of the nation – that was their guiding principle, for had not the Declaration of the Rights of Man declared that 'the principle of all sovereignty resides essentially in the Nation'? While they were not necessarily hostile to monarchy they had little love for the restored Bourbon regime, which they affected to despise because it had returned in the wake of the enemy, which they disliked because it had done away with the tricolour, and which they suspected because of the influence of the Ultras. They were largely recruited among the urban bourgeoisie who were jealous of the pretensions of the returned nobility, among purchasers of national property who feared that they would be dislodged, and among former soldiers who regretted the glories of the Empire. They included Bonapartists, Liberals[10] who would have preferred to see an Orléans on the throne, a handful of Republicans, and a number of freemasons and anti-clerical admirers of Voltaire. They were the Rationalists as opposed to the Romantics, the Left-wing party of the day. In Lafayette they had their 'flag', in Benjamin Constant and Manuel two brilliant parliamentary orators, in Paul-Louis Courier their pamphleteer, and in Béranger their song-writer. In the press their views were expounded by the *Minerve* and subsequently by the *Mercure* and the *Constitutionnel*.

The third party, the Constitutionalists, who came to embrace or combine with a small group known as the Doctrinaires, was the party of the centre, which tried to preserve a balance and which was most sincerely concerned to secure stability for the regime on the basis of the Charter. Opposed alike to revolution and to reaction, it included several men whose past allegiance was varied but who had an equal desire to make the new order work, men of great intellectual ability and oratorical powers such as Camille Jordan, Royer-Collard and Guizot, the future Minister of Louis Philippe. It was the party with which the King himself was most in sympathy and on which he chiefly relied for the carrying on of his Government during the first five years after his return from Ghent. It was the party on which Richelieu and Decazes depended mainly for support, but, although it had the backing of an influential section of the bourgeoisie, it had no deep roots in the country as a whole.

The fact that the Ultra Chamber of 1815 was confronted by a moderate ministry led to a curious inversion of roles – the Ultras espousing the doctrine of parliamentary sovereignty and the Constitutionalists maintaining that, provided the King did not govern unconstitutionally, he might choose his Ministers as he wished. The apparent liberalism of the Ultras went still further when they advocated the extension of the franchise and a measure of decentralization. These proposals, however, were dictated solely by immediate party interest; their authors calculated that a wider franchise would increase the influence of the lesser nobility and their adherents, and that decentralization would likewise augment the political power of local aristocracies at the expense of the prefects, many of whom were still recruited from former officials of the Empire. Moreover, other demands made by the Ultras, demands for the abolition of the University and the national debt and for the restitution of the national property to the owners from whom it had been confiscated at the time of the Revolution, showed that their true intentions were very far from liberal. While the Ministry did what it could to temper the zeal of the majority in the Chamber it was the Upper House which at first played the main part in frustrating Ultra policy. Strangely enough, the House of Peers was by no means packed with the old aristocracy, and these proposals and the new electoral law voted by the deputies were rejected by a Chamber largely composed of former Imperial officials who had astutely contrived to hold on to rank and fortune. Thus at the outset of the new regime the Second Chamber appeared to justify the bicameral system and fulfilled its role as a block or brake upon ill-considered or excessively partisan legislation. In this way the course of aristocratic reaction, which had incidentally provoked two minor insurrections, was stayed, but the enemies of the Ultras were not content with this victory, and finally, in 1816, the King was induced to intervene. In April he brought the session of the Chamber to a close, and in September he yielded to the pressure put upon him both by his Ministers and by the Allied Conference of Ambassadors, and dissolved a house of representatives embarrassing both for its conservative ardour and its financial irresponsibility. It was hard for him to be as severe as the Constitutionalists could have wished against men who had shown such devotion to the Royalist cause, but at last he acted and the Ultras learnt to their bitter regret that they had presumed too much upon their strength.

The new Chamber which met in November 1816 contained a large majority of Constitutionalists who gave the Richelieu Ministry a support it had never yet enjoyed. The Liberals were still only a small group and the Ultras whose strength was much reduced entered the Opposition. The number of deputies had been once more limited by royal ordinance to 258, as in 1814, and their age limit restored to forty.

Having obtained a majority to their liking, the King and the Government sought to pursue a policy of appeasement and reconciliation and to make one people of the two who, as Louis XVIII was to admit in 1818, still unhappily lived side by side under the same sovereign. Now that the relations between Government and Chamber were more harmonious serious legislation became possible. There were certain important tasks of reconstruction which the Ministries of Richelieu and Decazes carried out with singular success. The finances were overhauled and French credit was re-established owing to the skill of two exceptionally able Ministers, Baron Louis and Count Corvetto. A new system of accounting was adopted and in 1818 for the first time it became obligatory on each Minister to present an annual report for his department. As a result of all this, French finances only three years after Waterloo were sounder than those of any other European state except Great Britain.[11] Furthermore, this re-establishment of credit and the prompt payment of the heavy war indemnity enabled France to be rid of the Allied army of occupation in the shortest possible time. In 1817 Wellington had already consented to reduce it by 30,000 men. By November 1818 the evacuation was complete and Richelieu, content to have accomplished the liberation of the territory, resigned his office. In the meantime an important law was passed which established the basis on which the army was to be recruited for the next fifty years. Since the abolition of conscription by the Charter in 1814 and the disbandment of Napoleon's men after Waterloo, the army had been recruited entirely by voluntary enlistment. This method had produced but a very small force and the Law Gouvion St Cyr of 1818 supplemented it, despite the Charter, by the annual conscription of a levy not exceeding 40,000 men. The conscripts were chosen by lot, but those who wished could escape service by paying a substitute to take their place, and priests and teachers were in any case exempt. The peace-time effective of the army was fixed at 240,000 men and the period of service at six years for the infantry and eight for other arms. As a result, the French army was to become essentially a professional army, recruited mainly from the peasantry, since most of the upper classes who drew 'a bad number' paid for substitutes (curiously enough, the nobility, in spite of their traditional interests in the army do not seem to have attempted to reserve any specific privileges for themselves). The numbers and the periods of service might be altered – in 1820 the complement was increased to 400,000 and the annual levy from 40,000 to 60,000 – but the Law Gouvion St Cyr laid down the basic principle of a small professional army, sedulously cultivating the *esprit militaire*, and regarded by successive Governments as a bulwark against internal disorder as well as against external aggression. The main omission of this and subsequent legislation for many years to come was the provision for an effective trained reserve. The middle-class National Guard was hardly a substitute, yet Governments shied at the prospect of arming the nation in time of peace.

The new Chamber also tackled the question of the electoral regime, which the *Chambre Introuvable* had failed to solve, and legislated for the control of the Press. The Ultras again pressed for a wider franchise, but they were defeated. What, asked Royer-Collard, would be the effect of 'calling upon the multitude' but to 'stir all the depths and to make it drunk with false hopes and promises of proscriptions and spoils?'[12] The laws of 5 February 1817 and 25 March 1818 confirmed the provisions of the Charter which stipulated that the vote should be confined to men over thirty who paid 300 francs in direct taxes and that only men of forty or more who paid 1000 francs should be eligible as deputies. They also continued the arrangement whereby the Chamber was renewed by fifths each year and laid down that, for the first time since 1793, there should be direct election by *scrutin de liste* held in the chief town of the department, the electors meeting as a single electoral college for the purpose. This was a blow to the Ultras who would have preferred *scrutin d'arrondissement* – a system whereby the elector would have cast a single vote at the chief town of his local *arrondissement*,[13] instead of voting for as many deputies as were allotted to the department. *Scrutin d'arrondissement* was always believed to tell more strongly in favour of rural interests and, as we shall see, the conflict between these two rival systems of election continued throughout the greater part of the next hundred years.

The question of the control of the Press was a subject which aroused scarcely less passion than that of the electoral regime and it continued to be regarded as a major problem for many years to come. The Charter had laid down that Frenchmen had the right to publish and print their opinions 'in conformity with the laws which should restrain abuses of this liberty', but the Hundred Days and the conflict with the Ultras had delayed the passage of definite Press laws. In France, however, as in most countries at this time, the political Press was regarded as a potentially dangerous and subversive force which must be kept under strict supervision. Thus Napoleon had maintained it as an arsenal reserved for those who had the confidence of the Government, and the philosopher Maine de Biran could write of 'these papers which can bring life or death'.[14] In fact, although the number of daily papers was extremely small – in 1827 the twelve biggest daily papers had only 56,000 subscribers between them – and although they were expensive and obtainable only by subscribers, within their limited circle of readers they exercised great influence. Moreover, this circle naturally corresponded closely to the privileged electorate, whose views might largely be moulded by the able but often irresponsible journalists of a Press which in France has always tended to place doctrine before news. Hence Governments were bound to be sensitive to the influence of the Press upon the electorate,[15] while the more they betrayed their sensitiveness, the more the power and prestige of the Press were enhanced. The laws of 1819, introduced by de Serre and modelled, like much else at this time, upon English usage, were in fact the most liberal of the Press laws of the Restoration monarchy, but they reflected the prevalent notion that the production and perusal of a newspaper should alike be reserved for men of substance, men who could be presumed to be educated, who were likely to enjoy a vote and who ought also to have a sense of political responsibility. Newspaper proprietors were obliged to pay a deposit which was fixed at such a high figure – 10,000 francs for daily papers in the Parisian area – as to ensure that only men of wealth could afford to start a paper. In addition, the retention of a stamp duty meant that the papers would continue to be expensive to buy. The liberalism of the laws lay in the important provisions abolishing censorship and permitting Press trials to be decided by jury instead of courts of summary jurisdiction.

Meanwhile the balance of forces in the Chamber had been shifting. The annual renewal of the Chamber by fifths meant a partial election each year, and each year saw an accretion in the strength of Bonapartist Liberals, which reflected the growth, even before the Emperor's death, in 1821, of a Napoleonic legend and the influence of men like Béranger. Béranger's songs, satirizing the Royalists and providing the first popular glorification of the armies of the Empire and the Revolution, had indeed a vogue which extended far beyond the electorate, and it was said of him: 'He is more than the poet of the people, he is the people turned poet.' From twenty-five deputies in 1817, the Bonapartists and Liberals rose to forty-five in 1818 and to ninety in 1819, and they included men of note, such as Lafayette, Benjamin Constant and Manuel, or of notoriety, such as the Abbé Grégoire, a former regicide. This rising tide of Liberalism alarmed Richelieu to such an extent that he advocated revision of the electoral law and a rapprochement with the Ultras. As so often happens with Governments or parties of the Centre the moderates tended to be torn in two directions by the opponents on either side of them. So now the result was a split in the Ministry and its resignation in December 1818. The King preferred to continue to steer a middle path and a new Cabinet was formed in which his 'dear son' Decazes still played a leading part, ably assisted by the Comte de Serre; but it met with considerable opposition in the Chamber of Peers, which was overcome only when Louis XVIII increased the number of Peers from 208 to 270, restoring to the Chamber a number of Bonapartists who had been ejected after the Hundred Days. Decazes was subjected to ardent criticism from both Left and Right and the growth of the Liberal representation served only to emphasize the continued existence of the 'two peoples' whom the King would fain merge into one; men who remembered the vicissitudes of the last thirty years now became uneasy and began to doubt the stability of the existing regime, however much they desired it.[16] The King was put under increasing pressure from the Royal Family and the Ultras to change his Ministers, and the assassination on 13 February 1820, by a lunatic, of the Duc de Berry, the Comte d'Artois' second son, together with the outbreak of a series of Liberal risings and revolutions in various parts of Europe in the same year, forced him to give way. For the Ultras and Right-wing Constitutionalists, the assassination was the final proof of Liberal conspiracy to overthrow the regime and the Ministers were denounced for their weakness, if not indeed their direct complicity in the crime. Consequently, as a result of the storm of Royalist indignation on the Duc de Berry's death, Louis XVIII, to his bitter grief, was obliged to get rid of Decazes and his colleagues. Richelieu returned to power, but at the head of a Cabinet in which Ultra influence was strong and which openly proclaimed its intention of making war upon the Liberals.

The Right, which was now to enjoy power for seven years, immediately set about undoing or modifying the work of the previous governments. Control of the Press was at once tightened; the censorship was re-established, new papers were forbidden to appear without Government authorization, and all printed or engraved drawings had similarly to be approved before they could be published, displayed, distributed or sold. These measures taken in 1820 were followed by a law of 1822 which made papers liable to prosecution for their general tendency and once again removed Press cases from trial by jury and handed them back to the royal courts. The electoral law was also promptly modified to suit the party in power. Instead of widening the franchise, the Government substituted *scrutin d'arrondissement* for *scrutin de liste* and introduced a system of double voting. The electors were now to meet in colleges of arrondissements instead of in a single departmental college – this measure gave greater scope for local and official pressure[17] – and, whereas they all elected the 258 deputies, those who were in the class which paid 1000 francs direct tax were empowered to meet again as a departmental college to elect a further 172 representatives. The total number of deputies was thus increased to 430 by a system which gave a double vote to the 16,000 wealthiest citizens. The result of the first elections held under this arrangement in 1820 was entirely satisfactory to those who devised it. The Ultras emerged with a large majority in the new Chamber, the compromise Richelieu ministry gave way to one headed by Villèle, and the triumph of the Right was complete when the posthumous birth of a son to the Duc de Berry assured the continuance of the male succession in the elder branch of the Bourbon family which hitherto had been childless.[18] But the *enfant du miracle*, as the infant Duc de Bordeaux (later known as the Comte de Chambord), was called by ardent and pious Royalists, was destined never to reign. The folly of his grandfather was to deprive him of the throne and his own obstinacy to prevent him from regaining it.

The effect of the severe measures taken by the party in power was naturally to drive some of the elements of opposition underground and to encourage those very conspiracies which the Ultras had feared. Thus a secret society, known as the Charbonnerie and adapted from the Neapolitan Carbonari, was formed with the definite object of overthrowing the

Bourbon dynasty. Its activities were probably not unknown to intellectuals like Victor Cousin and Jouffroy and were connived at by Liberal deputies like Manuel and Lafayette, but its attempts to foment revolution by the insurrectionary outbreaks which occurred in four or five towns during 1822 were quelled without difficulty. The time for a successful rising was not yet, and under the new Government France was in fact free to take the leading part in crushing an insurrectionary regime in Spain. Intermittently, however, secret societies with more or less revolutionary aims were for many years a feature of French political life and objects of governmental fears and repressions.

Meanwhile, as a result largely of Richelieu's able diplomacy, France had escaped from the tutelage which had been imposed on her after Waterloo and was now once again in a position to play an independent part in European politics. In March 1814 the four principal Allies had, by the Treaty of Chaumont, formed a sort of league to guard against further peril from France. Renewed again in Paris in November 1815, it had then provided for periodic meetings for the discussion of matters of common interest and the maintenance of peace. As a result, the conference of Aix-la-Chapelle took place in 1818 for the final settlement of the war damages to be paid by France, and France, having with the aid of the English banking house of Baring acquitted her obligations, was invited to join the Big Four and to sign with them a protocol declaring the intention of the five powers to maintain the peace of Europe on the basis of the existing treaties and to confer again as need be. Accordingly, although the four Allies, still suspicious, secretly renewed the Chaumont Treaty, France was publicly readmitted to the Concert of European Great Powers. With her finances re-established and a new army in the making, she could afford to take an independent line, and once the Ultras gained the ascendancy, French foreign policy, although it never lay in a single directing hand, began to reassume its traditional aspect of hostility to Great Britain both in the New World and the Old. In the New World it showed an ambition to establish spheres of French influence in South America which was disquieting to the British Foreign Secretary, Canning, and which he was able to frustrate. In the Old it intervened so successfully that, when Canning in 1826 described how he had called the New World into being to redress the balance of the Old, he represented his action as a direct riposte to French action in Spain.

In 1820 a military revolt had obliged the Bourbon King of Spain, Ferdinand VII, to re-establish the Spanish constitution of 1812 and to submit to the election of a Cortes or parliament. Such a regime was wholly distasteful to the monarch and, in consequence of disturbances which arose when he was discovered to have been plotting against his Liberal ministers, he was kept more or less a prisoner in his own capital. A party armed itself in his support, but was as unable to win control as the Liberals were to exert their authority effectively over the whole country. In these circumstances, the French Government saw an opportunity of reviving French prestige by means of an easy military and diplomatic triumph, and also of acquiring merit in the eyes of the continental Great Powers, who were increasingly disturbed by the manifestations of unrest in various parts of Europe. At the same time they were not unaffected by what has been and still is a recurring preoccupation of French Governments whatever their political colour, namely the desirability of securing in Spain a regime whose political outlook would accord with their own. So at the Congress of Verona in 1822, Montmorency, now Foreign Minister in the Cabinet headed by Villèle, secured the blessing of the Great Powers other than Great Britain for an expedition to Spain to re-establish the authority of Ferdinand VII. In 1823 a French army, commanded by the Comte d'Artois' elder son, the Duc d'Angoulême, crossed the Pyrenees. The expedition was at first, like so many French military ventures in the nineteenth century, hampered by the inefficient organization of its supplies, but compared with the forces opposed to it it was a model army. Spain had relapsed into a veritable state of anarchy and the Liberal Government, unable to put up any really effective opposition, took the King with them and withdrew to the south-western and remotest corner of the Kingdom, where after the capitulation of the Trocadero fortress at Cadiz, they eventually gave in.

The success of this 'military promenade' through a country which had caused Napoleon so much trouble had the desired effects of enhancing French prestige, consolidating the loyalty of the army and strengthening the Government's position at home. But apart from this the gains were slight; the war was costly and the operations of Ouvrard, the biggest French financier of the day, who had demanded exorbitant terms for his services in compensating for the defects of the army intendance, were much criticized; the Liberals in France were naturally bitterly opposed to this 'crusade' on behalf of a reactionary Bourbon King – indeed some of them even went off to fight under the Spanish tricolour against their own forces, thus setting a precedent for their spiritual descendants 113 years later – and the reactionary King himself showed little gratitude to his liberators. Furthermore, the failure of the French Government to exact any guarantees that the King would be moderate in his conduct, or to prevent him from inaugurating a regime of repression, lost them much of the sympathy they might otherwise have gained at home and abroad.

Meanwhile Villèle exploited the Spanish victory to ensure the perpetu-ation of the power of the Right in the Chamber. In 1823 he obtained a dissolution. Early in 1824 fresh elections, in which civil servants were openly admonished to vote for the Government candidates, resulted in the assembly of a Chamber so reminiscent of the *Chambre Introuvable*, by reason of its large majority of fanatical Ultras, that it was dubbed '*la Chambre retrouvée*'. One of its first measures did away with the system of partial renewals and declared that henceforth the life of the Chamber should last seven years instead of five. This time there would be no Louis XVIII to restrain them from acts of intemperance which ill accorded with the mood of the nation as a whole, for it was evident that for some while past the King's physical powers had been failing and with them his power of independent decision. Since he had been forced to abandon the *via media* of conciliation in 1820 he had fallen increasingly under the influence of the charming Comtesse du Cayla, who sympathized with the Ultras, and he had bowed more and more frequently to the stronger will of his brother, the Comte d'Artois. At length, after much suffering, he died in September 1824. Artois ascended the throne as Charles X and Artois was the chief of the Ultras.

Notes

1 In *Mémoires d'outre-tombe*, vol. 4, p. 25, cit. Woodward, E. L., *Three Studies in European Conservatism*, p. 122.
2 I.e. he had never supposed that a Chamber so Royalist could have been found.
3 *Mémoires d'outre-tombe*, vol. 4, pp. 115–16.
4 Morgan, Lady, *France*, p. 162.
5 Talleyrand's wry comment on his successor's qualifications was: 'He is certainly the Frenchman who is best acquainted with the Crimea.'
6 One, the Comte de la Valette, escaped through the courage of his wife who changed clothes with him in prison.
7 Resnick, Daniel P., *The White Terror*, p. 118.
8 The word Jacobin, which originally denoted the name of a club, became that of the extreme Republican party which set up the dictatorial regime of 1793–4, commonly known as The Terror. In consequence, it was commonly applied by Conservatives in both the New World and the Old to Republican or democratic movements which they disliked.
9 See Appendix 1 for a genealogy of the Bourbons.
10 The term 'Liberal' in Continental politics has a wider application than in this country, where it has come to be associated with a highly organized political party. In general, it refers to those who believe in the Liberal or Girondin theory of parliamentary government developed at the time of the Great Revolution: a theory according to which national sovereignty should be constitutionally exercised through freely elected assemblies.
11 Marion, M., *Histoire financière de la France depuis 1715*, vol. 4, p. 433. For a criticism of some of Baron Louis' measures, see Bertier de Sauvigny, G. de, *La Restauration*, pp. 111–12.
12 Cit. Weil, G. D., *Les élections législatives depuis 1789*, p. 81.

13 The *arrondissement* is a subdivision of the department. It contains a number of cantons which are in turn subdivided into communes.
14 *Journal intime*, vol. 2, p. 11.
15 They were not above helping friendly papers by grants from secret funds.
16 E.g. Biran, Maine de, *Journal intime*, vol. 2, pp. 111 and 138.
17 For interesting details of the forms official pressure took see Frederick B. Artz, *France under the Bourbon Restoration*, pp. 71ff.
18 Neither Louis XVIII nor the Duc d'Angoulême, the Comte d'Artois' elder son, had any children.

Bibliography

Artz, Frederick B., *France under the Bourbon Restoration*, Harvard, 1931.

Bagge, D., *Les ideés politiques en France sous la Restauration*, Paris, 1952.

Beck, Thomas D., *French Legislators 1800–1834: A Study in Quantitative History*, Berkeley, 1974.

Bertier de Sauvigny, G. de, *Le Comte Ferdinand de Bertier (1782–1864) et l'énigme de la Congrégation*, Paris, 1948.

Bertier de Sauvigny, G. de, *La Restauration*, 2nd edn, Paris, 1963, English trans., Philadelphia, 1966, *Au Soir de la monarchie: la Restauration*, revised with amended title 1974.

Bertier de Sauvigny, G. de, *La Révolution de 1830 en France*. Paris, 1970.

Bertier de Sauvigny, G. de, *Nouvelle histoire de Paris: la Restauration 1815–1830*, Paris, 1977.

Charléty, J., *La Restauration* (vol. 4 of Lavisse, E., *Histoire de France contemporaine*), Paris, 1921.

Chateaubriand, *Mémoires d'outre-tombe*, vol. 3, ed. M. Levaillant, Paris, 1948.

Collins, I., *Government and Society in France, 1814–1848*, London, 1970.

Cooper, Duff, *Talleyrand*, London, 1932.

Deniel, R., *Une image de la famille et de la société sous la Restauration (1815–1830)*, Paris, 1965.

Fouques Duparc, J., *Le troisième Richelieu*, 2nd edn, Lyon, 1940.

Fourcassie, J., *Villèle*, Paris, 1954.

Hudson, Nora E., *Ultra-Royalism and the French Restoration*, Cambridge, 1936.

La Gorce, P. de, *La Restauration*, 2 vols, Paris, 1926–33.

Maine de Biran, *Journal intime de, 1792–1824*, ed. A. de Lavalatte-Montbrun, 2 vols, Paris 1927 and 1931.

Mellon, Stanley, *The Political Uses of History: A Study of Historians in the French Restoration*, Stanford, 1958.

Noailles, Marquis de, *Le Comte Molé, 1781–1855, sa vie – ses mémoires*, vols 2–5, Paris, 1922.

Pasquier, *Mémoires du Chancelier*, 4th edn, vols 3–5, Paris, 1894.

Resnick, Daniel P., *The White Terror and the Political Reaction after Waterloo*, Harvard, 1966.

Spitzer, Alan B., *Old Hatreds and Young Hopes: The French Carbonari against the Restoration*, Harvard, 1971.

Vidalenc, J., *La Restauration (1814–1830)*, 2nd edn, Paris, 1968.

Vidalenc, J., *La société française de 1815 à 1848*, Paris, 1970–3.

4

The reign of Charles X

Charles X, a widower like Louis XVIII, tall and active in spite of his sixty-seven years and a great huntsman, like so many Bourbons before him, possessed a charm, elegance and graciousness unknown to his brother. But his political views were far from reassuring in one who was called upon to be a constitutional monarch and to consolidate a dynasty. More passionate, but at the same time more light-hearted than Louis XVIII, he lacked his brother's balance and sound judgement. When he acted like a sensible King, said Guizot, he did so from a sense of propriety, 'from timid and short-sighted complaisance, because he was momentarily carried away, or from the desire to please, and not from conviction or natural choice'.[1] As Comte d'Artois he had been the acknowledged leader of one of the main parties in the State, and that the very party which had the most reactionary views and was most inclined to scoff at the Charter which as King he was now bound to uphold. Moreover, dissolute in his earlier years, the new sovereign was now a devotee much under clerical influence. As an Ultra and a pious son of the Church he therefore fully believed that the Revolution was the work of the Devil and disbelieved as fully in constitutional limitations upon the divine right of Kings. The Duke of Wellington in 1818 might well wish that 'Monsieur would read the histories of our Restoration and subsequent Revolution, or that he would recollect what passed under his own view and probably at his own instigation in the Revolution'[2] – Charles, if he did indulge in such reading or reflections, came only to the conclusion that he would rather chop wood than be a King like the King of England. With such a past and such an outlook it would have been difficult indeed for him to raise himself to be a King above party, even had he so wished.

Nevertheless the circumstances under which the new King ascended the throne were not unfavourable. France was at peace and economically prosperous. The value of foreign trade notably increased during the first year of his rule. The elections had produced their intended results; the new reign began with harmony between the sovereign, the Government and the majority in the Chamber, and the head of the Government, Villèle, though scarcely popular, was widely recognized as a man of great ability. Furthermore, the King began his reign by abolishing the censorship and according a limited amnesty to political prisoners, gestures which made a favourable impression. Thus it might have been expected that under such conditions the Ultras of the *Chambre Retrouvée*, supported by King and Government, would have had little difficulty in imposing the programme which they had failed to carry in 1815; that they would hand over the control of education and the keeping of civil registers to the clergy; that they would indemnify the *émigrés* for their confiscated property; that they would re-establish a territorial aristocracy and amend the provisions of the Civil Code relating to the equal division of inheritance; and that such measures would be accepted quietly, since the ranks of the parliamentary Opposition were so much reduced although the principle of parliamentary government was still maintained.

In fact, however, although the Opposition were weak in the Chamber, they were strong outside it. They won much support in an increasingly youthful population (67 per cent were under forty in 1826) and in an electorate most of whom had by now been under twenty in 1789. Moreover, Villèle had blundered when in 1824, because of Chateaubriand's lukewarm support of a conversion loan, he had persuaded Louis XVIII to dismiss his Minister of Foreign Affairs in summary fashion. Chateaubriand, who 'aspired to all things and complained of all' and who, as Guizot remarked, was much hurt if he were not regarded as the rival of Napoleon as well as of Milton,[3] might be an awkward colleague, but he was still more dangerous as an opponent and the Opposition now gained a powerful ally. In the press the Opposition papers, such as the *Constitutionnel*, in which the young Thiers made his début, and the *Journal des Débats*, which Chateaubriand carried with him into opposition, commanded 40,000 subscribers, whereas the organs which supported the Government could boast no more than a mere 15,000. In such circumstances the Ultra programme was less easy to fulfil; it was bitterly opposed outside Parliament, while within three years the ardent Royalists in Parliament were themselves so divided upon certain of its proposals that Villèle was forced to dissolve a Chamber with which he had hoped to govern for seven years.

This is not to say that the programme was not in part carried out. Control of education was in effect given to the Church when a Bishop, Mgr. Frayssinous, was in 1822 made Grand Master of the University and in 1824 appointed Minister of Education and Ecclesiastical Affairs; and the vexed question of compensation for the *émigrés* who had been dispossessed of their estates was not unfairly settled when in 1825 they were voted an indemnity. This indemnity was often referred to by its opponents as the *émigrés'* 'milliard' but in tangible form it would not appear to have amounted to more than 650 million francs at most. It had, however, been strenuously opposed by many of the bourgeoisie because the money was originally to be provided by the conversion of 5 per cent annuities into 3 per cents. As yet the principle of a conversion loan, subsequently so familiar in government financial operations, was new and strange in France, and the holders of annuities were sore and indignant at losing in such a cause. Other issues, however, aroused still more contention, and above all it was the clerical question which excited passions and caused the ranks of Tuscany to break.

Louis XVIII had been too infirm to undergo the strain of a five hours' coronation service; Napoleon had crowned himself; but one of Charles X's first acts was to be crowned at Rheims with most of the elaborate religious ceremonial of the Ancien Régime. To the critical in a country long unused to such scenes, the ceremony seemed symbolic of a will to restore some of the substance as well as of the forms of pre-revolutionary society. In particular, many men, like the terrible Béranger (who scoffed at the ceremony in his *Coronation of Charles the Simple*), feared that it heralded the revival of clerical influence in matters of state. Those who shared the fear of clericalism included not only deists and free-thinkers, Bonapartists and Liberals, but also Catholics who had come to accept the idea of the neutral lay state as a necessary concomitant of civil equality and Royalists who were full of the old Gallican fire against the pretensions of Rome to direct the clergy. Under Louis XVIII proposals for the restoration of unsold national property to the Church had been rejected for fear of the opposition of the Chambers, and for similar reasons the Government had dropped a suggested new Concordat which it had negotiated and of which the main effect would have been a reversion to the Concordat of 1516. Among the public, however, it was the reappearance of the Jesuits and suspicion of the alleged occult power of the Congregation which did most to revive anti-clericalism. The true Congregation was simply a body of priests and others dedicated to the renewal of religious observances in a country which had partially relapsed into paganism through lack of clergy, and as such it did excellent work. But many of its members belonged also to a remarkable secret society called the Chevaliers de la Foi, which had been founded under the Empire with the object of restoring the monarchy, and which continued to exercise great political influence in Ultra-Royalist circles until its dissolution in 1826. Its secrecy was such that the nature of its organization has but recently been revealed. Its existence, however, gave substance to public distrust, and the attribution of its sinister, because secret, activities to the Congregation or the Jesuits did much to increase the unpopularity of religious orders. Moreover, under the new King a multiplication of religious manifestations (in some of which the King and members of the Royal Family took part), ecclesiastical control of education, the measures taken against critics like Cousin, Béranger, P.-L. Courier and Guizot, who were imprisoned or obliged to suspend their lectures, the persecutions of publishers who reprinted the works of the eighteenth-century Rationalists such as Helvetius and D'Holbach, the suppression of the École Normale or teachers' training school on account of its *mauvais esprit*, and an extraordinary law, passed despite Villèle's opposition, which made sacrilege a crime punishable by death, all increased the fears that 'hidden forces' directed by Rome were gaining control of the State. Fantastic rumours circulated about the aims of the Jesuits[4] and the Congregation, and the King himself was reported to have become a Jesuit.

This issue of clericalism came to a head in 1826 when a Royalist but ardently Gallican noble, the Comte de Montlosier, published a book denouncing the existence of 'a religious and political system tending to the overthrow of religion, society, and the throne' and declared that it was due to four 'scourges' – a number of religious and political congregations which had spread throughout France, various establishments of 'the odious and forbidden society of Jesuits', the more or less open profession of Ultramontanism, and priestly encroachments upon civil authority.[5] Already the Villèle ministry had been under heavy fire from the Left and from the Royalists who followed Chateaubriand and, as we have seen, the figures of the relative circulation of Opposition and Governmental papers – 40,000 compared with 15,000 only – showed how far it was from carrying even educated opinion with it. Now Montlosier's action divided the Royalists still further: several Bishops even went so far as to make a declaration against the Jesuits and the Royal Court debated a new Denunciation of the Jesuits addressed to it by Montlosier and showed its sympathy with his case, although it had no power to prosecute. The anti-clericalism of the Opposition papers increased and there was a veritable spate of pamphlets and brochures – no less than 5000 in 1826 alone – denouncing the influence of the religious orders in general and of the Jesuits in particular. In salons and in clubs, and even in the Académie Française as well as in the press, Villèle and his colleagues were bitterly attacked for countenancing the growth of clerical influence; and their denials carried little conviction when it was they who had had the unwisdom to sponsor the law on sacrilege. Faced by such a virulent campaign, they decided that it could only be checked by more drastic control of the press. Accordingly, a bill was introduced which imposed the obligation to prior deposit (*dépôt préalable*) or a stamp duty on printed matter. This bill, described by its main sponsor as a 'law of reason and love', but condemned by Chateaubriand as a 'law of the Vandals', would virtually have stifled the printing business, and though it was carried in the Chamber it was, to Villèle's extreme vexation, as good as rejected by the Peers. Once again, as in 1815, the members of the Upper House showed that they were prepared to stand out against excessively reactionary measures.

Ironically enough, while Villèle's policy at home was disliked on account of its reactionary vigour his foreign policy was no less criticized on account of its caution. In particular, the cause of Greek independence had won widespread sympathy in France as well as in Great Britain, and Villèle's failure to give the Greeks more active support increased the unpopularity of his Government. In April 1827 an ill-advised attempt of the King to try and rally opinion by a grand review of the Paris National Guard only made tension worse, for some of the Guards shouted for the downfall of the Ministry and the Jesuits, and Villèle unwisely insisted on their dissolution. Finally, the Minister decided that he could retain control only by packing the House of Peers and by securing a still more disciplined Chamber. In November the King issued three ordinances, the first dissolving the Chamber and ordering new elections, the second creating seventy-six new peers – a precedent for an English sovereign four years later – and the third, a conciliatory gesture, abolishing the recently reimposed censorship.

Villèle's confident expectation that official pressure would give the Ultras a fresh majority was grievously disappointed. The forces of the Opposition gained a majority of over sixty, and after an attempt to carry on notwithstanding this check Villèle resigned in January 1828. He was the most unpopular Minister the Restoration monarchy had known, yet even his enemies admitted that he was a great administrator and in particular perhaps the ablest French Finance Minister since Colbert. He had crowned the work of Baron Louis and Corvetto by further stabilizing French finances and putting public accounting on a regular basis. Whatever the shortcomings of the Bourbon Governments in other directions it could no longer be said that they were incapable of financial reform, and after 1821 the credit was due to Villèle. But he had not proved himself a statesman: largely dependent upon a majority which was still more out of touch than he with the main currents of French opinion, he had allowed himself to carry out a policy with which he was not wholly in sympathy, in order to retain the power of which he was over-fond.

The fall of Villèle was a bitter blow to Charles X, but for a while he made the best of his discomfiture and succeeded in forming under the Vicomte de Martignac, a new Ministry, recruited mainly from men of the

Right Centre who were prepared to follow a conciliatory policy. The censorship of the Press was not restored and Guizot was allowed to resume his lectures; unauthorized congregations were forbidden to direct schools and a limit was placed upon the number of pupils who could be taken by seminaries. Such measures effectively served to relieve tension, but they were far from palatable to the monarch, and the Ministry of the Centre was, as usual, liable to be attacked from the Right and Left. At length, in April 1829, Charles X, who, from a successful tour in Eastern France, long hostile to the Bourbons, had gained the illusion that he was universally popular, decided after the rejection of a Government bill by a combination of Right and Left to be rid of his too moderate Ministers at the first convenient moment. Like Louis XVIII in 1815 he preferred to work with men after his own heart: so in the new Cabinet formed in August one of the two chief Ministers was an intimate personal friend, a former *émigré* and Ultra of the deepest dye, Prince Jules de Polignac.

The new Ministry was formed when the Chamber was no longer sitting, but the announcement of its composition came like a thunderbolt to France and to Europe. Apart from Polignac it included Bourmont, a general notorious for having deserted Napoleon before Waterloo, and, for a short time, La Bourdonnaye, one of the Ultras most bloodthirsty in demanding vengeance after the Hundred Days. The choice of men so unpopular was either a piece of blind tactlessness or deliberate provocation. Under Louis XVIII the first Richelieu Ministry, if it had not the backing of the majority of the Chamber, was well regarded by public opinion as a whole both at home and abroad. But the Polignac Cabinet was bound to antagonize both. Abroad, the Austrian Chancellor, Prince Metternich, at once recognized its formation as tantamount to a counter revolution. At home, Opposition papers like the *Journal des Débats*, hailed it with scorn: 'Coblentz! Waterloo! 1815! Those are this Ministry's three principles: Squeeze it, twist it, nothing but humiliation, misfortune and danger oozes out!'[6] Many feared that it was the prelude to a *coup d'état*, and, during a winter of great severity which followed a run of bad harvests and coincided with growing economic difficulties, all the forces opposed to clericalism and reaction and loyal to government according to the Charter girded themselves for a fight. Some men resigned rather than serve such a Government, while political societies, such as the one which rejoiced in the name of 'Help thyself and heaven will help thee' (it was supported by Constitutionalists as eminent as Guizot and Broglie) began to contemplate passive resistance and refusal to pay taxes. The Opposition Press was powerfully reinforced by the creation, in January 1830, of *Le National*, a new paper which had the blessing of the aged Talleyrand; under the direction of Armand Carrel and two distinguished young historians, Thiers and Mignet, it extolled the Glorious English Revolution of 1688 and hinted that an unsatisfactory monarch might well be replaced by a member of his own family with broader views. The allusion to the Duke of Orléans was understood by all.

The clash between Cabinet and Chamber came as soon as the new session opened in March 1830. The speech from the throne carried a scarcely veiled threat that opposition would be overcome by force. The Chamber replied with an address of no confidence. 'The permanent harmony of the political views of your Government with the wishes of your people is the indispensable condition for the conduct of public affairs. Sire, our loyalty, our devotion oblige us to tell you that this harmony does not exist.'[7] Thus the constitutional problem latent throughout the Restoration came to a head. Could the King choose and keep his Ministers as he pleased or must they be chosen from the majority in the Chamber and resign when defeated or censured? The Prince de Polignac was a man of considerable personal charm but extremely stubborn, complacent and self-assured. Unfortunately Charles stood by him. He first prorogued and then dissolved the Chamber but kept his Ministers.

The Government and country now prepared for new elections, but no amount of official pressure could secure a majority for the supporters of so unpopular a Cabinet. In the elections of July 1830 the Opposition returned 274 strong instead of 221. Still the King was undaunted. In spite of this vivid proof of public opinion, in spite of advice from the Tsar and Metternich, he was determined to have his way. On 25 July he invoked Article XIV of the Charter which empowered the King, if need be, to make 'the necessary regulations and ordinances for the execution of the laws and for the safety of the State'. As it depended upon the King and his advisers to decide when Article XIV should be called into play, he could still argue that he was acting according to the letter of the constitution. But in all the circumstances the four ordinances published on 26 July,[8] virtually suppressing the liberty of the Press, dissolving the Chamber, modifying the electoral law in such a way that the electorate was reduced to some 25,000 people mostly landowners, and fixing a date for new elections, amounted to a *coup d'état*. The immediate reactions in Paris did not threaten revolution. Deputies still contemplated only passive resistance; and, although at the *National*'s offices Thiers and his fellow journalists drew up a protest declaring that the Government had lost its legal character and inviting the country to decide 'how far she ought to carry resistance against tyranny', the first demonstrations of printers on strike and of stray bands of workmen and students did not seem serious. But Paris, now grossly overcrowded and still in the throes of a recession, was a city where an explosion might easily occur.

It was the astonishing lack of preparedness on the part of the King and Government which allowed a demand for the dismissal of the Ministry to swell rapidly into a revolution beyond their control. Nothing indeed is more extraordinary than the blind insouciance of Charles X and Polignac. It was they who were effecting a *coup d'état*, it was they who controlled the armed forces, and yet they took no steps to ensure that their forces should be adequate to ensure their success. They believed that if the *coup* were prepared with secrecy the public would be too surprised to react, and so, having signed the ordinances, the King went off to hunt at Rambouillet, leaving the Deputy Minister of War to learn of them for the first time from the official *Moniteur* and to deal with the situation as best he could. No troops had been concentrated in case of emergency, no measures taken to occupy all strategic points in and about the capital or to arrest potential leaders of opposition. The Paris garrison was actually much below strength, since some men had been drafted to take part in an expedition against Algiers and others were away on manoeuvres. As if this were not folly enough, the King appointed Marmont, the Duke of Ragusa, to command these diminished forces. Marmont, like Bourmont, had betrayed Napoleon, and 'raguser' for the Parisians was a word which meant 'to betray'. His appointment was provocative, while the anonymous hoisting of the tricolour on the top of Notre Dame rekindled latent patriotic resentment against the Bourbons. Events suddenly took a revolutionary turn. Barricades went up all over the city; it was above all artisans from traditional crafts and shopkeepers and their employees who bore the brunt of the fighting, often led by veterans of the revolutionary and Napoleonic armies. Swept by a wave of romantic revolutionary enthusiasm, the majority of the Parisians clamoured for the fall of the dynasty and Marmont's small force struggling in the labyrinth of narrow streets soon suffered heavy casualties. On 29 July 1830, the decisive day, two of his regiments went over to the insurgents. Meanwhile, Charles, now back at St Cloud, within sound of the firing, had resumed the customary routine of court etiquette, and continued to remain obstinately optimistic, refusing either to call up reinforcements or to make the concessions urgently entreated of him by some of the moderate leaders in Paris, the Constitutionalists, who feared a Republic every whit as much as they detested absolutism. Not until the 30th did he at last consent in writing to change his ministers and revoke the ordinances. But by then it was too late. When the royal messengers reached the capital the moderate leaders had decided to replace him by Louis Philippe, Duke of Orléans. Charles X could only have regained control by the exercise of an overwhelming force which he did not possess. There was nothing left but to abdicate, escape the mob which set out to search for him at St Cloud and Rambouillet, and make his way into exile for the third and last time.

Thus ingloriously and unnecessarily the restored Bourbon monarchy came to an end through the folly of the monarch only fifteen years after Waterloo. A fresh shock was given to French political stability and new cleavages were added to those which already divided Frenchmen from Frenchmen. And yet, despite its miserable ending, the Restoration was no inglorious period. In these years France had achieved a rapid national recovery from the strain and disorganization of prolonged war and the effects of invasion. Her population had increased by three millions; until the depression which began in 1825 and was intensified at the end of 1827, she had enjoyed a relative commercial prosperity:[9] her credit had stood high, there had been a marked increase in public wealth and from 1819 to 1826 the budget showed a surplus. Banking operations had enormously increased in scope and the support of Villèle had helped to establish the French branch of the Rothschilds which soon rivalled the Swiss and Protestant houses founded a generation or so earlier. A first savings bank had been established in Paris in 1818, joint stock companies had begun to appear and a fine new Bourse or stock exchange had been opened in 1826. Communications, too, had been improved if only very slowly: main roads neglected during the last years of the Empire had been repaired and macadamization had been introduced; the canal system had been lengthened by an additional 921 km; a first steamboat crossed the English Channel, regular services had made their appearance on several rivers and, most revolutionary of all the changes in modes of transport, the advent of the railway had been heralded by the opening in 1827 of a short line for the carriage of coal by horse-drawn wagons. In these same years some textile and metallurgical industries had made progress behind the shield of protection with which France had, like most continental states, guarded herself, and which manufacturers and landowners alike had forced successive governments to maintain or reinforce. Paris had witnessed three industrial exhibitions. She had seen the development of street pavements and horse-drawn omnibuses; and a plant run by an Englishman named Manby had helped to supply the gas lighting which had become general in the city by 1829. Thus in the material sphere Restoration France had some solid, if unspectacular, achievement to her credit. It might have been greater still had her Governments been less frugal.

In politics many distinguished men had upheld the country's reputation. Great orators or able men such as Berryer, Benjamin Constant, Royer-Collard, de Serre and Chateaubriand had been among the protagonists in the Chambers and had contributed to the high standard of debate which had won admiration far beyond the frontiers. In literature and the arts there had been a remarkable, exhilarating outburst of creative activity. The Romantic movement, of which Chateaubriand and Madame de Staël had been eminent precursors, had received fresh impetus from a new study of Shakespeare and from the works of Byron and Scott; and Hugo, Lamartine, Vigny and Musset, the young Royalist champions of the revolt against classicism, had contributed to a literary revival which gathered pace from 1820 onwards. The Restoration had thus seen the momentous years of the great struggle between the Classics and the Romantics which had culminated in the battle over Victor Hugo's play, *Hernani*. Here Charles X, foolish in so many things, had been wise enough – wiser no doubt than a Napoleon in that he refused to interfere: 'In matters of comedy, gentlemen, I am no more than one of the audience in the stalls.' These had been the days when Ingres returned to France from Italy to continue his painting and when Delacroix arose to carry the standard of Romanticism into the realm of art; when fashionable companies had been delighted by the plays of Scribe and the music of Auber, by the dancing of Marie Taglioni, the singing of La Malibran and the acting of Mademoiselle Mars; when Italian music was the vogue, the interest in opera revived and the Concerts of the Conservatoire were founded; when the greatest names of literature, art and politics assembled in the brilliant salons of ladies such as Madame Récamier, the Duchesse de Duras, Madame Ancelot and Madame Vigeé-Lebrun: when science and natural history were adorned by men such as Cuvier, Sadi Carnot, Fresnel and Ampère, philosophy by Maine de Biran and de Maistre, and when, through the lectures of men such as Guizot, Villemain and Cousin, the Sorbonne gained a fresh reputation as the centre for the diffusion of new ideas. These, too, had been the days of the founding of such notable institutions as the École des Chartes (1821), the École des Arts et Manufactures (1828) and the École des Beaux Arts (1830).

Finally, however unfortunate the domestic policy which eventually brought Charles X to his fall, it must be remembered that the Restoration Governments had done much to restore French prestige abroad. 'In their foreign policy,' as an eminent French historian has written, 'the Bourbons, as though by hereditary vocation, displayed an understanding of French interests.'[10] In the affairs of Spain as we have already seen, and later, after the fall of Villèle, in those of Greece and the Eastern Mediterranean, France had played a conspicuous part. Her navy had shared in the victory of Navarino over the Turks in 1827, and her troops had cleared the Morea of Turkish and Egyptian forces in 1828. Moreover, Charles X and Polignac, for all their shortcomings at home, had a wide vision of foreign affairs. An ambitious plan they had devised for the overthrow of the Vienna settlement and the rearrangement of the map of Europe by France and Russia had indeed come to nought,[11] but with the conquest of Algiers in July 1830 Charles had defied the hostility of Great Britain, had laid the foundation stone of a vast new African Empire and finally put an end to a nest of pirates which had been a menace to Mediterranean trade for more than three centuries. The transport to Africa of a force of 38,000 men and 4500 horses by 103 warships and 469 merchant vessels was no mean symbol of France's renewed strength, and the expedition had had the additional merit of paying for itself, since a treasure greater than its whole cost was found in the hoard of the Algerian Dey. Such a success, however, had counted for nothing with Frenchmen who had been wholly preoccupied by the constitutional crisis. The glory of an African conquest had diverted men, but not public attention, from France. Indeed it is unlikely that the French public could have been roused to enthusiasm even had there been no clash of King and Chamber. The exploitation of Africa still lay far in the future and the men of 1830 'could only conceive of war and glory as something in Europe, across the Rhine and across the Alps'.[12] But, although they knew it not, Charles X's last foreign venture had been one of momentous importance for the future of France. He had been quick to seize a great opportunity. Had he not done so the conquest of Algiers might have been postponed for many years or not been possible at all, for it is highly doubtful whether his cautious successor would have embarked upon such an enterprise.

Notes

1　Guizot, F., *Memoirs to Illustrate the History of My Time*, vol. 1, p. 265.
2　Cit. Aldington, Richard, *Wellington*, p. 244.
3　Guizot, op. cit., p. 86.
4　The number of Jesuits in France was probably not more than 300. Dansette, A., *Histoire religieuse de la France contemporaine*, p. 278.
5　*Mémoire à consulter sur un système religieux et politique tendant à renverser la religion, la société et le trône*, par M. le Comte de Montlosier, Paris, 1826.
6　Cit. Lucas-Dubreton, J., *La Restauration et la monarchie de juillet*, p. 134.
7　Cahen, L. and Mathiez, A., *Les lois françaises de 1815 à 1914*, p. 57.
8　For the text in English see Butterfield, H., *Select Documents of European History, 1715–1920*, pp. 111ff.
9　But see Bertier de Sauvigny, G. de, *La Restauration*, pp. 307ff. for the difficulties of assessing the position.
10　La Gorce, P. de, *Napoléon III et sa politique*, p. 48.
11　Cf. Bourgeois, E., *Manuel historique de politique étrangère*, vol. 2, p. 771ff.
12　Halévy, D., *Trois épreuves*, p. 36.

Bibliography

Artz, Frederick B., *France under the Bourbon Restoration*, Harvard, 1931.
Beach, Vincent W., *Charles X of France: His Life and Time*, Boulder, 1970.
Beck, Thomas D., *French Legislators 1800–1834: A Study in Quantitative History*, Berkeley, 1974.

Bertier de Sauvigny, G. de, *Le Comte Ferdinand de Bertier (1782–1864) et l'énigme de la Congrégation*, Paris, 1948.

Bertier de Sauvigny, G. de, *La Restauration*, 2nd edn, Paris, 1963. English trans. Philadelphia, 1966, *Au soir de la Monarchie: la Restauration*, revised with amended title 1974.

Charléty, S., *La Restauration* (vol. 4 of Lavisse, E., *Histoire de France contemporaine*), Paris, 1921.

Chateaubriand, *Mémoires d'outre-tombe*, vol. 3, ed. M. Levaillant, Paris, 1948.

Collins, I., *Government and Society in France, 1814–1848*, London, 1970.

Fourcassie, J., *Villèle*, Paris, 1954.

Garnier, J.-P., *Charles X. Le Roi – le Proscrit*, Paris, 1967.

Hudson, Nora, E., *Ultra-Royalism and the French Restoration*, Cambridge, 1936.

Jardin, A. and Tudesq, A.-J., *La France des notables*, Paris, 1973.

Lucas-Dubreton, J., *Le culte de Napoléon 1815–1848*, Paris, 1960.

Mellon, Stanley, *The Political Uses of History: A Study of Historians in the French Restoration*, Stanford, 1958.

Noailles, Marquis de, *Le Comte Molé, 1781–1855, sa vie – ses mémoires*, vol. 5, Paris, 1922.

Pasquier, *Mémoires du Chancelier*, ed. Duc d'Audiffret-Pasquier, vols 3–5, Paris, 1894.

Pinkney, David H., *The French Revolution of 1830*, Princeton, 1972.

Rader, Daniel L., *The Journalists and the July Revolution in France*, The Hague, 1973.

Richardson, N., *The French Prefectoral Corps, 1814–1830*, Cambridge, 1966.

Schapiro, J. Salwyn, *Liberalism and the Challenge of Fascism*, New York, 1949.

Sussel, P., *La France de la bourgeoisie*, Paris, 1970.

5

The July Monarchy

Charles X can never return to Paris; he has shed the blood of his people. The Republic would expose us to dangerous divisions; it would involve us in hostilities with Europe.

The Duke of Orléans is a Prince devoted to the cause of the Revolution.

The Duke of Orléans has never fought against us.

The Duke of Orléans was at Jemappes.

The Duke of Orléans is a Citizen King.

The Duke of Orléans has carried the tricolour under the enemy's fire; the Duke of Orléans alone can carry it again. We will have no other flag.

The Duke of Orléans does not commit himself. He awaits the expression of our wishes. Let us proclaim those wishes and he will accept the Charter as we have always desired it. It is from the French people that he will hold his crown.[1]

Thus succinctly did Thiers and his friend, Mignet, put the case for a French 1688 and such was the proclamation that the belated envoys of Charles X found placarded in Paris on 30 July 1830. That same day, after much hesitation, Louis Philippe, Duke of Orléans, who was above all animated by the desire not to be obliged to go into exile once more, entered Paris and accepted the post of Lieutenant-General of the Kingdom offered to him by a group of deputies. But the Chamber dissolved by Charles X's ordinances was not the only power in the insurgent capital, and the problem of government could only be solved with the consent or acquiescence of a municipal commission of Republican tendencies which had installed itself in the Hôtel de Ville and of the veteran Lafayette, whom the re-emergent National Guard had invited to command them and who now appeared the hero of the hour. Accordingly, on the 31st, the Duke, who had never lacked personal courage, proceeded through the crowded streets to the Hôtel de Ville. Lafayette, 'a Republican at heart who never had the strength or daring to proclaim the Republic', preferred a constitutional monarchy to a Jacobin dictatorship, and was prepared to welcome him. The crowd, at first hostile, cheered when Louis Philippe appeared on the balcony holding the tricolour flag and publicly embraced the venerable Commander of the National Guard. This was the kiss that helped to make the July monarchy. Republican opposition was stifled by a gesture which momentarily made the Duke of Orléans appear the best of Republicans.

Two days later Charles X, bowing tardily to realities, in turn appointed Louis Philippe Lieutenant-General of the Kingdom and abdicated in favour of his grandson, the boy Duc de Bordeaux, henceforth to be known to his adherents as Henri V. Charles left the protection of his grandson's rights to Louis Philippe; but when he and the boy were both on their way to exile it could be argued that the throne was vacant. Louis Philippe accepted this view, and accordingly on 7 August the Chambers declared the throne to be vacant and two days later he was proclaimed King. Perhaps it was true that no compromise of Regency would have been acceptable to the men of the Left, but the Royalists who remained loyal to Charles never forgave what to them was a base act of treachery.

The Revolution thus accomplished by Paris was endorsed elsewhere often with anti-Bourbon demonstrations. It was a blow to the Church, which for some time was greatly discredited. It was also a blow to the Royalist nobility who had in many ways exercised a predominant influence since 1814; moreover, it split their ranks, thus introducing yet another cleavage among Frenchmen, for the majority, henceforth known as Legitimists or Carlists, remained faithful to Charles and his grandson and retired to their tents, nursing a bitter hatred against those of their fellows who had rallied to the new regime. It was also a disappointment to the handful of ardent Republicans who had hoped for the abolition of Kings and were far from being satisfied with this fresh experiment in constitutional monarchy. It was not, however, as used to be said, a triumph for a *grande bourgeoisie* of wealthy businessmen. The men who now came to control the state were mostly landed proprietors much like their predecessors. But they looked to parliament to secure opportunities and freedoms they cherished. Thus the days when men feared that the *émigrés* would overthrow the revolutionary land settlement had gone for ever. The newcomers had now made a King, and their sovereignty as representatives and leaders of the nation was demonstrated in the terms of his creation. The new monarch was not to be Philip VII, King of France, but Louis Philippe, King of the French 'by the Grace of God and the will of the nation'. The Chamber of Deputies took upon itself to revise the 1814 Charter and did away with the preamble on the grounds that it was

'wounding to the national dignity'.[2] Thus instead of Louis Philippe granting a revised Charter, like Louis XVIII, of his royal prerogative, he had one
imposed on him by the deputies who represented the will of the nation.
And these deputies displayed a somewhat niggardly delight in curtailing
the privileges of royalty in other ways. Charles X had enjoyed a civil list of
40,000,000 francs: but the deputies, in Guizot's words, 'scrutinized and
passed' the bill for Louis Philippe's allowance as though they were 'dis-
puting and determining the price of a machine'[3] and reduced it to a mere
12,000,000 francs. In the same way they made a fresh attack upon the
hereditary principle by securing the transformation of the Chamber of
Peers into an upper house of life members nominated by the King, many
of them former civil servants or army officers. Characteristically the passage of this reform was obtained by the creation of a further batch of new
noblemen.

The new King, scion of a branch of the royal house which was tra-
ditionally on bad terms with the reigning sovereign, was a son of that
Duke known as Philippe Égalité, who had intrigued against Louis XVI,
adopted revolutionary ideas, and none the less perished on the scaffold.[4]
He was fifty-seven years of age when he came to the throne. His boyhood
and early manhood had thus been passed in the years of the Revolution;
he had known poverty and exile and had had exceptional opportunities of
observing the workings of democracy abroad. Now one of the wealthiest
men in France, careful in the management of his fortune, though often
generous to individuals in distress, excellent father of a large family,
simple and unaffected in his habits and tastes, although a man of wide
interests, he appeared admirably fitted to preside over a regime directed
by the bourgeoisie, so many of whose virtues he seemed to epitomize.
Shrewdly opportunist, he understood how to play to the gallery. Committed to being a Citizen-King, he performed the part with assiduity,
received delegation upon delegation of fellow citizens, discarded the
pomp and etiquette of the Bourbon Court, mixed freely with the Parisians
in his daily walks, and appeared like an ordinary bourgeois in top hat and
with an umbrella instead of in uniform. In the first months of revolutionary enthusiasm the Parisians were entranced by such a novel and model
sovereign; later they were to find him drab, to pine for more splendour,
cruelly to caricature his homely virtues and criticize even his manifold and
manifest abilities.[5]

The main immediate changes in regime of the revised Charter were
naturally enough in the direction of greater liberty. The creation of extraordinary tribunals and judicial commissions was forbidden and the censorship was abolished 'for ever'. The age qualification for electors and those
eligible as deputies was lowered to twenty-five and thirty respectively;

and laws were passed reducing the property qualification for electors from 300 to 200 francs. The National Guard was reorganized; the term of military service was reduced from eight to seven years; and the tricolour flew once again as the national flag of France. The alliance of Throne and Altar was at an end and Roman Catholicism was now recognized as no more than the religion 'of the majority of Frenchmen'. Certain religious orders were expelled and the funds allotted to the Ministry of Public Worship were reduced. Press cases were once again referred to trial by jury; the county and municipal councils were made elective, and though they were to have relatively little power, they now became a permanent feature of local administration. Last, but not least, by Guizot's law of 1833 state-aided primary schools, in which religious instruction was given and clergy were free to teach, were set up in every commune.[6] This was the beginning of a momentous educational reform, but only a beginning, for there was no compulsion, and illiteracy remained widespread for many years to come.

These measures which constituted the main legislative changes of the first three years of the new reign were by no means unimportant, yet there still remained the great question – to what end had the revolution been made? The 'Three Glorious Days' of July 1830 had released an extraordinary ferment of ideas and passions which continued to work long after the formal establishment of the new regime. All the latent discontents and grievances came to a head, and all who wanted change, or believed they would profit from it now it had come, vociferously demanded new men, new methods and new ideas. Mobs of place hunters besieged each Ministry and the new Government made sweeping changes of prefects and sub-prefects, generals and high army officers, magistrates, Counsellors of State and Rectors of Academy; among these new men were many erstwhile servants of the Empire or their sons. At the same time the belief that a new era of liberty had dawned led to an extraordinary efflorescence of political clubs and societies, accompanied by constant street demonstrations and by a spate of literary propaganda on behalf of all kinds of political and social reform. Bonapartists and Republicans, and social reformers such as the followers of Fourier and Saint Simon all believed that their hour was at hand. Even within the Church, the extraordinary fire and eloquence of Lamennais seemed in his paper *L'Avenir* to herald a revolutionary movement of Liberalism and democratic trend. Moreover the incursion into the political arena of a Romanticism which had deserted Royalist for new Liberal, Philhellenist enthusiasms – the *Globe*, for instance, so influential in the first four years since its foundation in 1824 in doing battle against the Classicists, had begun to join issue in political matters in 1828[7] – momentarily carried a cloak and dagger extravagance of action into political demonstrations.[8] At the same time economic difficulties which the revolution and a hard winter accentuated led to manifestations of another kind, strikes and processions of workers demanding 'bread'.

Thus the months immediately following the revolution were extremely disturbed. There were many, especially in the younger generation, who for one reason or another believed or hoped that the revolution was but the beginning of a series of further changes and who did not cease to agitate for fresh reforms; but there was also an important body of opinion which was alarmed by such demonstrations and held that in effecting a change of dynasty and a new guarantee of essential liberties through the revised Charter the Revolution had accomplished its object. These contradictory views both had their representatives in Louis Philippe's first government. On the one hand there was the so-called Party of Movement, with Lafayette, Laffitte, Dupont de l'Eure and others, who carried with them many Romantic idealists and held that the events of July were but a prelude to further reform and to an active foreign policy. On the other, there was the Party of Resistance whose most prominent members, Casimir Périer and former Doctrinaires such as Guizot and the Duc de Broglie, maintained that the Revolution was complete with the victory of constitutional legality and that it was essential to conciliate the great powers of Europe. But the revolutionary momentum could not be stopped at once, however much the King might wish it, and in November, not long after Parisian mobs had demonstrated under his windows and marched to Vincennes to demand the heads of Polignac and his colleagues who were imprisoned there, Louis Philippe thought it prudent to give the Party of Movement some rein and to form a new Ministry headed by the banker Laffitte. This was a sop to public opinion but did not prevent further disorders. There were furious demonstrations when the Chamber of Peers condemned Charles X's late Ministers to life imprisonment instead of to death, and again, in February 1831, hostility to the late regime showed itself afresh when a mob, angered at a Legitimist commemoration and swept by one of the most violent waves of anti-clericalism witnessed in the nineteenth century, sacked the palace of the Archbishop of Paris and the church of St Germain l'Auxerrois. The Laffitte Government, unable or unwilling to maintain good order, and unable either to prevent a financial crisis and a sharp rise in unemployment or to indulge a popular clamour for a crusade in aid of national risings in Belgium, Poland and Italy was soon discredited. Accordingly, in March 1831, Louis Philippe turned to the Party of Resistance and with a Ministry headed by another banker, Casimir Périer, secured a much stronger government. Casimir Périer was indeed a man of most forceful character, a veritable Prime Minister, ruling

King and colleagues alike and by no means patient of royal interference. This struggle for power between the more adventurous and the more conservative was to continue throughout the reign, but, although the King himself spoke of pursuing the policy of the happy mean (*juste milieu*) his temperament and native caution naturally inclined him to the Party of Resistance and it was this which enjoyed office for the greater part of his rule.

Louis Philippe, as we have seen, represented a compromise. In other words it was once again a case of the solution which would divide Frenchmen least. But after the failure of the Restoration to recreate unity, and after the events of July 1830, the task of founding a regime acceptable to all was still more difficult. Once again the Government had to face insurrectionary fire from two flanks. The absence of any sort of rising in support of Charles X in 1830 had shown how little real hold the Ultra-Royalists had had in the country, but none the less they were now ready to plot against the Government, even on occasion joining forces with the Republicans, who were much more experienced conspirators. During the first ten years of the new regime there was a whole series of plots and disturbances of varying gravity, and between 1835 and 1846 no fewer than six attempts were made on the life of the King. In spite of the fact that men such as Berryer still championed the Legitimist cause,[9] and of an attempt in 1832 by the young and once popular Duchesse de Berry to raise the Vendée for her son, 'Henri V', Legitimist hostility was much less serious than that of the Republicans. The Vendée rising proved to be a fiasco only less ridiculous than the later efforts of Louis Napoleon to raise the Bonapartist standard at Strasbourg and Boulogne in 1836 and 1840, and the strength of the Legitimists was to some extent further weakened by the growth of a Liberal Catholicism which ran counter to the Ultramontane tendencies of the Bourbon exiles. The real peril lay to the Left and it was the abiding and eventually fatal weakness of Louis Philippe's Government that it failed to conjure the peril by broadening its electoral basis or by timely social legislation.

For the first time since the Great Revolution the condition of the workers in industry now came to the fore as an important social and political problem. The fundamental reasons for this were the striking increase in population during the last decade of the Restoration together with the development of certain big industries. These had resulted in a crowding and migration of population into the Parisian and other areas, unchecked by considerations of health, sanitation or a minimum living wage. This did not mean that France had ceased to be a country in which small industries were the rule – by 1846 the numbers employed in large-scale industry were not much over a million[10] but it did mean that 'the industrial revolution' (a phrase first used in France by Blanqui in 1837) was developing apace and that the scale and scope of industrialization had rapidly increased, especially in the cotton and textile industries of Alsace, Normandy and the Nord, in the silk industry in the Lyons area, and the metallurgical industries of the Loire basin and Lorraine. Thus, for example, the numbers employed in the Haut Rhin textile industry increased by 135 per cent during the seven years 1827–34, and the population of Roubaix jumped from 8000 to 34,000 in the ten years 1831–41 and that of St Etienne from 16,000 to 54,000. Crowded and insanitary living conditions gave a free field to terrible epidemics such as the cholera, which raged both in Great Britain and France in 1831–2, but caused a heavier mortality among the French;[11] and these conditions, together with the uncontrolled exploitation of female and child labour and long hours of work, led to widespread tuberculosis, immorality and drunkenness. The damage to health is vividly brought out by the fact that 'in 1840 out of every 10,000 young men called up for military service from ten French departments which were predominantly manufacturing in character, 9000 were rejected as physically unfit.'[12] Apart from their wretched living conditions, the main misfortune of these workers was the uncertainty of employment. Research has shown that on the whole their average consumption per head increased under the July monarchy, that there was a general rise in agricultural and industrial productivity and that many workmen were able to entrust earnings to the growing number of savings banks; but all too often salaries (which varied enormously in different industries and different localities) failed to keep pace with rises in the cost of living, and all too seldom did they allow a margin to guard against the big emergencies of unemployment or illness. Contemporary observers calculated that a working class family would be in distress if their earnings were less than 750 francs per annum and there were times of economic crisis or of epidemic when all too many families failed to reach this figure.

Living in such precarious conditions, many workers, especially in Paris, had been led to believe that the July Revolution would mean an improvement of their lot. Had not *Le National*, for instance, declared on 30 July: 'It is the people which has done everything . . . it has been powerful and sublime; it is it which has won the victory and all the benefits of the victory should be for it'? But the workers of different trades in Paris who demonstrated, demanding shorter hours and minimum wages, got no encouragement from the new authorities. The Revolution had dislocated business and the political uncertainty which naturally followed the establishment of the new regime only brought with it an intensification of unemployment which continued into 1831. Disappointment and desperation led to a series of demonstrations in Paris and Lyons of workers demanding bread or work and finally in November 1831 to a veritable insurrection in Lyons during which the city was for a time in the hands of the 'canuts' or silk-weavers. These months were indeed critical. They determined whether the authorities would be sympathetic to large numbers of Frenchmen in distress, and upon the answer largely depended the extent to which the Republican opponents of the regime could swell their ranks by recruits from the workers.

The Lyons insurrection of 1831 which has been called 'the first appearance of armed socialism'[13] – since many of the men involved in it are known to have been influenced by Socialist ideas – was a tragic blow to the cause of conciliation. In the silk trade, which at this time accounted for 29 per cent of France's exports, wages had lagged sadly behind the cost of living. The workers therefore demanded that joint committees of workers and employers should meet to fix a minimum wage scale. The proposal was approved by the Chambers of Commerce, and the Prefect himself lent his good offices, with the result that a tariff was duly fixed. The principles of collective bargaining and peaceful settlement of disputes appeared to have won a signal success. But 104 out of some 1400 manufacturers refused to observe the agreement and threatened to close their works. Then it was that the whole body of weavers rose in exasperation and for a short time controlled the city, the challenging words *'Vivre libres en travaillant ou mourir en combattant'* inscribed upon their banners. The Government was scared and replied by an overwhelming display of force, dispersed the rebels, denounced the tariff, and declared collective bargaining illegal. Thus in their alarm the authorities rallied to protect the interests of the manufacturers and reaffirmed the sacred doctrine of *laissez-faire* – each individual must be free to contract as he liked. In the Chamber, the workers were told by Casimir Périer that patience and resignation were their only remedies.

This insurrection was not primarily political in its objective; but its repression and the repression of many lesser disturbances in Paris and elsewhere all led the workers to seek more effective association for their own interests, to distrust the Government and to realize that to improve their conditions they would have to rely on their own efforts. So they became amenable to Republican propaganda which made great efforts during these first years 1831–4 – no less than 6,000,000 copies of Republican pamphlets were distributed in three months – and many were tempted to join secret Republican groups such as the Société des Droits de l'Homme, the 'Familles' or the 'Saisons'. Thus to some extent events moved in a vicious circle. The Republicans, frustrated in the achievement of their goal in July 1830, less numerous than the Legitimists, but better versed in revolutionary technique, kept the authorities on edge by a series of disturbances and strikes and so led them to deal severely with all manifestations, even those with no political objective. In consequence many who were not primarily concerned with political issues turned to Republicanism in the hope that it would help them in their struggle for existence.

Casimir Périer, the strong man of the first years of the reign, died in May 1832 during the first cholera epidemic in France, a fearsome visitor which carried off some 20,000 victims and increased the bitterness of the poor. The Vendée rising was still flickering and in Paris in June the funeral of a popular Opposition deputy, General Lamarque, afforded a pretext for further Republican demonstrations so serious that for three weeks the city was put in a state of siege. It was clear to the King that the policy of resistance must be continued. Accordingly in October a new Ministry was formed with Marshal Soult as titular head, but Broglie as the real director. The death of the Duc de Reichstadt, Napoleon's son, and the arrest of the Duchesse de Berry, who was soon discredited by a liaison with an Italian count, by weakening the Bonapartists and Legitimists seemed to strengthen the Orleanist dynasty and to introduce a period of relative calm.

But it was not to be for long. After a brief respite there was a fresh eruption of Republican propaganda and incitements to violence, and the *Tribune*, the Republican paper directed by Armand Marrast, which in four years was the subject of 114 prosecutions, now published a programme for the establishment of a 'social Republic'.[14] For more than three years the Press had enjoyed unbridled liberty, the King and Government had been unmercifully caricatured by Daumier and Monnier, Republican papers had deliberately fomented disturbances, the life of the capital and often the existence of the regime had been threatened by insurrectionary movements. At length, their patience exhausted, the Government decided that liberties must be curtailed in the interests of order and stability. In April 1834 legislation was passed restricting the right of association. In Lyons, where there had just been a strike, the news of the law produced fresh disturbances organized by friendly societies of Republican sympathies and six days of bitter fighting followed. In Eastern Paris there was an almost simultaneous rising, at the call of the Société des Droits de l'Homme. Its repression, largely directed by Thiers, was savage, involving as it did the so-called massacre of the Rue Transnonain, a foretaste of the repression after the June Days of 1848 and the Commune of 1871, when Thiers was again in control. It was, however, effective and the Republican movement was driven underground for several years to come. In 1835 a fresh attempt to kill the King, which caused the loss of many lives, provoked a further revulsion against the romantic cult of political assassination. The Government was impelled by the pressure of parliamentary and public opinion to introduce the so-called September laws bringing the

Press under stricter control and modifying judicial procedure in order to secure more speedy results. Henceforth insults to the King or attacks on the principle or form of government by Charter were to be treated as threats to the security of the State. The Press, which had shown its power in 1830 had subsequently abused its new-won liberties and indulged in the unbridled violence so characteristic of French journalism. It had over-shot the mark and was now to pay the penalty.

The main period of disorder was now at an end, and during the next four years interest in internal matters centred rather on the battles in Parliament and the instability of Ministries. Louis Philippe had appreci-ated the need for the firm hand of Casimir Périer and his successors, but he had chafed under their domination. He had no notion of being a King who would reign but not govern, and after the fall of the Broglie Ministry in February 1836 he sought ministerial combinations in which he hoped himself to keep control. The young and ambitious Thiers seemed likely to be a more supple instrument and was tempted into leading the next Cabinet – a momentous decision, for it meant a break between Thiers and Guizot. Henceforward one of the dominant features of the reign was to be the rivalry between these two historians who were to be its most notable Ministers. This first Thiers Cabinet, however, did not last long. Thiers came to grief over foreign policy and in August he resigned.

Foreign affairs had been of vital importance from the outset and nowhere had the King shown greater firmness and good sense. The July Revolution had had immediate repercussions throughout the Continent. In imagination men's thoughts had inevitably flown back to 1789 and Europe had been torn by a complex of fears and hopes. Conservative Governments were indignant and alarmed at the outbreak of revolution in France, and when it inspired Belgians, Poles and Italians to rise in revolt and German Liberals to make demonstrations, the Russian Tsar beheld the menace of universal revolution and was eager to parry it with all the armed might of the quondam Holy Alliance. At the same time in France itself there were many hot-headed and enthusiastic supporters of the Party of Movement who burned to help the Poles and other foreign insurgents and who envisaged a march across the Rhine as a natural corollary of revo-lution. The new Government had therefore to walk warily. Mistrusted by the Eastern Powers, insecure at home, it could not afford to launch upon any ill-considered revolutionary crusade, even had it so wished. Equally its origin forbade it to play a reactionary role. Louis Philippe himself was the last man to wish to embark upon foolhardy adventures abroad. He wanted peace to consolidate his government and he wanted to obtain from other European Governments recognition that the July Monarchy could be a stable and stabilizing force in Europe. Although the presence of large numbers of Polish exiles in Paris and the romantic and dramatic quality of the Polish risings aroused more sympathies on behalf of the Poles than of the Belgians or Italians, Poland was too remote for there ever to be any serious question of French intervention. On the other hand, the Belgian and Italian revolutions presented the new regime with test cases from which it emerged with flying colours and enhanced prestige.

The rising in Belgium, originally a demonstration for Home Rule under the House of Orange, had soon turned into a move for complete separation from Holland. Such a disruption of the Kingdom of the Netherlands meant a flagrant breach of the 1815 settlement. The Dutch King appealed for military aid and the Eastern powers thought seriously of giving it. But in the west, close at hand, there was another power, Great Britain, which was much less disposed to join in or encourage armed intervention on behalf of the *status quo*. By co-operating with her, France saw an opportunity to play an honourable part in procuring a peaceful settlement and by none was this course more skilfully urged and executed than by the veteran Talleyrand, who now emerged to serve his fifth regime as French Ambassador in London, a post he had first held nearly forty years before, in 1792. 'Whether other States are or are not disposed in favour of peace, France and England must declare that they wish it, and this wish of the two most powerful and civilized countries in Europe must be heard with the respect to which their power entitles them.'[15] Thus Talleyrand argued, and, playing with the principle of non-intervention as skilfully as in 1814 he had played with that of legitimacy, he won Britain's support. His reckoning was correct. Instead of troops to the Netherlands the eastern sovereigns sent envoys to a conference in London to settle the Belgian question; and the settlement was virtually a recognition of the *fait accompli*. The new kingdom of Belgium came into being – French troops and an English fleet forced the Dutch king to submit – and its neutrality was guaranteed by the four Great Powers in 1839. Thus in its first great diplomatic trial the July Monarchy had at once emerged from isolation, effected a rapprochement with Great Britain, with whom France's relations at the end of the Restoration had been distinctly cool, and played an important part in imposing a peaceful settlement, which at the same time confirmed the breach in the 1815 treaties. As a result, on her northwest frontier France now had a new, weak, and friendly state, with a constitution still more liberal than her own, in place of the larger one which the settlement of Vienna had designed as a barrier against any recurrent French aggression. In securing this result Louis Philippe had had to resist great temptations; many Belgians and French had hoped for a union of Belgium and France and one of Louis Philippe's sons, the Duc de Nemours, had actually been elected King by the Belgian National Congress.

Acceptance of either proposal would have meant not merely alienation from but probably hostilities with Great Britain: and such a prospect the new King could not contemplate. It was much to his credit that he kept his head, contented himself with marrying one of his daughters to the Coburg Prince Leopold who eventually became King of the Belgians, and withstood the lure of realizing the age-old French dream of incorporating the Belgian lands in France.

In the Belgian problem France intervened in the name of non-intervention and yet avoided a clash with Great Britain. So, too, in Italy the French Government proclaimed a policy of non-intervention which Italian patriots hoped would mean that France would prevent Austria from intervening. But Louis Philippe had no desire to come to blows with Austria and so, to the disgust of the Italian patriots, Casimir Périer had explained that non-intervention actually meant what it said and that France could not give armed help to every foreign revolution. In 1832, however, when a second rising occurred in the Papal States, the Vatican once again called in Austrian troops and the French Government replied by occupying Ancona. By now the July Monarchy was more firmly established and by this action it demonstrated its fidelity to another classical principle of French foreign policy: that France had an abiding interest in Italian affairs and could not allow any other power to dominate the peninsula exclusively. The Austrian soldiers were not withdrawn until 1838, and so for six years French troops were maintained at Ancona facing them. As has been remarked, 'they had only to raise a tricolour on top of the hill-fort at Ancona and it might easily send a flame of revolution running northwards to the Alps and southwards to the Gulf of Taranto'.[16] But Louis Philippe did not aspire to give revolutionary signals. He had successfully made his demonstration on behalf of French prestige and the balance of power and at the same time avoided a clash with Austria. That was enough – he had no Napoleonic plan of fathering Italian unity – probably he had too shrewd a notion of France's real interests. In the west, meanwhile, further somewhat uneasy co-operation with England had resulted in a fresh triumph for constitutional monarchy. The Quadruple Alliance of 1834 between Great Britain, France, the Queen of Portugal and the Regent of Spain was speedily followed by the collapse of the absolutist forces of the two Iberian pretenders, Don Miguel of Portugal and Don Carlos of Spain.

Thus by 1837 the most serious disturbances which followed on the French Revolution of 1830 had been either quelled or settled. The main battle between the Liberal and the Conservative forces in Europe was over for the time being. Both had consolidated their positions and were prepared to observe a truce. Co-operation with Great Britain had been one of the main planks of French policy; but it had not been easy. Palmerston had been an exacting and suspicious associate, commercial rivalry was strong, and many Frenchmen deplored that their Government should work hand in hand with the power whom they still regarded as the 'hereditary foe'. Accordingly Louis Philippe, once his regime was established, was disposed to play a more independent role and eventually to seek rapprochement with the Conservative powers, especially Austria. The English *entente* began to cool, and was soon virtually shattered by a crisis in the Near East.

In general, France and Great Britain had been agreed in wishing to bolster up the sick man of Europe against his most persistent adversary, the Tsar. But in the 1830s Turkey was menaced with destruction from the south as well as from the north, and the attitude of the two Western powers to this new danger to Turkish interests was by no means identical. The most powerful of Turkish vassals, Mehemet Ali, the Pasha of Egypt, the Porte's main supporter in the war of Greek Independence, had been promised Syria as a reward for his help, and when the Sultan had tried to evade his promise he had seized the province and threatened Constantinople itself. Peace was patched up between the Sultan and his vassal by the good offices of the powers, but the Sultan could not brook his humiliation and in 1839 tried to take his revenge, only to be once again decisively defeated by the Egyptian forces. The European Powers once again prepared to intervene, but only one of them, France, was sympathetic to Mehemet Ali. France had maintained a close interest in Egypt ever since the time of Napoleon, and the Egyptian army had been largely trained and the Egyptian administrative services organized by Frenchmen. Mehemet Ali had responded by a policy which tended to be pro-French and markedly anti-British. Thus Great Britain had little love for him while Russia dreaded the prospect of a strong Egyptian ruler at Constantinople who might really reinvigorate the Turkish Empire. Aware of this situation Thiers, now for the second time head of a French Government, tried to bypass the intervention of the powers by bringing about a direct settlement between the Sultan and the Pasha which would safeguard the Egyptian's position. Instead of succeeding, however, this manoeuvre led only to France's isolation and humiliation. Palmerston denounced the French action as a bid for exclusive control in the Near East and induced the other powers to conclude the Treaty of London imposing a settlement distinctly unfavourable to Mehemet Ali. The news of this treaty was received with intense indignation in France. There was much talk of tearing up the 1815 treaties and fighting 'the new Quadruple Alliance'[17] on the Rhine. Even the King allowed military preparations to be set on foot: the army was increased to 500,000 and 12,000,000 francs were voted for the fortification of Paris. In fact, however, Louis Philippe was as loth as ever to embark upon risky adventures. He would not go to war to preserve Syria for Mehemet Ali, and, after a further attempt on his life had given him new popularity, he took the opportunity to be rid of the bellicose Thiers and to form a new ministry headed by Soult, but really directed by Guizot. Peace was thus assured and in 1841 France joined with the other four Great Powers in signing the Straits Convention. She thus returned to the Concert of Europe, but her client, Mehemet Ali, had been irreparably weakened and was now confined to Egypt alone. Moreover her own brief explosion of martial spirit had been answered by an unexpected thunder of warlike patriotism from the Germanic Confederation. The English bombardment of Beirut and the German songs, 'Die Wacht am Rhein' and 'Deutschland über alles' were warnings of the dangers of war and the risks of isolation. In France, however, 'the young, the passionate, the lovers of liberty and action', had ignored the dangers and thought only of the glory.[18] Disillusioned by an outcome which they thought humiliating, they believed the Orléans monarchy was pursuing a policy of peace at any price and they began to despise it accordingly. 'France', said Lamartine in a famous phrase, 'is bored' – and she failed to recognize the importance of the work which her Government was accomplishing in slowly and painfully building up the foundations of a new Empire in North Africa which would be of vital importance to her a century later, or to derive much satisfaction from the acquisition of a few remote territories such as Nossi Bé, Tahiti or the Ivory Coast. None the less the most significant decision of the July Monarchy, in foreign policy, apart from the decisions to avoid war, was indeed the decision to retain Charles X's conquest of Algiers. 'It is our opera box,' Louis Philippe is reported to have said, 'but a terribly expensive one,'[19] and Corcelle told an English visitor to France in 1857 that he did not believe that France would have retained it had not Great Britain hoped that she would give it up.[20] At first the policy pursued was one of a limited occupation of the coastal area, but constant raids by the tribes of the interior eventually led the Government to the decision that the whole of Algeria must be brought under French control. This work of pacification opened up a field for eventual colonization and a base for the later development of a vast new continental territory, but its immediate significance was mainly military. Not only did it add picturesqueness to the French army by giving rise to the creation of special corps such as the Zouaves and the Foreign Legion, but it was for a long time to be the main theatre in which French troops could gain direct experience of military operations. Moreover, since the conditions of this warfare were highly specialized, there came into being, under the command of men like Bugeaud, what was virtually a separate African army with its own technique and equipment, necessarily very different from those required by the army of the metropolis. Training in Africa, however, was no necessary asset to the men and officers who would be required to fight in Europe, and the existence of an African training ground certainly did not compensate the old adherents of the party of Movement and the young men who were bored for the absence of a European battlefield.

But their boredom was unlikely to be relieved by the Minister who now directed French policy in conjunction with the King. 'Let us not talk about our country having to conquer territory, to wage great wars, to undertake bold deeds of vengeance. If France is prosperous, if she remains free, rich, peaceful and wise, we need not complain.'[21] These words, spoken by Guizot on 17 November 1840, well summarize the policy of the man who was to be Louis Philippe's chief adviser during the last seven and a half years of his reign.[22] Guizot was a man of impressive learning, a Protestant of austere character, a man whom both Lord Acton and John Morley thought the greatest all-round statesman of the nineteenth century.[23] Yet he maintained his majority in the Chamber by a system of judicious bribery reminiscent of Sir Robert Walpole. Under him, said Tocqueville, the Government of France 'came to resemble a limited company in industry which undertakes all its operations with a view to the profit to be extracted from them by the shareholders'.[24] The theory that power was the prerogative of the upper classes was indeed the essence and the weakness of Guizot's view of politics. For him the notion of political equality was a dangerous illusion and universal suffrage an instrument of destruction or deceit. Such a theory required above all the maintenance of peace, order and prosperity and aimed at the conservation and consolidation of the gains made by the middle class in 1830 rather than at any extension of liberties. Thus it was not surprising that towards the end of his official career Guizot came to work in harmony with the leading figure among European Conservatives, Prince Metternich, or that he obstinately resisted proposals for an extension of the franchise to people whom he believed to be without political capacity since he was certain it would lead to internal disturbance. Unfortunately for him, this inflexibility was in the end to lead directly to the very trouble he sought to avoid. Unfortunately, too, for the stability of the regime, Guizot's views were largely shared by the King. Louis Philippe enjoyed politics too much not to wish to exercise personal influence. Casimir Périer, Broglie and Thiers had all been difficult to manage: in Guizot he found a perfect collaborator. Indeed, under the new dispensation, it was for the most part the King himself who, like George III of England, pulled the strings and manipulated the *'pays légal'*, as the electorate was called.[25] Unhappily this meant that once again the French sovereign was prone to be a party man and unable to lift himself above party politics. Moreover, Louis Philippe was vain enough to let it be known that he, too, was a king who governed. In consequence, when the corruptness of the system of government was exposed, the sovereign who boasted of his share in the direction of policy, inevitably shared also in the discredit.

To begin with, however, under the new combination all seemed to prosper. The Anglo-French *entente* was renewed when Lord Palmerston was replaced at the Foreign Office by Lord Aberdeen with whom Guizot formed close and friendly relations. Although the old struggle between Church and University for control of secondary education (by which the electorate was formed) was once again renewed the country as a whole was tranquil, since the turbulent Republican elements had been driven underground or into exile. Commerce and industry progressed; the population increased by another three million; agricultural production rose and the railway era was at hand. France was in appearance rich and peaceful. But was she also wise and free?

In a pamphlet published in 1821 attacking the Ultra Government of the time, a young critic had written as follows: 'France is prosperous and does not stir; that is enough for them (the Ministers). There is no need to fear anything; no need to do anything; and if contrary to expectation, contrary to right, some misfortune were to happen, the misfortune would be in the wrong. . . . Nothing is more deceitful than the material happiness of peoples . . .'[26] and he had complained that 'the Counter-Revolution' feared 'movement' above everything. How well might these words have been applied some twenty years later to Guizot's Government and how extraordinary that their author was none other than Guizot himself! His wisdom was indeed short-sighted. In the Chamber he won oratorical victories and in elections, by adroit manipulation, he secured safe majorities. But beneath the veneer of ministerial stability and industrial and commercial prosperity there lay a depth of misery among workers as well as peasants. Their freedom was a mockery. Here there was a social question of growing seriousness which sooner or later was bound to lead to grave complications unless the Government took steps to solve it. As early as 1819 Sismondi in his *Principes d'économie politique* had attacked the policy of *laissez-faire* and argued that the state should intervene to regulate the use of property for the well-being of the whole community. Already the writings of Saint-Simon, who died in 1825, had sowed a seed-plot of ideas which provided a basis for the Positivist philosophy of Auguste Comte and inspired on the one hand many Socialist thinkers and on the other many masters of new forms of capitalist enterprise. For Saint-Simon's whole emphasis was transferred from politics to economics. He looked upon society as one great workshop or industrial community whose efficient organization was the main task of modern times. And so there had arisen a whole series of thinkers and writers who were preoccupied by the problems of industrialism and economic inequalities and whose criticisms of the existing order served to focus discontent. When the Government did nothing, the investigations of individual researchers and philanthropists and the writings of theorists and reformers such as Louis Blanc with his *Organisation du Travail* (1839), Flora Tristan with her *Union ouvrière*, Lamennais with his *Paroles d'Un Croyant* (1834), and Proudhon with his *Qu'est ce que la Propriéte?* (1841) and his ruggedly individualistic Socialism, all helped to rouse a social conscience which was inevitably more and more critical of the July Monarchy and tended to look elsewhere, to Republicanism, for salvation.

At the same time, it must be remembered that the primary education law of 1833 and the development of a cheaper press was tending to increase the numbers of the literate. When enterprising speculators like Émile de Girardin and Dutacq introduced advertisements and spiced their newspapers with serial stories, a device which helped to bring wealth and fame to men like Eugène Sue, Alexandre Dumas and Balzac, they were able to sell their new journals such as the *Presse* (1836) and the *Siècle* (which was soon dubbed 'the grocers' paper') at half price. By 1846 some twenty-six dailies were published in Paris with about 180,000 subscribers, more than three times the number there had been twenty years earlier, and these now included quite new kinds of paper such as the workers' *L'Atelier*, founded in 1840, which advocated many of the social reforms which would appear in the Republican programme of 1848. Simultaneously there had taken place a corresponding development of the provincial press, and the number of papers of one kind and another published in the provinces had doubled during the decade 1835–45. Thus the circle of the reading public, that is to say of potential critics of the Government, had greatly widened since Louis Philippe's accession. Furthermore, there were other factors which belied the apparent stability of the regime during the 1840s. In 1842 the dynasty had suffered a serious loss through the death of the heir to the throne, the Duc d'Orléans, the eldest and decidedly the most popular of the King's numerous sons. At the same time there was a disquieting tendency for Frenchmen to make a cult of other regimes than the one under which they lived: a little book by Prince Louis Napoleon published in 1839 under the title *Des ideés napoléoniennes* contributed not a little to the legend of a Liberal Emperor, while the cult of Napoleon grew with the return of his ashes from St Helena in 1840 and their interment at the Invalides in a ceremony of portentous splendour; moreover, the publication of Michelet's *Le Peuple* in 1846 and of his *Histoire de la Révolution* and Lamartine's *Histoire des Girondins* in 1847 revived interest in the Great Revolution. [27] When we remember also that Paris in the 1840s was the home of many revived secret societies and a refuge for every kind of *émigré* forced to leave his own country on account of his political or social views, we shall see that it was open to all sorts of subversive influences and a harbour for advanced or revolutionary thought. Nevertheless, despite or because of this intellectual ferment, the elections of 1846 were the only ones in the reign which gave the government of the day a coherent majority.

Paradoxically, the real turning-point in the second half of Louis Philippe's reign came with the year 1846. Then good fortune seemed to desert the Government, which was confronted by a grave economic crisis and embarked on a very questionable foreign policy. The result was that it incurred more and more criticism and soon became as unpopular as the ministry of Villèle in the days of Charles X.

The root cause of the economic crisis lay in the widespread bad weather of 1846 and 1847 which led to the failure of a great part of the corn harvests and the blighting of the potato crops of most of northern and western Europe. By May 1847, a year long remembered in France as 'the year of dear bread', wheat had more than doubled in price since 1844. Fear and disorders were rife in rural areas. Consumers had less money to spare for less essential purchases and there was an acute depression in the textile and other industries with a consequent increase in unemployment and sometimes reductions in wages. 'The metallurgy, coal mining and building industries were hard hit. Railway construction was stopped. Prices and profits collapsed to an . . . unprecedented degree.'[28] All this came on top of a financial crisis which had for some time been brewing in consequence of overspeculation in railway shares and a shortage of capital for investment. In the second half of 1846 the gold reserves of the Bank of France sank to a dangerously low level and the French Bank was obliged not only to follow the example of the Bank of England and raise its discount rate which went up to 15 per cent for the first time since 1817, another year of dear corn, but also to obtain a credit of £1,000,000 from the Bank of England through Baring's. There had been many economic crises in France before. The July Monarchy had come into being during a period of depression and there had been another difficult period during 1837–9, but none since 1815 had been so severe as this. In spite of the Government's prompt measures to import corn and of a good harvest in 1847, discontent remained widespread and the financial crisis persisted on into 1848. By then Guizot no longer had any reason to contemplate the state of France with complacent satisfaction.

In the meantime his foreign policy had in 1846 led to a rupture of the *entente* with Great Britain over the so-called Spanish Marriage Question.

The shades of the war of the Spanish Succession and of various eighteenth-century dynastic quarrels seemed to have been resurrected by this strange nineteenth-century quarrel between two constitutional monarchies for influence in Spain. The issue was indeed, as Lord Aberdeen remarked, no adequate cause for national quarrel, but Aberdeen was no longer in office in England, and with his successor, Palmerston, the man who had helped to break the *entente* in 1840, Guizot's relations were far from friendly. The Queen of Spain and her sister were both in the marriage market and Great Britain hoped either to secure a Coburg relation of Queen Victoria's as one of the husbands, or at least to ensure that the House of Orléans should not carry off both the prizes. Thus it had been a British stipulation that the marriage of the Infanta to a French prince should take place only after the Queen had married and had a child; and when in 1846 notwithstanding this supposed understanding with France, a double wedding took place between the Queen and the Duke of Cadiz and the Infanta and one of Louis Philippe's sons, the Duc de Montpensier, Palmerston was furious and believed that he had been tricked, while Guizot's supporters hailed the event as a splendid triumph of French diplomacy.

It was an empty triumph, for the establishment of a precarious domestic influence in the troubled Spanish kingdom was hardly worth the determined hostility of the British Foreign Secretary and the rupture of the *entente* which had been the mainstay of French foreign policy during the greater part of Louis Philippe's reign. Temporarily the rupture left France in isolation and although the conservative tendencies of Louis Philippe and Guizot led them to gravitate all the more easily towards co-operation with the Conservative Governments in Eastern Europe,[29] this evolution was far from palatable to an increasingly critical public opinion at home. The capture of Abd-el-Kader, the most redoubtable of the native leaders of resistance to French rule, in Algeria in 1847, was of no avail to offset the rebuffs to French prestige elsewhere. In Italy, where nationalist and liberal movements were growing, it was to England rather than France that the patriots looked for support in the cause of constitutional reform, and when Switzerland was rent by civil war it was England and not France which won the chief credit for the success of the Federal (and Liberal) cause. Thus there were no military or diplomatic successes in Europe to compensate for misfortune at home and France, from being merely bored, became all the more carping and critical of the foreign as well as the domestic policy of her governors.

Nor was this all. In spite of the economic crisis and the criticisms of home and foreign policy, the Government made no attempt to meet its opponents half-way. 'What has been done during these last seven years?' asked an Opposition Deputy in 1847, 'Nothing! Nothing! Nothing!'[30]

and in fact, apart from the first Factory Act of 1841, a measure which restricted the use of child labour in undertakings which employed more than twenty persons, but which was largely ineffectual for lack of a proper system of inspection, and from measures taken to relieve distress and encourage benefit societies, there had been no social legislation of any significance. Moreover, in spite of the growing criticism and of the revival of a movement for parliamentary reform which had first begun before 1840 with a petition, rejected by Thiers, for the grant of the vote to National Guards, the Government refused to consider any extension of the franchise.

This was their last and most fateful error; for they claimed to be the Government of the middle classes and of the *juste milieu*, yet continued to exclude from the *pays légal* an important section of that middle class, confining it to the wealthy among whom the new class of rich manufacturers formed a veritable new aristocracy, 'one of the harshest,' said Tocqueville, 'that has yet appeared on earth'.[31] The tax qualification had been arbitrarily fixed in 1814 and as arbitrarily modified in 1830. There was no logical reason why it should not again be lowered, especially since it confined the franchise to some 240,000 men and debarred from it many National Guards and educated people already used to electing their municipal councillors or National Guard officers. As a brilliant writer of the Second Empire later pointed out, with his income he would in 1847 almost certainly have been neither eligible for parliament nor qualified to be an elector and 'the fact that I was a doctor of letters, a former Faculty teacher, a member of the Institute and even a landed proprietor would have been of no avail'.[32] Thus the government of the country was still confined to an extremely small circle, and the occurrence of political scandals, such as that which led to the conviction of a former Minister, Teste, of corruption and social scandals such as that of the murder of the Duchesse de Choiseul-Praslin by her husband, at a time when there was already so much discontent, made it very easy for the reformers and the critics to denounce the whole circle as rotten. The government of the 200,000 electors became almost as much a subject of abuse by the Left as the 'government of the 200 families' eighty or ninety years later.[33]

The English Anti-Corn Law League with its lectures and tea-parties had recently shown what vigorous propaganda could do; similarly, in France in July 1847 some members of the Opposition sponsored a widespread campaign of banquets in favour of parliamentary reforms. Though it failed to unite the Opposition and to win many converts, the campaign helped to reanimate political life and went on into February 1848 when a banquet was planned for the 22nd in Paris. After some hesitation the Government decided to ban this meeting which looked like being a pretext for street demonstrations. But the decision did not avail to prevent crowds from gathering and demonstrating against the Guizot ministry. At the same time, the appearance of barricades and red flags in certain working-class districts of the capital showed that there was a dangerous revolutionary spirit in the air. Even the entreaties of the Queen and the Princes, who were alarmed lest the hostility to Guizot should extend to the King, had failed ten days earlier to induce Louis Philippe to part with his Minister, but now he relented. Guizot was dismissed and the royal summons first to Molé and then to Thiers, the chief Opposition leader, to form a new Cabinet, seemed to show that the King was ready to change his system, that the cause of reform had triumphed and that the crisis was over. Unfortunately this bloodless 'revolution' was already being transformed into one of violence which was to sweep away the throne as well as the Government. On the evening of the 23rd, as the result of an incident in front of the Ministry of Foreign Affairs, troops were impelled to fire upon a crowd of demonstrators. At once the mood of the Parisians changed for the worse. Republican agitators had already made much profit out of the abnormal public excitement; streets in the eastern part of the city were quickly blocked by insurrectionary barricades and armed mobs began to descend to the centre. Louis Philippe, who was now 75 years old, had been recently much depressed by the death of his sister and confidante, Madame Adélaide. He was further disheartened by the lukewarm reception he had received from the National Guards whom he had ridden out to review on the 24th. When they, who had been his special protégés, no longer greeted him with warmth he felt that all was over. Paris, now a great city of over a million, could only be regained by military conquest and on that he was not prepared to embark. So, in spite of the opposition of some members of his family, he decided to abdicate in favour of his grandson, the Comte de Paris, the ten-year-old son of the late Duke of Orléans. On that same 24 February the old King and his family followed in the footsteps of Charles X and trod the melancholy road to exile into England.

In many ways there were striking resemblances between the Revolutions of 1830 which brought Louis Philippe to the throne and of 1848 which led to his fall. In both, when a large part of Paris comes into rebel hands, the King decides to abdicate in favour of a child. But in 1830 it was the King who had courted revolution without preparing to meet it should it break out, whereas in 1848 the King had already yielded to the outcry against Guizot and the further disturbances took him and the authorities generally so much by surprise that they had been unable to react with the necessary vigour to restore order. In consequence, it was the initiative of the extremists which carried the day and swept not only Louis Philippe but also his dynasty from the throne. The majority of deputies in the Chamber were ready enough to accept the Comte de Paris and the Regency of his mother, but, when the Chamber was invaded by a crowd and the Republic was proclaimed at the Hôtel de Ville, it was clear that constitutional forms had no validity against the will of an excited people. This time the Republicans were determined that their Republic should not be side-tracked by any monarchical compromise. They swept aside the claims of the boy Comte de Paris and by revolutionary acclamation the Second French Republic came to birth.

Thus for the second time since 1815 a monarchy in France had fallen because of its failure to bridge in time a widening gulf between itself and public opinion. A second attempt to found a lasting system of government on the English model had come to grief and once again a revolution made in Paris was meekly accepted by the provinces. Nowhere was there any attempt to raise the standard in defence of the Orleanist cause. The Orléans family did not represent either a principle or a national glory; they had merely been a useful expedient, 'an administrative monarchy', as Armand Carrel had predicted,[34] and when they ceased to be useful to an important section of the middle classes who had been their mainstay their power collapsed – there was no other section of French society on whom they could depend. But their fall also meant the end of the experiment by which the middle and upper classes had sought to reserve to themselves the exclusive enjoyment of political influence by means of a limited franchise. The bourgeoisie might quickly recover and long enjoy great political as well as economic influence, but if they did so it would no longer be founded upon exclusive electoral rights. The days of *la monarchie censitaire* were over for ever.

It is easy to criticize the failings of the July Monarchy, but this criticism must not blind us to the facts that during the eighteen years from 1830 to 1848 it presided over or witnessed great material changes which did much to transform the conditions of life of large numbers of the French people and add to their amenities; and that during this period individual Frenchmen continued to achieve eminence in the most varied spheres of activity.

It would be impossible for us to leave the reign of Louis Philippe without mention of the law of 1836 for the improvement of country roads or of the inauguration of the first railway worthy of the name, the Paris–St Germain line in 1837, or of the sailing of the first transatlantic steamer in 1840.[35] These initiated developments, due to the Government, private enterprise, or a partnership of the two, which soon brought distant countries into communication with France and distant parts of France into contact with one another in ways and to a degree undreamed of fifty years earlier. Although she lagged behind England and Belgium, by the end of the reign France could boast 1931 km of railway track – a first stage in a process that transformed the conditions of trade and war – while the construction of her steam navy had contributed not a little towards the veritable invasion scare which swept through England after the rupture of the *entente* in 1846. By 1848 the improvement of local roads had led to an acceleration of local transport, to a widening of the areas to which farmers could send their produce and so to the beginning of a gradual revolution in agricultural technique which included a greater specialization and a greater reliance on artificial aids. An incidental consequence of these changes in communications was the introduction of a regular postal service and the appearance of what was soon to be the familiar figure of the *facteur* or postman. These were changes which affected life in every commune. There were others, too, but we cannot do more than mention one example, namely the fall in cotton prices in 1842, which Michelet, with some characteristic exaggeration of language, described as meaning a revolution in France: 'a revolution in property, a sudden embellishment of the poor man's household; whole classes now had underclothes, and linen for their tables and windows, who never had had such things since the world began. All the women formerly wore black or blue dresses which they kept for ten years without washing them for fear they would fall to pieces – today their husbands, poor workmen, for the price of a day's labour can clothe them in dresses of flowers. All these women who now display a rainbow of a thousand colours in our streets used to go about in mourning.'[36]

The July Monarchy was also a period of great cultural achievement. It did much for higher education and it witnessed the publication of some of the greatest works in French literature, further plays or poems by the great Romantics, Lamartine, Vigny, Hugo and Musset, books such as Stendhal's *Le Rouge et le Noir* (1831), Balzac's tremendous *Comédie Humaine*, Hugo's *Notre-Dame de Paris* and Dumas' *Count of Monte Cristo* (1844), Mérimée's *Colomba*, and social novels by George Sand. It was a period which could boast of an historian such as Tocqueville and of others so popular in their own day as Thiers, Lamartine, and Michelet, as well as of a prince of literary critics in Sainte-Beuve; in which the début of the young tragedienne Rachel in 1838 and the failure of Hugo's play *Les Burgraves* in 1843, marked the decline of the Romantic movement and the revival of an interest in classical drama; when the exhibition of paintings by the Barbizon School in 1831 brought a new galaxy of talent, including the exquisite Corot, to the fore; when the same year helped to make the reputation of a noted sculptor in David d'Angers; when the skill of Monnier, Philipon, Gavarni and Daumier now for the first time raised caricature to the level of art, and when the daguerreotype, precursor of the photograph, was to doom the silhouette and to bring the possession of a family portrait gallery within the means of the most modest purse, thereby providing a democratic complement to the aristocratic art of portrait painting. Nor was this all: the eloquence of the Chambers was outdone in the pulpit, and Lacordaire and Ravignan, the first to deliver the famous Lenten sermons at Notre Dame, are to be numbered amongst the greatest of all French preachers; in architecture Viollet-le-Duc began his career as the exponent of the Gothic revival; the Abbé Huc, intrepid missionary explorer, penetrated to the capital of the mysterious kingdom of Tibet; the Orientalist Burnouf won a foremost place among those who advanced the study of eastern languages; and the astronomer Leverrier discovered Neptune. These are but a few of the many names which might be mentioned to illustrate the continued diversity of French talent. During these same years Paris, the chief centre of so much intellectual activity, grew apace; several new quarters were constructed; the Pont du Carrousel was opened; the Luxor obelisk was erected in the centre of the Place de la Concorde; and last but not least, the Panthéon was reconverted from its use as a Church to serve as a mausoleum for great men with the words '*Aux grands hommes la patrie reconnaissante*' inscribed over its portal. There were many in the roll we have just cited, many of the men of Louis Philippe's day, who were to deserve this gratitude and find a resting-place within its vaults.

Notes

1 Cahen, L., and Mathiez, A., *Les lois françaises de 1815 à 1914*, p. 63. See also Butterfield, H., *Select Documents of European History, 1715–1920*, p. 114.
2 For the Declaration of the Chamber of Deputies and the modified clauses in the Charter see Appendix 4.
3 *Memoirs to Illustrate the History of My Time*, vol. 2, p. 213.
4 See the genealogical tree in Appendix 1.
5 For a striking character of Louis Philippe see Tocqueville, A. de, *The Recollections of*, ed. J. P. Mayer, p. 4ff.
6 For the text, see Cahm, E., *Politics and Society in Contemporary France (1789–1971)*, pp. 542–9.
7 Sainte-Beuve, *Portraits littéraires*, vol. 1, p. 317.
8 The Romantic cult of the 1830s, like the Existentalist cult of the 1940s led to strange exaggerations of dress and behaviour, 'Even schoolboys were now dressed as pages with little daggers. . . . Young men endeavoured to float companies for reviving the tourney or formed societies like the so-called Francs-Archers.'
9 Chateaubriand refused to acknowledge Louis Philippe and resigned his peerage, but he remained Achilles-like in his tent and did not actively work for a Legitimist restoration.

10 Woodward, E. L., *Three Studies in European Conservatism*, p. 213. These figures are quoted by L. Blanc in *Organisation du travail*, p. 66.

11 Clapham, J. H., *Economic History of Modern Britain*, vol. 1, p. 317.

12 Woodward, E. L., *French Revolutions*, p. 137. This was no doubt one reason why gymnastics now became a significant element in military training.

13 Cit. Rudé, F., *Le mouvement ouvrier à Lyon de 1827 à 1832*, p. 739.

14 It was during the 1830s that the terms 'Socialism' and 'Socialist' first came to be widely applied to advocates of social reform.

15 Pallain, G., *L'ambassade de Talleyrand à Londres 1830–1834*, p. ix.

16 Berkeley, F. F. H., *Italy in the Making 1815 to 1846*, p. 123.

17 I.e. an alliance against France like the Quadruple Alliance of 1814.

18 Bourgeois, E., *Manuel de la politique étrangère*, vol. 3, p. 176.

19 Senior, N. W., *Conversations with Thiers, Guizot, etc.*, vol. 2, p. 139.

20 ibid.

21 Lavisse, E. and Rambaud, A., *Histoire générale du IV. siècle à nos jours*, vol. 10, p. 399.

22 He did not actually become President of the Council of Ministers until September 1847.

23 Woodward, E. L., *French Revolutions*, p. 135.

24 Cit. Charléty, S., *La Monarchie de juillet*, p. 315.

25 The fact that civil servants were not debarred from sitting in Parliament provided obvious opportunities for Government pressure: at one time no less than 184 out of 459 deputies were 'placemen'. cf. Bourgin, G. in Fejtö, F., *1848 dans le monde, le printemps des peuples*, vol. 1, p. 183.

26 Guizot, *Des moyens du gouvernement et d'opposition*, p. 90.

27 The appearance of Lamartine's book could be described by a contemporary, Lanfrey, as 'the greatest political event of the time'. Louis Blanc also published a *History of the Great Revolution* in 1847. cf. Halévy, D., *Histoire d'une histoire esquissée pour le troisième cinquantenaire de la Révolution française*, p. 15.

28 Labrousse, E., *Summary of a paper on the Economic Crisis and the Political Crisis in France, 1847–51, given to an Anglo-French Historical Conference in Paris, Sept. 1945*, p. 1.

29 For instance, both Guizot and Metternich went as far as they dared in supporting the Catholic Cantons' league in Switzerland.

30 Cit. Seignobos, C., *Histoire politique de l'Europe contemporaine*, p. 135.

31 Cit. Weill, G., *L'éveil des nationalités et le mouvement libéral (1815–48)*, p. 324. A new phenomenon is the jealousy and fear of the new monopolistic plutocracy sometimes shown by the smaller traders and *petite bourgeoisie*.

32 Prevost-Paradol, *La France nouvelle*, pp. 324–5, n. 1.

33 The '200 families' were the families of the 200 largest shareholders in the Bank of France, who alone of the whole number of 40,000 shareholders had the right to vote at the annual meeting. For this reason they were attacked as the representatives in the financial oligarchy which was accused of exercising a new *pouvoir occulte* in French politics.

34 Sainte-Beuve, *Portraits littéraires*, vol. 2, p. 144.

35 Grand-Carteret, J. *Le XIXe siècle*, vol. 2, p. 636.
36 Michelet, J., *Le peuple*. Cit. Duveau, G., *La vie ouvrière en France sous le second Empire*, pp. 162–3.

Bibliography

Allison, John M. S., *Thiers and the French Monarchy*, London, 1926.

Bastid, Paul, *Les institutions politiques de la monarchie parlementaire française (1814–1848)*, Paris, 1954.

Beck, Thomas D., *French Legislators 1800–1834: A Study in Quantitative History*, Berkeley, 1974.

Beik, Paul H., *Louis Philippe and the July Monarchy*, Princeton, 1965.

Blanc, Louis, *The History of Ten Years 1830–40*, London, 1844.

Blanc, Louis, *Organisation du travail*, ed. J. A. R. Marriott, Oxford, 1913.

Bonaparte, Prince Napoleon-Louis, *Des idées napoléoniennes*, Paris, 1860.

Charléty, S., *La Monarchie de juillet* (vol. 5 of Lavisse, E., *Histoire de France contemporaine*), Paris, 1921.

Chevalier, L., *Le Choléra, la première épidémie du XIXᵉ siècle*, La Roche-sur-Yon, 1958.

Cooper, Duff, *Talleyrand*, London, 1932.

Dolléans, Edouard, *Histoire du mouvement ouvrier*, vol. 1, 1830–71, Paris, 1936.

Dunham, A. L., *The Industrial Revolution in France 1815–1848*, New York, 1955.

Fortescue, W., *Alphonse de Lamartine: A Political Biography*, London, 1983.

Guizot, F. P. G., *Memoirs of My Own Time*, vols 2–4, trans. J. W. Cole, London, 1859–61.

Howarth, T. E. B., *Citizen-King: The Life of Louis-Philippe King of the French*, London, 1961.

Jardin, A. and Tudesq, A.-J., *La France des notables*, Paris, 1973.

Johnson, D., *Guizot. Aspects of French History 1787–1874*, London, 1963.

Kent, Sherman, *Electoral Procedure under Louis Philippe*, New Haven, 1937.

Lucas-Dubreton, J., *Le culte de Napoléon 1815–1848*, Paris, 1960.

Ponteil, F., *La monarchie parlementaire 1815–48*, 3rd edn, Paris, 1966.

Rémusat, C. de, *Mémoires de ma vie*, vols 3–5, Paris, 1960–2.

Schapiro, J. Salwyn, *Liberalism and the Challenge of Fascism*, New York, 1949.

Sewell, William H., *Work and Revolution in France: The Language of Labor from the Old Regime to 1848*, Cambridge, 1980.

Sussel, P., *La France de la bourgeoisie*, Paris, 1970.

Vigier, Philippe, *La Monarchie de juillet*, 3rd edn, Paris, 1969.

Woodward, E. L., *Three Studies in European Conservatism*, London, 1929.

6

The Second Republic

The proclamation of a Republic in Paris evoked an extraordinary variety
and intensity of emotion both in France and throughout Europe, emotion
which ranged from the deepest alarm and anxiety to the most extravagant
hopefulness and enthusiasm. The young Prince de Broglie, then a diplomat in Rome, was one of those who heard the news with alarm: 'Country,
family, honour,' he wrote later, 'ambition, interests, personal security –
all seemed to be threatened at once and to fall engulfed in the same abyss.
Men could think only of 1793. The Republic meant bloodshed, confiscation, terror and war.'[1] All those who had possessions were indeed
anxious. Within a week, more than 1300 English people had hurried
home. Business, already slack, came almost to a standstill; unemployment
increased and there were outbreaks of machine smashing. Stocks fell; rich
people sold their effects, while at the same time there was a run upon
banks, many of which were obliged to suspend payment; even the gold
reserve in the Bank of France sank to such a low level that on 1 March 1848
dealings in paper money had to be stopped. This was one side of the
picture, the gloomy side. On the other we see an extraordinary Romantic
ebullience manifest in many ways: in the sudden emergence of workers'
corporations and of clubs – no less than 450 appeared within a month in
Paris and its suburbs, clubs with names that echoed those of the Great
Revolution, clubs of Jacobins and Montagnards, and clubs for the emancipation of European peoples or of the feminine sex; in an abundance of
banquets, banquets of 'the Federation of European Peoples', of the
'Friends of Poland', of 'Democratic Women', of 'Les travailleurs de la
pensée' and a hundred more, banquets which always ended with some
resounding toast – 'To the Mountain of 1793' – 'To Mistrust, sister of
Vigilance' – 'To Jesus Christ' – 'To democratic Germany' – 'To Jean-
Jacques Rousseau' – 'To the oppressed peoples' – and to many others; in
the spate of newspapers and pamphlets which poured forth as soon as the
new rulers abolished the stamp duty and removed the restrictions imposed

by the law of 1835 on the liberty of the Press, papers and pamphlets which abounded not with news but with social and political programmes and doctrinaire declarations; in the planting of Trees of Liberty and their blessing by the clergy – for the Church, too, had been swept by liberal enthusiasms since the election in 1846 of a Liberal Pope; and in the cult of 'the people', as instanced by the opening words of the preamble to the Government's proclamation of 26th February announcing its intention to abolish the death penalty: 'The Provisional Government, convinced that generosity is the supreme part of policy and that each revolution effected by the French people owes it to the world to consecrate yet one more philosophic truth, considering that there is no principle more sublime than that of the inviolability of human life; considering that, in the memorable days in which we are living, not a cry of vengeance has arisen from the mouth of the people. . . .'[2] In short, among the people, the *gens du peuple* of Paris, Limoges, Rouen and elsewhere, the Revolution was hailed as the dawn of a new era. It was not long before their hopes were to be bitterly disappointed.

Although its breach with the immediate past was more complete, in many ways the Revolution recalled that of 1830. Once again journalists played a great part and rival sets of insurgents bid against one another for power; once again the Hôtel de Ville was a place of decisive importance; once again the period of unrest and popular demonstrations continued long after the Revolution itself was over; and once again there were two conflicting views of the object of the Revolution, each of which had its supporters within the Government itself. Accordingly, this Provisional Government which emerged represented a compromise. All its members save one, Albert, a workman, included in recognition of the part played by the people in the Revolution, were of bourgeois origin, more or less well-known Republicans, for the most part lawyers, orators and journalists by profession. On the one hand there were the men of the newspaper, *Le National*, people like Arago, Crémieux, Marie, Garnier-Pagès and Lamartine, for Lamartine had more or less abandoned poetry for politics and now became Minister for Foreign Affairs; on the other it included the men who supported the rival paper, *La Réforme*, such as Louis Blanc, Albert, Flocon and Ledru-Rollin. For the former the Revolution was a political event: it meant the completion of the political work of the Great Revolution by the substitution of a free and democratic Republic based upon universal male suffrage for a monarchy based upon a restricted franchise: but for the men of the *Réforme* it implied a social and economic as well as a political transformation, and in Louis Blanc, the author of *L'Organisation du Travail*, they had a social observer who was acutely aware of the evils of the new industrial age and who was most eager to abolish them. The great drama of 1848 lies in the conflict between those who want to seize the opportunity to solve the social problem by radical reforms of the conditions of labour and those who are determined to resist social changes which they fear will lead to chaos and anarchy. And herein also lies the great contrast between 1830 and 1848: in 1830 many middle class people stood to benefit, in 1848 they are for a while on the defensive.

The men of the *Réforme* were a minority in the Provisional Government, but they had sufficient influence and sufficient popular backing to make themselves felt at the outset. On 25 February only the eloquence of Lamartine saved the tricolour from being displaced by the Socialist red flag; this was symbolic of the conflict between the old and the new revolutionaries – but, if the Government compromised by allowing a red rosette to be affixed to the standard of the tricolour, they had to make more conspicuous concessions to the demand for social reform when they reduced daily working hours to ten in Paris and eleven in the provinces and when they issued a proclamation recognizing the right to work. Moreover, although they refused the request for the establishment of a separate Ministry of Labour, they set up a permanent commission which was to sit at the Luxembourg Palace and examine labour problems under the presidency of Louis Blanc. Finally, in order to deal with the acute problem of Parisian unemployment, they created National Workshops.[3] All this marked a radical departure from the *laissez-faire* attitude of the July Monarchy. The Government for the first time in French history were ready to guarantee work and to set about the task of organizing labour; but their organization of labour in the National Workshops was to be a parody of the 'Organisation du Travail' envisaged by Louis Blanc. None the less, these first social successes were sufficient to confirm the hopes of the enthusiastic workers. Was not one of their own kind, Albert, in the Government? Was not Louis Blanc in charge of labour questions? Was not George Sand who had echoed his charitable formula 'To each according to his needs',[4] busy helping the new ministers draft their decrees? And if the Government had not yet abolished the work-book or done away with the Combination Laws,[5] had it not guaranteed the right to work? All these considerations appeared signs of still better things to come and were hailed by many as a mere prelude to the complete transformation of society. But the fact that some of these social measures were extorted more or less under pressure by armed demonstrators had been enough to alarm both the moderates in the Government and most of their sympathizers outside it. The political course of the Revolution was soon to give the moderates and conservatives, the forces of order, the defenders of the existing society, an opportunity to rally, go over to the offensive and progressively disarm the extreme Left.

After preparing for the abolition of slavery in the French colonies, which was decreed in April', and abolishing 'monarchy of every kind without possibility of return'[6] the Provisional Government had hastened to arrange for the establishment of the Republic on a regular basis. On 5 March they decreed that elections to a National Constituent Assembly should be held on 9 April and that every Frenchman over twenty-one years of age should be entitled to a vote. Thus, by a stroke of the pen, universal male suffrage was introduced into France and the electorate was increased from some 240,000 to some 9,000,000. Moreover, in spite of the elementary education bill of 1833 and the growth of the popular press to which we referred in the last chapter, the majority of this vast new electorate was still illiterate. In his *Les Paysans*, written in 1845, Balzac has a striking passage on the meaning of legislation for the provinces:

> For twenty million beings in France the law is merely a piece of white paper stuck on the door of the Church or the Town Hall (Mairie). . . .
> Many mayors of cantons turn their copies of the *Bulletin des Lois* into bags for holding raisins and seeds. As for the mere mayors of communes you would be shocked by the number who cannot read or write and by the way in which the civil registers are kept.[7]

If such were the mayors, it is clear that the ordinary peasant or worker was unlikely to be more lettered. In these circumstances, although the Republic was giving them the vote, it was not at all certain that their vote would be for the Republic. Blanqui indeed had at once seen that if elections were held quickly they would be likely to produce conservative results, and Ledru-Rollin, Minister of the Interior, did his best to educate the new electors, replacing all the prefects by special Commissioners and circulating Republican propaganda. But the Government would only consent to postpone the elections for a fortnight and meanwhile events in Paris and various parts of the country served but to increase the moderates' distrust of the Republic and its capacity to maintain order. Thus the postponement of the elections was itself extracted from the Government by outside pressure. On 16 March the bourgeois National Guards of the western districts of Paris had demonstrated against a measure dissolving some of their companies: on the 17th clubs and crowds, one of whose leaders was Blanqui, had compelled the Government to postpone the elections but only until 23 April. On the 21st a Radical Republican 'Club of Clubs' was founded which opened branches in the provinces and associated itself with Ledru-Rollin in his attempt to republicanize the electorate. On 13 April another club, in which Armand Barbès was a prominent figure, called upon the Government to take over the Bank of France and to nationalize the insurance companies, railways, mines and canals. On the 16th, however, the National Guard dispersed a workers' demonstration.

This was a turning point. Nine days later, the Government felt strong enough to order five regiments of regular troops back to Paris. Meanwhile in many country districts also the Revolution had been a signal for serious disturbances, for attacks on clergy, rich proprietors, Jews and forest guards, and on justices of the peace, responsible for the collection of the unpopular *droits réunis* tax. The tales of these disturbances, of Paris disorder and of Socialist threats to property soon spread to the remotest parts of the country and were not diminished in retelling. Furthermore, acute financial difficulties had led the Government as early as 16 March to add an additional forty-five centimes to direct taxation. This was a measure which inevitably made them unpopular with a thrifty peasantry already alarmed by rumours of disorder. In fact, the difference between 1789 and 1848 was very marked, in spite of the conscious echoes of the Great Revolution which resounded in the clubs. In 1789 the great mass of the nation, the country dwellers as well as the bourgeoisie, had been eager for the abolition of feudal privileges and political inequality: but in 1848 the number of Frenchmen who genuinely desired a social revolution and the abolition of economic inequality was comparatively small. The peasantry, so many of them now proprietors, were only scared by the stories of the Parisian Socialists and their rumoured talk of redistributing or doing away with individual property by some new agrarian law. And so when election day came and 84 per cent of the electorate went to the polls, most of them for the first time and most of them village folk, often headed by their parish priests as they marched to the booths, the votes cast were above all votes for an orderly and liberal Republic. In other words, the result even in Paris, was a crushing defeat for the extreme Radicals and Socialists, who won only 100 out of 876 seats.

The new Assembly, which thus comprised a large majority of moderate Republicans, former Orleanists, and Legitimists, most of them middle-class men new to parliament, was bound to come sooner or later into conflict with the extremists still influential in Paris, despite their electoral setback. A few days after it met in May the Provisional Government resigned and the executive authority was entrusted to a so-called Executive Commission of five members of the late Government, but not including Louis Blanc or Albert. Already the Assembly was beginning to show its Conservative tendencies, and on 12 May there took place the first of a series of demonstrations against it which culminated in one on the 15th when the Palais Bourbon was invaded by a mob, a club orator pronounced the Assembly's dissolution, and most of the crowd, headed by Barbès and Albert, then proceeded to the Hôtel de Ville to concoct a new

Government. But the National Guard rallied and the new Mobile Guards, largely recruited from young unemployed, cleared the Assembly. The Hôtel de Ville was re-occupied and many of the leaders of this attempt at a second Revolution, including Barbès, Blanqui and Albert, were arrested and imprisoned. The apostles of a Social Republic had, as George Sand perceived, committed a moral as well as a political blunder: 'They had without serious cause . . . given the signal for a rising against the law of the Republic; they had thrown people into a permanent state of anxiety and in some sort justified future *coups de force!*[8]

Meanwhile labour problems again came to the fore. On 10 May Louis Blanc again proposed the creation of a Ministry of Labour and Progress, but the Assembly merely set up a committee to inquire into labour conditions in agriculture and industry, canton by canton, throughout the country. It was optimistic enough to hope that the inquiry would be completed in a few weeks, but such a vast operation was bound to be protracted and, despite far-sighted agrarian proposals, its enduring legislative fruits were small. A special problem was, however, presented by the National Workshops in Paris. In his *Organisation du Travail* Louis Blanc had conceived of state-aided 'social' workshops or factories as a means of combating unemployment and utilizing skilled labour in an orderly fashion. There was scope enough for a great programme of public works, as the history of the Second Empire was to show, but the Republican Government lacked the credit to finance one and the Workshops of Paris in 1848, as they were organized under the direction of Marie and Thomas, a travesty of Louis Blanc's conception, were like nothing so much as the *ateliers de charité* of the Ancien Régime. Set up too hastily, under revolutionary pressure and without adequate administrative services to control them, they had soon enrolled over 100,000 workmen when there was real work for only 10,000. The remainder had to be occupied and were therefore employed on tasks such as levelling the Champ de Mars for two francs a day, work of such little value that, as someone said, they might just as well have bottled the waters of the Seine. The presence of so many men so unprofitably employed was soon recognized by the Government as demoralizing for the men themselves, a drain on public funds, a danger to public order (many of the workers having taken part in the disturbances of 15 May) and in consequence an impediment to the recovery of business; and so it was decided that, after a census had been taken, the Workshops should be dissolved, that bachelors between eighteen and twenty-five should have the choice of dismissal or enrolment in the army; and that the rest should either accept what work could be offered by private employers or be sent to work on public enterprises in the provinces. After some delay the Assembly passed a decree on these lines and towards the end of June the Executive Commission of the Government decided to proceed immediately with the dissolution of the Workshops.

The result was infinitely tragic. The workers were furious at what they regarded as the Government's and Assembly's treachery in going back on the guarantee of the right to work. The persistence of the economic crisis, in spite of the rule of a Republican regime, had steadily hardened social antagonisms, making the employers sterner in their resolve to end what they regarded as social anarchy and the young workers all the more bitter at the choice now presented to them between conscription and unemployment. And so many, but by no means all, of the men of the National Workshops, and the unemployed who had been refused admission to them, determined to resist the order for dissolution, and all the eastern working-class quarters of Paris rose in sympathy. For a second time within a few months Paris saw the barricades go up. No persuasion could induce the men to disperse peaceably and on 24 June 1848 the Assembly gave General Cavaignac the title of Chief of the Executive Power with full authority to use force. Troops were hurried to the city by train, 100,000 provincial National Guards supported them, and three days of bitter fighting ensued. It was a remarkable insurrection – not led by any of the Socialist chiefs or deputies, but, in Tocqueville's words, one in which 100,000 insurgents fought 'without a war-cry, without chiefs, or a standard, and yet with a cohesion and a military skill which surprised the oldest officers'. It was 'not the work of a group of conspirators, but the rising of one part of the population against the other. Women took part in it as much as men . . . they hoped for victory to ease the lot of their husbands, and help to bring up their children.' 'It was not a political struggle . . . but class war, a kind of slave-war.'[9] As such it had all the ruthlessness of class or slave warfare, and was bitterly fought, and ruthlessly suppressed. Many were killed, 15,000 people were arrested and 450 eventually sent to Algeria.[10] All Socialists were now under suspicion and Louis Blanc hurriedly took refuge in England. Clubs were placed under supervision. New press laws reimposed a cautionary payment on those who wished to publish political papers and made attacks upon certain institutions indictable offences. In September the working day in Paris was once again increased to twelve hours and in many instances in the years to follow it became still longer. When the Assembly applauded Cavaignac for his achievement in suppressing the insurrection Lamartine exclaimed: 'The Republic is dead.' When Lamennais was obliged by the new press laws to cease publishing his paper *Le Peuple Constituant* he did so with the bitter words 'Silence to the poor man', and commented that the spectacle presented by France after the June Days was not that of Republican France but of the 'saturnalia of reaction around its bloodstained tomb'.[11]

Whatever the bitterness in Paris, this was not true of the provinces. There in July and August the first elections of local councils by universal suffrage passed off quietly. Country people were again exercising political rights and had no reason to feel cowed.

Nevertheless there is much to be said for the view of Lamartine and Lamennais that, although the Republic still continued for more than four years, it was really only a Republic in name. After the June Days it was experienced Orleanists or Legitimists like Thiers, Falloux, Montalembert, Odilon Barrot, and Berryer, who carried most weight in the inexperienced Assembly; and, when the Assembly had completed its work of endowing the country with a Republican constitution, the nation was to elect as President a man who would work patiently to give this strange accidental Republic the *coup de grâce*.

In November, after six months of labour, the new Constitution was ready. It has been called 'the most democratic that France has ever enjoyed',[12] yet it reflected both the retreat from the social aspirations of February and the reaction against the English parliamentarism imitated by the Charters of 1814 and 1830. The Republic now no longer guaranteed the right to work, but only undertook more cautiously to guarantee 'the existence of citizens in distress, either by procuring them work within the limits of its resources or by giving relief to those who were not able to work'. In its political arrangements the Constitution laid down that separation of powers was the first condition of a free Government and, in spite of Orleanist opposition, provided that the legislature should consist of a single chamber or Legislative Assembly. Thus its authors harked back to the traditions of the Great Revolution, but failed to ensure that the separated parts of their new structure would work in harmony together. What, for instance, would happen if the new Legislative Assembly, to be elected by universal suffrage, should conflict with the holder of the office, new to France, of President of the Republic, who was also to be elected by universal suffrage and to enjoy very wide executive power? In vain had the moderate Republican, Jules Grévy, argued that it would be more prudent not to have a President at all. His objections had been swept aside by the eloquence of another Republican, Lamartine, who himself aspired to the presidency and said that it would be an error to have the President elected by the Assembly instead of by direct universal suffrage; for an Assembly would be suspect, whereas 'a nation is as incorruptible as the Ocean'.[13] Again, if there were difficulties in operating the new machinery, would it not be as well to make it easy for the Constitution to be revised? But the Constituent Assembly had too much respect for its own work and held that a constitution was not a thing to be lightly tampered with. Accordingly the provisions laid down for revision were elaborate and required a vote of no less than three-quarters of the new Legislative Assembly before any changes could be made.

In December the sovereign people, Lamartine's 'incorruptible nation', went once again to the polls: this time to elect the first President of the Second French Republic. Three of the Republicans, who had played a prominent part in the events of the last ten months were among the candidates, Cavaignac, Lamartine and Ledru-Rollin. But these names spelt little to a nation which was by no means Republican at heart compared with another which had a meaning for the humblest peasant, a name known to all, a name covered with glory and which had gained such fresh popularity in recent years as the result of a romantic cult that it was capable of sweeping the country, almost regardless of the character and personality of its present bearer: the name of Napoleon. Already in by-elections to the Constituent Assembly in June and September a number of departments had chosen Prince Louis Napoleon, nephew of the great Emperor and, since the death of his elder brother in March 1831 and the Duc de Reichstadt in 1832, head of the House of Bonaparte, to be their deputy. Now in December, aided by the clever and assiduous propaganda of his agents, the Prince was carried to the Presidency by an overwhelming majority.

To those who knew the Prince, without knowing the strength of the Bonapartist legend and how weary France was of a Republic which had done nothing but accumulate disorders, perpetuate instability and increase taxation, such a result might well have appeared wholly astonishing. His attempts to raise the Bonapartist standard in 1836 and 1840 had been ludicrous fiascos. He had spent most of his life out of France and spoke French with a German accent. He was unprepossessing in appearance – with his black clothes, heavy thick moustache and pale immobile features, almost a caricature of a Romantic conspirator. His manners were awkward, shy, and irresolute, and his first speeches in the Assembly led experienced politicians to dismiss him as a nonentity. Indeed, ironically enough, the protest he made against a motion that all members of former ruling houses should be ineligible for the Presidency was so halting and embarrassed that the mover of the motion was led to withdraw it, saying that it was clearly superfluous 'after what we have just seen and heard'. But he still had two great assets, his name and his extraordinary faith in his star, which had so far enabled him to triumph over every obstacle. For the peasants and old soldiers[14] he stood for order and glory; for many of the workers 'Poléon', the Prince who in 1844 had written an essay called *L'Extinction du paupérisme* and who might like his uncle continue the work of the Great Revolution, was preferable to Cavaignac, the Butcher of June; for most of the Royalists he appeared likely to be a useful stopgap

until such time as the Legitimists and Orleanists should succeed in com-
posing their differences and restoring the monarchy; and even some
Republican politicians, like the Jewish Crémieux, gave him their vote on
the grounds that he represented the clearest protest against the Treaties of
1815.[15] And so the vote for Louis Napoleon in December 1848, had been
in the words of Emile de Girardin 'not an election, but an acclamation'.[16]

It remained for the other parts of the new constitutional structure to be
set up. The elections to the Legislative Assembly in May 1849, contested
by more highly organized groups than those of April 1848, still further
emphasized the discredit of the Republicans. Nearly two-thirds of the
deputies belonged to the 'Party of Order'; the moderate Republicans were
reduced to eighty and, to the alarm of the Conservatives, outdistanced by
the extremists now known as 'the Mountain', who retained a considerable
hold upon Paris and had won some ground in parts of the south and
south-east of France which have ever since tended to remain bastions of
the Left. The Spanish Ambassador might well comment on the strange
spectacle of an Assembly filled with monarchists who could not establish a
monarchy and who groaned under the weight of a Republic which had no
Republicans to defend it. Yet it was not so much true that the Republic
had no defenders as that its deputies were an impotent minority. The
meeting of the new Assembly, like that of the Constituent Assembly a
year earlier, provoked another Parisian insurrection, but this time it was
not the people who wanted leaders so much as the leaders, Ledru-Rollin
and his friends, who wanted troops. The rising of 13 June was a fiasco,
although it was supported at Lyon and elsewhere. It led Ledru-Rollin[17] and
others to follow Louis Blanc and flee to England, and it was followed by a
tightening of the press laws and a ban on public meetings of a political
character.

Meanwhile the President, although many of the politicians as yet did
not realize it, set about patiently preparing for the final step which would
lead him to the fulfilment of what he believed to be his destiny, the restoration of the Empire. He had a number of faithful personal followers, but
there was as yet no organized Bonapartist party. He could not hope to
appeal to Orleanists and Legitimists as such, but by his acts he might well
win over the influential body of French Catholics, who now included a
growing number of bourgeois scared out of their scepticism by the events
of 1848. And so 1849 and 1850 are marked by important developments in
foreign and educational policy which did much to consolidate Louis
Napoleon's position.

As we have seen, the Revolution of February 1848, was followed by
much grandiloquent talk of emulating the deeds of the ancestors of the
Great Revolution, and it was believed by many at home and abroad that

the proclamation of a Republic would inevitably lead to war and a crusade to tear up the 1815 treaties and carry the blessings of liberty to less fortunate peoples. It is indeed arguable that such a crusade would have solved the problem of unemployment and averted the civil strife of the June Days; but the rulers of 1848 were influenced as much by the new Romantic pacifism with its cult of the peaceful brotherhood of peoples as by militant Jacobinism, and with more than enough trouble on their hands at home they had no wish to add to their burdens the perils of war. Thus, although the February Revolution had been an European event of the first magnitude because it had given the impetus to revolution in Berlin, Vienna, Budapest and many other lesser cities, Lamartine had resolutely resisted the pressure of extremists like Barbès and Blanqui, who demanded that France should help to recreate an independent Poland, and he and his successors had been no less firm in refusing to go to war on behalf of the Italians against Austria. But the extreme Republicans never lost sight of their international connections. One of the avowed objects of the manifestation of 15 May 1848 against the Constituent Assembly had been to secure a Government which would reconstitute a free Poland; and now again the rising of June 1849 was partly a demonstration on behalf of the Republic which had been set up four months earlier in Rome, after the murder of his Prime Minister, Rossi, had led the Pope to flee to Gaeta. In March 1849, the expiring Constituent Assembly had voted credits for the dispatch of a French expeditionary force to maintain Roman liberties against the danger of suppression by Austria – once again the desire to maintain France's traditional influence in Italy was a powerful force in the diplomacy of 1848–9. But this was not the goal designed for the expedition by the Prince-President, for the French Catholics, for whose support he was angling, wanted not the preservation of Mazzini's Republic but the restoration of the Pope. And so it was that the expeditionary force intended by French Republicans to defend the Roman Republic was used to destroy it. After sham negotiations, its commander, General Oudinot, at the end of June, proceeded to besiege the city of Rome and on 3 July it fell. France, the chief of European Republics, then put an end to one of the few others born of the revolutionary wave of 1848 which still survived. The Pope was restored but, like Ferdinand VII of Spain in 1823, stubbornly refused to reintroduce any liberal reforms, in spite of Louis Napoleon's expressed wish. However, Catholic support was more important to the Prince-President than Liberal institutions. The result was that French troops henceforth appeared as the natural defenders of the temporal power of a Papacy which had reverted to reaction and was soon to denounce most of the works of modern civilization.

In foreign affairs Louis Napoleon had thus played his part. The countenance he gave to the Loi Falloux of 1850 was the equivalent gesture to the French Catholics in domestic matters. In spite of anti-clericalism, which had continued into the 1830s and revived again with renewed attacks on the Jesuits in the 1840s, the Church had continued to try and improve its position in the State. Above all, it had fought against the University monopoly of higher and secondary education and in its struggle it had been most eloquently served by some of the new school of Liberal Catholics of whom the Comte de Montalembert was the chief. Now at last its efforts were to be rewarded. The Loi Falloux was to secure the position of the Catholics in education for more than thirty years and seemed so great a victory that the illustrious Dominican preacher Lacordaire could hail it as a nineteenth-century Edict of Nantes.[18] The State monopoly was broken down and henceforward two categories of school were accorded official recognition: the public schools founded and maintained by communes, departments or the State; and the already flourishing free schools founded by private individuals or associations. In effect this meant that any authorized or tolerated religious association could now open a school – as for private individuals few were wealthy or interested enough to do so – and that religious orders, including the Jesuits, came to play an increasingly important part in education. To a detached English observer this might seem a fair solution, but to Frenchmen of the Left it appeared another sign of the strength of reaction, a measure of a piece with the electoral law of the same year, 1850, which resulted from the majority's profound alarm at the return of twenty-one Montagnards in recent by-elections in Paris and elsewhere. This law required evidence of three years' residence for inclusion in the electoral roll and effectively disfranchised some 3,000,000 people, many of whom would undoubtedly have tended to vote for the now more highly organized Mountain.

The discredit of the Republicans and the continued inability of the Monarchists to agree upon a King facilitated the Prince-President's task of achieving his personal ambitions. The two acts to which we have just referred were largely successful in bringing many French Catholics to regard him with sympathy as the defender of their interests. By a series of tours of the provinces he made himself more widely known, learnt to play his new part more easily and won a considerable personal triumph by his gracious demeanour and the unexpected felicity of the speeches in which he dwelt upon the blessings of order and prosperity and recalled how they had been provided of old by a greater than he whose name he bore. At the same time he had not been slow in showing the Legislative Assembly that he did not intend to be its mere tool. As time passed and Louis Napoleon's confidence in his ability to pursue an independent policy increased, the growing friction between the Executive and the Legislative became more and more apparent. In February 1851, the Assembly rejected a proposal to increase the President's civil list, and in July they defeated a proposal to revise the constitution so as to permit of Louis Napoleon's immediate re-election and turned down his suggestion that they should rescind the electoral laws of 1850. Meanwhile the term of both was running out. The President had been elected at the end of 1848 for four years, the Legislative Assembly in May 1849 for three years. 1852 would therefore be a critical year in which many feared anarchy and a resurgence of 'red' Republicanism. Louis Napoleon who had played his cards against the Legislative Assembly with so much adroitness exploited this fear and decided not to wait. By the end of November his plans were made, he was sure of the army, he had prepared his justification and during the night of 1–2 December he acted. The chief party leaders were arrested and the Chamber was occupied by troops. On the 2nd Frenchmen awoke to find the capital placarded by proclamations announcing the dissolution of an Assembly which the President accused of 'forging arms for civil war'. 'My duty,' said Louis Napoleon, 'is to maintain the Republic . . . by invoking the solemn judgement of the only sovereign I recognize in France . . . the people';[19] and he posed as the people's champion by at once reintroducing the full universal suffrage which the Assembly had refused to restore in the summer, and by announcing that a new Republican constitution would be submitted to the verdict of a plebiscite.

Wiser in his generation than Charles X, Louis Napoleon had prepared his coup with thoroughness. Yet it met unexpected resistance: 220 deputies protested and were briefly imprisoned; the Montagnards of the South and Centre took up arms to defend the constitution and redress local grievances, and a few Republican deputies, including Victor Hugo, tried to raise the eastern quarters of Paris. But there the workers were now mostly sceptical or indifferent, and the death of a deputy, Baudin, on a barricade, hardly caused a stir. This did not mean that there was not still a strong Republican feeling, which showed itself in the plebiscite and the elections to the new Legislative Assembly in February 1852 when two Republicans, Carnot and Cavaignac, were returned; but the workers had no taste for a second June Days war.

Attempts at resistance were ruthlessly repressed. Nearly 27,000 people were arrested or prosecuted in default; some 15,000 were condemned to various sentences; and some 9000 to deportation to Algeria. The Montagnard movement was destroyed and discontented peasants never again resorted to armed revolt.

Although the Republic, which Louis Napoleon acknowledged it was his duty to maintain, survived in name for another year, everyone knew that the restoration of the Empire was only a question of time. 2 December 1851 was virtually the *coup de grâce* for the Second Republic, so long already only a shadow of its original self, and it led to the institution of an authoritarian regime very different from the parliamentary governments enjoyed by France since 1815. The reluctance of Louis Philippe and Guizot to grant parliamentary reform and the violence of the Parisians had thus led to a further violent interruption in the peaceable and regular development of constitutional government in France. The political changes in French society resulting from the French Revolution had been emphasized anew and in addition the bitter social cleavages resulting from the industrial Revolution now stood revealed. The first Napoleon had been nearer than any French ruler since 1789 to recreating a unity among Frenchmen. It remained to be seen whether 'The man of December' would have equal success.

Notes

1 *Mémoires du Duc de Broglie*, vol. 1, p. 185.
2 *Les murailles révolutionnaires de 1848*, p. 58.
3 The new administrations in some provincial towns, e.g. Limoges and Rouen, likewise set up municipal workshops: see Merriman, John M., *The Agony of the Republic*, pp. 7, 15–16.
4 In *Le péché de M. Antoine* one of the characters says '*Si après votre formule à chacun selon ses capacités vous n'ajoutez pas aussitôt à chacun selon ses besoins, c'est l'injustice qui règne.*' Cit. Ponteil, F., *1848*, p. 15.
5 See ch. 2, p. above.
6 For the provisional Government's proclamation of 26 February cf. Butterfield, H., *Select Documents of European History, 1715–1920*, pp. 125–6.
7 Cit. *Bulletin No. 10* of the *Société d'histoire de la Troisième République*, p. 87. According to F. Ponteil the number of primary schools had increased from 30,586 to 63,028 between 1829 and 1847 and the number of pupils from 1,937,000 in 1832 to 3,000,000 in 1847, 'but as late as 1857, 33.5 per cent of the conscripts could neither read nor write', op. cit., p. 108.
8 Cit. Ponteil, op. cit., p. 116.
9 Cit. Namier, L. B., *1848: the Revolution of the Intellectuals*, p. 10.
10 The statistics for killed and arrested vary, for instance, those given in Philippe Vigier's *La seconde République*, p. 43, are considerably higher. The official number of killed is 1460, but no one ever counted those who died in hospital or who were buried immediately. One of the most notable casualties was Mgr Affre, the Archbishop of Paris, who was shot while attempting mediation.
11 Cit. Ponteil, op. cit., p. 154.
12 Pouthas, Ch.-H., *Démocraties et capitalisme*, p. 114. For the text see Appendix 5.
13 Cit. Falloux, Comte de, *Mémoires d'un Royaliste*, vol. 1, p. 352.
14 'I canvassed for Louis Napoleon one of my own peasants,' Montalembert told Nassau Senior. '*Comment veut-on*,' he answered, '*que je ne vote pas pour ce*

monsieur: moi, qui ai eu le nez gelé à Moscou!' 'Et quand,' added his wife, *'nous avons eu deux fois la maison pillée!'* Senior, N. W., *Conversations with M. Thiers,* vol. 1, p. 365.

15 Namier, op. cit., p. 34.

16 Cit. Bellessort, A., *La société française sous Napoléon,* III, p. 27.

17 It was at this time that Ledru-Rollin, a reluctant revolutionary, uttered his famous phrase, *'Je suis leur chef, il faut que je les suive,'* cf. Halévy, D., *La République des comités,* p. 16.

18 There was, however, a body of intransigent Catholics, led by the great polemical journalist Veuillot, who were not satisfied and denounced it as a miserable compromise. For the text, see Cahm, E., *Politics and Society in Contemporary France (1789–1971),* pp. 544–6.

19 Proclamation to the people. Cit. Cahen, L. and Mathiez, A., *Les lois françaises de 1815 à 1914,* p. 121.

Bibliography

Agulhon, M., *The Republican Experiment 1848–1852,* Cambridge, 1983.

Amann, Peter H., *Revolution and Mass Democracy: The Paris Club Movement in 1848,* Princeton, 1975.

Anderson, R. D., *Education in France, 1848–1870,* Oxford, 1975.

Bastid, P., *Doctrines et institutions politiques de la Seconde République,* Paris, 1945.

Bluche, F., *Le Bonapartisme. Aux origines de la droite autoritaire (1800–1850),* Paris, 1980.

Broglie: *Mémoires du Duc de,* vol. 1, 1825–70, Paris, 1938.

Duveau, G., *1848: The Making of a Revolution,* London, 1967.

Falloux, Comte de, *Mémoires d'un Royaliste,* Paris, 1925.

Fejtö, F. (ed.), *The Opening of an Era, 1848, An Historical Symposium,* London, 1948.

Flaubert, G., *L'éducation sentimentale,* Paris, 1869.

Fortescue, W., *Alphonse de Lamartine: a Political Biography,* London, 1983.

Girard, L., *La IIᵉ République,* Paris, 1968.

Jennings, L. C., *France and Europe in 1848,* Oxford, 1973.

Luna, F. de, *The French Republic under Cavaignac,* Princeton, 1969.

McKay, D. C., *The National Workshops,* Cambridge, Mass., 1933.

Margadant, Ted W., *French Peasants in Revolt. The Insurrection of 1851,* Princeton, 1979.

Merriman, John M., *The Agony of the Republic: The Repression of the Left in Revolutionary France 1848–1851,* New Haven, 1978.

Padberg, John W., *Colleges in Controversy. The Jesuit Schools in France from Revival to Suppression, 1815–1880,* Cambridge, Mass., 1969.

Ponteil, Félix, *'1848'* (Collection Armand Colin, No. 204), Paris, 1937.

Pouthas, Charles-H., *Démocraties et capitalisme (1848–1860),* 2nd edn, Paris, 1948.

Price, R., *The French Second Republic: A Social History*, London, 1972.

Price, R., *Revolution and Reaction: 1848 and the Second Republic*, London, 1975.

Seignobos, C., *La Révolution de 1848 – le second Empire (1848–59)*, (vol. 6 of Lavisse, E., *Histoire de France contemporaine*), Paris, 1921.

Simpson, F. A., *The Rise of Louis Napoleon*, London, 3rd edn, 1950.

Tocqueville, Alexis de, *The Recollections of*, ed. J. P. Mayer, London, 1970.

Vigier, Philippe, *La Seconde République*, Paris, 1967.

The Second Empire

The experiment of the Second Republic ended in profound disillusionment. The extravagant hopes of the birth of a new society at home and of the liberation of peoples abroad had come to nought. Within a few months there had been civil war in Paris and the economic crisis had been intensified. This crisis had persisted in many branches of the national economy: credit was impaired, the metallurgical, mining, and building industries continued to be depressed, while farmers were now dismayed by harvests so abundant that corn prices were lower than at any time since 1787. More remarkable still, 276,000 people had been driven to emigrate since 1845. Thus for a large section of the community the Republic had come to be synonymous with an instability which was injurious to the economic as well as the political well-being of the nation. The Prince-President for his part did not scruple to encourage this disenchantment or to diffuse the belief that only by giving him a free hand and by the restoration of the Empire could France recover confidence in the future. So, on Louis Napoleon came to centre many hopes, and the *coup d'état* together with his assumption a year later, on 2 December 1852, of the Imperial title, with the name of Napoleon III, were generally welcomed. He had won the support of the army and gratified it by a special proclamation on the morrow of the *coup d'état*: now under a Napoleon it could hope for greater scope and prestige. His accession was accepted by most of the remaining Saint-Simonian economists and by members of the financial aristocracy who had previously supported the July Monarchy – men such as Fould, Magne and Billault, 'Orleanists of the second generation', as they have been called, were to hold office throughout the greater part of the Second Empire. It was welcomed by the industrialists, business men and shopkeepers, who hoped for economic recovery under a strong government and mistakenly believed that the Emperor was a whole-hearted protectionist. It was hailed by most peasants, who hoped for higher prices, and even by many workers who hoped that the Emperor might yet prove to be the champion of their interests against the employers. It pleased the majority of the Catholics who were now increasingly Ultramontane and looked forward to a new alliance of Throne and Altar although the new ruler was no believer. Napoleon had posed as a saviour of society, and for the most part society accepted him as such. The Empire stood above all for order and social security, and because, after the turmoil of the last years, the majority of Frenchmen now counted these as the chiefest blessings, it was with comparative equanimity that they saw the disappearance of the relatively free institutions which they had enjoyed since 1815. The plebiscite of December 1851 had approved the *coup d'état* by an overwhelming majority of 7,481,000 to 647,000, and the plebiscite upon the restoration of the Empire was almost as striking a victory for the Emperor. As an English historian has well remarked, 'For better or for worse the people had made the act their own. . . . If the *coup d'état* was a crime France was less its victim than its accomplice.' Only for a small minority, the half million or so who voted 'No' and the sullen abstainers, did he remain 'the man of December 2nd', yet, as the same historian has pointed out, while Louis Napoleon 'appealed to the French people not as a tyrant, but as a tyrannicide . . . the fact remains that the Constitution was suppressed by the one man in the world who had sworn to uphold it'.[1]

This was the fundamental weakness of his position which Napoleon's enemies never forgot. Men like Victor Hugo, the author of *Les Châtiments* with its bitter attack on the Second Empire, and his fellow Republicans, never ceased to inveigh against the 'criminal' and the 'crime' of 2 December 1851. At the same time it is to be remembered that the 'tyrant' was not really the Republic. If Louis Napoleon saved France from anything, he saved it from the perils of an unsatisfactory Constitution and from the possibility of a monarchical restoration. As Bainville has remarked, 'To read the *Châtiments* of Victor Hugo or the *Histoire d'un crime* one would think the Prince-President had strangled the Republic. In reality he smothered a monarchy in the cradle'.[2] Yet, in spite of the death of Louis Philippe in 1850, the Royalists were still unable to put an end to their divisions. But for the emergence of yet another competitor in the person of Napoleon, the Republic might have survived on the basis of Thiers' famous negative formula, which we have already had occasion to quote, namely that it was the regime which divided Frenchmen least.

The institutions of Empire were already partly in being before the Empire itself was restored. The Constitution of 1852 was an avowed replica of the first Napoleon's Constitution of 1800, with the important difference that the lower house or Legislative Body was now to be elected by universal suffrage,[3] for that, together with the abolition of slavery in the French colonies, was the one great innovation of the Second Republic which no subsequent regime dared to reject. But the Legislative Body had only 260 members compared with the 750 of the Legislative Assembly of 1849; it was to sit for only three months in the year; it was not allowed even to choose its own President or to have its debates published; and the general elections of deputies, to be held every six years, were, in accordance with a tradition now well established, liable to be subject to strong official pressure. Moreover, to make doubly sure of satisfactory results, the Imperial Government drew the boundaries of constituencies in quite arbitrary fashion. The upper chamber, the Senate, was to be a still smaller body of men who held their seats for life, either ex officio or through nomination by the President. Its main function was to serve as a vehicle for constitutional change – any such changes being promulgated by *Senatus Consultum* which might afterwards be submitted to a plebiscite for confirmation. This was indeed a typically Napoleonic device. 'The present constitution,' declared Louis Napoleon in a proclamation to the French people, 'proclaims that the Chief whom you have chosen is responsible to you; that he always has the right to appeal to your sovereign judgement, in order that, on solemn occasions, you may be able to continue or withdraw your confidence. . . . Since he is responsible his action must be free and untrammelled.' In other words he might at any time override the legislature by resort to a plebiscite; while his freedom of action meant among other things that Ministers were responsible to him and not to the Legislative Body, of which they need not be members, and that he alone initiated legislation, bills being, by what Prévost-Paradol called 'a strange inversion of public powers',[4] prepared by the Conseil d'État and presented complete to the Legislative Body, which could modify them only on the Conseil d'État's advice. There is, as Lowes Dickinson has remarked,[5] 'no sufficient reason to suppose that he was deliberately announcing a fraud; as he believed in his own mission, so he believed in its acceptance by the nation': but the plebiscite was hardly 'an adequate means of establishing his responsibility to the people'.

The Prince-President also appointed to all offices, was Commander in Chief of the forces and had the right of declaring war and making treaties. This authoritarian regime, which gave the man who was soon to be Emperor such wide powers, was buttressed by other measures. Clubs were suppressed, the National Guard was disbanded except in Paris, and a 'decree-law' of 1852 subjected the Press to more stringent control. Any newspaper dealing with political or social economy now had to obtain Government authorization before it could appear, and all had to give a financial guarantee. Direct Government censorship was, however, replaced by an ingenious system of warnings. If a paper offended, its director received a warning, and when this had happened thrice the paper was liable to be suspended. Such warnings might be given by the prefects, whose powers were generally increased. They meant that the censorship desired was exercised by the directors themselves, and this system now decreed in France was subsequently imitated elsewhere by Bismarck and ⊀ the Tsar Alexander II. In addition, Napoleon, who had not scrupled to break his own oath to the Republic, demanded that all Senators, deputies, magistrates and state officials should take an oath of allegiance to him. This meant that conscientious opponents of the regime, like the Republican Cavaignac, who could not bring themselves to take the oath, were unable to take their seats in the Legislative Body, which was thus more than ever an instrument of the Imperial will. Under such conditions active political life was effectively stifled, as indeed the Emperor intended that it should be. By the end of 1853 the number of avowedly political daily newspapers had dropped to fourteen: on the other hand, as in the days of Charles X, there was an increase in the numbers and circulation of literary and philosophical papers in which the critics sought to make political points indirectly. State education, too, assumed a still more rigid and disciplined character, reminiscent of the First Empire, and the rule of Napoleon III's first Minister of Education, Fortoul, it has been said, 'was the time in which every class in France did exercises at the same hour; the time when teachers were ordered to shave off their moustaches in order to remove the last vestiges of anarchy from their costume as well as from their morals'. The France of Napoleon was strictly regimented in political matters, and the police organization whose extensive powers had more than once been criticized under previous regimes, was strengthened in order to keep watch on malcontents and subversive elements.

But if political activity was repressed, there was great activity in other spheres, and at this moment in French history this was a compensating fact which counted for much. The year 1851 had already marked a real improvement in the economic state of the country. The long depression was over and the fortunate coincidence of the beginning of a new period of prosperity with the advent of the new regime redounded greatly to the advantage of the Emperor. In spite of cholera and poor harvests again in 1853–5, a slight depression in 1854, and the worldwide crisis of 1857, which hit France less severely than any other countries, relative prosperity continued until 1860, when a change in economic policy, coinciding with a set-back in foreign policy, unsettled France's internal stability. Until then, however, Napoleon's reign could be said to have gone far to fulfil the hopes of many of those who had voted 'Yes' in 1851 and 1852; and the successes of the new regime were more striking than those of its predecessors in that they were shared or appreciated by more people. Plebiscites and elections by universal suffrage helped to maintain the illusion of popular sovereignty. The economic prosperity, stimulated by a great programme of public works, contrasted favourably with the lean years of the end of the July Monarchy and of the Second Republic. The Emperor's marriage in 1853 to the beautiful, red-haired Spanish Countess, Eugénie de Montijo, and the consequent development of a gay and brilliant Court contrasted with the stiffness of Bourbon etiquette and the bourgeois dullness of Louis Philippe's household. A series of fêtes and military reviews and the great Paris Exhibition of 1855, the French answer to the London Exhibition of 1851, all displayed the splendour and well-being of the new order. Moreover, prosperity at home was matched by success abroad. The Anglo-French *entente* was re-established, Russia was defeated in war, and in 1856 the statesmen of Europe gathered together in Paris at the first general Congress to be held since 1822. Once again their object was to make a peace settlement, but this time France was one of the victors. There is no doubt that in 1856 under Napoleon III the prestige of France stood higher that at any time since the First Empire. Once again she appeared to be without question the foremost power on the Continent. And yet in the end it was the weakness and contradictions of Napoleon's foreign policy which was to bring his whole edifice crashing to the ground.

'The Empire means peace': such were the oft-quoted words uttered by the Prince-President in a speech at Bordeaux in October 1852. They were enough at the onset of the new regime to reassure opinion both at home and abroad and may have been sincerely meant at the moment at which they were spoken. But the name he bore, his system of government and his personal interest in new movements abroad, all impelled the Emperor to an active foreign policy which was soon to lead him into war. The very name of Napoleon was in itself a challenge to the treaties of 1815; the Napoleonic system of government required success abroad as well as prosperity at home to compensate for the deprivation of liberty, while Napoleon III's quixotic sympathy with the aspirations of other nationalities, particularly the Italians, led him to war against Austria. So here, too, the Second Empire is in striking contrast to previous regimes; it is dominated not by internal political struggles or by the development of industry and commerce, important though they are, but by foreign affairs.

The character of Napoleon provides the main clue to a foreign policy in which he himself took the main decisions. But it was a character compounded of contradictions which often made the Emperor's purposes appear obscure and enigmatic to his contemporaries. If the third Napoleon was un-Napoleonic in appearance he was no less dissimilar from his great uncle in other ways. Although personally brave and imperturbable in

moments of danger, he had none of the military genius of Napoleon I.
Often obstinate and tenacious in adhering to designs once formed, he yet
lacked the vigour and ruthlessness to carry them out to the full. In exile and
prison he had meditated long upon the lessons of his uncle's reign with the
result that while in some ways the Second Empire was a sort of somnambu-
list's revival of the First, in others, especially in foreign policy, its ruler
deliberately pursued a different path, hoping thereby to avoid the mis-
takes of the great Napoleon. Thus while England was Napoleon I's great
enemy Napoleon III sought to base his policy upon English friendship.[6]
This un-Napoleonic aspect of the new Emperor's demeanour was enhanced by his attachment to certain dreams of his youth and by his almost
Republican belief in the virtues of nationality, the greatness of Prussia and
the possibilities of disarmament. Withal, the Emperor was grave,
courteous and gentle: 'If surnames were still given to Princes,' said Émile
de Girardin, 'Napoleon would be called Napoleon the well-meaning.' No
journalist would ever have attributed such qualities to the Little Corporal
or given such a name to Napoleon I. And it was precisely this gentleness
and idealistic humanitarianism, which by blurring the traits of the
Napoleonic model, made the Emperor so strange a figure among the
crowned heads of his day. The Saint-Simonian 'Socialist' who wrote
L'Extinction du paupérisme' still cared for the welfare of the workers, the
conspirator who had associated with the Carbonari still wished to do something for Italy and believed that the idea of nationality was a good one,
which it was his mission to bring nearer fulfilment. Unfortunately for
France these dreams were woven into the realities of Napoleon's foreign
policy. Heine had once described Louis Philippe as a 'secret, boxed-up
character',[7] but the words were far more truly applicable to Napoleon III.
There was in French foreign policy of the 1850s and 1860s almost always
'un secret de l'Empereur', just as a hundred years earlier there had been
'un secret du Roi', and French Foreign Ministers were too often 'not counsellors, but mere executors of designs of which they only see fragments'.[8]

To begin with, however, as we have seen, Napoleon's foreign policy
met with a great measure of success. The British Government had at first
viewed his accession with alarm and there had been another invasion scare;
but when it seemed that Napoleon was as pacific as his Republican predecessors, they had been prepared to be friendly. As after 1830 and after
1848, so after 1851, the best means of restraining France seemed to be to
co-operate with her, and soon, when the affairs of the Near East came to a
crisis, the two powers were to be allied on the battlefields. Thus a renewal
of the dangerous Anglo-French rivalry which had embarrassed Louis
Philippe's last years was averted and the new partnership greatly enhanced
Napoleon's prestige.

In the first new phase of the Eastern Question France played a leading part. When a dispute arose between Latin and Orthodox monks over the guardianship of the Holy Places of Jerusalem, Napoleon was quick to seize the chance of restoring France's traditional interests in the Levant, which had been reviving with the renewed activity of French missionaries in the 1840s, hoping thereby to make the support of the French Catholics still more secure. But Russia soon intervened on behalf of the Orthodox and widened the issues by demanding that the Turks should grant her a virtual protectorate over all Orthodox Christians within their Empire. To Britain, long suspicious of Russian designs, and to France, whose parvenu Emperor had been treated scornfully by the Tsar as an upstart, such claims were intolerable. France had long taken the British view of the Eastern Question and held that the balance of power and her own Mediterranean interests required that Constantinople and the Straits should be kept out of Russian hands; and so, when in 1853–4 Russian troops entered the Principalities of Moldavia and Wallachia and attempts to negotiate a settlement broke down, the two powers went to war to prevent the Turkish Empire from being crushed by Russia.

Marking as it did such an early departure from the announcement that the Empire meant peace, the Crimean War was far from being universally popular in France. Yet Catholics, as we have seen, had had reason to welcome Napoleon's championship of the interests of Latin Christianity, while Liberal opinion rejoiced at the attempt to curb the pretensions of the most reactionary power in Europe. Moreover, the war brought considerable prosperity to certain sections of the community which were concerned with the equipment of the troops. The new screw-propelled warships first laid down under Louis Philippe had proved their worth as also did the first iron-clad boats, whose construction, with the Emperor's support, was to revolutionize naval architecture.[9] The alliance with England, the traditional enemy, made an extraordinary impression and led Queen Victoria to pay an official visit to Paris. Moreover, although it brought no territorial gains and although the defects of the French military administration were once again exposed, the war ended victoriously. Such a result and the splendid assemblage of peacemakers in Paris, coinciding as it did with the birth of an heir to the Emperor, the Prince Imperial, seemed to emphasize the solidity and brilliance so quickly acquired by the new regime and was therefore very gratifying to French pride.

The Crimean War could be said to have been a war which accorded with French interests. This was much less evidently so with the war of 1859 which Napoleon plotted against Austria. Here Napoleon's Italophil sentiment, due partly to his ancestry, partly to his early associations with the Carbonari and to his participation in the 1831 rising in the Romagna, and partly to his liberal dreams, led him into a course of action which ran wholly counter to France's traditional policies. In his own entourage he had many people who were Italian in origin or sympathies, including Prince Napoleon his cousin, Conneau, his doctor, and others who urged him to do something for Italy, the northern part of which was still largely under Austrian rule. In January 1858 an attempt on the Emperor's life by an Italian named Orsini enhanced the Emperor's popularity in France and provoked a wave of anti-Italian feeling because of the number of casualties it caused. But, curiously enough, it was precisely this which impelled the Emperor to develop his Italian policy. Orsini's attempt had been made because of Napoleon's inaction; now the Emperor allowed Orsini's appeal to him from prison to espouse the Italian cause to be read in court and to be published. Thus he began to prepare public opinion for eventual French intervention. In July at the Vosges watering place of Plombières he had a secret interview with the Sardinian Foreign Minister, Cavour, and promised him French aid in a war which was to be undertaken against Austria with the object of freeing Italy 'to the Adriatic' and of setting up a Central Italian Kingdom, which, together with Sardinia-Piedmont, enlarged to form a Kingdom of Upper Italy, Naples and the Papal States, was to form an Italian Confederation under the presidency of the Pope. In return for her services and in compensation for the aggrandizement of Piedmont it was suggested that France might receive Nice and Savoy thereby attaining her 'natural' south-eastern frontier.

It had long been a cardinal point of French policy to keep Italy and Germany weak and divided, and even the Republicans of 1848–9 had been loth to see the creation of a strong North Italian kingdom. It might, however, still be hoped that an Italian Confederation which owed its existence to French support would be a valuable friend and client of the Empire. All might have been well had Napoleon been able to secure and maintain the rearrangement of the map of Italy as he had planned it at Plombières, for it was neatly devised to satisfy his own conscience and to appease all sections of French opinion. The expulsion of the Austrians might be expected to please the Liberals as much as the place reserved to the Pope in the projected Federation would appeal to the Catholics; while those who thought first of material gains would be placated by the acquisition of Nice and Savoy. Furthermore, and this was a fundamental point for the Emperor, the social aspirations of the Bonapartes were to be gratified by the marriage of Prince Napoleon with a Princess of Savoy. The marriage duly took place, but subsequent events outran the Emperor's control. Pius IX was no longer the popular liberal Pope of 1846, but, as a result of his experience of the revolutions of 1848–9, a die-hard reactionary, maintained at home by the aid of French bayonets; and soon after war began a series of risings against the existing rulers in Central Italy was followed by popular votes for union with Piedmont which threatened to sweep away Napoleon's Papal Confederation before it had begun to take shape. Moreover, the ravages of malaria among troops most inadequately provided with medical services, Catholic pressure at home and the menacing attitude taken up for the second time in twenty years by Prussia on the Rhine, all impelled Napoleon to seek peace without attempting to storm the redoubtable Austrian fortresses of the so-called Quadrilateral, which stood between the French army and the Adriatic. Thus he failed to keep his promise to free Italy as far as her eastern coasts and caused the Italians bitter disappointment. Furthermore, by the preliminaries of the Peace of Villafranca,[10] he impaled himself upon the horns of a dilemma. He still wished to obtain Nice and Savoy; at the same time he had agreed with Austria that the old rulers in Central Italy should be reinstated without the use of force: but if this happened when the people of Central Italy were clamouring for union with Piedmont, Piedmont could hardly be expected to relinquish Nice and Savoy. In this dilemma he abandoned the idea of a rapprochement with Austria and the restoration of the dukes and decided on a bargain with Piedmont whereby she would incorporate the peoples of the revolted areas and would cede Nice and Savoy to France. But the revolted areas included part of the Papal States, the Romagna. Could Napoleon, hitherto so stalwart a champion of the Pope, allow such a diminution of Papal territory? To secure his ultimate territorial aim he was ready to sacrifice the Pope and to hazard a complete change of policy at home. Accordingly he replaced his pro-clerical Foreign Minister, Walewski, by the more liberal Thouvenel and allowed much publicity to be given to an inspired pamphlet entitled *The Pope and the Congress*, which suggested that the requirements of Papal independence could as well be met by the retention simply of the city of Rome as of a large temporal dominion – 'the rest is only secondary'. The Pope, who stigmatized the pamphlet as 'a notable monument of hypocrisy and an ignoble tissue of contradictions', which he hoped that Napoleon would condemn,[11] received an unpleasant shock when it was followed up by a letter in which the Emperor urged him to renounce his claims to his rebellious provinces in return for a European guarantee for the remainder. But he was obliged to yield to *force majeure* – the current of Italian nationalism was too strong – and before long saw his temporal power reduced to Rome and a small adjacent territory. Even then its maintenance still depended on the French soldiery.

The Italian question had thus landed Napoleon in unforeseen difficulties. The war had indeed been short and successful as far as it went. The Emperor and his troops were hailed as victors on their return to Paris in

August 1859, the last occasion on which the city would welcome a victorious French army for fifty-seven years,[12] and the acquisition of Nice and Savoy,[13] confirmed by the vote of an overwhelming majority of the population, had marked a fresh breach in the 1815 treaties and was France's first territorial gain in Europe since the fall of Napoleon I. But the Emperor's reluctance to use force after the end of the war and his subsequent policy of non-intervention facilitated the incorporation of the whole of the peninsula, save Rome and Venetia, with Piedmont, and the creation of a new Kingdom of United Italy. Yet he was still committed to the protection of the papal sovereignty in Rome, which every Italian regarded as the natural capital of the new kingdom, with the result that France once again appeared to bar the way to the achievement of Italy's natural aspirations and that the Roman question continued to be an embarrassment to French policy for the remainder of Napoleon's reign. Furthermore, his acquisition of Nice and Savoy, in spite of earlier denials that he had any designs upon them, had much offended Great Britain, which was shocked by his duplicity and distrustful of his ambitions. The affair thus played much the part which the Spanish Marriages had played in Louis Philippe's reign towards breaking the Anglo-French *entente*. Last, but not least, his Italian policy had greatly offended those people in France who had hitherto been his warmest supporters, the French Catholics. He had in consequence made overtures to the Liberals; but, as events were to show, it was highly questionable whether Liberalism and Bonapartism were genuinely reconcilable.[14]

The year 1860 thus marked a turning-point in Napoleon's fortunes and in his policy towards the Catholics. Henceforth the relations of Church and State were less friendly. The Church no longer enjoyed such freedom of action, and the State system of education made notable progress under the direction of a man personally selected by the Emperor, Victor Duruy, who proved to be one of the greatest of all French Ministers of Public Instruction. The year was no less a turning-point in economic policy. The conclusion of a commercial treaty with Great Britain in that year, followed in 1861 by trade agreements with Belgium, Italy and Switzerland, and in 1862 by one with Prussia, gave an important impulse to greater freedom of international trade. But the Anglo-French Treaty, in many ways reminiscent of an earlier treaty of 1786, marked a striking departure from the rigid protectionist policy pursued by successive French Governments ever since the early years of the Restoration. As such it met with bitter hostility from some of the big landowners and from many industrialists, especially the textile manufacturers of Normandy and the north and the iron masters of the east. The change was a victory for the Saint-Simonians and evidence of Napoleon's desire to bolster up the Anglo-French *entente*, and although its most obvious effects were political it had some important economic and social consequences. More intensive competition from England hastened the concentration of certain industries in fewer firms and in many cases led to a renewal of plant or modernization of equipment. When factories had to be rebuilt there was generally a resulting improvement in the working conditions of the employees. On the other hand, many weaker firms went to the wall and others were obliged to reduce wages so that there was a considerable amount of temporary distress. This had unusually significant consequences, for it was partly responsible for the attempt of French workers to get into touch with the working classes of Britain which resulted in the formation of the First Workers' International. Nevertheless, in spite of the temporary distress and the political resentments caused by the new policy, the statistics of French exports in general, and to Britain in particular, continued to show an upward trend. On French industry as a whole there can be little doubt that the 1860 Treaty acted as a healthy stimulant.

This wind of free trade was not the only breath of fresh air which the Emperor now let into France. Irritated by the opposition of the clergy and their sympathizers to his Italian policy, Napoleon had sought to conciliate the other main body of opinion, the Left, by an amnesty in 1859 and by greater leniency towards the Press. In 1860 he went further and issued a decree permitting the Senate and Chamber to discuss and vote an annual address in reply to the speech from the throne, and allowing reports of debates to be published in full. In the following year the Legislative Body was granted a wider measure of control over national expenditure. Thus public opinion once again had a certain restricted opportunity to form judgements about political issues and to exercise pressure. But instead of winning converts to Bonapartism these so-called Liberal reforms, by giving greater freedom to the enemies of the regime, tended only to confirm them in their intransigence. Already indeed, in 1857, five Republican deputies had been elected to the Legislative Body and had taken their seats, treating the oath of allegiance as a mere formality. The extreme Left may have welcomed the Italian war and the 1860 Treaty of Commerce, but they remained Republicans. Equally, many of the men who re-emerged on the Right were monarchists avowedly or at heart. The old parties which had confronted one another under the Second Republic, the conservative and clerical party of order on the one side and on the other the Republican and democratic Left, had both re-formed, and this was in itself a grave setback for Napoleon who had wished to destroy both. After nearly a decade Napoleon had failed, as his predecessors had failed, either to win over or to annihilate the adherents of previous regimes. The Emperor now had to face a double opposition which was drawn from the most live elements of the nation; and the opposition of the Republican Left was particularly dangerous, since it, and not the official Bonapartist candidates, more and more won the sympathy and suffrages of the industrial workers. Moreover, his new policies caused serious rifts in his own entourage. His Liberal concessions, favoured by Walewski and Magne, were ridiculed by Prince Napoleon, who adopted an irresponsibly democratic attitude, and strongly opposed by men like Baroche, Fould and Rouher. His Italian policy, on the other hand, was no less unpopular with the Empress, who took an increasing interest in politics, and with Walewski, both of whom were ardent supporters of the Pope. Thus the strength of the regime at home was conspicuously weakened in the 1860s – it was being sapped by parliamentary opposition, by Press criticism, and by divided counsels, which meant that Government policy was increasingly hesitant and lacking in direction. This weakness became still more conspicuous towards the end of the decade when the Emperor, who was ageing fast, was frequently crippled by an extremely painful disease which impaired his power of decision. Already, however, the strength of the new forces of opposition was strikingly shown in the elections of 1863. Then a broad coalition of the opponents either of the regime itself or of the Emperor's personal policy, was formed under the name of Union Libérale. It contained men as varied as the Legitimist Berryer and the moderate Republican Jules Simon, and, although it won only thirty-five seats, it polled some 2,000,000 votes.[15] Moreover, most significant fact of all, the big towns, Paris, Lyons and Marseilles voted almost solidly Republican.

The Opposition deputies in the new Legislative Body, who now included such notable advocates of former regimes as Berryer, Thiers and the Republican Jules Favre, naturally demanded further Liberal reforms and urged a return to full parliamentary government with the right of interpellation and ministerial responsibility. But although his half-brother, the Duc de Morny, who presided over the Legislative Body, urged him to be generous, Napoleon was not ready for further political concessions. Instead he sought to gain the favour of the workers by concessions in social legislation. Thus in 1864 they were permitted to form combinations and the right to strike was legally recognized. Yet, important as such measures were, they failed to achieve Napoleon's object. Increasing pressure at home and serious set-backs abroad eventually obliged him to give way to the demands of the Opposition and in January 1867 he announced his intention of conceding further Liberal reforms. In the meantime the European balance of power, so recently and strikingly modified by the creation of the Kingdom of Italy, had undergone further significant changes.

The Italian question had shown the contradictions inherent in Napoleon's attempt to defend French interests and at the same time to give a

practical demonstration of his sympathies with the idea of nationality.
Nevertheless, Napoleon had acquired Nice and Savoy as the reward for his
services to the cause of Italian liberation. In like manner he hoped that a
fresh extension of French territory might be his recompense for assisting
the unification of Germany and even that it might be obtained merely
through astute diplomacy without any need to draw the sword. It is
remarkable how readily Frenchmen talked of annexing Belgium or the
Rhineland as the most natural thing in the world should there be another
war.[16] If Napoleon could succeed in securing one or the other for them
without war he might expect to win their undying gratitude and could
well afford to abandon further projects of Liberal reform. After 1860 two
main objectives emerge from the fog of Napoleon's secret diplomacy: his
wish to complete the unification of Italy by securing Venetia for her from
Austria; and his ambition to obtain either the Rhineland or part, if not the
whole, of Belgium for France by way of reward for helping or giving a free
hand to either Prussia or Austria in Germany. It is impossible not to be
struck by the cynical indifference with which he turned first to Austria and
then to Prussia and then back again to Austria, seemingly quite indifferent as to which power gained the hegemony of Germany provided that
France obtained additional territory as compensation. But unfortunately
for him and for France, as in Italian affairs he had met his diplomatic
match in Cavour, so in German affairs he was to meet his master in
Bismarck.

The Polish question of 1863, the Schleswig-Holstein question of
1864–6 and the Austrian war of 1866 all marked stages on Bismarck's
progress towards the unification of Germany, and in each of them France
was unable to play an effective part either because of the breakdown of the
entente with England or because of the Emperor's errors of judgement
and lack of military preparedness. It was indeed difficult for England or
for France with all her Polish exiles, to do anything but protest when the
Tsar not only crushed a Polish rising in 1863 but also revoked the Polish
Constitution of 1863: but their protests antagonized Russia, whereas Bismarck not only did not protest but assisted the Russians in dealing with
the rebels. Thus he later claimed to have won Russia's friendship thereby
ensuring that if France were again at war with a German power she would
not, as in the days of the Ancien Régime, have a traditional ally to help her
in the East. By the time of the Schleswig-Holstein affair mutual distrust
between England and France made effective Anglo-French co-operation
impossible, so that once again Bismarck had things his own way. In 1865
he prepared for the conflict with Austria which he hoped would make
Prussia master of Germany. Russia could be counted on to remain
friendly, but the attitude of France was less certain. In October Bismarck

had an interview with Napoleon at Biarritz but the Emperor would not commit himself. In 1866, however, he gave his blessing to the idea of an alliance between Prussia and Italy – yet a few months later he signed a convention with Austria whereby he promised to make every effort to induce Italy to abstain from intervention. In fact, he calculated that the struggle would be protracted, that France could step in and mediate or tip the scales on one side or the other, and that in the meantime it was to her interests to stand as well as possible with both parties.

Unfortunately his judgement of the balance of forces between Austria and Prussia was completely astray. He was indeed not alone in being amazed at the swiftness and completeness of Prussia's victory in the war of 1866. Within a few weeks the Austrian army had been routed at Sadowa and the Austrian Emperor, Francis Joseph, had appealed to Napoleon for his good offices in securing an armistice. When Austria ceded Venetia to Napoleon and Napoleon magnanimously handed it over to Italy the French Emperor might once again appear to be the arbiter of Europe, and in a circular issued not long afterwards he claimed credit for the overthrow of the 1815 settlement, the break-up of the Holy Alliance of the Eastern Powers, the progress made towards the realization of German national aspirations, and also for confining Prussian expansion to the north of the Main. In reality, however, these successes were purely illusory. Not one of them brought any real advantage to France. As a result of the war of 1866 Prussia had emerged as the leader of a closely knit confederation comprising more than half Germany; and none could doubt that her next objective would be the incorporation of the states south of the Main which still enjoyed a nominal independence. Moreover, this new and ominous change in the balance of power had occurred without any territorial compensation for France. Napoleon had lost his opportunity. Had he been ready, as his Foreign Minister, Drouyn de Lhuys, and others had urged, to place an observation corps on the Rhine frontier as soon as war broke out and to back his mediation by force of arms he might well have secured the Rhineland territory which had been the object of so many fruitless negotiations during the past five years. As it was, he had hesitated until it was too late. Once the victory was won Bismarck could afford to snap his fingers at what he called Napoleon's 'hotel-keeper's bill', asking for the frontiers of 1814 and the fortress of Luxemburg, and at a French draft convention which contained a secret clause providing for the French annexation of Belgium. More than that, he used this evidence of Napoleon's covetousness against him. He kept the draft convention for publication at a later date when it should suit him publicly to expose French ambitions, and he promptly utilized an alternative French suggestion that France might acquire the Bavarian Palatinate to put pressure upon Bavaria to sign a treaty of friendship with Prussia.

The Second Empire

Thus Napoleon's diplomacy played into the hands of the man w.
to be his mortal enemy and he was outmanoeuvred at every turn.
memorandum of 1829 Polignac had written that it was of great impo.
ance to France to prevent the reunion of Germany into one or two big
states. 'If ever this circumstance was to occur, this country, which is today
divided between Princes who have need of our protection, would confront
us with rival forces which would be jealous and soon hostile, and our
relative power would be seriously affected.' The jealousy and hostility of
nationalist forces in Germany had already been shown in 1840 and 1860;
but Napoleon and many other Frenchmen had failed to appreciate their
significance. His departure from the fundamental French policy which the
Ultras, heirs of the Ancien Régime, had understood so well was fatal for
France. Napoleon had failed to give protection to the small South-
German states, who had at one time or another looked towards France; he
had misjudged Bismarck and Prussia; and he had been unsuccessful in
securing an adjustment of frontiers in order to compensate France for the
change in the balance of power. As has been well said, 1866 marked the
end of that old order of things in Central Europe which had been so agreeable and so safe from the French point of view.

Nor had the Emperor been able to compensate for this check in Europe
by his many ventures overseas, although some of them were of great
importance for the future growth of France's new colonial Empire. The
conquest of Algeria had been virtually completed by 1857, but this was an
event which caused little enthusiasm, particularly among those sections of
the community who viewed the new colony as a tiresome commercial rival,
since its products were not so much complementary as similar to those of
the metropolis. Moreover, the Emperor's well-meant but misguided
attempt to apply the theory of nationality to Africa and treat Algeria not
as a colony but as an 'Arab Kingdom', discouraged French colonization
and retarded the material development of the country, which was to be
further hampered by a terrible famine in 1867–8. Elsewhere, indeed,
there was great activity. French troops fought in places as distant as China
and Mexico. They intervened with England in China in 1857–8 and took
part in an expedition to Pekin in 1859–60; an expedition to Syria in 1860
reaffirmed France's interest in the Levant; in Africa France's footing in the
Senegal area was extended by Faidherbe and new settlements were made
on the coasts of Guinea and Dahomey; in the east of the continent and off
it the old rivalry with England continued and France replied to the English
settlement of Perim by purchasing the territory of Obock and contested
with her for influence in the rich island of Madagascar.[17] Farther east again
New Caledonia had been occupied in 1853 and the persecution of French
missionaries by the Emperor of Annam had led to another military

expedition. In 1859 Saigon had been captured and within a few years France had gained full sovereignty over three of the provinces of Cochin China and established a protectorate in Cambodia. Furthermore, in Egypt, which French capital was rapidly helping to transform into a great cotton-growing country, the Frenchman, Lesseps, by cutting the Suez Canal, was engaged in a work which was to transform the strategic and commercial communications of the world. Thus in the new era of exploration and exploitation which was the prelude to the great 'Scramble' for Africa and other lands outside Europe in the last quarter of the nineteenth century, France of the Second Empire played an active and enterprising part. But the French public, as ever, was little concerned or interested in these distant happenings. Algeria was still widely looked upon as a source of military weakness and doubtful economic advantage which France would have been glad to abandon had she been able to do so without loss of prestige, and the potentialities of more remote territories were even less understood by the general public. Moreover, the success of French arms in the distant valleys of the Senegal or the Mekong was soon completely overshadowed by the tragic failure of Napoleon's policy in Mexico.

Begun as a debt-collecting expedition of three powers, Great Britain, France and Spain in 1861–2, the Mexican venture developed into an attempt by France alone to establish a new Latin Catholic Empire in the New World. Napoleon appears to have hoped that, with French support Mexico might become strong and prosperous enough to counterbalance the power of the United States. The venture would reassert Catholic power and provide easy compensation for the humiliation of the Pope and the set-back to French policy in Italy in 1860. In so far as it was a sort of Catholic crusade it did indeed at first help to appease Catholic opinion in France, while at the same time it held promise of satisfaction to French financial interests. But unfortunately the Emperor and his advisers were sadly ignorant or misled about the real conditions, both geographical and political, of the country they set out to conquer. The Mexican expedition was to be no easy promenade like the Spanish war of 1823. The French intruders met with savage resistance. For five years they fought for the establishment and maintenance of the Hapsburg Archduke Maximilian on the newly created throne as Napoleon's puppet Emperor; but, although more than 38,000 men were involved and 6000 were killed or died of sickness, their efforts were in the end of no avail. The Mexican Republicans remained indomitable and, once the American Civil War was drawing to an end, the United States Government, angered by Napoleon's flouting of the Monroe Doctrine, began to adopt a threatening attitude. Unable to face the prospect of war with the U.S.A. and worried by events in Europe, Napoleon had no choice but to withdraw his troops.

Left to its own feeble resources the artificial Mexican Empire speedily collapsed and the news of the death of the hapless Maximilian at the hands of his Republican opponents reached Napoleon to mar the Paris Exhibition of 1867 when he was acting as host to many visiting sovereigns and grandees. Once again he had been seduced by a chimera. The 'most profound conception of the reign', the establishment of a Mexican Empire might indeed have served French economic interests and strengthened the Latin Catholic forces in America, making them better able to resist the encroachments of Yankee 'Manifest Destiny': but the tangible advantages for France were not obvious and once again Napoleon had shown that his schemes were apt to fail through lack of adequate preparation. The war of 1866 had already dimmed France's prestige; the Mexican disaster and further failures of the diplomacy of *pourboires* or compensations in Europe in 1867 tarnished it still more. In September of that year Napoleon might well confess that France had met with reverses and that the horizon was darkened by *des points noirs*.

Under the cloud of such disappointments, Napoleon was impelled in his hesitant fashion to seek to appease public opinion at home by further Liberal reforms. Since the 1863 elections there had grown up a so-called Third Party, largely Orleanist in personnel and generally moderate in tendency but eager to limit the Emperor's personal power and to convert the Empire into a parliamentary regime. Already in 1866 its demand for further Liberal reforms had won sixty-three votes. Now, early in 1867, the Emperor made a gesture to it by granting the Legislative Body the right of interpellation and by relaxing the laws controlling the Press and public meetings. Characteristically, however, he kept the old Ministers, the men who were opposed to concessions, so that his ultimate aims remained in doubt. None the less the Legislative Body continued to show a growing independence: so much so indeed that on two matters of vital importance it was able to frustrate the Emperor's policy and to impose its aim. In the first instance, showing, as is too often the case with Parliaments, an ill-timed sense of economy,[18] it rejected a proposal by the Government, alarmed at Prussia's victory, to strengthen the French army by the creation of an effective trained reserve. In the second, it wrung from Rouher the rash promise that France would never abandon Rome. 'This,' says a French historian, 'was the solemn undertaking which, in spite of clerical pressure, Napoleon had so far always refused to give; his Government yielded at last to the Legislative Body. Contemporaries were alive to the significance of this: "There you have Parliamentary government in full swing," wrote Sainte-Beuve to the Princess Mathilde.'[19]

This was however an exaggeration: the elections of 1869, a fresh Third Party demand for parliamentary government, this time backed by

116 deputies, and a further set of half measures, were necessary before the Emperor finally brought himself to the experiment of ministerial responsibility and government through the Third Party. After an appeal in November 1869 to the Legislative Body to help him to found liberty in France, in January 1870 he asked Émile Ollivier, formerly one of the five Republican deputies of 1857, to head a Ministry which would be responsible to Parliament as well as to the Emperor. Ollivier, was a notable example of an erstwhile opponent of the Empire who had rallied to its support, and it was therefore fitting that he should lead the experiment of reconciling the country at large to a revived parliamentarism under the Bonapartes and of giving a new lease of life to the Empire on a new basis. But that basis was still equivocal, and, when the Emperor ingeniously contrived once again to make use of the plebiscite, two of the Orleanist members of the Ministry resigned in protest against resort to such extra-parliamentary machinery. The plebiscite of 1870 was, however, an event of considerable importance. The people were asked whether or not they approved the Liberal reforms introduced since 1860 and in particular the *Senatus Consultum* of 20 April 1870, whereby the Constitution of 1852 was revised and constituent power transferred from the Senate to the people. In spite of the vigorous opposition of the Republicans, who had been increasingly active since 1863, who had once again carried most of the great urban seats in the 1869 elections, and who had all along denounced the new parliamentarism as a sham, the result was a resounding endorsement of the Emperor's policy. It was not so much a specific vote of confidence in the Ollivier Ministry as in the Empire, and as such it greatly heartened the authoritarian Bonapartists who had viewed the Emperor's latest concessions with the utmost dismay. Over 7,000,000 people, nearly as many as had approved the *coup d'état* of 1851 and the proclamation of the Empire in 1852, again voted 'Yes'. Against them there were 1,500,000 'Noes': the various opposition forces, who in the 1869 elections had polled 3,000,000 votes, appeared to have received a grave set-back.

It may be idle, but is none the less interesting, to speculate whether the Empire might now have continued for many years more had not Bismarck intervened and the Emperor made a last fatal blunder in foreign policy. In spite of the impressive support it received in the plebiscite, signs of weakness in the Empire had been growing. For the last five years at least it had been apparent that Napoleon was failing, that his powers of decision had been affected by disease, that he was tired and saddened, torn between the contrary advice of those who opposed and those who favoured concessions to Liberalism, and no longer imbued with that confident belief in his star which had been such a remarkable feature of his rise to power. And as the Emperor had begun to lose grip, so too, as it seemed, had the

Government and administration in general. The growing weakness of the master had communicated itself to the servants. Several of the ablest of the Old Guard of Bonapartists who had assisted Napoleon to power were either dead, like Morny, or in retirement, like Persigny, and the men to whom he had since given preferment were of lesser stature. Moreover, the Liberal reforms set the administration more difficult problems. The 1859 amnesty had given an impetus to Republican journalism and, although the Government-sponsored papers had a wider public and were more effectively edited than their forebears of Restoration days, it was a moderate Republican paper, Le Siècle, which by 1866 had a far larger circulation (44,000) than any other. The relaxation of the Press legislation in 1868 had put an end to the warning system and the necessity for prior government authorization before a paper could be launched and had led to an efflorescence of new journals, particularly in the provinces, reminiscent of 1848. Many were ephemeral, but there were some Parisian newcomers, like Le Rappel of Victor Hugo and Le Réveil of Delescluze, which mingled mutual criticism with violent attacks on the Empire; and the Government could find no friendly journalist to vie with the renegade Republican aristocrat Rochefort for biting wit. The first number of his La Lanterne, with its famous opening sentence, 'The Empire contains 36,000,000 subjects, not counting the subjects of discontent' sold no less than 120,000 copies instead of the 15,000 expected.[20]

The authorities did their best to curb or suppress the most virulent or impudent critics of the regime. Prosecutions and Press trials multiplied, but they did not always have the desired results, for they sometimes created martyrs or, as in the Baudin trial of 1868, provided the publicity for some new recruit to the Opposition, in this case the young Gambetta, to win his spurs by a fresh denunciation of the imperial regime. Thus, in the climate of opinion of the late 1860s, the ablest of the younger men, whether in the universities, in journalism, in politics, or at the bar, were more tempted to oppose than to support a regime which had so obviously lost prestige that the mere fact of deriding it might itself provide a passport to renown. To maintain or regain authority the Empire needed to renew its personnel and to attract the rising generations. At the end of 1869 it was in a situation not unlike that of the July Monarchy under Louis Philippe, but unlike Louis Philippe, Napoleon had been ready to concede reform without waiting for insurrection to force him to it. At the same time, as in 1847, the critics, growing vehement, had been all the more eager to smell out scandals. The great public works were decried as too costly and financed by irregular means; the famous Prefect of the Seine, Baron Haussmann, who had transformed the centre of Paris and done so much to make it the city we know today, was forced to resign owing to 'alleged financial impropriety'; and in 1870 when an obscure but irascible cousin of the Emperor, Prince Pierre Bonaparte, shot a young Republican journalist, Victor Noir, the sensation caused was as great as that of the murder of the Duchesse de Praslin in 1847. It was disquieting, too, that the great cities remained strongly Republican, that revolutionary bodies and secret societies, many of them now more or less connected with the First Workers' International, were beginning to operate again and that they were active in fomenting street demonstrations from which Paris of the Empire had been singularly free; and that in the same year, 1870, troops had, for the first time since Napoleon came to the throne, been called in to repress a serious outbreak of strikes.

All these signs seemed to suggest that the Empire was slowly decomposing. Yet it is possible that some French Republican historians have been easily led to exaggerate the strength of the Opposition and the unpopularity of the Empire. The voters in the plebiscite of 1870 were above all votes for peace and order – too many people remembered the disorders of the Second Republic to wish for their recurrence – but the Republican deputies' recognition of this fact meant that they at least would not begin a revolution though they would be ready enough to profit by one. Moreover, the plebiscite, as we have suggested, was still a vote for the Empire and, in the opinion of a French historian of the working classes during this period, nearly twenty years of power had done little to impair the hold of Napoleon upon the loyalty of the masses: 'Napoleon III, still strong in his 7,000,000 votes, retained a singular prestige.'[21] Furthermore, the economic situation showed a marked improvement in 1870, the Prince Imperial was growing up and likely to be popular, and, last but not least, the concessions to Liberalism seemed to open the door to precisely that renewal of personnel which was so necessary. The Ollivier Government had gone so far as to appoint notable Orleanists like Guizot and Odilon Barrot to various commissions: Ollivier himself, as we have seen, had once been a Republican; and there was more than one observer who believed that, given time, even a young 'irreconcilable' like Gambetta might one day emerge as a Minister of the Crown.[22] Ill though he was, Napoleon had by no means lost his personal charm and power of fascinating individual opponents.

But the experiment of parliamentary empire was all too brief. On 3 July 1870 the appearance of a fresh *point noir* came to darken the political horizon. News reached Paris that a Hohenzollern prince had consented to stand as a candidate for the vacant throne of Spain. As we have already seen from the history of the Restoration and July Monarchies, France had long been accustomed to regard Spain as a natural field for French influence. The sudden intrusion of a prince related to the ruling house of

Prussia appeared to be part of a Machiavellian manoeuvre to encircle France and, in Thiers' well-known phrase, 'recreate the Empire of Charles V' at her expense. French public opinion was therefore immediately aroused. Since 1866 there had indeed been a growing belief that a collision between France and Prussia would sooner or later be inevitable. 'There must,' Prévost-Paradol had written in 1869, 'be a struggle for supremacy. Until this collision has taken place everyone will instinctively feel that nothing has been decided. For Germany to become unified in spite of France, or while France remains passive, would be an irrevocable abdication of French greatness.'[23] This fatalistic feeling was perhaps itself a factor which helped to precipitate events in 1870.

Meanwhile the French Government at once attempted to secure the withdrawal of the candidature. Many Ministers and diplomats were on holiday, but after a few days, Benedetti, the French Ambassador to Berlin, succeeded in inducing the King of Prussia, the Head of the House of Hohenzollern, to arrange that his relative's candidature should be withdrawn. This renunciation was regarded by the two most experienced statesmen of the July Monarchy, Guizot and Thiers, as the greatest diplomatic victory they had ever seen. Had the French Government rested content with it the prestige of the Empire would have enjoyed a remarkable recovery. But Ollivier and Gramont, his Foreign Minister, disastrously overplayed their hand. Instead of being satisfied with the word of one of the foremost European sovereigns, they sought to improve upon their success by requiring a formal guarantee that the candidature would never be renewed. Moreover, they did nothing to calm public opinion at home. Thus the incident, which should have been swiftly and successfully closed, was prolonged and its prolongation gave Bismarck the opportunity to intervene, to influence opinion on both sides of the Rhine and to goad the French into war. The famous Ems telegram was an immediate cause of hostilities, but not the only one. Still more important was the lack of calm and balance on the part of the French Ministers who had made a false move and then feared to draw back in face of their own public opinion which they had allowed to become increasingly bellicose.

Thus it came to pass that in spite of Thiers' grave warning that the moment was very ill-chosen, on 19 July 1870 France, having failed to secure the guarantee she had demanded, declared war upon Prussia, taking up the sword against a formidable opponent without any ally to support her. Here, too, Napoleon's diplomacy had failed. Since 1868 tentative negotiations had been in progress for a triple alliance between Austria, France and Italy; but Austria, more interested in securing an ally against Russia than in giving help against Prussia, had hung back, and Napoleon, in view of the attitude of the Legislative Body, had hesitated to play what has been called France's last strong diplomatic card – 'the fact that Rome was still hers to give or to refuse'[24] – in order to make sure of Italy. Thus, when July 1870 came, the projected alliance had still not been concluded. Diplomatically unsupported, France was still further handicapped by her lack of military preparedness. In conversation with an Austrian Archduke earlier in the year Napoleon had said that he could put 400,000 men on the frontiers within fifteen days, but, in fact, by 5 August he was unable to mobilize more than 250,000. Unfortunately for France, the Emperor's own complaint in 1859 of the inefficiency of French military organization which, he said, meant 'that we are never ready for war', still held good in spite of all his efforts to improve it in the meantime. Napoleon, indeed, in military as in other matters, was often more far-sighted than the experts,[25] but he had been unable to overcome the resistance of the comfortably routine-loving War Office and High Command to his proposals for reform. Even the shock of 1866 had failed to stimulate a thorough-going overhaul of the military system. In 1865 the military school at Metz had been solemnly taught that the Prussian army was no better than a training school for a Landwehr: 'It is a magnificent organization on paper, but a doubtful instrument for defence and would be very imperfect during the first period of an offensive war.'[26] In 1870 the power of that army was still underestimated, and, although in the meantime the Emperor had secured the introduction of the chassepot, a quicker firing gun (rejected as quite useless by a committee of experts eleven years earlier), his endeavours to introduce conscription and create a proper reserve had been frustrated. In 1867 he changed his War Minister, but through Marshal Niel, too, he was able only to obtain half-measures. The Niel Plan for forming a mobile National Guard which would receive a summary training in peacetime and be drafted into the regular army upon mobilization was ludicrously amended by the Legislative Body. On the one hand Conservative deputies jibbed at the extra expenditure; on the other, the Republicans maintained their distrust of standing armies and argued that France should renounce offensive wars and be content, if attacked, to rely upon the nation in arms for her defence. Thus the four months' training period for the Mobile Guard proposed by Niel was reduced to fifteen days and an absurd provision was introduced providing that no muster should entail more than one day's absence from work. In 1870, therefore, when war broke out, the Guard was in fact little better than a paper force and its equipment and training were to take many weeks. The diplomatic blunders of the Emperor and his Ministers were indeed responsible for France's commitment to war; but the need for preparedness had been obvious to all who had eyes to see for at least four years. Yet all save the Emperor, Niel, and a handful of prophets, had been only too eager to bury their heads in the sand. So too, in a somewhat different way, it was to be again seventy years later. On each occasion the Nemesis was swift and terrible.

'Formerly,' wrote Prévost-Paradol, 'when the military power of the Continental States was discussed the only question was whether France could resist a European coalition: today the question is whether France will defeat Prussia.'[27] But the majority of his compatriots had no doubts. Accustomed to victory in every European campaign in which France had taken part since 1815, forgetful of Waterloo, but mindful of Jena, still ill-informed about Prussian efficiency, they looked for a triumphal march to Berlin. All the more bitter and stunning, then, was the news of defeat upon defeat. By the end of the first week in August Alsace and most of Lorraine lay open to German invasion. The French armies had fought and continued to fight with gallantry, but they were out-numbered, out-generalled and out-manoeuvred by a force which was superior in discipline, equipment[28] and mobility. At home in Paris the gravity of the situation led the Empress, who was acting as Regent in the absence of the Emperor with the armies, to recall Parliament for a special session and the Ollivier Ministry was at once defeated and resigned. In an unhappy moment in July Ollivier had said that he entered the war 'with a light heart' – that phrase was never forgiven him, his political career was at an end, and he spent most of the rest of his long life writing the history of the short-lived parliamentary Empire in seventeen volumes. Before the special session began some of his colleagues had urged that the Republican deputies should be arrested and sent to Belle Île. But the Empress rejected the proposal on the ground that it would be more likely to provoke than to prevent the risk of civil war. This failure to take strong action and the formation of a new Ministry by Palikao, an elderly general who took many sound measures but lacked the popularity or dynamic qualities necessary in such a crisis, showed that the authorities, too, were stunned by France's reverses and that they had lost confidence in their ability to maintain control. In the Legislative Body it was now the Opposition deputies who took the initiative, and radical proposals which a few weeks before would have aroused storms of protest were now listened to with silent fear or apathy by the chastened Bonapartists. As early as 16 August the British Ambassador reported that the new Foreign Minister, Prince de La Tour d'Auvergne, was the only person he knew who still spoke like a loyal subject.[29] In fact the belief rapidly grew that the end of the Empire was at hand. At such a moment there are always men to desert the sinking ship, and the number of the defenders of the Bonapartist cause rapidly dwindled.

By 20 August it was known that the army commanded by Marshal Bazaine was blockaded at Metz. The fate of the Empire depended upon the movements of the Emperor and upon the only remaining force of any size, the army of Châlons under Marshal MacMahon. The Liberal General Trochu, to whose appointment as Governor of Paris the Empress had reluctantly consented, and others were insistent that the Emperor should return to the capital, but the Empress, who feared for his life, would have none of it, and in order that he might be kept away MacMahon's army was sent off on a foolhardy attempt to make a junction with Bazaine. Thus the Emperor was, in the words of a contemporary observer, 'like King Lear driven out of his palace'[30] and the last main French army set out to court disaster.

Retribution was not slow in coming. On 31 August and 1 September a great battle raged near the Belgian frontier only to end in the French defeat so vividly described by Zola some years later in his novel *La Débâcle*. On the 2nd the whole of MacMahon's army of 84,000 men, 2700 officers and thirty-nine generals capitulated. With them Marshal Mac-Mahon and the Emperor himself were captives. 'There had been no disaster in French history more complete or more humiliating.'[31]

The political consequences were speedily to follow. The unhappy and unpopular Empress had no chance of maintaining a regime which had brought France to such disaster and which now had scarcely any defenders. On 4 September after a bloodless revolution, the Republic was once again proclaimed in Paris. The Empress fled to England, now the habitual refuge of France's fallen sovereigns, where she was joined by the Emperor in the following year. Two years afterwards, in 1873, Napoleon III died, once again an exile and now a broken man. He too had failed to unite all French-men and to end the struggle of Revolution and Counter-Revolution; but none the less he had come nearer than any of his predecessors since 1815 to winning the sincere allegiance of the great mass of Frenchmen.

It was easy for the Republicans to dismiss the Second Empire as a tissue of meretricious grandeur and political and social corruption which invited an inevitable collapse. But we who can take a more detached view must remember that economically and culturally, as well as on account of its achievements overseas and its political successes or failures in Europe, the eighteen years of its existence from 1852 to 1870 were of singular import-ance in French history. It was during these years that the economic struc-ture of the country as it was to continue until the Great War of 1914–18 was largely moulded. It was during these years that the capital began to assume its modern form and that the social structure was further crystal-lized, while developments in thought foreshadowed the ideological battles of the Third Republic.

If first we glance at the Paris of 1870 and compare it with that of 1840 we shall see that economic developments and the great building programme

Railway System

——— 1852
+—+—+ Extensions 1852-70

Miles

0   50   100   150

Map 1: Railway system

of Baron Haussmann, one of the most notable town planners of his age, had changed much of it out of all recognition. The modern tourist would have little difficulty in finding his way in the Paris of 1870, but were he transported to that of 1840 with its tortuous labyrinth of narrow streets he would indeed be lost. Haussmann's new Boulevards, broad and straight, bewailed by the Goncourts as suggestive of 'some future American Babylon',[32] opened up the centre of the city and gave it the spaciousness of a modern cosmopolitan capital. Some 20,000 old houses were pulled down and more than 40,000 new ones built. New squares and new churches multiplied; the new Opera and the new Louvre were begun: the Parc Monceau and the Buttes de Chaumont were converted into public parks; the Bois de Boulogne and the Bois de Vincennes were made into agreeable places for promenades; and cafés, hitherto select and closed, opened up on to the streets and earned a new popularity. Omnibuses and local railways increased greatly in number, and, now that long-distance railways and steamship services were developing, Paris more than ever became a centre of attraction to foreigners, 'the café-concert of Europe', the city of gaiety and vice from which France was to derive such a reputation for depravity among the peoples of austerer northern nations. At the same time the area of the city was greatly extended. By a decree of 1860 it took in all the outskirts and villages between the *octrois* (customs barriers) and the fortifications, thus increasing its administrative area from twelve to twenty arrondissements. The social effects of reconstruction and enlargement were considerable. In the old city, which in 1851 contained just over a million inhabitants, bourgeois and worker had often lived cheek by jowl in the same buildings. Now the destruction of old houses and building of new ones at higher rents forced many workers to the miserable outskirts, parts of which were becoming industrialized.

In consequence of this enlargement and of an influx from the countryside (rural depopulation was already causing concern) the Paris of 1870 counted more than 1,800,000 residents and in it the divisions between bourgeois and working-class quarters were much more marked. The *'banlieue rouge'* – the 'Red' precinct of the twentieth century, so-called from the political sympathies of the workers who congregated there – was already foreshadowed. At the same time, within the city there were many new buildings which marked the arrival of a new economic era. It is from the Second Empire that there date the earliest of those vast stores, the 'Bon Marché', the 'Louvre', the 'Belle Jardinière', the 'Printemps' and the 'Samaritaine', which are still such paradises for shoppers. It was then that great new joint-stock banks, such as the Société Générale and the Crédit Lyonnais, and enterprises like the Crédit Foncier and the Crédit Mobilier, opened their doors, supplying thereby on the best Saint-Simonian principles the credit necessary for an ever-increasing commercial and industrial activity. It was from Paris, too, that there radiated most of the great railway lines, extended during these years by the addition of some 14,000 km of track to the 3685 existing in 1851, so that it became more than ever the economic, social and intellectual hub of France. So it came to pass that the capital of Napoleon III with all its material transformations, its imperial fêtes and splendid exhibitions, did indeed shine forth before the world as La Ville Lumière.

Similar developments, though on a different scale in different places took place in the provinces. The organization of country pleasures for the fashionable world was marked by the foundation of seaside resorts, such as Deauville, the creation of the Duc de Morny, while Imperial visits gave a new vogue to spas like Vichy.

On the other hand, the populations of industrial cities also made striking growth: that of Roubaix was trebled; in Lyons, Lille, Toulouse and St Etienne the numbers doubled; and in other towns such as Marseilles, Bordeaux and Rheims the rise was of the order of 50 per cent to 70 per cent. In fact the Californian gold discoveries of the 1840s were largely responsible for facilitating the acceleration of industrial development and of business enterprise. As a result France had enjoyed a period of remarkable prosperity especially in the 1850s: industry had boomed; there was an orgy of speculation, a large amount of capital available for foreign investment, and a great increase in the number of small investors; and the total value of the French import and export trades had risen from 2615 million francs in 1851 to 8008 millions in 1869. At the same time the growth in numbers and in power of the big industrialist or capitalist was still more notable than in the reign of Louis Philippe. Vast interests were concentrated in the hands of a few families such as the Jewish Péreires and Foulds and the Schneiders and Paulin Talabots; before the end of the Empire an observer estimated that most of the money of the country was handled by some 183 firms. In certain industries, such as that of iron – the most remarkable new building material displayed in the Paris Exhibition of 1867 – this development was particularly marked, and the famous Comité des Forges, founded in 1864, was soon to become a power in the land, the weight of whose influence has still to be correctly estimated. Such great interests soon formed connections which transcended national boundaries, and it is in this intensely active period of the Second Empire that the international aspects of French finance and industry begin to assume a real importance. Thus although the artisan and the small workshop had by no means disappeared – individualism and the persistence of small industries were long to be characteristics of French economy – the Second Empire had witnessed a profound transformation. France, basically still a land of artisans and poor and backward peasants, could now in 1870 also be counted as 'a big industrial power',[33] not nearly so big as Great Britain already was or as Germany was soon to become, but none the less a highly important factor in the increasingly industrialized world. In this development the reign of Napoleon III had been the period of decisive advance, and the patronage of the Emperor and of highly placed people like the Duc de Morny had done much to encourage it.

It was amid such changes, then, that the intellectual and cultural life of the country continued to flourish; and, as the emphasis in social and economic matters was on material progress, so in these spheres a new realism marks much of the most notable work of this period – the realism of Courbet in the realm of painting, soon to be followed by the first pictures of the Impressionists led by Manet; of Flaubert in the resonant periods of *Madame Bovary*, and of Gautier in the exquisite vignettes of *Émaux et Camées*; of Augier, and Dumas *fils* in their problem-plays; and the scientific determinism of Taine and Renan in historical study. But if this was a dominant note it was far from being the only one; as ever France was rich in the variety of her talents. While Hugo, now in exile, was publishing lyric and epic poetry as prolifically as ever, Daudet wrote *Lettres de mon Moulin*, and Sainte-Beuve was doing much to make literary criticism an art to which a man might be proud to devote all his gifts and energies. It was now that Leconte de Lisle brought a serene and luminous paganism into poetry and that other so-called Parnassians shared his love of plastic form, while Baudelaire in his *Les Fleurs du Mal* laid bare the agonies of a tortured Christian soul. It was in 1860 that Gounod's *Faust* was first performed, and it was during these years that Offenbach launched the *opéra bouffe* which was to have such an extraordinary success in the fashionable world, and that Labiche delighted enthusiastic audiences with his gay comedies. In the world of art Corot was joined by other landscape painters of great talent such as Millet and Harpignies, and Puvis de Chavannes began his monumental frescoes; while Méryon and Doré showed their skill as etchers and illustrators. In the realms of political thought and philosophy, however, there was little originality; after the death of Comte in 1857 it was his pseudo-scientific creed of Positivism that became dominant, under the direction of men such as the lexicographer, Littré. Here too the effect of the material progress of the age was marked in popularizing man-made systems which affected to dispense with the aid of religious beliefs, and Positivism in particular was to play a great part in strengthening the secularist, anti-clerical tendencies of many a Republican. Throughout Napoleon's reign, indeed, the age-long struggle between clericals and anti-clericals continued, and the Roman Question of the 1860s and the challenging pronouncements of the Pope caused it to become ever more passionate. But the superior intellectual talent was on the whole on the side of the unbelievers and the Church was fighting a losing battle. Last, but not least, we must note the remarkable achievements, often despite grossly inadequate facilities, of French scientists, such as the physiologist Claude Bernard, Deville the discoverer of aluminium, Marcellin Berthelot and, greatest of all, Louis Pasteur, who now began his work on fermentation and bacteria. With men such as these France, in spite of the shortcomings of her rulers and the collapse of her armies, could still hold her head high: whatever her social and political failings there was no intellectual or artistic débâcle.

Notes

1 Simpson, F. A., *Louis Napoleon and the Recovery of France 1848–56*, pp. 163, 168–9.

2 Bainville, J., *Histoire de France*, p. 486.

3 For the text of this Constitution, see Appendix 6.

4 *La France nouvelle*, p. 96.

5 *Revolution and Reaction in Modern France*, p. 229.

6 This influence of Napoleon III's study of history upon his policy was the subject of an interesting article by F. A. Simpson in *The Times' Napoleon Supplement* of 5 May 1921.

7 *French Affairs*, vol. 2, p. 35.

8 La Gorce, P. de, *Napoléon III et sa politique*, p. 70.

9 See Temperley, H. W. V., *The Crimea*, p. 295, for the part played by the screw in inducing the Turks to decide the Holy Places issue in favour of the French, and Baxter, J. P., *The Introduction of the Iron-Clad Warship*, p. 4.

10 For the English text see Butterfield, H., *Select Documents of European History, 1715–1920*, pp. 137–8.

11 Cit. Arnaud, R., *La deuxième République et le second Empire*, p. 164.

12 That is, apart from troops who returned from successful colonial expeditions.

13 See Map 2, pp. 122–3.

14 It is to be noted that the achievement of Roumanian unity in 1859 was a triumph for Napoleon III who had been the chief foreign sponsor of the Roumanian cause. But this success of his nationality policy was entirely overshadowed by the Italian problem.

15 The candidates of the Union Libérale had their consciences about taking the oath of allegiance set to rest by Jules Simon, who explained that it really meant an undertaking not to conspire against the Empire. Yet rather than take the oath a few years earlier he himself had resigned his chair at the Sorbonne.

16 See e.g. Senior, N. W., *Conversations with Thiers, Guizot, etc.*, vol. 1, p. 27; vol. 2, p. 94.

17 See Map 4, p. 201. French explorers did notable work in West Africa in these years.

18 Simpson, F. A., in *The Times' Napoleon Supplement*, 5 May 1921, also speaks of 'surreptitious economies designed to conceal the true costs of that forlorn adventure into world-policy'; i.e. the Mexican expedition.
19 Hauser, H., Maurain, J. and Benaerts, P., *Du libéralisme à l'impérialisme (1860–70)*, pp. 27, 28.
20 Zévaès, A., *Henri Rochefort, le pamphlétaire*, p. 43.
21 Duveau, G., *La vie ouvrière en France sous le second Empire*, p. 56.
22 Cf. Saint-Valry, G. de, *Souvenirs et réflexions politiques*, vol. 1, p. 134, who says that the rural masses up to 1870 were '*dans un état de confiance réel*' towards the Empire.
23 *La France nouvelle*, pp. 386, 389.
24 Simpson, F. A., *Louis Napoleon and the Recovery of France 1848–1856*, pp. 88–9.
25 He has been well described by a French historian as 'l'homme de son temps qui a le mieux prévenu l'avenir et le plus mal dirigé le présent', A. Dansette, *Histoire religieuse de la France contemporaine*, p. 334.
26 Cit. Monteilhet, J., *Les institutions militaires de la France, 1814–1932*, p. 39.
27 *La France nouvelle*, p. 377.
28 The French were much inferior in artillery but their infantry was on the whole better equipped. Cf. Brogan, D. W., *The Development of Modern France*, p. 20.
29 Bury, J. P. T., *Gambetta and the National Defence*, p. 43.
30 *Letters from Paris, 1870–75*, ed. R. Henrey, p. 56.
31 Bury, op. cit., p. 45.
32 Cit. Duveau, op. cit., p. 209. The Emperor himself took the greatest interest in Haussmann's plans.
33 Duveau, op. cit., p. 105.

Bibliography

Anderson, R. D., *Education in France 1848–1870*, Oxford, 1975.
Bellet, R., *Presse et journalisme sous le second Empire*, Paris, 1967.
Blanchard, M., *Le second Empire*, Paris, 1950.
Bury, J. P. T., *Napoleon III and the Second Empire*, London, 1964.
Case, L. M., *French Opinion in War and Diplomacy during the Second Empire*, Philadelphia, 1954.
Case, L. M., *Édouard Thouvenel et la diplomatie du second Empire*, Paris, 1976.
Corley, T. A. B., *Democratic Despot: a Life of Napoleon III*, London, 1961.
Dansette, A., *Du 2 décembre au 4 septembre*, Paris, 1970.
Desmarest, J., *La France de 1870*, Paris, 1970.
Dunham, A. L., *The Anglo-French Treaty of Commerce of 1860 and the Progress of the Industrial Revolution in France*, Ann Arbor, 1930.
Duveau, Georges, *La vie ouvrière en France sous le second Empire*, Paris, 1946.
Girard, L., *Nouvelle Histoire de Paris, La Deuxième République et le Second Empire 1848–1870*, Paris, 1981.

Hanna, A. J. and K. A., *Napoleon III and Mexico: American Triumph over Monarchy*, Chapel Hill, 1971.

La Gorce, P. de, *Histoire du second Empire*, 7 vols, Paris, 1894–1905.

Payne, Howard C., *The Police State of Louis Napoleon Bonaparte, 1851–1860*, Seattle, 1966.

Plessis, Alain, *De la fête impériale au mur des fédérés, 1852–1871*, Paris, 1973.

Prévost-Paradol, *La France nouvelle*, Paris, 1876.

Rohr, J., *Victor Duruy, ministre de Napoléon III*, Paris, 1967.

Schefer, C., *La grande pensée du règne: les origines de l'expédition du Mexique (1858–1862)*, Paris, 1939.

Schnerb, Robert, *Rouher et le second Empire*, Paris, 1949.

Seignobos, C., *La Révolution de 1848 – Le second Empire* (vol. 6 of Lavisse, E., *Histoire de France contemporaine*, Paris, 1921).

Seignobos, C., *Le déclin de l'Empire et l'établissement de la Troisième République* (vol. 7 of Lavisse, E., *Histoire de France contemporaine*), Paris, 1921.

Simpson, F. A., *Louis-Napoleon and the Recovery of France, 1848–56*, 3rd edn, London, 1951.

Steefel, L. D., *Bismarck, the Hohenzollern Candidature and the Origins of the Franco-German War of 1870*, Cambridge, Mass., 1962.

Thompson, J. M., *Louis Napoleon and the Second Empire*, Oxford, 1954, reprinted 1975.

Zeldin, Theodore, *The Political System of Napoleon III*, London, 1958.

8

The Franco-Prussian war
and the Commune

'France,' wrote Prévost-Paradol in 1868, 'is approaching the most formidable trial she has ever had to encounter.'[1] He was a true prophet; and the men who from September 1870 onwards had to face it were, like the Republican leaders of 1848, comparatively little-known lawyers, journalists and politicians whose experience of government was either nonexistent or dated from the Second Republic. In February 1848 the Republicans had come into power as the result of a revolution which had taken everyone by surprise and had found themselves under the necessity of ruling France at a time of severe economic depression and of almost universal unrest in Europe. In September 1870, the situation with which the new Provisional Government was confronted was much more alarming; and yet it contained many striking parallels with 1848. Although the revolution of 4 September was bloodless, it was not 'legal' – that is to say, all the constituted authorities had been swept aside or ignored. As in 1848, while the deputies were dispersed in their committee-rooms debating the transference of powers – this time to some sort of Executive Commission which should carry on the government of the country until a Constituent Assembly could be elected – the Chamber was invaded by a motley crowd, probably with the connivance of some of the Republican deputies. The clamours of this mob soon made debate impossible and deprived the legislators of all authority. But, as in 1830 and 1848, the people looked again to the Opposition deputies to give a lead, and so two of them, Jules Favre and Gambetta, assented to the demands for the proclamation of a Republic, but declared that as in 1830 and in 1848 it should be proclaimed at the Hôtel de Ville – to such a point had Revolution in France now developed its ritual. Once again crowds converged on the Hôtel de Ville and once again there was a race between moderate and extreme Republicans to seize power. In order to forestall growing disorder, a convenient formula was hastily devised by the parliamentarians – the new Government should be formed by the deputies of Paris, including those who had originally been elected there, but who, under the system whereby a man could be a candidate in more than one constituency at the same time, had chosen to sit for some other constituency. Thus the 32-year-old barrister Gambetta, who sat for Marseilles, and Jules Simon, one of the members for Bordeaux, both became members of the new administration which assumed the title of Government of National Defence. In addition, because of the military situation General Trochu, the Governor of Paris, was made President of the Government. On the other hand, Thiers, who was also a deputy for Paris, while ready to serve it on diplomatic missions abroad, prudently abstained from entering a Government so uniformly Republican in its composition. This abstention was indeed a loss; but it meant that on the whole the men in the new Government were people of much the same outlook. With the exception of the journalist Rochefort, who had to be fetched from the prison of Ste Pélagie, where he was serving one of his numerous sentences for infringement of the Press laws, they were all relatively moderate in their Republican views. There was not the sharp cleavage between the advocates of social revolution and the others which had weakened the Government of 1848.

The name 'Government of National Defence' rightly stressed the urgent overriding task of the new authorities. In spite of the pacifist tendencies not so long since exhibited by some of the more doctrinaire among them, and in spite of the seemingly hopeless military situation, there was little thought of peace. Had Napoleon still been on the throne he might perhaps have appealed to England to mediate and peace might have been concluded as rapidly as it was between Austria and Prussia in 1866. But this would have been possible only if the Emperor had been able to persuade opinion to accept territorial concessions. It would have been difficult for a Bonaparte to do this. It was no less difficult for a Republican Government. In Paris, the great stronghold of Republicanism, apathy and dejection had been transformed into a frenzy of patriotic fervour, and many naïve enthusiasts appeared to think that the mere existence of a Republic was as good as a rout of the enemy in the field. Indeed the new Government's very first proclamation encouraged such a way of thinking when it declared 'The Republic was victorious against the invasion of 1792. The Republic is proclaimed. The Revolution has been made in the name of the right of public safety'. With characteristic love of historical parallels the minds of Frenchmen at once went back to 1792. Once again German armies were advancing towards Paris; once again the country was in danger and would be rescued by the united efforts of all her citizens. The regular soldiers might be captive or besieged, but still the nation would rise in arms and the *levée en masse* would sweep the sacrilegious invader from the land. Such thoughts even found their way into the first circular issued by the new Foreign Minister, Jules Favre, to French representatives abroad: 'We shall yield neither an inch of our territory nor a stone of our fortresses. . . . Paris can hold out three months and conquer. If it fell, France, ready at its call, would avenge it; she would continue the struggle and the aggressor would perish.' Between such a spirit and the German determination to annex Alsace and a large part of Lorraine on the grounds that they were historic German lands and that their chief cities, Metz and Strasbourg, were, in Bismarck's phrase, 'the keys of the German house', there could be no compromise. Thus the revolution of 4 September meant not peace, but *guerre à outrance*, war to the knife.

Such a war presented tremendous and pressing problems. The German armies were rapidly advancing upon Paris. The city must be prepared to stand a siege, but was the Government to stay and be immured in the capital? The provinces must be galvanized into mobilizing all their resources of men and materials, but who was to galvanize them if the Government remained in Paris? The Government's solution of these two questions was a strangely unsatisfactory compromise. To the deputies of Paris, even more than to most Frenchmen, Paris naturally seemed all-important. It was the heart of the country: in it were concentrated some 75,000 of the remaining regular troops and the best of the Garde Mobile. The Government had some justification for thinking that if they quitted it they would be accused as deserters, that political control of the capital would be in danger of falling into the hands of the extreme Left, and that civil disorder and a weakening of morale might ensue. So they decided to stay in Paris, but to send the 74-year-old Minister of Justice, the Jewish Crémieux, as a Government delegate to Tours. A few days later they dispatched two more of their oldest and least-known colleagues to join him. They left only just in time. Two days afterwards the Germans completed the investment of the capital, and on 23 September its last certain means of communication with the outside world disappeared when the telegraphic cable in the bed of the Seine was cut. Henceforward, the Parisians and all but three members of the Government of National Defence were dependent upon carrier-pigeons and balloons for their contact with the rest of France and the world beyond. Such a siege of a city of nearly 2,000,000 inhabitants, the cultural capital of Europe, such isolation of the Government of a Great Power, constituted one of the most extraordinary spectacles of the nineteenth century. There were few indeed outside Paris, either among the Germans or in neutral countries, who believed that the siege could last for more than a week or so. But the Parisians tightened their belts, and, although it is very questionable whether they made the most of their manpower and military resources under the military direction of a general, Trochu, who had no belief in the possibility of victory and profoundly distrusted the National Guards, they held out for four months, far into the depths of one of the severest winters of the century. Thereby they won the respect and admiration of the world and did much to make foreign opinion, which at the outbreak of the war was largely unfriendly to France, more sympathetic.

Meanwhile the provinces were far from being galvanized by the elderly Delegation at Tours, and the question had arisen whether their authority should not be reinforced by some sort of elections. The Government of National Defence, like the Government of February 1848, was a purely *de facto* administration, the offspring of a revolution. But in war it was diplomatically desirable for the country to have a regular Government and it could well be argued that such a Government with the nation behind it would have much more authority and prosecute the defence more successfully than an improvised regime like that of 4 September. The Government of National Defence had debated this issue from the outset and, in spite of considerable divergence of opinion, had on 9 September decreed that elections for a Constituent Assembly should be held in October. A few days later Jules Favre had interviewed Bismarck at Ferrières in an endeavour to obtain an armistice which would enable the elections to be held all over the country, in the invaded as well as in the free departments. But Bismarck's conditions for such an armistice had been unacceptable and in consequence the Government had decided to postpone the elections indefinitely and to devote their whole energies to the war. They were therefore much astonished when only a week later they heard that their Delegates at Tours had reversed their decision on the grounds of 'a general demand of the departments' and of 'unavoidable necessity'. In fact the three elderly Ministers were quite unable to dominate a situation which was going from bad to worse. Toul and Strasbourg had fallen and the advance of Bavarian troops towards the Loire had necessitated the evacuation of Orléans. The Delegation themselves inspired neither respect nor confidence – to many of the military and Conservative elements they represented a crowd of demagogues and the coincidence of demagogy and invasion seemed to have brought the country to the 'very bottom of the abyss, the last circle of Dante's Hell'.[2] The Generals and military authorities were constantly at loggerheads with the new Republican prefects appointed throughout the country by Gambetta. Disturbances were reported from various southern towns, and the formation of a so-called Ligue du Midi, however patriotic its purpose of regional defence, threatened still further to weaken the Delegation's hold upon the country.

France 1814 - 1940

.... Boundaries between Departments

▨ Territory retained by France in 1814 and ceded in 1815

▨   " ceded to France by Sardinia in 1860

▤   "   " by France to Germany in 1871

ooooooooo Line of military occupation by Allies according to
               Treaty of Paris, 20 Nov. 1815

⋯⋯⋯   "   "   "   " by German troops 26 Feb. 1871

xxxxx   "   "   "   "   "   "   " according to Armistice
                                           of June 1940

Miles

0   20   40   60   80   100

Map 2: France 1814–1940

Thus very naturally the Delegates felt that elections were essential to reinforce their waning authority. But they reckoned without their beleaguered colleagues, who at once sent Gambetta to Tours by balloon to express their disapproval and impart to the direction of the war in the provinces that energy which had been so lacking. With him he bore a fresh decree, cancelling the elections, and instructions which gave him a casting vote in the councils of the Delegation and full power as Minister of the Interior to recruit, call up and equip all the forces of the nation which might be required for the country's defence. On his arrival at Tours on 10 October he found that one of his colleagues, Admiral Fourichon, had just for the second time resigned the post of Minister of War and that no one else was willing to assume it. Gambetta had no such hesitation. Within forty-eight hours of his coming he had become Minister of War as well as of the Interior and had virtually concentrated all powers in his own hands. It was now up to this young Cyclops of thirty-two to improvize the defence of the invaded country and emulate the feats of a Carnot or a Danton.

Gambetta's arrival very quickly had a tonic effect. At once the country felt that here was a man who, however little he knew about waging war, was full of energy and determination and that action would succeed to apathy and confusion. Within a short time he had appointed a tireless, supple, ambitious civil engineer, Charles de Freycinet, to be his deputy at the Ministry of War and together they had organized the small part of the War Office which had been evacuated to Tours with the Delegation. The civilians and the amateurs were now in control and the last chance of salvation lay in the hope that their readiness to dispense with military routine and red tape would so accelerate the defence measures already under weigh and so hasten new ones, as to enable fresh armies to take the field while Paris still held out. They did their utmost: many changes were made in commands; all formations which did not constitute part of the regular army were enrolled into a new auxiliary force; and the National Guards, who had been revived as a result of Opposition pressure in August, were mobilized for active service. Indeed there was no lack of manpower; the crux of the problem of organization was to train and equip a sufficient number of men to enable the new provincial 'Army of the Loire' to go into action well before 1 December, the date which, as Gambetta and Freycinet believed, would mark the limit of effective resistance by the Parisians.

At first their efforts met with success beyond expectation. At the beginning of November the new Army of the Loire was able to relieve Orléans and to win a battle at Coulmiers, but it could not exploit its victory and all attempts to break through to relieve Paris were as ineffectual as the efforts of the Paris garrison to effect a sortie. Disaster soon followed upon disaster. Already at the end of October, the capitulation of Bazaine and his army of 154,000 men at Metz had released large additional German forces and darkened the military prospects still further. By the beginning of December the Army of the Loire was being rapidly forced back and cut in two; and the re-entry of the Germans into Orléans and their advance down the Loire compelled the Delegation to quit Tours for Bordeaux. The defeated Army of the Loire was reorganized – one half executing a brilliant retreat westwards under a new commander, Chanzy, the other being formed into a new Army of the East under General Bourbaki, which Freycinet dispatched to attempt the relief of Belfort and to threaten German communications. But it too was thrown back and only escaped the annihilation which threatened it at the end of January 1871, as the result of Jules Favre's omission to cover it in the terms of a general armistice, by crossing the Swiss frontier and being interned. Finally, on 28 January, Paris itself capitulated. During the last month of its ordeal it had experienced many of the trying experiences now so familiar in modern war, including bombardment, sheltering in basements, firewatching and food rationing.[3] By the end of that time supplies were nearing exhaustion and the failure of a last effort to effect a sortie had seriously impaired morale. The news of the capitulation reached Bordeaux on the 29th together with information that the Government in Paris had agreed to a twenty-one days' armistice and that a National Assembly to be elected on 8 February was to meet on 12 February. Gambetta was furious. He had often told his colleagues that the provinces could carry on the war even after the fall of Paris and he still believed that he could raise and equip new armies and wear the Germans down by refusal to surrender. Yet now, as he thought, the Government in Paris had betrayed him and meekly given in. At least if there were to be elections he would ensure that they would have a reasonable chance of giving a Republican result and so, since he had not received a copy of the Paris Government's election decree, he issued one of his own for which he obtained the reluctant consent of his elderly colleagues of the Delegation. This laid down that no one who had served Napoleon III as a Minister, Senator, Councillor of State or official candidate should be eligible. The armistice terms, however, had stipulated that the elections should be free, and free the Government in Paris were determined that they should be. For a moment, when Gambetta refused to listen to Jules Simon whom they dispatched to Bordeaux to explain their policy and to effect liaison with the Delegation, it looked as though a major conflict between the Government in Paris and the Government in the provinces would still further complicate the affairs of the unhappy country. But, when more Ministers from Paris reached Bordeaux and upheld the armistice conditions, Gambetta rejected the promptings of enthusiasts who urged him to make a coup and assume a dictatorship; he bowed to superior numbers and resigned. That resignation removed both the danger of civil war and the last obstacle in the way of peace.

Thus the desperate, heroic, and largely improvised national defence, the French 'people's war', as it has been called by a military historian,[4] came to an end. The sufferings of the often ill-equipped, ill-prepared, hastily raised new forces had been intensified by bitter weather. By the beginning of February 1871 the Paris garrison and three other armies had capitulated or been interned, the remaining forces, Chanzy's Army of the Loire and Faidherbe's Army of the North, were in retreat, and forty-three departments or half the country had been overrun by the enemy. Furthermore, although Great Britain had made a friendly offer of mediation, no ally had come to France's aid. Under such circumstances further resistance might well seem hopeless. It was true that the Germans had at first been angered, inconvenienced and perplexed by the rising of new forces whose extent and worth they were for some time unable to gauge and whose existence had created a veritable 'fog of war'; but this fog had not been thick enough to mislead them into a single serious defeat and all Gambetta's energy and indomitable resolve could not have availed to restore the morale of the people after such a series of unrelieved disasters. France was weary of war and the elections of 8 February held so hastily and in such conditions that campaigning was scarcely possible, were first and foremost a vote for peace. By her resistance she had saved her honour and had reminded men of what had not been seen in Western Europe since the days of the Spanish war of Napoleon I, the immense possibilities of organized resistance by a whole people to a foreign invader. For the future, his organization of the provincial armies and his role as champion of war without thought of surrender would serve Gambetta and the Republicans in good stead and give rise to a legend: but for the moment, in spite of his election by no less than nine constituencies, they were to bring him and most of his colleagues of the Government of National Defence into temporary eclipse. The Republic, formerly associated with social disorder, had not succeeded in dispelling this impression in 1870 and now in addition it was coupled with military defeat. Gambetta and his prefects had not succeeded in their short period of power in converting the mass of the people to Republicanism, any more than had Ledru-Rollin and his Commissioners of 1848. So the electorate turned to the forces of order which had not been compromised by the war. In their result the elections of 8 February were reminiscent both of the elections to the Chamber of 1815 and of those to the Legislative Assembly in May 1849, and incidentally they were held under the same electoral law as the elections of 1849.

The Legitimists reappeared and along with Orleanists and other Conservatives gained a majority – some 400 seats compared with 200 won by the
Republicans and thirty by the Bonapartists. The eclipse of the Empire was
confirmed, the Republicans were scarcely stronger than the Mountain in
1849. Once again the Monarchists appeared to have a great opportunity to
put France's house in order and to set her back upon the path of constitutional monarchy from which she had by such an unhappy accident
departed in 1848. Unfortunately for them they were still, twenty years
after, divided as to who should be king.

Apart from being a vote for peace and a triumph for the Monarchists,
the elections were also an extraordinary personal success for a single man,
Adolphe Thiers. Thiers, now a veteran elder statesman of seventy-three,
was returned by no less than twenty-six departments. Alone among the
foremost politicians he enjoyed a prestige which was unimpaired. Prominent ever since the days of Charles X, this little man who had been the
protégé of Talleyrand and the opponent of Guizot and Palmerston had an
unrivalled experience of public affairs. Since 1863 he had distinguished
himself as a leader of the Opposition and as one of the most trenchant and
clear-sighted critics of Napoleon III's foreign policy: his warnings of the
German menace had fallen unheeded at the time, but now they were
remembered all over the country. By refusing to enter the Government of
National Defence he had avoided being compromised by its ill success,
while by his diplomatic missions on its behalf he had shown his patriotic
readiness to serve his country. Even had the Monarchists not been divided
they might well, remembering Louis XVIII and the Treaties of Paris, have
preferred that someone other than the King should bear the responsibility
for making a peace which must be humiliating. As it was, all were agreed
that Thiers was the obvious head of the new provisional Government
which must function until a new constitution had been devised and could
come into operation. Accordingly, on 17 February, the National Assembly,
which had met at Bordeaux and accepted the resignation of the Government of National Defence, nominated Thiers as 'Chief of the Executive
Power of the French Republic' – this title being without prejudice to the
eventual form of Government which might be decided upon by the
deputies or their successors. Thiers at once accepted the post, undertook
by what was to be known as the Pact of Bordeaux to observe neutrality as
between the different parties, and formed a Government which, amongst
a number of men of various shades of opinion, included three of the
members of the late Government of National Defence; they were to share
in the responsibility for the peace which followed the war they had waged
and not to be left free to criticize it like the Left under the Restoration. At
the same time he was given a free hand to negotiate for peace, and the

representatives of Alsace and Lorraine made a first moving protest against the cession of their provinces, which everyone knew that the Germans intended to demand, and which was in fact inevitable.

Before France was free to consider her future form of government she had more bitter trials to undergo. Already on 18 January she had experienced the humiliation of seeing the King of Prussia proclaimed German Emperor in the Hall of Mirrors at Versailles. Now Bismarck was ready to consolidate the new Empire forged in war by territorial aggrandisement at France's expense. Not only was she obliged by the preliminaries of peace, eventually confirmed in the Treaty of Frankfurt,[5] to pay a war indemnity of five milliard francs within three years and to submit to the occupation of several departments by German troops, who would be withdrawn gradually as the instalments of the indemnity were paid, but she also had to surrender two of her richest provinces. Alsace and Lorraine could not be saved, and with them she lost great iron ore deposits, important textile works, rich forest and agricultural land and a population of some 1,600,000. Thiers' tenacity as a negotiator had succeeded in securing a reduction of one milliard francs in the indemnity and in retaining in return for the concession of a triumphal entry of German troops into Paris on 1 March, the fortress of Belfort, but more than this he could not wrest from the conqueror. When the terms of peace were announced to the Assembly the deputies from Alsace and Lorraine once again made a moving protest and swore that their people would ever remain faithful to France. By this annexation of two unwilling provinces and their erection into a German Reichsland, or territory common to the new Empire, Bismarck may have helped to cement the unification of the new Germany but he also bequeathed to Europe a problem which bid fair to endanger her peace and made almost impossible any reconciliation between France and Germany such as took place between Austria and Prussia after 1866. Henceforward until 1918 the statue of Strasbourg in the Place de la Concorde in Paris was to be veiled in crêpe. Henceforward, although the mass of the people was quickly resigned to the new situation, the thoughts of many Frenchmen were long to be dominated by the idea of *revanche*. Like the partition of Poland, the 'rape of Alsace-Lorraine' was a wound in the body politic of Europe, a wound which would not be healed for nearly fifty years.

The preliminaries of peace, voted by the National Assembly on 1 March 1871, were only one of the trials which France had to face. A few days later the Assembly decided to adjourn and to resume its sittings at Versailles on the 20th. Before it met again the country was involved in civil war. On 18 March there broke out the revolutionary movement in Paris known as the Commune.

This tragic and complex affair was the outcome of a variety of causes and to understand some of them we must go back to the June Days, which in certain aspects this new Parisian rising so much resembled. The June Days insurrection of 1848 had, as we have seen, been ruthlessly suppressed, but it had left among certain classes of Parisian workers a deeper hatred than before of the bourgeoisie, which none of Napoleon III's gestures had been able to eradicate. The economist, Michel Chevalier, was obliged to admit that there were two opposing mentalities, the bourgeois and the proletarian,[6] and it seemed more than ever difficult to reconcile them. In the by-elections of 1864 sixty French workers had issued a manifesto declaring that social emancipation had still to come and that political rights implied social rights which could only be won by the workers' own efforts. In the following years the opening in Paris in 1865 of the first French office of the International and the gradual extension of branches to other parts of the country, the influence of Proudhon and Blanqui, combined with continued long hours and poor conditions in several industries, had all tended to keep open the gulf between workers and bourgeoisie and to revive dreams of the Socialist Republic of which the workers had been disappointed in 1848. The International, still an essentially working-class organization,[7] had soon fallen into the hands of extremist leaders in France, and when it had aroused the suspicion of the Government and was prosecuted, it had quickly become another thorn in the flesh of the weakening Empire.

So, Paris in the late 1860s, as in the 1830s and 1840s, was once again honeycombed by extremist societies and clubs of political and social revolutionaries, all of them anti-clerical, all of them hostile to the Empire, but at the same time far too individualist and varied in the sources of their inspiration to constitute anything like an organized party or even a movement. As the Empire had become more Liberal and restrictive legislation had been relaxed, so the extremist attacks upon the regime had been ever more virulent and the likelihood of some attempt at insurrection had increased. On 4 September 1870, there is little doubt that had the Republican deputies been less prompt, some of the extremist group would have seized power. As things were, they all hoped, like their forebears of 1848, to be able to bend the new Government to their will. The Government of National Defence, like that of Lamartine and his colleagues, were subjected to frequent pressure from clubs, from demonstrations of armed National Guards from working-class quarters, and from self-appointed district Watch Committees, often composed of extreme Republicans, who set up a Central Committee in the offices of the International and sought to impose their own military and political ideas. The National Guards in particular had in the siege conditions of Paris and with the shortage of regular soldiers become a veritable power whom the Government had great difficulty in handling. They, too, developed a general organization in Federations, and many extremists worked their way into positions of command. Once Paris was cut off, the Government were under constant criticism from all these extremists and patriots; their failures to proclaim a *levée en masse*, to attempt sorties sufficiently frequently and to hold municipal elections were all held against them; and when the news of the capitulation of Metz had reached the city on 3 October, they had nearly been overthrown by a crowd of excited demonstrators who had surrounded and invaded the Hôtel de Ville demanding elections to a Commune or municipal council and a *levée en masse*.

In both these demands the preoccupation was with the prosecution of the war; for the Commune at this moment was envisaged less as an organ of municipal autonomy than as a means of imposing a Jacobin dictatorship which would save the country and wage war with more ruthless energy. For a short time, until loyal forces came to the rescue, most of the members of the Government of National Defence had been held prisoner by the mob. After this escape they had reinforced their authority by a plebiscite which gave them a handsome majority, and had sought to govern with a stronger hand by entrusting the administration of the city to the firm and capable Jules Ferry. Nevertheless, clubs and extremist papers had continued their attacks and as the siege dragged on, food gave out, the cold became more severe, news of the outside world was rare, and the Germans began their bombardment, these grew more bitter. In one way or another many of those in the beleaguered city came to be overwrought and to suffer from what was known as 'siege fever'. And so, soon after the dismal failure of another attempt at a sortie, on 22 January, there was another revolutionary demonstration. Breton Mobile Guards were obliged to fire on National Guards who had sided with the demonstrators, and General Vinoy, who had just succeeded Trochu as Governor of Paris, closed several clubs and suspended a number of newspapers. When the city capitulated a few days later feelings inside it were passionately divided; and in the subsequent elections there was a violent campaign against the 'men of the capitulation', the Government of National Defence, with the result that workers and extremists like Tolain, Benoît Malon, Gambon and Félix Pyat, were elected alongside Republicans of all shades from Gambetta to Henri Martin. Out of forty-three deputies all but six were in favour of the continuation of the war. Such a result was a striking indication of the emotional state of the populace.

But in the provinces, as we have seen, the elections were overwhelmingly a vote for peace. Thus there was yet one more parallel with 1848. Once again the contrast between the will of the capital and the will of the country stood out in sharp relief. Paris was dismayed by the election of what it regarded as an Assembly of reactionary rural notables, and the Assembly had little understanding or sympathy for the feelings of the Parisians. Capital and country had both fought the same war, but in totally different conditions and the fact that they had been isolated from one another for four months greatly increased their mutual incomprehension. A series of acts of the new Government was soon to cause the city's latent tendency to insurrection to flare up again in exasperation. The Parisians were humiliated by the Germans' entry into the city on 1 March, although the exceedingly prompt ratification of the peace preliminaries had obliged them to withdraw two days later; they were slighted by the decision of the National Assembly to sit at Versailles instead of in Paris; and they were greatly embittered by two other measures. The first, in mid-February, provided that the National Guards should no longer automatically receive a payment of 1 fr. 50 a day; they must prove indigence. The second, a law of 10 March, ended the moratorium on payment of commercial bills and required that those outstanding since the middle of August should be settled forthwith. This requirement bore particularly hardly on tenants whose livelihood had been affected by the war and who owed rents to absentee landlords. And so when in March the Government proceeded to demand that the Parisians should hand over to the military authorities some 220 guns, which had been subscribed for by the people and concealed from the Germans, they met with a blank refusal. The test of force was about to begin, for the Government had committed a major blunder in depriving many National Guards of their pay without having first deprived them of their weapons. Jules Favre, to his eternal sorrow, had refused to consider their disarmament when he negotiated the armistice with Bismarck and no step had been taken to enforce it since.

But for local incidents in which two Generals were killed it is possible that some peaceful settlement might have been reached. But once again, as so often in French history, the unforeseen local clash, unexpectedly involving the loss of human life, at once changed the course of events, quickly embittering the opposing forces beyond hope of reconciliation. To a large number of Parisians it now seemed that a reactionary Government was bent on humiliating the capital in spite of its gallant defence. To the Government it appeared that insubordinate and dangerous revolutionary elements were bent on defying them and discrediting their authority while the invader looked on. They believed that their first task must be to restore their authority. But such regular troops as could be mustered were unreliable. And so on 18 March when Thiers and the army commanders heard that the regiments sent to recapture the guns had begun to fraternize with the people, that National Guards and demonstrators had

disarmed soldiers in various barracks, and that insurgents were masters of
several parts of the city, they decided that it should be evacuated at once.
This was what Thiers had urged Louis Philippe to do on 24 February 1848,
to withdraw with the regular troops, reorganize them and then take the
city by force. Now, in a similar situation, he lost no time in carrying out
the policy which Louis Philippe, with fatal results for his dynasty, had
hesitated to adopt. The seat of government was transferred to Versailles
and the evacuation left Paris once more in the hands of revolutionaries.
There was thus to be civil war, war between the regular troops of the
Versailles Government and the Federalists, as the National Guards of Paris
were known on account of their federal organization; and after the repulse
of the Federalists' attempt to march on Versailles Paris was to undergo its
second siege within six months.

The extremists thus had their chance to create a Commune under the
impetus of the National Guards' Central Committee, installed at the
Hôtel de Ville and of a number of followers of Blanqui, and several more
or less obscure Radical and Socialist politicians and journalists. The handful of moderates soon resigned, but since the Commune still included
doctrinaires of every kind, atheistic Blanquists, Proudhonians, Jacobins of
the 1848 variety and various independent revolutionaries (but only one
Marxist) it was more successful in hunting 'reactionaries' and priests than
in evolving an agreed and coherent constructive programme. Indeed the
Communards were soon at loggerheads with one another; and when the
threat from Versailles grew and it was known that Communards taken
prisoner were shot out of hand, their violence became more extreme and
they tended to imitate the Terror of the Great Revolution. Numbers of
suspects, including the Archbishop of Paris, were thrown into prison as
hostages, and buildings and monuments such as Thiers' house and the
Vendôme Column were destroyed. The Communard forces had abundant
arms, but they were relatively few and ill-disciplined; it was soon evident
that they would be no match for the reorganized Government forces
under Marshal MacMahon, whose numbers the Germans had permitted to
be increased from 40,000 to 80,000 by the incorporation of returned
prisoners of war. By the middle of May their position was hopeless, and
then, in a terrible frenzy of despair, when Government troops began to
pass into the city they began an orgy of destruction. Fifty-six of the
hostages, including the Archbishop of Paris and several priests, were shot,
and many of the finest buildings in Paris, among them the Tuileries, the
Palais de Justice and the Hôtel de Ville were set in flames. By the 28th,
after a brief existence of little over two months, the Commune was at an
end. Paris was subjugated and order restored, but at a terrible price. As in
the June Days, the fighting on both sides had been characterized by all the

savagery and ruthlessness of civil war; now, as then, fear and resentment made repression equally ruthless. The forces of order had been all the more exasperated by this insurrection at a time when the foreign enemy was still within the gate and when the country was in crying need of peace and reconstruction after the war against Prussia. Small wonder, then, that in the last week of the fighting, the *'semaine sanglante'* or 'bloody week' when the Government troops fought their way into the city street by street, they indulged in wholesale executions and undoubtedly made many innocent victims. The exact number of those who perished will never be known but it was probably about 20,000. In addition 38,000 were taken prisoner, 13,450 sentenced to various terms of imprisonment and 3500, among them the journalist Rochefort, deported to New Caledonia.

Hitherto, since the Great Revolution, it had been an oft-repeated axiom that in politics Paris led the way and gave the law to France.[8] The failure of the Commune marked the end of that supremacy.[9] As a movement of defiance against a conservative Assembly and a protest against peace it had had its imitators in other towns, particularly in the south, where extremist influence was still very strong. But the Communes of Toulouse, Narbonne, Lyons, St Etienne and Marseilles had been suppressed with little difficulty and 'the Commune', without qualification, remains for history above all a specifically Parisian phenomenon. Although it displayed the red flag, although members of the International took a prominent part in its direction, and although most of its troops were supplied by the Parisian workers, it was, like the insurrection of the June Days, a spontaneous uprising, not a long-planned, carefully co-ordinated, conscious attempt at social revolution; an uprising dictated in the first instance, as we have seen, as much by patriotic indignation as by political ambition or doctrinaire theory. Unhappily the results had been death and destruction on a scale still greater than in 1848. As after the June Days, executions, arrests and deportations disorganized and virtually silenced the extremists thereby greatly delaying the growth of organized Socialism in France. Among the victims we must also note the National Guard whose abolition was decreed by the National Assembly in August despite the opposition of Thiers. Thus there finally disappeared a 'democratic' force which had played a notable part in French history during the best part of a century. The Commune was an unhappy prelude to the Third Republic, a tragic climax to the misunderstandings of half a century between capital and provinces and between workers and bourgeoisie. Yet without it, it is possible that the birth of the Third Republic might have been much more difficult than it was. The proscription and exile of so many extremists enabled the new Republic to attain constitutional legality and to develop in a peaceable and orderly fashion during its first formative years. Last but not least, this absence or quiescence of the turbulent extremist elements enabled it at length to cast off that association in men's minds with violence, instability and social peril, by which it had been inextricably bound and hampered for so long. Only then could it be certain of winning the allegiance of the majority of hard-working, peaceable, Frenchmen.

Notes

1 *La France nouvelle*, p. 373.
2 *Mémoires du Duc de Broglie*, vol. 2, p. 21.
3 There was also a serious epidemic of smallpox both in Paris and in the provinces. Cf. Ashworth, E., 'Pestilence and War', *Spectator*, 2 November 1945.
4 Hale, Colonel Lonsdale, *The People's War in France, 1870–71*.
5 For texts see Butterfield, H., *Select Documents of European History, 1715–1920*, pp. 165–6, and Thomson, D., *France: Empire and Republic*, pp. 328–34.
6 Cit. Duveau, G., *La vie ouvrière en France sous le second Empire*, p. vii.
7 See *Société d'histoire de la Troisième République, Bulletin No. 8*, p. 66.
8 The elections of 1848 and the June Days were, of course, notable exceptions.
9 It is, however, to be noted that the Communards no longer claimed supremacy for Paris like the Jacobins of old, but demanded liberty for all the Communes of France. In doing so they spoke a language much like the Anarchists of Bakunin. Halévy, E., *Histoire du socialisme européen*, p. 158.

Bibliography

Baldick, R., *The Siege of Paris*, London, 1964.
Bourgin, G., *La Guerre de 1870–1871 et la Commune*, Paris, 1939.
Bury, J. P. T., *Gambetta and the National Defence*, London, 1936.
Dreyfus, Robert, *Monsieur Thiers contre l'Empire, la Guerre, la Commune, 1860–71*, Paris, 1928.
Edwards, S., *The Paris Commune, 1871*, London, 1971.
Hale, Lonsdale, *The 'People's War' in France, 1870–1*, London, 1904.
Horne, Alistair, *The Fall of Paris: The Siege and the Commune 1870–71*, London, 1968.
Howard, Michael, *The Franco-Prussian War*, London, 1967.
Hutton, Patrick H., *The Cult of the Revolutionary Tradition: the Blanquists in French Politics, 1864–1893*, Berkeley, 1981.
Kranzberg, Melvin, *The Siege of Paris, 1870–1871*, Ithaca, New York, 1950.
Mason, Edward S., *The Paris Commune*, New York, 1930.
Rihs, C., *La Commune de Paris: sa structure et ses doctrines*, Geneva, 1955.
Rougerie, J., *Paris libre, 1871*, Paris, 1971.
Tombs, Robert, *The War against Paris 1871*, Cambridge, 1981.
Williams, Roger L., *The Commune of Paris, 1871*, New York, 1969.

9

The establishment of the
Third Republic

Once France could take stock of her position after the terrible year of 1870–1 she found herself in a world which had greatly changed since the triumph of Napoleon III at the Treaty of Paris in 1856, only fifteen years earlier. Then she had been incontestably the foremost power in Europe. Italy and Germany were still only geographical expressions, Russia had been vanquished, Great Britain was an ally. Now France's débâcle had completed that rapid transformation of the map of Europe which had begun with the Italian war of 1859. It had obliged her to recall her troops from Rome – without any quid pro quo – and this withdrawal had spelt the doom of the Temporal power of the Papacy. The establishment of the Italian Government in the Eternal City had completed the unification of the new Italian kingdom. At the same time Russia had seized the chance afforded by war between two of the great powers of Europe to secure a modification of the Black Sea clauses of the Treaty of Paris. Most momentous of all, Germany, through war with France, had at last attained national unity and France had been without an ally. Consequently, while France was prostrate, three of the other principal European states had profited from her fall. The balance of European power was completely altered. The new German Empire had proved to be the most formidable military state; it already outnumbered France by over 4,000,000 people[1] and bid fair also to become the greatest industrial country on the Continent. The hegemony of Europe had passed from France to Germany, and Bismarck, not Thiers, was now the chief arbiter of continental destinies.

Willy-nilly, therefore, France had to adjust herself to a position which was painful and humiliating. Isolated, to some extent an object of mistrust to other Powers because of the Revolution of 4 September and the Commune, she could no longer think of ambitious foreign policies. As after 1815, so now her main preoccupations were internal – reconstruction after the ravages of war, fulfilment of the terms of the peace treaty, and last but not least the establishment of a stable form of government. The elections of February 1871 had shown clearly enough that the crying desire was for peace and this was long to remain true for the vast majority of the people – peace and quiet and steady work at home were the heartfelt needs, and they go far to explain the public dislike of new colonial adventures and the slight enthusiasm evoked by clerical campaigns for the restoration of the Temporal power. But was France capable of the positive effort of setting her house in order? Notable among the pessimists were men of letters such as Renan and Taine[2] who wielded such influence in the opening years of the Third Republic. After all, what had the last half-century been but a dismal tale of the failure of one regime after another? And now the Terrible Year had brought defeat by Germany, civil war at home, and insurrection in Algeria.

In fact, however, France once again showed the economic resiliency which had been so striking after 1815. Many a thrifty citizen had managed to put a good deal aside during the prosperous years of the Second Empire, and Europe and France herself were surprised and impressed by the way in which the two principal loans raised to meet a war indemnity, which all had regarded as crushing, were covered not once, but twice and thirteen times. As a result it was possible to secure the evacuation of France by the occupying German troops much before the date originally contemplated. By 30 July 1873 the whole country was cleared, except for Verdun, and in September the last German soldier left French soil. Thiers, whose steadying hand and skilled negotiations had largely contributed to this success, well deserved the title of Liberator of the Territory.

In general the early measures of reconstruction were marked by a conservative imprint. As Johnson in England is still Dr Johnson and Gladstone still Mr Gladstone, so Thiers in France is still M. Thiers, that is to say the type of the prudent bourgeois. For good or for ill, any chance the disappearance of the Empire might have afforded for a radical change in administrative organization was ignored. The traditionalist Thiers stood out against any wide measure of decentralization, although there had been a strong Opposition movement in favour of the so-called Nancy Regionalist Programme in the last year of the Empire. Indeed for a time the Right, like the Ultras in 1815, appeared to be more liberal than the Chief of the Executive Power who refused to allow free election of mayors to be accorded to any but towns of under 20,000 inhabitants, not including chief towns of departments and arrondissements. So it was, too, that while the general councils,[3] bodies still composed mainly of local notables, were now free to choose their own Presidents and to set up standing departmental Commissions, they were also still very much under the control of the prefects and far from achieving the independence as a unit of local government which some of the advocates of decentralization desired that they should enjoy. It was no less significant that neither he nor his Republican successors made any attempt to control the powers of the Prefecture of Police. In fact the highly centralized administrative structure inherited by France from Napoleon survived another crisis of regime without substantial modification.

In financial and commercial policy the traditionalism of Thiers was also marked. The proposal to introduce an income tax was rejected and under stress of competition from the New World he secured the first steps towards a return to the protectionist policy so characteristic of France before 1860. Thus innovations were few. 'The Republic will be conservative or it will not be at all,' said Thiers, and his attitude was no doubt reassuring to the bulk of the French middle classes and the ever-growing ranks of investors: but it is arguable that in the long run France would have benefited still more had a greater breath of freedom been introduced into local government and had the French people accepted an income tax in the 1870s instead of waiting for the crisis of the 1914–18 war.

No less striking, both as a measure of reconstruction which was to have European significance and as a further example of the strength of traditional habits in colouring French institutions, was the law of August 1872 and subsequent legislation reforming the army. This law, the counterpart of the Law St Cyr of 1818 reorganizing the army after the Napoleonic wars, bore the stamp of Prussian example. Victorious Germany enforced three years' general conscription. So in theory France must have conscription too, and for no less than five years. But in practice the application of the theory was singularly modified in the interests of economy. France could not, did not wish to carry the perennial burden of an enormous standing army, and so the old system of drawing lots was re-introduced. Only those who drew 'bad numbers' were obliged to serve the full period of five years, while their more fortunate brethren were let off with a year or six months. In addition, numerous categories of people, including priests and seminarists, were exempted altogether and volunteers who provided their own equipment were also required to serve only for a year. Thus, though deprived of the right to vote, the new French army was in many ways strikingly like the old. Three years later, however, the financial position had so much improved that the National Assembly was able to pass a bill providing for the increase of the size of the army by 150,000 men, and in the following years much thought was given to modernizing equipment and developing a reserve. This increase, coupled with the patriotic agitation of exiles from Alsace and Lorraine and the open talk of *revanche* which still persisted in certain circles, led to the so-called war scare of 1875. There is no evidence that Bismarck actually intended to embark upon a preventive war, but it suited him to unleash the German Press and to adopt an attitude sufficiently menacing to cause considerable alarm and to lead Decazes, the French Foreign Minister at the time, to rouse England and Russia to awareness of a possible danger to peace. Both powers answered his appeal for good offices. The British Government made representations in Berlin and the Tsar intervened personally with the German Emperor. The incident was significant. It emphasized another aspect of French recovery; it suggested that other Great Powers would not always let Germany invade France with impunity; and in particular it pointed to Russia as a possible future ally.

In the meantime, once the Commune had been quelled and the peace treaty signed at Frankfurt on 10 May 1871, the problems of government could be tackled anew. In view of the composition of the National Assembly the logical solution in 1871, as in 1849, would have been the restoration of a monarchy, and in June, in spite of the opposition of Thiers, the Assembly hastened to repeal the legislation exiling the princes of the royal houses of Bourbon and Orléans. But the Royalists, as in 1849, were still divided among themselves. Although mostly drawn from the aristocracy and wealthy bourgeoisie, half were Legitimists devoted to 'Henri V', the Comte de Chambord, and half were Orleanists who recognized Louis Philippe's grandson, the Comte de Paris, as their chief. Again, while one group was strongly Ultramontane, another was closely associated with the Liberal Catholic school which had just been worsted at the Vatican Council of 1870. Moreover, the cause of the Republic was by no means hopelessly lost. The Assembly had allowed the name of Republic to continue to be attached to the provisional regime and it had elected a moderate Republican, Jules Grévy, to preside over it, mainly because he had been highly critical of the continuation of the war and of the Government of National Defence. More important still, the Chief of the Executive Power, M. Thiers himself, former Orleanist Minister that he was, yet convinced that in the circumstances the Republic would prove to be the regime which divided Frenchmen least, was a convert to the Republican faith. Furthermore, the by-elections of July 1871 were highly significant. As a consequence of the election in February of many deputies for more than one constituency, and of subsequent resignations and deaths, as many as 118 seats had to be filled and of these the Republicans won no less than 100. This striking reversal of the trend in February strongly suggested that the voting then had been for peace rather than for monarchy. If this current continued the handsome Royalist majority would soon be seriously reduced. Thus it behoved the Royalists to make their Restoration quickly if it were to be achieved at all.

But this was just what they were unable and what perhaps many Orleanists were unwilling to do.[4] Although the fact that Chambord was childless should have made the fusion of Legitimists and Orleanists an easy matter, the Orleanists were not ready to give him unqualified support. Moreover, he himself was a grave obstacle. After forty years spent largely in an exiled circle remote from the realities of French politics, the Pretender paid a secret visit to France, and on 5 July issued a manifesto which caused consternation among his supporters. He would, he said, be ready to accept a constitutional form of government based upon universal suffrage, but he must retain the white flag: 'Henri V cannot abandon the white flag of Henri IV.' 'With the symbol of the Revolution,' he had told one of his followers, 'it would be impossible for me to do any good, or set aright any evil.'[5] This reaffirmation of an attachment to a forgotten and 'reactionary' symbol, so out of harmony with the national sentiment of a country from which he had been absent since the age of ten, was a bitter blow to the Royalists' hopes. They saw at once that the French people would never consent to abandon the tricolour, which now evoked so many glorious memories, and that until the Comte de Chambord consented to modify his attitude there would be no prospect of his becoming king. Thus there was an extraordinary situation: 'Henri V' invoking the name of Henri IV to justify his fidelity to the white flag, whereas Henri IV, who thought Paris worth a mass, was the very man to think Paris worth the tricolour, the more so since this was a flag under which Royalists of both groups had served with distinction during the recent war; 'Henri V' thus as good as turning down a throne which was virtually his for the asking and for which he had waited forty years; 'Henri V's' supporters, loth to believe that he really meant what he said and therefore themselves commending the tricolour and doing their utmost to keep the way open for his restoration; while Thiers, the man chosen by them to be head of the Provisional Government more and more clearly exhibited his preference for a Republic.

For the moment there was, then, no alternative but the continuation of the provisional regime: but as a result of a bargain at the end of August its nature was rather more clearly defined. The majority of the Assembly were anxious to secure beyond a doubt that when any constitution came to be framed they should be the framers – the door might then be left open for monarchy. Accordingly they formally arrogated to themselves the constituent power which was strenuously denied them by the Republican Radicals, Gambetta at their head, and in return they conferred upon Thiers the title of President of the Republic. In fact this was to prove a fresh stage in the consolidation of the Republic first provisionally established on 4 September 1870. But the position remained a strange one, for, as a correspondent of the London House of Rothschild wrote shortly after the passage of the new law, anything might happen: 'We are living under a Provisional Government run by an old gentleman of seventy-four!'[6] In fact the old gentleman of seventy-four, who had been the protégé of Talleyrand and the rival of Guizot, was still remarkably vigorous.

Omniscient, a shrewd debater, and tireless talker until overcome by sleep, M. Thiers with his vast experience thoroughly enjoyed the position of being *faute de mieux premier*.[7] As temperamental as a prima donna, he always dominated his Cabinets and generally succeeded in controlling the Assembly. 'No personal power' was ever so personal as that of M. Thiers, said one of his critics on the Right. While negotiations concerning the fulfilment of the peace treaty had still to be completed he was indeed indispensable. But long before the territory was finally liberated there came an open breach with the Right which foreshadowed his downfall. The President's conduct was indeed increasingly unsatisfactory from the Royalist point of view. The return of Gambetta to the Assembly after the elections of July 1871 had led to a rapid growth of Radical Republicanism. A great series of speeches delivered at banquets in various parts of the country – the continuation of a state of siege debarred public meetings – the foundation of a paper called the *République Française*, and the results of further by-elections, including one in Paris where Thiers' own friend and Foreign Minister the former Orleanist, Rémusat, was beaten by an obscure Radical named Barodet, showed that the 'ex-Dictator' was by no means a spent force. Now a Conservative Republic ruled by Thiers might be supportable to the Royalists as a necessary stopgap, but the kind of 'red' Republic which they believed to be represented by Gambetta was anathema to them, and when Gambetta called for the dissolution of the Assembly and the definite establishment of a Republic they demanded that Thiers should govern as a resolute Conservative and combat Radicalism without mercy. Thiers' refusal to give any undertaking to do so led to a breach which was widened virtually beyond repair when on 13 November 1872, in a presidential message to the Assembly he declared himself unequivocally in favour of a Republic. 'The Republic exists,' he said, 'it is the legal government of this country; to wish for anything else would be tantamount to revolution, the most formidable of all revolutions.'[8] Such a flagrant violation of the Pact of Bordeaux meant war between Thiers and the majority, war mitigated only by the anxiety of all not to prejudice the final negotiations with Germany for the evacuation of French territory. M. Thiers had always impressed upon Louis Philippe that the King reigns but does not govern; the Right now began to administer to M. Thiers a dose of his own medicine. On 13 March 1873, a law was passed preventing the President from communicating directly with the Assembly except on special occasions. Thus he became less of a Prime Minister and more of a President and was no longer able to sway the Assembly as he pleased by his skill as a debater. Two months later the climax came in a debate on a motion demanding that the Government should pursue a resolutely Conservative policy. Unable to wean Thiers back to the paths of strict Conservatism if not of monarchy, the Right brought about his downfall. He resigned at once and that same evening, 24 May, the Duc de Magenta, Marshal MacMahon, was elected President in his stead. Three hundred and ninety votes were cast in MacMahon's favour, but virtually the whole of the Left abstained.

There could be no greater contrast than that between M. Thiers and his successor, who was eleven years his junior. Marshal MacMahon was a devout Catholic and Conservative who had served many regimes, commanded with distinction in Italy, contrived to maintain a certain prestige in spite of the capitulation at Sedan, and been appointed Commander-in-Chief of the Government troops in the campaign against the Commune. Honest and loyal, he was as limited in conversation as M. Thiers was expansive. He accepted the Presidency because he had been persuaded by his wife and the Right that it was his duty to do so, but whereas M. Thiers adored politics the Marshal knew little of them and was bored by them. He was the despair of Ministers and politicians who, out of Cabinet hours, had the greatest difficulty in getting him to talk of anything but the weather, food and hunting.[9] For most of the Right, however, the Marshal appeared far more likely to be a satisfactory provisional President than M. Thiers. With his election we enter upon the period of the truly conservative Republic, the Republic of the Dukes, as it has been called by Daniel Halévy, since, in addition to the President, the Duc de Magenta, three Orleanist Dukes were now to play a prominent part in government and in a second attempt at bringing about a Restoration, namely the Duc de Broglie, who, though nominally only Vice-President of the Council, was to lead MacMahon's first ministry, the Duc Decazes, son of Louis XVIII's favourite, and Foreign Minister from 1873 to 1877, and the Duc d'Audiffret-Pasquier, President first of the National Assembly and then of the Senate.

Now that Thiers was out of the way the Right appeared to have a clear field for the application of their own policies. Although the Radicals had won some more by-elections, the death in 1873 of Napoleon III, who after his release from captivity in Germany had joined his wife in England, a sick and broken man, made it possible for the time being for the thirty Bonapartist deputies to co-operate with the Right. The new Broglie Ministry thus included even a Bonapartist as well as Legitimists and Orleanists. Its head was a man of great culture as well as of ancient lineage,

th little experience of parliamentary politics and hampered by a
ence which was too often and too easily mistaken for disdain. For
him the term Republican was synonymous with revolutionary. To him it
appeared that 'Religion, the army, the magistrature, the ascendancy of
the educated upper classes, in fact everything which was in any degree
representative of moral authority, everything which commanded
respect'[10] was odious to the Republican party. For him, therefore, the
immediate programme was that of the vigorous offensive against Radical
Republicanism upon which Thiers had refused to embark. Termed the 're-
establishment of moral order' it was a fight for the continued authority of
the upper classes and the Church. It entailed a thoroughgoing purge of
the administration and the magistrature in which many posts had, since
September 1870, continued to be held by Republicans. It entailed the
resumption by the Government of all appointments of mayors and a
determined effort to check Republican Press propaganda. Furthermore, it
meant open support for the Church which was so often the subject of
bitter Radical attacks. Civil funerals were permitted only in the waking
hours. The numerous expiatory cults which had grown up after the war
and the great pilgrimages to Lourdes, Paray-le-Monial and elsewhere
received official encouragement. The catastrophe of 1870 was attributed
by many of the Right to the general laxity of thought and morals which
had been characteristic of the Second Empire, and now, by way of
reaction, they were, in the words of one of them, M. de Marcère, overcome
'by a passionate desire for virtue'.[11] It was in something of this spirit that
on 4 July 1873 the Assembly voted for the construction, as 'a measure of
public utility', of the Basilica of the Sacred Heart, the great church on the
hill of Montmartre which dominates the city of Paris to this day. Thus the
dissolute revolutionary capital, which had let the Commune separate
Church and State and use its churches as clubs and debating halls, was in a
sense made to do public penance for its infidelity and sacrilege. At the
same time, under the sway of moral order, Ultramontane hopes of a
crusade for the restoration of the Temporal power revived. In many of its
aspects this strange resurgence of aristocratic and clerical ascendancy recalls
the days of Louis XVIII and Charles X.

Meanwhile the question of the restoration came to the fore once again.
In August 1873 a long-deferred visit by the Comte de Paris to Frohsdorf,
the Comte de Chambord's Austrian home, where the Orléans prince
greeted 'Henri V' as 'the representative of the monarchical principle in
France', seemed at last to ensure the complete fusion of the two main
monarchist parties. A period of muddled negotiation between the Pretender and Royalist emissaries ensued, which led the majority of Royalists
in France to believe that the difficulty of the white flag had been overcome

and that restoration was imminent. Elaborate preparations were made by enthusiastic supporters to welcome the King when he came into his own again. Dresses and carriages and flags and bunting were got ready for the triumphant day. Stocks rose on the Bourse, responsive to the belief that restoration by ending the provisional state of things would bring greater stability and prosperity. But all these expectations were doomed to bitter disappointment. On 27 October Chambord reiterated his earlier declaration. In no case would he abandon the white flag. If he did so he believed that he would be no more than legitimate king of the Revolution, liable to be swept aside by any gust of popular disapproval. 'Without my principle,' he is stated to have said in private, 'I am but a fat man with a limp.'[12] Thus Royalist hopes were finally dashed. When all was ready the Comte de Chambord, clinging with all the smiling serenity of a Pius IX to an outmoded principle, made his accession to the throne of his ancestors finally impossible. No wonder Thiers had already gleefully dubbed him the Washington of the Third Republic.[13]

In the circumstances the Orleanists would have gladly substituted the Comte de Paris immediately for the Comte de Chambord, but they had no chance of imposing such a solution, since the Legitimists still regarded Chambord as their chief and he refused to abdicate. There was no alternative, then, but to try and ensure that MacMahon, 'that Bayard of these modern times', as Chambord once described him,[14] should keep the King's place warm as long as possible in the hope that the *Deus ex machina* of Death might intervene and remove Chambord and that meanwhile the Republic should continue to be governed in a spirit of moral order. Accordingly in November a bill was passed prolonging MacMahon's term of office for seven years. This further extension of the provisional appeared to be a striking witness to the truth of the French adage '*Il n'y a que le provisoire qui dure*', but in fact the Assembly could not for ever be debarred from its self-appointed task of constitution-making, and a Commission of thirty was also appointed to report on the organization of 'public powers'. Although the majority of the members of this Commission were Royalists, they could not spin out their labours indefinitely, and in January 1875, when their proposals came before the Chamber, the decisive debates upon the proper Constitution of the French state at last began.

From the debates of 1875 there emerged two laws concerning the organization of the public powers and one relating to the organization of a second Chamber or Senate. These, together with two later so-called 'Organic Laws', which dealt with the procedure for electing Senators and deputies, form what is generally known as the 'Constitution of 1875';[15] and the 'Constitution of 1875', with but few modifications, was to be that under which Frenchmen were to live and have their being for no less than sixty-four years. It was the Constitution not of the monarchy but of the Republic.

The Monarchist intention was far from such a result. The Right wished merely to support the 'Seven Year' Marshal by providing him with conservatively designed institutions to assist his task of government. They intended, in fact, to prolong the provisional and give it further definition, but not to prejudice the future beyond the seven years' term; therefore their proposal for the organization of public power contained no mention of the word 'Republic'. But the Right had continued to lose ground during the last year. The Broglie Ministry, like so many later Ministries of the Third Republic, had succumbed to a momentary coalition of the extreme Left with the extreme Right who resented the Orleanists' treatment of Chambord. Further, the alliance with the Bonapartists had been short-lived, since the coming of age of the Prince Imperial and fresh election results had revived his party's aspirations. Indeed in the electoral field the Bonapartists were now the only Monarchist party to make any headway, with the consequence that many Orleanists, rather than encourage a revival of the Empire, tended again to gravitate towards the Republic. And so, as a result of this general situation and of much complicated manoeuvring, a motion known as the Wallon amendment introducing the word 'Republic' into the new legislation was carried by 353 votes to 352. 'The President of the Republic,' said the amended article, 'is elected by an absolute majority of votes by the Senate and the Chamber of Deputies met together as a National Assembly. He is appointed for seven years. He is re-eligible.' Thus by a single vote the Republic crept in furtively and as though by a side door, for its mention in this way, however apparently incidental, meant in fact that the constituent National Assembly formally recognized it as the proper and continuing mode of government. The President was already in office. As soon as elections to a Chamber and Senate had been held the new constitution would begin to function.

On 31 December 1875 the National Assembly met for the last time. The provisional regime which had endured for the best part of five years was finally at an end. The Assembly has too often been lightly dismissed by Republican historians as a concourse of 'rustics', reactionary representatives of a dying order, whose only desire was to put back the clock and prolong a state of uncertainty in their own narrow interests. In fact, few French parliamentary Assemblies have ever included so many men of eminence in all walks of life, generals, ecclesiastics, historians, economists, philosophers, as well as the expected lawyers, journalists and professional politicians. Ability and distinction were by no means the monopoly of any one party. Debating was of a remarkably high order, and in conjunction with the various governments of Thiers and MacMahon, the Assembly had directed the fortunes of the country in a period of singular difficulty. The measure of its achievement is best understood when the position of France in December 1875 is compared with her situation in February 1871 when the new Assembly first met at Bordeaux. Then the picture was one of defeat, disorganization and hopelessness; now it was one of striking recovery, reorganization and revival of optimism. Finally, as the result of much strenuous labour, the Assembly had hammered out a set of constitutional laws which were to serve France more than three times as long as any since the Great Revolution. Perhaps it was just because they were in the nature of an agreed compromise rather than of a doctrinaire Diktat that they proved so durable.

Marshal MacMahon's soldierly sense of duty made him tenacious of office. When he became President his motto was said to be, '*J'y suis, j'y reste*' – but after the voting of the Constitutional laws and the elections to the new Chambers the mot was wittily turned: '*J'y reste, mais je n'y suis plus.*'[16] He had managed well enough with Broglie and other Conservative Ministers, but the working of the new institutions brought him face to face with men of a very different type. Confronted with a growing tide of Republicanism that was by no means wholly conservative, he was soon irritated and perplexed. In fact, the Republicans had won further victories since the Wallon amendment of 30 January 1875. The Senate of 300 members of at least forty years of age, was to consist of seventy-five life members nominated by the Assembly and of 225 who were to be elected for nine years. The elective part of the body was to be renewable by thirds every three years. Both the provisions for life senators and those for the composition of the electoral colleges were designed to weight the Chamber in a conservative sense. It was therefore a bitter blow to the Right when a coalition of Republicans and Bonapartists secured the nomination of no less than fifty-seven Republican life senators some of whom were very recent converts to the Republican cause. The elections of January 1876 redressed the balance so as to secure a Conservative majority in the Upper House as a whole, but it was far less safe than the Right had hoped. Nor was this all; the elections to the Chamber of Deputies, held in February and in March, resulted in a sweeping victory for the Republicans who won no less than 360 seats, whereas the Monarchists obtained only 153, seventy-five of which went to the Bonapartists. This was largely the success that follows success – now that the Republic had been legally established many electors would have seen no sense in not supporting it. At the same time it was no doubt due also to the prestige of Thiers and to the growing popularity and authority of

Gambetta, who towered head and shoulders above most of his colleagues, both as an orator and as an adroit politician. The Monarchists had no popular leader to put up against such men, and their clericalism had earned them unpopularity; their inability to establish a monarchy discredited them and their attempts at exercising official pressure frequently reacted against them.

The passage of the laws of 1875 had virtually settled the question of the regime. A restoration of monarchy by constitutional means was now out of the question and MacMahon was hardly the man to lend himself to a *coup d'état*, although, at one moment, as we shall see, he does seem to have allowed himself to contemplate one upon a different issue. There was still, however, another question of vital importance to be resolved and that was one of the balance of power in the new Constitution. The confrontation of a Conservative President and Senate by a much more Radical Chamber threatened a conflict which was soon to develop.

After a brief experiment with a Ministry headed by a representative of the Left Centre, the Marshal reluctantly brought himself in December 1876 to request a moderate Republican, Jules Simon, to form a Cabinet. The policy of the new Ministry, however, whose term of office coincided with a fresh clerical offensive against Radicalism, was too liberal for the Marshal's tastes and when it acquiesced in a motion denouncing 'Ultramontane manifestations' he resolved to be rid of it. On 16 May 1877 he sent a letter to his Prime Minister which was tantamount to a dismissal and, although he had not been defeated in the Chamber, Simon took it as such and resigned. The Marshal's letter included a phrase which declared that if he had no responsibility towards Parliament he had a responsibility towards France for which he must have regard. This had an ominous Bonapartist ring about it and when the Marshal then proceeded to commission the Duc de Broglie to form a Cabinet, adjourned the protesting Chamber for a month and finally secured the Senate's assent to its dissolution, it was evident that a first-class constitutional conflict had arisen.

Once again the old issue of 1830 was raised. The Marshal was strictly within his rights. M. Thiers had been given the right to appoint and dismiss Ministers as he chose; he had done so freely without incurring hostility and the Marshal had succeeded to the same powers which had not been taken away from him by any subsequent legislation. Similarly, one of the laws of 1875 empowered the President to dissolve the Chamber before the expiration of its term, provided the Senate concurred. But was he justified in choosing his Ministers as he wished in defiance of the majority of the Chamber and in using his power of dissolution simply in order to try and obtain a Chamber which would work with those

Ministers? From the Republican point of view the Marshal's claims naturally made a mockery of parliamentary government.

Thus in the summer of 1877 there took place one of the most strenuous and exciting electoral campaigns in modern French history. The Duc de Broglie's Ministry, almost a replica of his Cabinet of 1873, used to the full all the traditional means of pressure so highly developed under the Second Empire and natural to any party in power. Once again there were sweeping changes in administrative personnel, and official candidates were general. Even the President himself took a hand in the struggle, making speeches in various parts of the country. But all these efforts met with little success. Although Gambetta's confident boast in June that the 363 Republican deputies of the last Chamber would return 400 strong in the new was not fulfilled and the Republicans lost thirty-six seats, the loss was far too small to give the Right the majority. They polled only 300,000 votes less than their opponents,[17] but won only 207 seats. Thus a fresh clash was bound to occur when the Broglie Government met the new Chamber. 'When the sovereign voice of France has been heard,' cried Gambetta in one of his election speeches, 'submission or resignation must follow.' But were these the only alternatives? Or would the Marshal, like Charles X, try yet another dissolution or a military *coup d'état*? It is certain that he had about him some who urged these high-handed solutions, but he resisted the tempters and when the Broglie Government met its inevitable defeat as soon as it encountered the new Chamber, he sought to temporize by forming a new Cabinet in which most of the Ministers were not members of either house and of which the head was an obscure general. This was no less unacceptable to the Chamber, who made short shrift of it by refusing to vote the budget unless the Ministry was chosen from the majority. Now indeed submission or resignation were the only alternatives. The Marshal submitted, and on 13 December 1877, the formation of a Ministry under Dufaure, which included Gambetta's former colleague at Tours and Bordeaux, Freycinet, was a triumph for parliamentary democracy.

This crisis of 1877 and the Marshal's submission were of vital importance for the future of the 'Constitution of 1875'. Henceforth no President could hope to have any success in pitting his personal responsibility against that of the Chamber. The crisis deepened the distrust of 'personal power' which was already so marked among Republicans since the *coup d'état* of 1851, and thus left an unhappy legacy, whereby it became all the more difficult for the chief executive office to be held by a man of commanding personality. It meant that the Presidential power to dissolve the Chamber fell into desuetude; that Ministries would henceforward be formed from the majority in the Chamber (almost invariably from a coalition of groups which together formed a majority); and that the

President of the Council would henceforth select all his Ministers, not, as hitherto, leaving the President of the Republic free to appoint to certain offices, such as the departments of Foreign Affairs, War and the Navy: in short it meant a decisive change in the balance of forces in the Constitution. The Executive had been humiliated and the Legislature was henceforth to be the preponderant power in the State, especially the Chamber with its guaranteed life of four years. How much this was to affect the character of the Republic we shall see when we come next to consider the Republic of the Republicans.

Notes

1 Germany's population in 1871 was 41,000,000, France's in 1876 nearly 37,000,000. Clapham, J. H., *Economic Development of France and Germany*, p. 278.
2 See Renan's *La réforme intellectuelle et morale de la France*, and Taine's *Origines de la France contemporaine*.
3 See p. 48 above.
4 'If the Republic didn't exist we should have to invent it in the interest of the Orleanist princes' wrote Montalivet to Thiers in February 1871. Cit. Lomenie, E. Beau de, *Les responsabilités des dynasties bourgeoises*, vol. 1, p. 220.
5 Cit. Brabant, F. H., *The Beginning of the Third Republic in France*, p. 327.
6 *Letters from Paris, 1870–75*, ed. R. Henrey, p. 171.
7 *Vanity Fair* published an excellent cartoon of him over this legend on 6 January 1872.
8 Cit. Hauser, H., Maurain, J. and Benaerts, P., *Du libéralisme à l'impérialisme (1860–78)*, p. 180. Cf. *Mémoires du Duc de Broglie*, vol. 2, p. 126.
9 See Cambon, P., *Correspondance, 1870–1924*, vol. 1, pp. 63–4.
10 *Mémoires du Duc de Broglie*, vol. 2, p. 44.
11 Cit. *Letters from Paris, 1870–75*, ed. R. Henrey, p. 181.
12 de Roux, Marquis, *Origines et fondation de la Troisième République*, p. 169. I am indebted for this reference to Canon F. H. Brabant.
13 Bourgin, G., *La Troisième République*, p. 43.
14 ibid., p. 56.
15 For the text of these laws see Appendix 7.
16 Cambon, op. cit., p. 69.
17 The Republican vote was approximately 4,000,000, the Conservative 3,700,000, cf. Halévy, D., *Décadence de la liberté*, p. 32.

Bibliography

Barral, P., *Les fondateurs de la Troisième République*, Paris, 1968.
Bertocci, Philip A., *Jules Simon*, New York, 1978.
Brabant, F. H., *The Beginning of the Third Republic in France*, London, 1940.

Broglie, Duc de, *Mémoires*, Vol. 2, *1870–5*, Paris, 1941.

Brown, Marvin L. Jr, *The Comte de Chambord: the Third Republic's uncompromising King*, Durham, NC, 1967.

Bury, J. P. T., *Gambetta and the Making of the Third Republic*, London, 1973.

Chapman, Guy, *The Third Republic of France: the First Phase 1872–1894*, London, 1962.

Chastenet, J., *L'enfance de la Troisième, 1870–1879*, Paris, 1952.

Dreyfus, Robert, *La République de Monsieur Thiers (1871–3)*, Paris, 1930.

Elwitt, S., *The Making of the Third Republic: Class and Politics in France 1868–1884*, Baton Rouge, 1975.

Gambetta, L., *Lettres, 1868–82*, ed. D. Halévy and E. Pillias, Paris, 1938.

Gouault, J., *Comment la France est devenue républicaine 1870–1875*, Paris, 1954.

Halévy, D., *La fin des notables*, Paris, 1930, English trans. Middletown, 1974.

Halévy, D., *La République des Ducs*. 6th edn, Paris, 1937.

Locke, Robert R., *French Legitimists and the Politics of Moral Order in the Early Third Republic*, Princeton, 1974.

McManners, J., *Church and State in France 1870–1914*, London, 1972.

Mayeur, J. M., *Les débuts de la Troisième République 1871–98*, Paris, 1973.

Pisani-Ferry, F., *Le coup d'état manqué du 16 mai 1877*, Paris, 1965.

Rudelle, O., *La République absolue 1870–1879: aux origines de l'instabilité constitutionnelle de la France républicaine*, Paris, 1982.

Wormser, G., *Gambetta dans les tempêtes*, Paris, 1964.

10

The Republic of the Republicans

The triumph of parliamentary government in 1877 was also a triumph for the Republic represented by Thiers and Gambetta. In 1871 Thiers had appeared to be poles apart from Gambetta, the man whom he had dubbed a 'raging madman', but since, through his breach with the Right, he had moved towards the Left while Gambetta had moved away from it. 'If the Republic is a form of government,' wrote the Duc de Broglie in his memoirs, 'the French Republican Party is not a party capable of governing,' and he made it clear that for him the term Republican was still synonymous with Revolutionary.[1] 1792, 1830, 1848, 1870, 1871 all seemed to bear this out; but since 1871 Thiers and Gambetta each in his way had done their best to divest it of its revolutionary connotation. Thiers' first contribution had been to make the form of government respectable; his second was to begin to make the Party respectable, since his example and their own interest had split the original Conservative bloc of 1871 and led to the formation of a Republican Left Centre largely composed of deserters from Royalism.

In this second aim he found an unexpected but powerful ally in Gambetta. In 1869 Gambetta had subscribed to the famous Belleville electoral programme, which included demands for the election of all public officials, the suppression of standing armies and the abolition of 'privileges and monopolies'; but by 1875 he had shed much of his Radicalism and assumed a new task which, as an acute observer, Saint-Valry, remarked in May of that year, was fundamentally the same as that of Ollivier a few years earlier. It was to organize and discipline the democracy; to give it 'cadres'; to raise from it 'a new governmental personnel, a new ruling class'.[2] The heroic age of the Republican movement, the age of the men of 1848, the Armand Barbès and the Louis Blancs, was now over. The 1870s were to prepare for the ascension to power of what Gambetta called 'a new social stratum'. Essentially this meant the rise of the class from which Gambetta himself had sprung, the *petits bourgeois*, small shopkeepers, clerks and artisans, the class which had shown its economic importance by the way in which it swelled the ranks of investors and by its active part in the work of reconstruction after the war. Gambetta was determined that these people who were such a vital element in the life of the nation, and potentially in the Republican movement, should be fit to share in the responsibilities of democratic government and that Republicans generally should show themselves ready for power. In seeking this end he ceased to be a Radical and became what he called an Opportunist – a name which was to stick to his followers down to the 1890s. In other words he was now the advocate of a policy of realism: doctrinaire tenets were shelved in favour of immediately practical tasks and the electorate was reassured that if Gambetta was a stalwart opponent of monarchy and clericalism he was far from being revolutionary and red. Thus in the crisis of 1877 there was co-operation between the veteran Thiers and Gambetta, and it was believed that, if all went well, Thiers would before long once again preside over a Republican government in which Gambetta would then take a chief place. The mantle of Thiers would give Gambetta respectability beyond question, and would ensure the final establishment of a Republic which would be fully Republican in spirit as well as in name, and would guarantee rather than menace social order. Unfortunately this great partnership was never consummated, for Thiers died suddenly during the election campaign of 1877. It was left for Gambetta to complete the work with the aid of lesser men and under a President in whom he was to find an enemy instead of a friend.

But before Republican policies could be freely introduced it was necessary for the Republicans to capture the two strongholds of power which still remained in the hands of their antagonists. In little over a year after the Presidential 'submission' of 1877 their victory was complete. As a result of the first triennial elections to the Senate, in January 1879, they gained a comfortable majority of fifty or so in the Upper House. At once they proceeded to exploit their success and to reverse the work of Conservative governments by filling the administration and judiciary with loyal Republicans. This was but a natural swing of the pendulum, but when the Cabinet went further and proposed to remove a number of elderly generals, his old comrades, MacMahon could stand no more. A lonely figure now, more and more uncomfortable in an uncongenial, if not actively hostile political world, he had retained his post so long only from a sense of duty. But this tampering with the army was the last straw and after refusing to sign the decree of removal on 30 January 1879 the Marshal, first president of the Republic under the 'Constitution of 1875', resigned his office nearly two years before his term was due to expire.

Chosen originally by the National Assembly to keep the succession open for a sovereign, he had the humiliation of handing over his post to an elderly Republican lawyer of humble ancestry. That same evening the Chamber and Senate, meeting together as a National Assembly or Congress, elected Jules Grévy to be his successor.

Thus, with the disappearance from the political stage of the Duc de Magenta the Republic of the Dukes came finally to an end. And its end meant more than the end of a particular form of Republicanism – of Republicanism without Republicans. It was a social as well as a political revolution; for although Conservatism was still, as we shall see, to be a considerable force in the country owing to its continued association with the clergy, the army, big banking interests, and for a brief time still, with some members of the civil service, the old aristocracy and its allies were never again during the Third Republic to wield such power as they had in the 1870s. They might still serve with distinction in the army and the diplomatic or colonial services, but in all the numerous Cabinets between 1879 and 1940 it is rare to find even the particle 'de' in front of a Minister's name. The new social strata which gradually replaced them had no such adornments.

Now that the Republicans held all the levers of power they were concerned to consolidate their victory and free to carry out a truly Republican policy. They, too, had early assumed the cloak of virtue and, like the Monarchists, attributed the débâcle of 1870 to the levity and licence of the Second Empire. Accordingly they liked to picture their regime as one in which austere excellence and elevated morals would go hand in hand with Republican simplicity. But foreign observers soon became sceptical of the virtues and showed little enthusiasm for the simplicity in so far as M. Grévy's drab and economical establishment at the Élysée was its model. At the same time, though far from revolutionary, the Republic was placed under the sign of the old revolutionary slogan 'Liberty, Equality and Fraternity' and all Republicans would have held that one at least of its missions was now to give real content to those words by the establishment of a true political democracy.[3] It is, however, a particularly striking fact, especially when we remember 1848, that in 1879, thirty years later, no Republican group of any significance in parliament goes seriously beyond this political aim. The Radicals of 1869 in a singularly laboured phrase of the Belleville programme referred to the social question in only the vaguest terms. Ten years later their successors, the Radicals of 1879, the Opportunists and the Moderates are hardly more explicit or, if they are, the social part of their programmes definitely takes second place. The reasons are not far to seek. The social revolutionary aspect of the Second Republic was the one which had done most to turn the electorate against Republicanism, just as its social revolutionary possibilities had done most to rouse them against the Commune, with the result that until 1879 most of the socialistically inclined Republicans were in exile. The others – Radicals, Opportunists and so on – sprung almost wholly from the bourgeoisie themselves, had for the most part received their political education by participating in a political struggle against the Second Empire. Thus they and their successors in power in the 1880s and most of the 1890s either, like Thiers, distrusted social change; or were simply not interested; or feared it since it was dangerous. In fact, as we have seen, the Republicans' success in the critical struggle against the Monarchists in the 1870s was not a little due to the conversion of important Orleanists. Such a conversion would have been impossible had social and economic change loomed large in the Republican programme, for the Orleanists, like some of the Opportunists such as Jules Ferry and Scheurer-Kestner, were closely associated with the big bourgeoisie. There is also another factor which may perhaps help to explain why political and not social problems were the main preoccupation: France was still predominantly a land of peasants – a land in which some 65 per cent of the population were still country dwellers with little direct interest in the social problems of workers in the towns.

Hence the first measures of the Republicans in power are concerned with the political consolidation of victory, the political education of the democracy and the extension of political liberties. In the first place the advent of the Republic of the Republicans is confirmed by a number of acts which have a symbolical significance. The return of the Chambers to Paris in 1879 and the partial amnesty for Communards, followed by a full one two years later, were evidence of the spirit of Fraternity which actuated the new regime, marked the reconciliation of government and capital, and showed that the Republicans proposed to welcome at least all Republicans into the fold. In 1880 the observance of 14 July, the anniversary of the Fall of the Bastille, as a day of national festival for the first time since the Great Revolution (it had been observed as a religious festival in 1790), and its celebration amongst other things by a great military review, emphasized both that the Republic was the heir of the Great Revolution and that it was a patriotic regime, proud of the revival of a national army. Similarly the inauguration of an extravagant programme of public works by Freycinet seemed to show that the Republic had a care for the well-being of its citizens and the dignity of the State, and may have served to convert many lukewarm electors by giving them work.[4] An egalitarian, democratic breeze blew through the Senate and certain administrative services when, by a constitutional revision in 1884, the creation of more life senators was abandoned, provision being made for the remaining quarter of the Upper House

Density of population c 1885

	0 - 20	inhabitants per square kilometre
20 - 60	"	"	"	"
60 - 100	"	"	"	"
100 - 200	"	"	"	"
200 and more		

Miles

0   50   100   150

The nine towns with over 100 000 inhabitants each are marked
— · — · — Borders with neighbouring states

Map 3: Density of population c. 1885

to be elected for nine years just like their brethren, and when recruitment by competitive examination was introduced into the Diplomatic Service and later into other branches such as the Conseil d'État, the Cour des Comptes, and the Inspection des Finances. No less important were the laws restoring or extending certain freedoms; the laws of 1884 leaving all French communes, except Paris, free to elect their mayors (although they were still subject in various ways to a considerable measure of prefectorial control) and admitting a partial freedom of association by the grant to workers in the same profession of the right to form unions for the defence of their economic interests. But of all the reforms of these early years those to which many Republicans attached supreme importance, which were most contentious, roused the deepest passions and had the most far-reaching consequences, were undoubtedly the education laws sponsored by Jules Ferry.

After Thiers and Gambetta, Jules Ferry was undoubtedly the third most commanding figure among the founders of the Republic. Born near St Dié in the Vosges, trained like Gambetta at the bar, he had won his political spurs in the same opposition struggle at the end of the Second Empire and shown a faculty for mordant wit in a series of articles with the felicitous title of 'Les Comptes fantastiques d'Haussmann'. But in 1870, while the younger man was virtual ruler of the provinces, Ferry had had the narrower and more ungrateful task of being responsible for Parisian administration. This included the distribution and eventually the rationing of food supplies, and inevitably brought him unpopularity with a populace ill-accustomed to such privations. Hence the nickname 'Ferry-Famine', soon to be followed by that of 'Ferry-Massacre' on account of his part in putting down the attempted insurrection of 22 January in Paris. But, in spite of this unpopularity with a section of the Parisians, Ferry's stature and influence continued to grow in the 1870s. He, too, took an active share in convincing the electorate of the Republicans' fitness to govern and in time he became the acknowledged leader of one of their two main parliamentary groups, the Gauche Républicaine, the other being Gambetta's Union Républicaine. Finally he entered the Waddington Cabinet of February 1879, the first of Grévy's presidency, as Minister of Public Instruction and continued to hold this post both in the succeeding Ministry and in the Cabinet after that, which he himself headed. Thus, in spite of Cabinet changes, he was in charge of the country's education for nearly three years. This was time enough in which to put through a sweeping programme of reform.

'The most urgent of all reforms,' Gambetta had declared when he accepted the Belleville programme of 1869, 'must be the liberation of universal suffrage from every sort of tutelage, obstacle, pressure and corruption.' Universal suffrage had in 1849, 1851, 1852 voted and would again in 1870 and 1871 vote Royalist or Bonapartist. The problem was to ensure that it should vote Republican and the remedy persistently prescribed by Republicans was compulsory primary education, and moreover primary education which should be not only compulsory but also free[5] and above all in the hands of laymen. In fact we are now approaching another momentous stage in the great battle of Church and Revolution which had been waged on many fronts almost continuously throughout the century. During the Restoration and the July Monarchy, as we have seen, one of its main aspects had been the struggle for control of secondary and higher education: now the scene broadens to take in the field of primary education. In Republican eyes illiteracy – estimated by Ferry in 1879 at 15 per cent of the population – and clerical influence in education were the main obstacles in the way of the conversion of France into a free political democracy. The flirtation of Church and Republic in 1848 had been but a brief romantic embrace. Everything that had happened since had tended to force the two farther apart.

On the one hand the Church viewed with increasing alarm the development of new forces which seemed to be still further hastening the disintegration of France as a Christian society. Enthralled by the vista of indefinite material progress opened up by the Industrial Revolution and all its attendant discoveries, the young intelligentsia believed that science and free inquiry were the keys to all things. In their brave new world God and religion had little place and the fact that so many of them were Republican and therefore politically opposed to the Conservative Catholics increased their intellectual hostility. So it is that the majority of the brilliant young men trained at the École Normale after 1848 and the majority of the Republican leaders – that is, those who were not Protestants – and the small Protestant minority was to play a part in the Third Republic out of all proportion to its numbers – were agnostics, and many of them devotees of the pseudo-scientific creed of Positivism which was founded by Auguste Comte and had an extraordinary influence in the second half of the century. This new intellectual attitude undoubtedly widened the breach between the Conservatives and the Republicans for many of whom, too, the cult of the Great Revolution had become almost a religion, and, in so far as it affected their political thinking, intensified the political offensive of the Left against the Church. Long before 1870, many writers such as Edgar Quinet, Vacherot, Prévost-Paradol and others had demanded the separation of Church and State; it was one of the requirements of the Belleville programme, and, as we have seen, was actually put into effect by the Commune in Paris. Moreover, the anti-clerical materialistic propaganda was highly organized. The Ligue de l'Enseignment,

The Republic of the Republicans

founded by Jean Macé in 1866, the sectarian teaching of the free
who were now ardently Republican and whose numbers doubled
1862 and 1889, the publication of a host of cheap brochures and booklets
written for popular consumption, contributed to the diffusion through
ever-widening circles of French people of an intellectual and moral outlook wholly at variance with the traditional teaching of the Church. No
wonder then that in the rise of the modern Republican State the Church
and the Conservatives saw the gravest threat to all that they held most
dear.

On the other hand, the growth of Ultramontanism among French
Catholics, their loyalty to a Pope who was so openly at war with Liberalism, who had promulgated the Syllabus of Modern Errors and the Decree
of Infallibility, their violent campaigns for the defence or for the
restoration of the Temporal power before and after 1870, their uncon-
cealed support of the Royalists, and their outbursts against Radicalism[6] led
the Republicans to see in them a reactionary force which was constantly
guided by political ambitions and irreconcilably hostile to most of the
ideas for which they themselves stood. Moreover, since 1848, it was a force
which in many ways appeared to have gained ground. The Loi Falloux of
1851 had, as we have seen,[7] confirmed their freedom to have their own
schools. The number of religious orders, some legally authorized and
some not, had greatly increased so that in 1878, in addition to the
ordinary clergy, there were no less than 128,000 nuns and 32,000 monks
including teaching brothers (compared with 34,000 and 3000 respectively
in 1851), while some two out of five million schoolchildren were being
taught in Catholic *écoles libres* mainly run by the regular clergy. The value
of the property held by the authorized communities was no less than
421,000,000 francs, or £16,840,000,[8] while the unauthorized bodies, of
whom the Jesuits were the most notable, accounted for another
160,000,000 francs. The education of women, and the organization of
charitable relief, were still, as they had been for centuries, almost wholly
in the hands of the Church. The strength of clerical passion and anti-
clerical feeling had already been strikingly demonstrated in the 1860s
under the Second Empire, when more passion was aroused over clerical
than over almost any other issues in that momentous decade. After their
experience of the rule of Moral Order between 1873 and 1877 there was
hardly a Republican who could not have been firmly convinced that the
power of the Church had increased, was increasing and ought to be
diminished. Accordingly, when in 1876 Gambetta, echoing a cry already
uttered in the 1860s, thundered 'Clericalism – there is the enemy', he
knew that he would rally Republicans of every shade. It was therefore both
natural and logical that the first big offensive of the Republicans to

consolidate their power should be anti-clerical in direction. But it was also a happy coincidence that such a policy was likely to win the approval of such powers as Germany, Italy and Austria, which had their own struggles of Church and State, and that once the French Republican was engaged upon his favourite sport of *manger du curé* he would have less inclination to think about *revanche* or social problems. Finally, in addition to the other important aims of suppressing illiteracy and spreading the knowledge of French there was a further argument in favour of compulsory education – Prussia had had it before the war of 1870, and it was widely said that her victory was the victory of the Prussian schoolmasters as well as of the Prussian generals.

So the most significant of the education bills brought forward by Jules Ferry was the bill, eventually passed in 1882, which made primary education free, compulsory and secular – that is to say, which banned religious and clerical supervision from all state primary schools.[9] But another of his measures directed at strengthening state control over higher education won still greater notoriety since it contained article No. 7, which forbade members of unauthorized congregations to direct or teach in any educational establishment. After a tremendous debate this article was rejected by the Senate, but Government and Chamber were not prepared to admit defeat and immediately decided in favour of a rigid enforcement of the existing laws. Thus again, as in 1828 and 1845, there is a State offensive against the unauthorized congregations, of whom the Jesuits were the chief, once again an attempt to apply a law which had so often remained unobserved. In March 1880, decrees ordered the dissolution and disbandment of the Jesuits within three months and of all other unauthorized congregations who failed within a prescribed time limit to obtain permission to reside and operate in France. Conservatives and Catholics were passionately indignant, a number of communities refused to obey the decrees, some 400 magistrates and officials resigned rather than enforce them, and, when troops had in some instances to be called in to secure the expulsion of male communities (the female were unmolested), it seemed almost as though a new war of religion was at hand. But the Government remained unmoved – the nineteenth century was not the sixteenth – it had the full support of the Chamber and the numbers actually dissolved were small enough. Moreover, the resignation of conservatively disposed magistrates and officials simply gave an opportunity to replace them by others whose Republicanism was not in doubt. Indeed, in his second premiership, in 1883, Jules Ferry went further; he suspended for three months the legislation providing that magistrates should be irremovable, and thus was able to remove another 614 whose clerical sympathies had been too pronounced for Republican taste.

These measures were only part of a general offensive against clerical-ism. Three other educational laws deprived members of teaching congre-gations of the right to teach in State primary schools and Catholic Universities of the right to confer degrees and made State provision for the first time for secondary education for women. (Yet as late as 1930, André Siegfried could still write that there was no type of Frenchman more representative than the anti-clerical deputy whose wife was a devout Catholic and had her daughters educated in a convent.[10] The tradition of conventual education for women was deeply rooted and not to be broken in a day.) Furthermore, the clergy were eliminated from representation on the reformed council for the direction of higher education and from the administration of charitable organizations. Military chaplains were abolished, Sisters of Mercy were gradually ousted from hospitals, divorce was re-established and the estimates of the Ministry of Public Worship were cut down.

This offensive, backed by all the powers of the State, inevitably met with considerable success. The influence of the clergy upon many sides of French life diminished and there is no doubt that between 1880 and 1900 the decline in religious practice, already noticeable under the Second Empire, continued and was if anything accelerated. This was natural enough for, as Daniel Halévy once pointed out, the secular school, by eliminating from school teaching such fundamental words as 'God, soul, hope and prayer', suppressed the very instruments of religious thought.[11] In their place came as pale substitutes the jargon of civics and State morality. Furthermore, in the village schoolmasters the Republic now had a valuable new instrument for increasing its hold. Addressing a gathering of these men Ferry made quite clear what was expected of them: 'As citizens you have been enfranchised by the French Revolution; as teachers you are going to be emancipated by the Republic of 1880: how could you not love and through your teaching bring others to love the Revolution and the Republic? This policy is a national policy.'[12] When many school-masters, often the only educated people in the village apart from the priest, acted as secretaries to the local Mairie their value as local political agents was further enhanced. Moreover, although, officially, State schools were to be neutral so far as religious questions were concerned, the very circumstances of their creation as agencies for a secular State meant that the teaching in them often enough had a distinctly anti-clerical bias. In Great Britain parson and schoolmaster were often allies – in Republican France they were almost certain to be rivals and foes. And here indeed lies the tragedy of the France of the Revolution, a tragedy whose darkness was deepened by the laws of 1880–1. The abolition of religious instruction in state schools makes absolute the educational cleavage between the two

Frances – clerical and secular, black and red – and, in spite of the multitude of acute social and economic questions which have come to overlay it, this dichotomy is still of considerable importance. At the time, in the 1880s, the introduction of what Broglie called 'the Godless school', and all the accompanying anti-clerical measures, inevitably led most of the clergy and devout laity to regard the Republic as a rule of Satan, its 'Fraternity' and the emphasis on 'Unity' within the 'Patrie' in its new text-books as mere hollow mockeries. Once again, as for all previous regimes, the great problem was that of achieving a genuine national unity. Can the Third Republic ever succeed in having more than the negative quality of being the regime which divides Frenchmen least? Can it ever be a regime accepted freely by all parties, however vigorously they contend with one another within the Republican framework?

Much must obviously depend on the tact and political wisdom of the contending forces. On the Republican side the one man, who, had he lived long enough, might eventually have had the authority and power to rally the Conservatives was he who had launched the offensive against clericalism. Great hopes were entertained that Gambetta would at an early stage of the new regime form a strong Government which would do much both to consolidate the Republic at home and to make it a force to be conjured with abroad. But Grévy, who envied Gambetta's popularity and believed him to be dangerous because more than any other man he was identified by public opinion with the idea of *revanche*, refused to call upon Gambetta to form a Ministry and 'the great man' of the regime saw his supporters in office while he himself remained President of the Chamber. Inevitably he exercised influence upon policy through the men whom he had himself educated for government; but as Ministry succeeded Ministry and Gambetta still was not summoned, the intriguers, the jealous, and the henchmen of Grévy put it about that Gambetta preferred to evade responsibility and exercise a hidden dictatorship. When at last in November 1881 Grévy decided to ask him to form a Cabinet it was in the knowledge that Gambetta's influence had been largely diminished by his own manoeuvring. 'The Great Ministry', which public opinion had expected to be composed of all the foremost Republican politicians, could not be formed and instead Gambetta had to content himself with a Cabinet of personal friends and men who were comparatively little known. It lasted only two months and within less than a year of its fall Gambetta, still no more than forty-four, was dead of acute peritonitis. During these last years he had become steadily more moderate: meeting and fascinating the Prince of Wales and aristocrats like the Marquis de Galliffet and the Comte du Lau, welcoming and appreciating the great importance of the accession of Leo XIII to succeed Pope Pius IX, declaring that anti-clericalism was not an article for export, perhaps entertaining hopes that even the Alsatian question could be settled by diplomacy. Many competent observers were agreed that with him there passed away the one commanding figure of the Republic who was sufficiently generous and broad-minded to have created something like a real unity in France.[13] After his death Jules Ferry was the man who stood out as the ablest of the Republicans and it was to him that the men of Gambetta's 'Union 'Républicaine' rallied, so that for two years he was able to maintain a strong Government based upon a solid Opportunist majority. Then he in turn fell in circumstances which throw singularly little lustre upon the Chamber and virtually ended his political career.

The occasion of Ferry's fall was an incident in the process of colonial expansion which was the last great achievement of these early years of the Republican Republic, and which Ferry himself did more than any other politician to support and encourage. As we have seen, the first years after the débâcle of 1870 were necessarily years of *recueillement*, overseas as well as at home. The general opinion was that France must now conserve all her resources ready for any emergency in Europe, that she must think of *revanche* as her foremost duty, remember that Germany was the great enemy and keep her eyes fixed on 'the blue line of the Vosges', and it was in harmony with such a view that the Broglie Government in 1874 reduced France's Far Eastern commitments by the evacuation of Tonkin. Yet there was still a handful of men who, moved by the spirit of adventure, the love of exploration, the hope of financial gain, or the desire to extend French influence in the world, sought to carry on that expansionist movement which had received such a powerful impetus under the Second Empire; and at home there were men with vision enough to back them in spite of popular distrust or apathy. Moreover, as France's material recovery progressed and she became a factor once again to be reckoned with in international affairs, other powers took a hand in encouraging or discouraging these aspirations. In 1878, the year of the first great exhibition held in Paris under the Republic, when France formally re-entered the councils of the European powers by attending the Congress of Berlin, summoned to resolve the Eastern Question, both Lord Salisbury, ready to compensate France for Britain's annexation of Cyprus, and Bismarck, anxious to divert her attention from the Vosges and estrange her from Italy, encouraged her to move into Tunis.

Ever since the conquest of Algiers France had cast an eye upon Tunis, still nominally a dependency of the decaying Turkish Empire, but the subjugation of Algeria had been so long and costly that she had hesitated to take on more North African territory. Moreover, a formidable insurrection in Algeria in 1871 merely increased the general reaction against

overseas adventures. In the striking last chapter of his *France Nouvelle*
Prévost-Paradol had urged that France had no hope of maintaining her
relative position in the world unless there were a speedy and sufficient
increase in the number of Frenchmen. Her great opportunity, he said, was
to colonize Algeria which was rich, close at hand and easily defensible, and
then he went further: 'May the day soon come when our fellow citizens,
too straitly confined in our African France, will overflow into Morocco and
Tunisia and found the Mediterranean Empire which will be not only a
satisfaction to our pride, but certainly in the future state of the world, the
last resource of our greatness.'[14] Prophetic wish! for although the increase
in the number of Frenchmen was to be obtained not by colonization – the
French were, as ever slow to expatriate themselves[15] – but by assimilation
and a Roman extension of citizenship, in 1940 the African and
Mediterranean Empire, built by the Third Republic almost in despite of
public opinion, was indeed to appear the last resource of French greatness!

Between 1878 and 1881 it was 'greatness', the desire to recover her
position as a great power, as well as the wish to protect French financial
interests and to ensure that Tunisia should not become Italian, which
induced France to begin a new policy which was approved by Gambetta as
well as by Ferry. Italy, too, was showing expansionist ambitions, and her
considerable interests in Tunisia suggested that she, too, might wish to
annex it. So it was, that, after a short military campaign involving some
40,000 troops, France in May 1881 induced the Bey of Tunis to sign the
Treaty of Bardo which converted his territories into a French protectorate,
and by the end of the year, after punitive expeditions against tribes of the
interior, virtually the whole country was under French control.[16] But,
whereas anti-clericalism was a policy which united Republicans, colonial
expansion divided them, and the Radicals, clinging to a narrow *revanchard* patriotism, combined with the Right in a fierce attack on the
Tunisian venture. Ferry, whose position had been weakened by the
autumn elections, had already decided to resign and did so in November
immediately after the bitter Tunisian debate. Only the intervention of
Gambetta had saved the maintenance of the protectorate itself from being
called into question.

The fall of the Ferry Cabinet under such circumstances and the
passionately bitter campaigns of Left and Right had momentous consequences at the eastern end of the Mediterranean. The vast extravagance of
another nominal vassal of the Turkish Sultan, the Khedive of Egypt, had
brought him under the control of his French and English creditors and
given France and Great Britain such an influence in the Nile delta and
valley as to cause a nationalist rising in protest. Gambetta's policy during
his short-lived ministry was to co-operate with Great Britain in a vigorous

defence of European interests, but his successor, Freycinet, remembering Tunis, was far more timorous. He refused to join England in a naval bombardment of Alexandria, and, when eventually after much hesitation he plucked up courage to ask for credits for an expeditionary force to join with the British in an occupation of the Suez Canal area, the demand was rejected by the Chamber. Thus, once again, a Cabinet headed by one of the most prominent, if not the most forceful, of the Republican politicians was defeated on a question of overseas policy. Great Britain remained in Egypt alone and reaped the profits of a vigorous policy, whereas France had thrown away her opportunity to share in them. Unfortunately the knowledge that her loss was due to her own indecision and timidity served only to increase France's jealousy of her more successful rival and the sour grapes of Egypt were to play an important part in embittering Anglo-French relations during the next twenty years. Yet it is indeed doubtful whether those relations would have been much more cordial even if France had stayed in Egypt and exercised condominium there with Great Britain. The tradition of colonial rivalry was still very strong overseas and a condominium, instead of bringing the two countries closer together, might no less easily have been a cause of constant friction and intrigue.

Nevertheless, French expansion was not to be checked by the Chamber's censures either on the Tunisian or the Egyptian question. By now, after mature reflection, Ferry had become a convinced colonialist. He saw in colonial policy the inevitable result of the policy of industrialization to which France like the other great countries of Western Europe was irretrievably committed, and the secure majority which he enjoyed for a considerable time during his second premiership meant that the years 1883–5 witnessed a fresh forward movement. France's foothold in Madagascar, where Great Britain was again her chief rival, was strengthened; the explorations of Brazza in the Congo basin were so effectively followed up that the International Congress of Berlin in 1884–5 consented to give formal recognition to the creation of a French Congo – a colony larger than France herself, cheaply won at a cost of some 300,000 francs;[17] and last, but not least, in the Far East Tonkin was reconquered and a protectorate established over Annam. This advance in the Far East, however, led to an undeclared war with China, Annam's suzerain, and it was not until the summer of 1885 that the Chinese finally recognized France's new predominance. Before the achievement of this striking success, Ferry, the man at home who was mainly responsible, had been cast to the winds by a frenzied Chamber in one of the most extraordinary outbursts of passion and panic ever witnessed in a French Parliament. The report of a minor reverse at Langson in Tonkin followed by an urgent demand for reinforcements from the general on the spot, at once roused all the enemies of the Republic, all the enemies of the Ferry Ministry (which was not unnaturally tending to lose ground after two years of office) and all the antagonists of colonial expansion, both within and without the Chamber, in the press and in public meetings, to whip up a passionate campaign suggesting that Ferry's insensate imperialism after a prodigal expenditure of men and money was now leading France to a humiliating defeat. When the Government at once ordered reinforcements and asked the Chamber for a fresh credit of 200 million francs, the storm burst. All Ferry's opponents and all those who remembered Mexico and then thought of Germany rose up against the Prime Minister in fury and revolt. He was denounced as a tool of Germany. In a speech of extreme bitterness the formidable Radical leader Clemenceau even went so far as to accuse the Cabinet of high treason. All sense of proportion, all sense that the verdict should not be given until the facts were fully known, were swept aside and Jules Ferry, who already had certain but secret information that China was disposed to come to terms, could but bow before the storm and resign. Outside in the streets crowds shouted for the death of 'Ferry-Tonkin' and Ferry never fully recovered from the wave of unpopularity which virtually swept him out of public life. While, ironically enough, the same Chamber which had rejected his demand for credits granted them a few weeks later to his successor, the new Chamber of December 1885 rejected a motion for the evacuation of Tonkin by only one vote. Thus, as precariously as the Republic itself, the Republic's new Far Eastern Empire came to stay.

So, with the overthrow of Jules Ferry there ends the age, as we may call it, of the Founders of the Republic; but not the age of Opportunist government. That, as we shall see, was to continue for several years more in spite of much discomfiture, disturbance and discredit.

Notes

1 *Mémoires du Duc de Broglie*, vol. 2, p. 43, cf. also pp. 89–90.
2 Saint-Valry, G. de, *Souvenirs et réflexions politiques*, vol. 1, p. 119ff.
3 Barni, J., *Manuel républicain* (1872), '*L'admirable devise de nos pères: Liberté, Egalité, Fraternité, en résume les principes fondamentaux.*'
4 Cf. Halévy, D., *Décadence de la liberté*, pp. 45–6.
5 The abolition of fees had already been encouraged by Victor Duruy during the Second Empire and effected in 8000 Communes.
6 In all this the influence of Veuillot and his belligerent paper *L'Univers* was extremely important.
7 p. 00, above.
8 The contemporary sterling equivalent.

9 For the text, see Cahm, E. *Politics and Society in Contemporary France (1789–1971)*, p. 551.
10 *Tableau des partis en France*, p. 65.
11 *Société d'histoire de la Troisième République, Bulletin No. 16*, p. 135.
12 Cit. Reclus, M., *Jules Ferry*, p. 220. For his more guarded letter of 1883, see Cahm, p. 552.
13 Cf. e.g. Bodley, J. E. C., *The Church in France*, p. 52.
14 *La France nouvelle*, p. 416.
15 And when they did so, they often preferred to go to a country where they would not be liable to military service. It is noteworthy that nearly 1,000,000 Frenchmen emigrated to the New World during the nineteenth and twentieth centuries, mostly to the USA and the Argentine. Cf. Chatelain, A., 'Les Migrations Françaises', *Annales*, January–March, 1947.
16 See Map 4, p. 201.
17 Beaumont, M., *L'essor industriel et l'impérialisme colonial*, p. 96.

Bibliography

Auspitz, K., *The radical bourgeoisie. The Ligue de l'enseignement and the origins of the Third Republic 1866–1885*, Cambridge, 1982.

Baumont, Maurice, *L'essor industriel et l'impérialisme colonial (1878–1904)*, Paris, 1937, 3rd edn, 1965.

Brunschwig, H., *French Colonialism, 1871–1914; Myths and Realities*, London, 1966.

Bruun, G., *Clemenceau*, Harvard, 1943.

Bury, J. P. T., *Gambetta's Final Years: 'The Era of Difficulties', 1877–1882*, London, 1982.

Chapman, Guy, *The Third Republic of France: The First Phase 1872–1894*, London, 1962.

Chastenet, J., *La République des Républicains 1879–1893*, Paris, 1964.

Gambetta, L., *Lettres, 1868–82*, ed. D. Halévy and E. Pillias, Paris, 1938.

McManners, J., *Church and State in France 1870–1914*, London, 1972.

Mayeur, J. M., *Les débuts de la Troisième République 1871–98*, Paris, 1973.

Pisani-Ferry, F., *Jules Ferry et le partage du monde*, Paris, 1962.

Power, Thomas F., *Jules Ferry and the Renaissance of French Imperialism*, New York, 1944.

Reclus, Maurice, *Jules Ferry*, Paris, 1947.

Rudelle, O., *La République absolue 1870–1879: aux origines de l'instabilité constitutionelle de la France républicaine*, Paris, 1982.

Saint-Valry, G. de, *Souvenirs et réflexions politiques*, Paris, 1886.

Sorlin, P., *Waldeck-Rousseau*, Paris, 1967.

Vitzetelly, E. A., *Republican France 1870–1912*, London, 1912.

Watson, D. R., *Georges Clemenceau: A Political Biography*, London, 1974.

11

The years of crisis and scandal

The achievements of the Third Republic during the first ten years of the 'Constitution of 1875' were thus considerable: a great programme of public works, re-entry into the concert of Europe, and the acquisition of new overseas dominions all helped to restore prestige; while legislation at home, if it did little to make for unity among Frenchmen, at least strengthened the Republican hold on place and power and prepared the education of a new generation whose fidelity to the regime would be beyond question.

But there was a reverse side to this medal. Reviving material prosperity was tempered by a severe agricultural depression, which also affected many other parts of Europe and for which the huge influx of cheap wheat and meat from the newly developed prairies of the American Middle West was largely responsible. In France, where tenant-farmers were particularly hard hit, this depression had been aggravated by a deadly outbreak of phylloxera which wrought havoc in most of the vineyards and caused French wine production to fall from 83,000,000 hectolitres in 1875 to 24,000,000 in 1889; and the distress in country districts was made still worse by the crash in 1882 of the Union Générale Bank to which thousands of small farmers and rural investors had committed their savings. This depression had two main effects: it accelerated the movement of population from countryside to town, from agriculture to big industry; and it reduced the demand for many kinds of consumer goods, thus bringing on a parallel depression in industry. In consequence, by 1885 there was considerable economic distress and social discontent among various classes of the community; and the number of hostile critics of the regime had considerably increased.

The Republic, indeed, had its critics and foes on the Left as well as on the Right. The Radicals held that the Opportunists had stopped half-way; they still wanted separation of Church and State, a revision of the Constitution whereby the Senate would be abolished as a reactionary institution, and a much more thorough purge of administrative personnel. Further Left still there were many groups which had either come into being or gained new vigour as a result of the return of the Communard exiles in 1879 and 1881; and the workers had begun to organize anew in Congress and unions. In 1879, under the influence of Jules Guesde, a workers' congress at Marseilles had declared in favour of the formation of a Socialist Party to conduct a class struggle in accordance with the collectivist doctrines of Karl Marx. Accordingly, in the following year, the Parti Ouvrier Français was founded, and for the first time Marxism was to become an important disruptive influence within the French State and society. But it had no monopoly and while the economic distress afforded a fertile field for propaganda, there were rivals or dissident groups, the Blanquists, the Anarchists, the Possibilists after 1881, and the Alemanists after 1890, who competed with the Guesdists for influence among the working classes. The main characteristics of French Socialism at this time are its divisions, the struggles between authoritarian Marxists and non-Marxists and between those who looked primarily to violence and those who were ready to seek reforms within the existing state. Faced by bitter Radical criticism in Parliament and by quasi-revolutionary groups outside, it was no wonder that the Opportunists sometimes believed that the danger to the regime came as much from the Left as from the Right.

The reverse side of the medal also showed itself in the working of parliamentary sovereignty which had been far from shedding lustre on Republican democracy. In fact the crisis of 1877 had been a calamity, for it had in effect deprived the 'Constitution of 1875' of its most valuable safeguard against the irresponsibility of the legislature. Once the menace of dissolution was removed the deputies were veritable kings of the Republic, free to do what they liked for four years. 'The Chamber' it has been well said, 'did not want any person or institution to be potent save itself; to the degree that a large assembly can govern a country, the Chamber would govern it. What the Chamber could not do would not be done – and, in the Radical Republican tradition, there was a strong element of anarchical suspicion of all government. Above all, that tradition was suspicious of the government of one man.'[1] The result was that the Palais Bourbon became a preserve in which shifting groups played elaborate games of intrigue in order to gain office and in which Ministries were overturned with light-hearted impunity. The system of 'interpellation', which enabled any deputy to call upon a Minister to explain his policy on any issue and necessitated an immediate general debate before the business of the day could be proceeded with, also contributed to instability, the more so that if the vote in the debate went against the Government it was expected to resign, no matter how trivial the issue.

Thus legislation of national interest and continuity of national policy were alike at the mercy of political manoeuvring; envy in Bodley's words 'condemned excellence to obscurity and exposed capability to ostracism',[2] and the Third Republic became a byword for ministerial instability.

Moreover, with the instability of Cabinets went the mediocrity of the deputies. The contrast between the calibre of the men of the National Assembly of 1871–5 and the Parliaments of the 1880s and 1890s was glaring. The Republic might produce great administrators and ambassadors – its legislators were of a far lower order. Paul Cambon, Gambetta, Lord Lyons, all deplored it, and while some like Cambon or Renan believed that 'the advance of mediocrity was the law of democracies',[3] others like Gambetta thought that a change in the electoral law would provide a remedy. Under the system known as *scrutin d'arrondissement* whereby each arrondissement elected a deputy (or deputies, if its numbers exceeded 100,000) the nomination of Republican candidates for parliament tended to fall into the hands of small committees of petty bourgeois officials, shopkeepers, schoolmasters or rentiers, often self-appointed, whose one concern was to secure the return of a deputy who would look after local interests. Thus a parochial outlook or *esprit de clocher* too often prevailed over a national view in constituency and in Chamber alike. Gambetta believed that the substitution of the method known as *scrutin de liste* would lead to the election of men of greater intellect and broader vision and, when he was Prime Minister, he brought in a bill for the revision of the electoral procedure. The bill was rejected and the 'Grand Ministère' fell, but three years later what a jealous Chamber had refused to Gambetta it granted to Brisson. Accordingly the elections of 1885 were conducted on a departmental basis, each department being entitled to one deputy for every 70,000 inhabitants and the electors voting at the principal town or departmental capital for as many deputies as the whole department was allowed. It was not clear, however, that the quality of the deputies in the new Chamber of 1885–9 was notably superior to that of their predecessors and, in the reaction after the Boulangist crisis of those years, the Chamber hastily returned to *scrutin d'arrondissement*, which in spite of many subsequent demands that *scrutin de liste* be given a new trial was to remain the method of election to the Chamber until 1919.

Consequently the electoral habits of constituencies became confirmed, and in the 1890s men as different as Zola and the Vicomte de Vogüé were still to complain of the mediocrity of their parliamentary representatives; the power of local caucuses grew and under what a well-known writer was to call 'La République des Comités'[4] the *esprit de clocher* seemed more than ever to prevail.

These defects of the parliamentary regime had, as we have seen, already begun to appear during the first decade – as early as 1883 Bismarck had spoken contemptuously of France's democratic evolution *ad absurdum*[5] and, taken in conjunction with the economic distress and social discontent of the 1880s, they go far to explain the fact that in spite of many notable successes the Third Republic was soon to suffer a series of crises and scandals which shook it to its foundations. The internal history of the last fifteen years of the century is overshadowed by the Boulangist crisis, the Panama Scandal and the Dreyfus Affair.

The main results of the elections of 1885 were not the return of better deputies, but the revival of the Right, who, although they secured only 202 seats, polled but 600,000 votes less than the Republicans, and the election of some 180 Radicals. The strength of the Conservative vote was probably due as much to Catholic discontent with the Government as to any increase of Monarchist feeling; for although the death of the Comte de Chambord in 1883 had eliminated the obstacle of the white flag, and the tragic end of the young Prince Imperial in Zululand in 1879 had removed the Pretender who had the best prospect of making a popular appeal to Frenchmen, the Monarchists could not have been said to have made much advance in popular esteem. Their new head, the Comte de Paris, though conscientious, cultivated and liberal, was little known to the French people as a whole and had no personal magnetism. None the less, the Government were sufficiently scared by the election results and the renewal of Royalist hopes and activities to seize upon an incident in 1886 as a pretext to expel the Comte de Paris and all other heads of former ruling houses from France together with their heirs, and to decree that no member of their families should join the army or navy, occupy any public employment or be eligible for parliament.[6] The strength of the Radical vote, which reflected social and economic discontent and the unpopularity of overseas expansion, meant that the Opportunists had no clear majority in the new Chamber. They were, therefore, obliged to depend upon the support of Right or Left. As it was still inconceivable that a Republican party should make a working alliance with the Conservatives, the Radicals were in effect masters of the situation, and men asked, as they had asked once before of Gambetta, whether the Radical leader, the redoubtable Clemenceau, would now form a Cabinet or whether he would prefer to remain behind the scenes and exercise *le pouvoir occulte*. Once again the answer was the same. The aged Grévy, who was re-elected President of the Republic in December 1885, feared Clemenceau no less than he had feared Gambetta and nothing would induce him to choose him as Prime Minister. Thus, Clemenceau, most unfortunately perhaps for the Republic, was condemned to wield power without responsibility, making and remaking Cabinets without being in them himself and putting his own nominees into office.

The first notable consequence of this Radical mastery was the inclusion in the coalition Cabinet formed by Freycinet in January 1886 of General Boulanger, an officer with a brilliant record of personal gallantry, son of a Breton father and a Welsh mother, still under fifty, tolerably good looking and possessed of great personal charm. Although he had not scrupled to solicit the Orleanist Duc d'Aumale for help in his career, Boulanger now professed strong Radical views and Clemenceau imposed him on Freycinet as Minister of War because he believed that Boulanger was the man the Radicals required to carry out a more thorough Republican reform of the army. So to some extent he was: he made many changes in the Ministry of War, improved the armament and brightened the living conditions of the ordinary soldier; he also prepared a new scheme for implementing the Radical wish to reduce the term of military service to three years,[7] and for making it really compulsory for all by doing away with exemptions and giving the anti-clericals the delight of seeing the priest with a pack on his back (*le curé sac au dos*). These were measures that might have been applied by any vigorous Republican, but Boulanger was no ordinary Minister of War and he acted in no ordinary way. Every move was accompanied by extraordinary publicity, every move was calculated to win popular favour. The result was that after he had been only six months in office he had achieved an extraordinary reputation: people talked, said Lord Lyons, as though he were about to become a Cromwell or a Monk;[8] and when the General appeared at the military review at Longchamps on 14 July a martial, blond-bearded figure on a black horse, the Parisians went mad with delight. All the cheers were for Boulanger, scarcely any for Grévy, the President of the Republic. The song 'En revenant de la revue', composed that evening by the chansonnier Paulus, became the anthem of a new cult of hero worship. Naturally the Opportunists were alarmed and urged Freycinet to be rid of a Minister whose popularity looked dangerous and whose self-advertisement ill became a servant of the Republic. But Freycinet feared the Radicals, and Boulanger, scenting opposition, for a time drew in his horns, and used his personal fascination for a more discreet consolidation of his position in social and political circles. He was so successful in doing this, while keeping the goodwill of the Radicals, that in December he retained his position in a new coalition Cabinet – 'a Freycinet ministry without Freycinet'. Meanwhile it was being put about that Boulanger was the man of Destiny who would recover France's lost provinces, and exiled Alsatians and Lorrainers and patriotic societies like Déroulède's 'Ligue des Patriotes', founded in 1882, suggested that the hour of *revanche* was at hand. Bismarck's reply was characteristic – the system of government in the Reichsland was deliberately made more harsh; a bill was sent to the Reichstag for the increase of the German army, the Triple Alliance with Austria, Hungary and Italy was renewed in February 1887 and a German Press campaign was launched against French 'warmongers'.

Once again, as in 1875, there was a veritable war scare, and both in February and in April, when the Germans arrested a French police official named Schnaebele, the situation was tense. It is probable that Bismarck exploited France's seeming militarism in order both to force a German army bill through the Reichstag and also to weaken Boulanger's position. Indeed had not wiser counsels than Boulanger's prevailed in the French Cabinet it is possible that war might have broken out. Fortunately for France Grévy and some of the Ministers kept their heads better than Napoleon III and Gramont in 1870 and France was spared a new defeat. The French public, however, knew nothing of what had gone on in the Cabinet. What they believed, when Bismarck was conciliatory over the Schnaebele affair, was that in Boulanger France at last had a man who could make the German Ogre draw back. The new confidence of 1887 was in striking contrast to the timorousness of 1875. The affair at once made Boulanger a national hero and new songs acclaimed him as 'General Revanche'. By now, however, the Opportunists were thoroughly alarmed and soon determined to get rid of Boulanger by bringing about the fall of the Ministry. Grévy was only too delighted to be quit of a man whom he regarded as a dangerous demagogue, but it was not so easy to find a new Prime Minister willing to take the responsibility of offending the Radicals and forming a Government without Boulanger. At length after a prolonged crisis during which there was continuous popular clamour for Boulanger's retention, the Marseillais Rouvier, who was to be one of the ablest Finance Ministers of the Third Republic, succeeded in forming a Ministry, but only at the expense of breaking with the Radicals and depending on the tolerance of the Right. For the first time since 1875 Republicans were the allies of Monarchists against other Republicans.

The public were disappointed and furious at Boulanger's exclusion from the new Ministry and the cult of the popular hero grew apace, notwithstanding his fall from power. Afraid of what might happen on 14 July 1887, the Government hastily posted him to Clermont Ferrand, but the Parisians did their best to prevent him from leaving the capital. Astonishing scenes took place at the Gare de Lyon on the evening on which he was due to depart. Immense crowds gathered and 3000 people stood or lay on the lines in front of Boulanger's train so that it should not go. It was only by a stratagem which enabled him to mount an engine on another line that the embarrassed General was able to get away at all and take up his new command. This extraordinary manifestation showed that Boulanger had become the focus of a formidable revolt of public opinion against parliamentarianism. As such, others besides the Opportunists now saw in him a danger to the regime. While the journalist Rochefort, still a powerful iconoclastic force, remained true to Boulanger, Clemenceau and the more responsible Radicals withdrew their support and condemned the demonstrations at the Gare de Lyon. The 14 July celebrations went off without any undue disturbance and it might have been hoped that relegated to a provincial command – the Government would have done better still to have sent him overseas – the General would soon be forgotten. But new events soon occurred to cast further discredit on the regime and to provide Boulanger with an opportunity for return to the limelight. In the autumn of 1887 it was discovered that a deputy named Daniel Wilson, who had married Grévy's daughter and been allowed by his father-in-law to reside at the Élysée, had abused his position as the President's son-in-law to traffic in honours, to solicit subscriptions to the newspapers he owned and to conduct a vast correspondence free of charge by employing the President's frank. The Chamber appointed a Commission of Inquiry and Wilson was eventually condemned to two years' imprisonment, but acquitted on appeal. Meanwhile the scandal naturally enough led to the demand that Grévy should resign, and since he showed no inclination to do so the majority in the Chamber engineered the defeat of the Rouvier Cabinet and decided that it should be impossible for the President to find a new Prime Minister. For some days there was an unparalleled situation: crowds demonstrated in front of the Élysée and sang mocking songs such as 'Ah! quel malheur d'avoir un gendre!'; eligible deputies went on strike and refused the President's entreaties that they should form Cabinets, but still the old man of eighty-one remained obdurate. Not until 27 November did he promise his resignation for 1 December. Who was to be his successor? Suddenly the Radicals and the Right realized that Jules Ferry was likely to be the strongest candidate, and Boulanger re-emerged to take part in agitated conferences about the possibility of forming a Ministry which would after all serve under Grévy. Anything would be better than the hated Ferry.

When these manoeuvres came to nothing and Grévy's farewell message was at last read to the Chamber on 2 December, there were violent street demonstrations, organized both by Déroulède's 'Ligue des Patriotes' and by the revolutionary Blanquists of the extreme Left. There is little doubt that these signs of Ferry's unpopularity and the hostility of the extremely Radical Paris municipal council conjured up visions of serious disorders and frightened the National Assembly when it met at Versailles the next day to elect a new President. In addition Ferry's enemies were able to work upon the now traditional jealousy of a strong man. Senators and deputies therefore adopted Clemenceau's suggestion that the choice of a new President should fall on an outsider, and though his recommendation of Sadi Carnot 'He is not very bright, but he bears a Republican name' (popularly repeated as 'let's vote for the stupidest') was scarcely enthusiastic, it vividly illustrated the attitude of the legislature towards the executive and won the day. Ferry's return to a prominent position was prevented. Instead, Sadi Carnot, son of a deputy of 1848 and grandson of Lazare Carnot, the 'organizer of victory' in the Great Revolution, became the third President of the Third Republic. A member of a Republican dynasty, a bourgeois of some standing and unimpeachable integrity, he was in fact to preside over the Republic with considerable dignity and to achieve a much wider popularity than his predecessor.

Boulanger meanwhile had formed connections both with the Monarchist Right and with the Bonapartists. He had accepted a Monarchist proposal for a working alliance ('We have the same adversaries: let us first combat them together; afterward we shall see') and also a Bonapartist one that he should stand for election to the Chamber in as many by-elections as possible and so obtain such a strong personal position that he must either be admitted to the Government or sweep it away. Thus there began the extraordinary 'plebiscitary' campaign of 1888, largely financed by a Royalist Duchess, which seemed to introduce into French electioneering the vulgar hustling of American methods and in which Boulanger, soon placed on the army's retired list for indiscipline, headed a new 'National Republican Party', and carried six out of seven by-elections in various parts of the country on a programme demanding a dissolution of the existing Parliament, a revision of the Constitution and the election of a Constituent Assembly. Detached observers all bore witness that the country was swept by a kind of delirium – 'It is 1851 all over again and worse,'[9] wrote the staunch Republican, Paul Cambon. The climax came in January 1889 when the Boulangists decided to test the feeling of the capital itself and the General stood at another by-election in what was now a largely Radical stronghold. The Radicals and Opportunists made the error of putting up against him a colourless local politician who was presented as 'the candidate of the Republic' as though the very regime was in danger. To their great discomfiture Boulanger was elected by an enormous majority. Later, when his movement failed, disappointed supporters made out that when the historic poll was announced the enthusiastic crowd had called on him to march upon the Élysée and that, had his courage not deserted him, he could have carried all before him and played Cromwell or Monk as he wished. But this was an audacious invention. There seems to be no clear evidence that he ever planned a *coup d'état* or contemplated such an undertaking. From the first he and his mixed bag of supporters had proclaimed their faith in universal suffrage and it was in the ballot boxes of the general elections eight months later that they were eventually defeated.

However, 27 January 1889 had given a severe shock to the upholders of the existing regime. In consequence all Republicans who remained loyal to it temporarily sank their differences and rallied in its defence. In February a new Cabinet of so-called 'Republican concentration' was formed; *scrutin de liste* was once more abandoned in favour of *scrutin d'arrondissement* in order to minimize the danger of future electoral steeplechasing; a bill was passed forbidding multiple candidatures; an energetic Minister of the Interior, Ernest Constans, prosecuted the 'Ligue des Patriotes'; and preparations were for the first time made to implement article 12 of the Constitutional Law of 16 July 1875, whereby the Senate could act as a High Court for the trial of attacks against the safety of the State. In the meantime Boulanger himself gave the death blow to his movement and to the hopes of his supporters. It was rumoured that he was to be arrested. Instead of staying in Paris he and his mistress took train for Brussels. Had he stayed in France and boldly faced arrest and trial he might still have remained a popular hero, triumphant if acquitted, glorified by a crown of martyrdom if condemned. Indeed the evidence that he had actually plotted against the State was so flimsy that he should have been able to tear the prosecution case to ribbons. But he refused to return to France in spite of the most pressing appeals of his followers. 'Instead of being the saviour of France he preferred to save his own skin.'[10] The enthusiasm of January melted away in the disappointment and discredit of April. Although Boulanger himself was once again elected in a Paris constituency, in the general elections in September his party only won some forty seats. The Boulangism of Boulanger was effectively killed by the General's own lack of political courage and the end of the story was dreary and lamentable. Boulanger was duly condemned by the High Court – a condemnation which was hardly justice, but the Republic required a conviction; the movement fizzled out amid the mutual recriminations of the General's last adherents, and in September 1891 he committed suicide on his mistress's Belgian grave.

The astonishing enthusiasm which marked the Boulangist movement of 1888 had amazed and perplexed detached contemporary observers; for the General was no more than a regular soldier with a fine record of personal bravery who had shown some energy and humanity during a seventeen months' tenure of the Ministry of War, and those who met him were surprised by his limited intelligence though they might admit his personal charm. But the enthusiasm was not so much for what Boulanger had done as for what thousands of Frenchmen hoped he would do; and so long as his programme remained vague every hope was still possible. Thus he became the focus and symbol for all the aspirations of all the discontented; for those who hoped that a flame of purification would purge the State of corruption and give it new strength and dignity; for those who still longed for *revanche*; for those who wanted a revision of the Constitution; for Monarchists and Bonapartists who believed he was working for their private ends; and even for many extremists of the Left who looked for a transformation of the social order. And so it was that Boulangism was a movement which had cut across existing party groupings and divided them all according to temperament, the liberal sheep who opposed him from the authoritarian goats who flocked to his support. As such it was the last great upsurge of a Bonapartist spirit in France – a Bonapartism, but without a Bonaparte.

Though Boulangism was a fiasco, it had stirred the country to such depths that it left enduring marks upon French politics. It gave birth to a new anti-parliamentary nationalism which was to be both a continuing force and the monopoly of the Right. Hitherto during most of our period the noisy patriots, the militarists eager for crusades to carry arms through Europe, have generally been the Bonapartists or Jacobin Republicans, parties of the Left under Bourbon and Orleanist government or under Republics of Moral Order: but from the crucible of Boulangism the Right, Monarchists or Right-wing Republicans like Déroulède, emerge as the standard bearers of *revanchard* patriotism, and in consequence, by reaction, the pacifist anti-militarist tendencies of part of the Left, already perceptible during the Second Empire are much reinforced. So, too, Boulangism marks the beginning of a revolution in Paris. In the new era of rapid communications Paris is no longer the supreme political force overthrowing Governments and imposing new ones upon the laggard obedient provinces; although still true to itself in tending to be in opposition, its opposition begins to swing to the Right. Paris was the last city to elect a Boulangist deputy, and after the Dreyfus Affair the city which had given birth to the Commune became a stronghold of Nationalism and Conservatism. In other ways, too, Boulangism was of great importance. By menacing the very existence of the Republic it strengthened the conservative instincts of the Republicans, and so the Radicals, who had before been clamorous for constitutional revision and for the abolition of the Senate as a reactionary brake upon progressive legislation, soon abandoned revision; for all Republicans defence of the Republic came to mean defence of the Constitution of 1875, which the political scientist might therefore soon be inclined to classify as a distinctly 'rigid' form of government. But while

Boulangism was thus a force which made for the conservation of existing institutions it gave a leftward impetus to political parties. The Royalists had compromised themselves seriously by participating in a movement which had raised false hopes and caused them to jettison or modify some of their traditional principles. Farther than ever from the prospect of a speedy restoration, some of them were, as we shall see, soon disposed to rally to the Republic. Boulanger had, in effect, been the gravedigger of French monarchy in its traditional sense. At the same time, dissatisfied with the Opportunists, many of the *petits bourgeois* were to transfer their votes to the Radicals, while the allegiance of the workers passed more and more to the growing group of Parliamentary Socialists.

Immediately, the reassertion of Republican authority and the débâcle of Boulangism led to a striking revival in the popularity and prestige of the Republic. The centenary of the Great Revolution of 1789 was celebrated with éclat in a variety of ways, notable among them being a banquet to all the mayors of France:[11] At the same time a great exhibition which attracted 25,000,000 visitors, vividly displayed the wealth of France and endowed the capital with a new and wonderful landmark in the Eiffel Tower. The new President of the Republic took part in many of the ceremonies of commemoration throughout the country and made an excellent impression by his dignified bearing. The passage at last of the bill reducing the term of military service to three years and suppressing most of the exceptions hitherto permitted was a highly popular measure which may well have contributed to the Republican success in the elections of September. A new stability seemed to have been achieved when the Tirard Ministry of 1889 lasted for a whole year and the Freycinet Ministry which succeeded it for very nearly two. Nor was this all; with the experiment of what French historians know as the 'Ralliement' the Republic, more confident in its new strength, showed a more conciliatory disposition, and numbers of Conservatives and Catholics were led to abandon their hostility to the regime; and these signs of renewed vigour helped French diplomacy to lead France from isolation to the conclusion of an alliance with one of the greatest of European states. The Ralliement and the Franco-Russian Alliance were, as we shall see, two of the most remarkable attempts to consolidate the success of 1889.

The shock of Boulangism had brought home to many Republicans, and in particular to the Opportunists, the fact that the Republic was set on too narrow a basis for security. Although the Monarchists had lost a number of seats in the 1889 elections, the poll showed that a third of the French people were still hostile to the regime. For some time, indeed, various Opportunist leaders had shown a desire for appeasement in the struggle of Church and State; and even Ferry, the architect of the education laws, had more than once urged the need to open the doors of the Republic to all men of goodwill. Now, after the strain of the Boulanger crisis, both sides were tired of war and the conciliatory attitude of the moderate Republicans was met with equal goodwill on the part of the octogenarian Pope who, since his election in 1878, had shown himself one of the wisest Pontiffs and ablest diplomats of the century. Leo XIII had always resolutely refused to condemn the Republic as a form of government. It was with his approval that in 1890 one of the greatest of the French bishops of the time, Cardinal Lavigerie, the Primate of Africa, spoke in a formal toast to surprised naval officers of the need for unqualified adherence to that form of government which was willed by the nation; and in subsequent pronouncements in 1891 and 1892 the Pope himself explicitly ordered the Catholics of France to recognize the Republic: the constituted authority should be accepted as representing the authority derived from God.[12] This behest was so unpalatable to most of the hierarchy and many of the faithful that they were slow to obey, some arguing like Mgr Freppel, the Bishop of Angers, that the Republic was no mere form of government but a whole system of irreligion, others questioning the Papal right to pronounce on a matter of secular allegiance. Thus, although in 1892 some men of note such as the great Catholic orator, the Comte de Mun and the leader of the Right in Parliament, the Baron de Mackau, rallied to the Republic, there were still many who remained intransigent in their hostility and unswerving in their loyalty to the Pretender.

The task of those who were eager for the success of appeasement was not made easier by the incurable suspicion of the Radicals, who saw in the Pope's injunctions no more than a wily attempt to manoeuvre the Trojan horse of clericalism into the Republican fortress. For men like Clemenceau and Léon Bourgeois the Great Revolution of 1789 represented a bloc of doctrines and achievements which must be accepted in its entirety by the convert. In Clemenceau's words it was still an active force because the same men (the men of the Revolution) constantly found themselves face to face with the same enemies.[13] In so far as the Opportunists in the Chamber of 1889–93 had no clear majority and were dependent on Radical support it was, therefore, difficult for them to go very far in the way of conciliation. After 1893, however, the Opportunists, or Progressists as they now came to be called, had a clear majority and the Ralliement could make new headway when what Spuller, a moderate Minister of Public Worship, termed 'a new spirit' was in the air. This spirit was shown not by the repeal of anti-clerical legislation – no Government dared go so far as that – but by a new tolerance, if not laxity, in its application. But for the Dreyfus Affair, which was once again to throw France into turmoil, it is possible that the moderate Progressists, reinforced by a growing number of Ralliés, might have continued to govern France for many years and that a certain Catholic influence might once again have made itself felt in the councils of government. As things turned out, however, these years of Ralliement were to be no more than an interlude between periods of bitter strife. The experiment of 'appeasement' was incomplete and won only limited success. Yet, even so, it was not unimportant: it weakened the Monarchists still further and, although the Ralliés were too few and divided among themselves to enable the formation of a strong Catholic Centre party, their adhesion to the Republic strengthened the Conservative element among the Republican moderates and accentuated the cleavage between the Progressists and the Radicals. It was the first real attempt of the Republic to work for the achievement of a united France.

If the attempt to reconcile Frenchmen with Frenchmen was a failure, the attempt to ally France with Russia was a notable success. Although, as we have seen, France had re-entered the European comity of nations in 1878, she was still isolated in 1889. Europe was still dominated by the Germany of Bismarck, and Bismarck had bound all the other Great Powers save Great Britain to his own system. Austria, Hungary and Italy were harnessed by the Triple Alliance while a Reinsurance Treaty, which ensured Russian neutrality in case of a French attack upon Germany, kept Russia in check. Great Britain remained aloof, but their colonial rivalries gave Bismarck little fear that she and France would ever become close friends. None the less, many Frenchmen, from Thiers and Decazes to Déroulède and Boulanger, had believed that one day France must find a natural ally in Russia and few opportunities were missed to court the Tsarist state. Yet, if the rulers of Russia were far from friendly to Austria and chafed under the German hegemony, they had little respect for France, which Giers, the Russian Foreign Minister, had described as a 'mass of rottenness'.[14] Moreover, the old suspicions of French Republican and 'atheist' governments died hard and, as late as 1890, the Tsar told the German Chancellor that he would never ally with a Republic.[15] In that very same year, however, events occurred which were soon to lead him to do this very thing. That spring the new German Emperor, William II, 'dropped the pilot'. Bismarck was Chancellor of Germany and arbiter of Europe no longer, and the German ship of state seemed likely in less experienced hands to steer a disquietingly erratic course.

The change in policy was strikingly marked by Germany's omission three months later to renew the Reinsurance Treaty with Russia. Meanwhile, France's new stability, the Pope's readiness to recognize her form of government, the revival of her military power together with her willingness to restrain Russian Nihilist activities in France and to provide facilities for the manufacture of new weapons and loans to finance the growing industrial development of the Tsarist Empire – all these were facts which made a favourable impression upon the Russian Government. When in 1891 the Kaiser renewed the Triple Alliance and began a demonstrative courtship of England, Russia, afraid of being left in isolation, rapidly drew closer to France. In July a French naval squadron visited Kronstadt and a sensation was caused when the Tsar himself visited the French Admiral's flagship and listened bareheaded to the Marseillaise. In the following month an agreement for mutual consultation was concluded; a document very vague in its terms, but none the less sufficiently important for Freycinet and other French statesmen to declare publicly that a new situation had arisen and that France who had been 'isolated and almost forgotten' was now, 'thanks to the reorganization of her army and the wisdom of her diplomacy',[16] once more an important factor in the European balance of power. French opinion was now for the most part Russophil and public and Government alike were eager for a definite alliance. In fact the French authorities had immediately after the conclusion of the entente proposed to the Russians that it should be followed up and made more effective by a military convention. But the Tsar and Giers were in no hurry to bind themselves too closely – the Panama scandal and other incidents in France reinforced their hesitancy – and it was not until 4 January 1894, that an exchange of secret notes accepting the military agreement made the Franco-Russian alliance a reality. The form of the effective instrument of the alliance, the military convention, had a great advantage from the Russian point of view: there was no need for it to be debated by the French Parliament before it could come into effect. In the meantime, in October 1893, a Russian naval squadron had paid a return visit to Toulon, and the Admiral in command and the men who accompanied him on a tour of various French cities received a delirious welcome. A few years later the alliance received its formal consecration in an exchange of visits between the heads of state. The Tsar and Tsarina came to Paris in 1896 and President Félix Faure was received in St Petersburg in 1897.

The visit of the Russian naval squadron to France in 1893 was reported by *The Times* to have given rise to 'the most remarkable outbreak of international feeling ever witnessed'.[17] The enthusiasm for the alliance on the French side was much more noticeable than that of the Russians and yet, although during the next twenty years the Russians were the main gainers economically, since some £400 million of French capital was subscribed to Russian loans by French investors, and also diplomatically, since the security given them by the Alliance enabled them to act with much greater freedom in Asia – the intensity of French feeling is easily intelligible. Quite apart from the hopes of the Nationalists and patriots, of Madame Adam and her *Nouvelle Revue*, of Déroulède and his 'Ligue des Patriotes' and of all the exiled Alsatians and Lorrainers, that the day of *revanche* would now be brought immeasurably nearer, it was clear to all that the Russian connexion had greatly enhanced the prestige both of France and of the Republic even though France might appear to be no more than the junior partner, the 'brilliant second' of the alliance. But possibly still more important was the general feeling of relief that France was no longer alone in a hostile world. Now at long last the French people felt a sense of security such as they had not experienced for more than a quarter of a century.[18]

Unfortunately, however, the prestige of France's reorganized army and of her diplomatic service was not equalled by that of her Parliament. The Boulangists had not succeeded in eliminating corruption in high places, but the disclosures resulting from the failure of the Panama Canal Company in 1889 were to give the handful of Boulangist deputies in the Chamber of 1889–93 a superb opportunity of exposing a scandal and thereby covering the regime with fresh obloquy.

The construction of a Panama Canal by a company directed by Ferdinand de Lesseps of Suez Canal fame, with the help of Eiffel and other eminent French engineers of the day, should have been a great national enterprise, a triumph of French engineering skill, a source of wealth, and a means of strengthening French influence in Central and South America. Unfortunately the difficulties and expense of the undertaking, which was begun in 1881, proved to be far greater than Lesseps' estimate. The Company was constantly obliged to raise further loans and on each occasion the charges made by banks and publicity agents were more onerous: of the 1040 million francs raised only 640 million were eventually spent on construction work. In spite of the importance of the enterprise for French prestige the authorities refused to give it any official support, and it was not until December 1888 that the Chamber authorized an issue of lottery bonds. When they, too, were lamentably undersubscribed, the Company, unsupported by the State, had no alternative but to go into liquidation. The shareholders appealed to Parliament to safeguard their interests and eventually Lesseps, together with his son and certain other officials of the Company, were condemned for obtaining money by false promises and for malversation of the funds. Very few dispassionate inquirers could now agree that these charges had been substantiated, and in fact they were shortly afterwards quashed on technical grounds.

It was not the trial of 'the great Frenchman', as Lesseps was generally known, and of some of the most noted engineers of the day which stirred the political world to its depths, but another case which arose incidentally out of the Panama investigations. In September 1892 a rabidly anti-semitic paper, the *Libre Parole*, accused the Company of having distributed *pots de vin* to parliamentarians through a Jewish financier named Baron Jacques de Reinach. When the Chamber reassembled after the autumn recess there were immediate interpellations, and on 18 November it was agreed that a debate on the Panama question should be held on 21 November. On the 19th Reinach was found dead and Cornelius Herz, another financier of Jewish origin, who had been blackmailing him, promptly fled to England. On the 21st the Government, after a tense sitting in which a Boulangist Deputy had alleged instance after instance of corruption, giving the facts but refusing to disclose the names of the colleagues implicated, were obliged to agree to the appointment of a Commission of Inquiry. In the subsequent revelations it became clear that large sums of money had been distributed through Reinach, Herz and other agents for the Company to various members of Parliament in return for promises to vote for the authorization of its lottery bonds. Proceedings were instituted against five deputies – including three Ministers or former Ministers – and five Senators – including two former Ministers, a former Prefect of Police and a former Governor-General of Algeria – but in most of these cases they were dropped and in the end only one man, a former Minister of Public Works, who confessed to having accepted 375,000 francs, was condemned. But though Commissions of Inquiry and law courts were lenient, charges had been made and mud had been thrown which stuck. The career of Floquet, the President of the Chamber and a former Prime Minister, was virtually ended by the Affair, that of Rouvier checked for ten years, while a number of lesser men bore the stigma of having been *chéquards*, the receivers of tainted money. Most notable of all was the eclipse of the destroyer of Cabinets, the man whose tongue, sword and pistol (he was a skilled duellist) were feared by all, the Radical leader Clemenceau, who had been much too closely associated with the dubious Herz and was now on the basis of trumpery and forged documents denounced by his numerous enemies as a tool of the British Foreign Office. In the general elections of 1893 Clemenceau's meetings were punctuated by cries of 'A – Oh yes!' and he was not returned to the Chamber in which he had sat continuously since 1876.

Although previous regimes had had their notable scandals, the Restoration its Ouvrard, the July Monarchy its Teste and Cubières, none made such a lasting impression or did so much to poison the air as Panama. The country as a whole was apathetic enough, and the discredited Opportunists were returned in even stronger force in the 1893 elections; but in the political world the Affair created an atmosphere which, in the words of Lord Bryce, 'lasted for years, like the smoke that continues to hang over the spot where a high-explosive shell has struck the ground. A scandal so tremendous seemed to confirm the vague suspicions that had existed before; and it tended to render probable charges subsequently made . . .'[19] Immediately, it had a number of political consequences: it deprived parties of some of their old leaders and brought new and younger men to the fore; on the Progressist side, for example, along with Dupuy, some of the Presidents and Foreign Ministers of the twentieth century such as Deschanel, Poincaré and Barthou now made their first appearance – Poincaré and Barthou so young that they were known as the 'two boys' – and in the Radical camp a Léon Bourgeois succeeded Clemenceau; it gave a new impulse to anti-semitism which had been growing ever since Édouard Drumont, the editor of *La Libre Parole*, published his vitriolic *La France Juive* in 1886; it also encouraged the growth of a new Nationalism, which in some ways foreshadowed the ideas of German National Socialism, by its defence of the essentially French mode of life, its cult of French soil and its French dead, and its rejection of alien influences, whether Jewish or Gentile; it probably hindered the Ralliement even as it delayed the consummation of the Franco-Russian alliance; and it certainly reinforced the pessimism about the future of France and her institutions which marks the observations of so many contemporary writers. France in the momentous decade of the 1890s was, as General de Gaulle once wrote, like the Infanta weeping in the Palace Gardens, overcome with melancholy, while enjoying the good things of life.[20]

Panama also, perhaps, gave a further impetus to the growth of Parliamentary Socialism and encouraged various social theorists to put their ideas into practice. During the next few months and years the rise of the Socialists and their alliance with the Radicals in Parliament, the bombs of Anarchists, the growth of Trade Unions and of federations of unions of workers in the same localities known as Bourses du Travail, the new May Day demonstrations and numerous strikes, together with much talk of a general strike, combined to force the social question upon the attention of the public and upon Parliament. In the 1893 elections Radicals and Socialists joined forces and the results led to an increase in the Socialist representation from twelve to forty-nine, among them a great orator, Jaurès, an able lawyer, journalist and organizer, Millerand, and the apostle of Marxism, Jules Guesde. The continued co-operation of the Radicals with these Socialists further emphasized the cleavage between the two main Republican parties, Progressists and Radicals. At the same time the Anarchist outrages which began in 1892 and culminated in the assassination of President Carnot in June 1894, the violent Socialist attacks against his successor, Casimir-Périer, the wealthy grandson of Louis Philippe's Minister, and the formulation by Millerand in 1896 of a minimum Socialist programme for the peaceful conquest of power, all tended to force the Progressists and moderates back upon a programme of Republican defence which also implied the defence of the existing social order.

Thus the political situation in the middle 1890s was frequently disturbed and confused. Conservative hopes that Casimir-Périer would prove to be the strong man who would restore the authority of the Executive were disappointed by his resignation in January 1895 after only six months of office. A further shock followed with the formation of the first predominantly Radical Cabinet of the Third Republic and the Chamber's approval of the principle of a progressive income tax. But the Senate came to the rescue of property and after it had forced the Government to resign by its subsequent refusal to vote certain military credits the conservative Republican forces rallied round a new Cabinet headed by Jules Méline, the champion of the agricultural interests. In so doing they followed a natural if unconscious reaction – taking as their leader for a policy described as being 'neither revolution nor reaction' the man who had done most to benefit the naturally conservative rural majority of the French people. Under him, as Bainville put it, 'agriculture governed France. And all that could be done by means of corn and hay he did'.[21] 1896 and 1897 were thus years of relative prosperity and stability which might well have continued much longer, but for the growing tempest of the Dreyfus Affair. The social problem in these years had come more to the fore and the opposition of conservative bourgeoisie and rural interests to the left-wing workers had been sharper, but this opposition had if anything delayed the passage of social legislation and the Dreyfus Affair, like Boulangism and Panama, once again relegated social questions to the background.

In 1894 the intelligence services of the French War Office discovered that there had been a leakage of military information to the German Embassy. After some investigations a young Jewish staff officer named Alfred Dreyfus was arrested. The news of the arrest leaked out and there was at once an outcry in the anti-semitic press which demanded his head and attacked the Minister of War, General Mercier, because of reports that the General was not yet satisfied of Dreyfus' guilt and might be prepared to release him. In December Dreyfus was tried by secret court martial and condemned to deportation for life. In the following month, January 1895, he was publicly degraded and then dispatched to Devil's Island off the coast of French Guyana, where he was kept in solitary confinement. In view of the attitude of the Press, of the statements of General Mercier who had told the *Figaro* that he had crying proofs of Dreyfus' treason, and of the verdict, almost all Frenchmen were convinced of the Jewish officer's guilt and accepted the sentence without question. There, so far as the general public was concerned, the matter remained until the end of 1897. But the weakness of General Mercier in wishing to dispose of the matter and avoid trouble with the Press by securing a speedy conviction had laid a train which was to lead to an explosion far more tremendous than the original one which he or his colleagues had feared to face. Dreyfus' family were convinced of his innocence and at once went to work to find evidence which would clear him. At the same time, quite independently, an intelligence officer, Colonel Picquart, had come across conclusive evidence that a document in writing identical to that of the famous *bordereau*, or memorandum, which was one of the main papers on which Dreyfus' conviction had been based, had been written by a needy infantry officer of foreign extraction and dubious morals named Esterhazy. Picquart at once examined the Dreyfus case files and, surprised at the slenderness of the evidence against Dreyfus, came to the conclusion that Dreyfus had been wrongly condemned, that Esterhazy was the real culprit, and that there ought to be a revision of the Dreyfus case. But his superior officers were afraid of the discredit which might follow upon an admission that military justice had erred. They prevaricated, then told Picquart that further formal proof of Dreyfus' guilt had been obtained and, when he was still not satisfied, sent him away on a mission and subsequently posted him to North Africa. The new document, later known as '*le faux Henry*', was in fact a forgery, newly inserted in the Dreyfus dossier by Picquart's successor as head of the Intelligence Bureau, Colonel Henry.

Picquart, however, was able to communicate his suspicions to his lawyer, who in turn told the story to the Vice-President of the Senate, Scheurer-Kestner. Scheurer-Kestner, convinced of its substance, at once made representations to General Billot, Mercier's successor at the Ministry of War and to Méline, the Prime Minister. But General Billot had already stated in answer to an interpellation in the Chamber a year earlier that Dreyfus had been justly and legally condemned and he now stuck to his guns, while Méline, like most politicians anxious above all to avoid another scandal, stood by the Minister of War. By now, however, there was in being a small 'Dreyfusard' party determined to work for a revision of the trial – Dreyfus' brother and his friends joined forces with Scheurer-Kestner, and brought a formal charge against Esterhazy, public opinion began to be interested and while the majority of the Press was opposed to Dreyfus, the novelist, Zola, took up his cause and Clemenceau re-entered politics with a remarkable series of articles in a paper called *L'Aurore*, demanding that, whatever the circumstances, the truth should be told. In the Chamber, however, Méline declared that there was no such thing as a Dreyfus Affair – the case of Esterhazy was the only one to be considered – and Billot reaffirmed his belief in Dreyfus' guilt and appealed to the

Chamber to stop the campaign which was being pursued 'against the national honour and the honour of the army'. In January Esterhazy in turn was tried by secret court martial, acquitted and hailed as a hero by enthusiastic crowds. This, the Government and the War Office hoped, would be the end of the matter. But they were greatly mistaken. Two days later Zola published his famous open letter to the President of the Republic in which he accused a number of Generals and high officers of deliberately procuring the condemnation of Dreyfus on the basis of a second document not communicated to the defence and declared that the court martial of 1898 had acted on superior instructions in acquitting Esterhazy.

'*J'accuse*', as Zola's letter was called, was described by Anatole France as 'a revolutionary act of incomparable power'. It was a challenge which no Government could ignore. It roused passions to fever heat and forced all who were concerned for the character of the Republic to take sides. The guilt or innocence of Dreyfus became an article of belief about which even families were bitterly divided, for the issue had now been raised far beyond the personality of the individual Dreyfus and his sufferings. For most Frenchmen Dreyfus became no more than a symbol, either of the eternal Jewish traitor, or of the denial of Justice. On the one hand the Nationalists, the patriots, the anti-semites, the Catholics and all those who put social order before everything, believed that the whole affair was a deliberate plot to throw France into disorder and discredit the army, a plot hatched, said the anti-semites by an international Jewish syndicate. On the other the Dreyfusards held that injustice had been tolerated for alleged reasons of State and that if Reason of State were allowed to dominate in French affairs the citizen had no security against any form of arbitrariness; the Republic was no better than the Ancien Régime.

For the time being, however, the great bulk of public opinion, Republican as well as Conservative, was still against Dreyfus. Zola was twice tried and condemned for slander – the second time in default – and the verdict was hailed with delight by crowds which shouted for 'Death to Zola' and 'Death to the Jews'. In the summer of 1898, however, new and sensational developments occurred; a new Radical Minister of War, Cavaignac, abandoned the attitude of his predecessors and attempted to establish Dreyfus' guilt by public disclosure of some of the evidence in the Chamber. This, as Clemenceau wrote, at once made revision of the Dreyfus trial inevitable. 'That was inescapable from the day when the Government undertook to supply proof instead of being content with mere affirmations.'[22] And so in fact it turned out. The Dreyfusards were no longer up against a stone wall: they now at last had the chance of dissecting the evidence; and Picquart wrote to the Prime Minister,

Méline's successor Brisson, offering to prove that one of the documents mentioned by Cavaignac did not refer to Dreyfus, that another had been falsified and that a third, the *'faux Henry'*, was a forgery. Shortly afterwards a War Office intelligence officer confirmed the forgery of the third. Colonel Henry was questioned by Cavaignac, confessed and, on being confined to the fortress prison of Mont Valérien, committed suicide. The anti-Dreyfusards were thunderstruck by this news so damaging to their case, and Esterhazy, the real villain of the piece, scenting a change in the wind, slipped away to England, where he lived quietly under the name of Comte de Voilemont until his death in 1923.

Although the *'faux Henry'* was not one of the documents on which Dreyfus' conviction had been based, so much play had been made with it that discovery that it was a forgery convinced Brisson and many deputies that a retrial was necessary. Not so the Minister of War; Cavaignac resigned rather than hear of a revision of the case and the two Generals who succeeded him speedily followed suit. Meanwhile a formal request from Madame Dreyfus for revision had been handed to the Cour de Cassation and eventually a civilian Minister of War in the new Dupuy Government of Republican concentration, formed in November 1898, agreed to hand over the secret dossier to the Court. Revision was thus inevitable, but much might depend on who conducted the trial. Legally the case should have been dealt with by the section of the Court of Cassation, known as the Criminal Chamber, but this contained a number of Protestants and free-thinkers and so in February 1899 the anti-Dreyfusards managed to secure the passage of a special law transferring it to the whole court. A few days later still further excitement was caused by the sudden death of the President of the Republic, Félix Faure, in the course of an intimate meeting with a lady who was not his wife. As the President was Conservatively minded and had very little sympathy with the Dreyfusards the anti-Dreyfusards at once declared that the Dreyfusards were responsible for his death. Although there was no evidence of this, the influential Royalist writer, Charles Maurras, went on repeating it up to 1930. The death of the President, however, influenced feeling still more and the ensuing presidential election in which Émile Loubet defeated Jules Méline was tantamount to a Dreyfusard victory in that it was a defeat of the more Conservative candidate, of Méline, who as Prime Minister had done his best to prevent the Dreyfus Affair from being reopened. A few days later Faure's funeral gave the Nationalist Déroulède, an ardent anti-Dreyfusard, the chance to attempt a *coup d'état*. But the coup of Reuilly, in which the novelist Maurice Barrès was one of his accomplices, was a lamentable failure, ill-prepared and without even a Boulanger to capture the imagination of troops and crowds. Its only significance was to show that there were still groups of men faithful to the Boulangist tradition and that the general effervescence and state of feeling was such that they judged the time ripe for a coup; while Déroulède's acquittal in May was one more instance of the frequent partiality of French justice during these impassioned months.

In June the long-drawn-out affair began to move to its climax. The Court of Cassation, in spite of the anti-Dreyfusard February law and of the violence of the anti-Dreyfusard party, showed its independence, quashed the trial of 1894 and ordered a rehearing. The anti-Dreyfusards were furious and a Baron Christiani insulted the new President of the Republic by striking him on the hat with a cane at the Auteuil races, an absurd and pitiable incident, but one which had immediate consequences in Parliament. The Dupuy Ministry, accused of not having given the President sufficient protection, was defeated and resigned. After a prolonged Ministerial crisis one of the ablest barristers of the day, Waldeck-Rousseau, who had made his début in Gambetta's 'Grand Ministère', formed a Cabinet which was to mark a turning-point in French politics and to stay in office for the record length of nearly three years.

The immediate determination of the new Government was to restore public order which had been sadly disturbed by anti-Jewish riots and demonstrations of Dreyfusards and anti-Dreyfusards, and to dispose of the Dreyfus Affair as soon as possible. The Nationalist agitation, Déroulède's coup and rumour of further plots against the regime gave it the opportunity to pose, like the Tirard-Constans Cabinet of 1889, as a Cabinet of Republican defence. Accordingly, before the second Dreyfus trial opened, some sixty-seven people were arrested for plotting against the regime and three of them, including Déroulède, were in January 1900 condemned by the High Court and banished or imprisoned for ten years. On 7 August 1899, the retrial of Dreyfus, which aroused extraordinary interest throughout the world, began at Rennes and in September the new court martial gave their verdict. While two out of seven of the judges had voted for Dreyfus's acquittal, the majority found him guilty of 'intelligence with the enemy with attentuating circumstances' and sentenced him to ten years' detention. Except among the anti-Dreyfusards there was a wave of furious indignation at such a verdict when so many had expected acquittal. Shortly afterwards, however, the President of the Republic pardoned Dreyfus and at the end of the year the Government secured an amnesty for all concerned, their main object being that the whole Affair should be forgotten as speedily as possible. But the eager Dreyfusards were far from satisfied with such a result and in consequence of further strenuous efforts on their part there was a second revision of the case by the Court of Cassation in 1906. This time the Rennes verdict was also quashed, but the Court did not order a retrial. Instead the Chamber passed a special resolution for Dreyfus' rehabilitation; he was decorated with the Legion of Honour and he and Picquart were both promoted in rank.

This Affair, of the many Affairs in French history the one which is known simply as 'The Affair' without qualification, dragged on for twelve years from the original trial to the final rehabilitation, and during at least three appeared almost entirely to dominate the French political scene. Yet, though the educated classes not only in France but throughout a large part of the world were passionately roused by it, the great mass of the French people were unmoved and little interested in a question which soon became so complicated as to be far beyond their understanding. They tended to dismiss it as a soldiers' and politicians' quarrel which was no concern of theirs, and it is noteworthy that in the general elections of 1898 it was a very minor issue. None the less it was profoundly important for the development of French politics and its effect upon the orientation of the Third Republic.

The fragmentary and conflicting character of the evidence disclosed to the public was equally perplexing for the educated classes; hence the great majority of those who took sides did so in the last resort according to their ordinary political prejudices. Thus the Nationalist Barrès could write that his mind was made up even before he knew the judicial facts: 'I adhered to the opinion of the men whom society had pointed out as competent,'[23] and for him, as for so many others, at any rate at first, the competent judges were the army officers. But it was when serious doubts came to be cast upon the competence of the army that political passions came into play. While the foremost men of letters, artists, and 'intellectuals' went into battle on one side or the other – the 'Ligue pour la défense des Droits de L'Homme et du Citoyen' being countered by the 'Ligue de la Patrie Française' – each distilling the issue into a war of abstract principles (*Fiat justitia ruat coelum* against the idea that it were better that an innocent man should die 'and that the whole nation perish not') – all the forces of the Right tended to rally together against a new offensive of a Republican spirit which they disliked; while eventually the Radicals and Left, once again shocked by the strength of Conservatism (and the violence of the clerical, Nationalist, and anti-semitic elements in it) determined to break it once and for all.

At the same time the Affair soon provoked, as Clemenceau foresaw, an admirable opportunity for party intrigue, and this increased its complexity. 'It was utilized,' wrote Bodley, 'by the Reactionaries against the Republic, by the Clericals against the non-Catholics, by the anti-Clericals against the Church, by the military party against the Parliamentarians and by the revolutionary Socialists against the Army. It was even conspicuously used by rival Republicans against one another.'[24] Like the Boulangist movement it cut across parties.

The triumph of the Dreyfusards meant that the Republic was to swing back to the militant anti-Clericalism of the first decade. It signalized the decline and, as we shall see, the division of the Progressists and an advance of the Radicals to a position of ascendancy. Once again the enemy was on the Right and there must be no foe to the Left. Above all, the Conservative forces were routed and there was an end of the moderate conciliatory Republic of the 1890s under which the Ralliement had been such a notable experiment. All the latent bitterness and old hatreds revive and the Dreyfus Affair is the prelude to the most formidable of the secular Republic's offensives against its old enemies with whom we have so often already seen it at grips.

Notes

1 Brogan, D. W., *The Development of Modern France*, p. 166.
2 Bodley, J. E. C., *France*, p. 287. How many conscientious Ministers of the Third Republic might have echoed the words of the Duc de Richelieu: 'One is obliged to exert all one's strength and all one's faculties to maintain one's position, and there is neither the time nor the means to accomplish anything useful. . . . You would be very much mistaken if you supposed that during the five months since we have been Ministers we have spent any time on administering, there has been no time for it physically. Each one is so occupied by his petty Ministerial interests, by the Chambers and by the speeches he has to make that he has no time to concern himself with the State.' Cit. Fouques Duparc, J., *Le Troisième Richelieu*, p. 96.
3 Cambon, P., *Correspondance, 1870–1924*, vol. 1, p. 131.
4 Daniel Halévy.
5 Cit. Baumont, M., *L'essor industriel et l'impérialisme colonial (1878–1904)*, p. 155.
6 This law was not abrogated until 1950.
7 This became law in 1889.
8 Newton, Lord, *Lord Lyons*, p. 519.
9 Cambon, op. cit., p. 318.
10 Baumont, op. cit., p. 155.
11 A remarkable meal, at which 15,000 people sat down to table, 80,000 plates were used and 45,000 bottles of wine uncorked.
12 For the text of the Pope's pronouncement in 1892, see Cahm, E., *Politics and Society in Contemporary France (1789–1971)*, pp. 630–2.
13 Cit. Halévy, D., *Histoire d'une histoire . . .* p. 55.
14 Cit. Baumont, op. cit., p. 142.
15 Langer, W. L., *The Franco-Russian Alliance, 1890–4*, p. 105n.
16 Freycinet, C. de, *Souvenirs*, vol. 2, 1878–93, p. 475.

17 Cit. Langer, W. L., *The Franco-Russian Alliance, 1890–4*, p. 356.
18 Siegfried, A., *Tableau des partis en France*, p. 106.
19 Cit. Jackson, J. Hampden, *Clemenceau and the Third Republic*, p. 79.
20 de Gaulle, C., *France and her Army*, p. 82.
21 Bainville, J., *La Troisième République 1870–1939*, p. 198.
22 *L'iniquité*, p. 460 (8 July).
23 Barrès, M., *Scènes et doctrines du nationalisme*, vol. 1, p. 218.
24 Cit. Leslie, Shane, *Memoir of John Edward Courtenay Bodley*, p. 269.

Bibliography

Barrès, Maurice, *L'appel au soldat*, Paris, 1926.

Barrès, Maurice, *Leurs figures*, Paris, 1943.

Baumont, Maurice, *L'essor industriel et l'impérialisme colonial (1878–1904)*, Paris, 1937, 3rd edn, 1965.

Byrnes, Robert F., *Antisemitism in Modern France*, vol. 1. *The Prologue to the Dreyfus Affair*, New Brunswick, 1950.

Carroll, E. M., *French Public Opinion and Foreign Affairs, 1870–1914*, New York, 1931.

Chastenet, J., *La République triomphante 1893–1906*, Paris, 1955.

Clemenceau, Georges, *L'iniquité*, Paris, 1899.

Dansette, Adrien, *Les affaires de Panama*, 3rd edn, Paris, 1934.

Derfler, L., *The Dreyfus Affair: Tragedy of Errors?* Boston, 1963.

Jaurès, Jean, *Les preuves*, Paris, n.d.

Johnson, D., *France and the Dreyfus Affair*, London, 1966.

McManners, J., *Church and State in France 1870–1914*, London, 1972.

Maitron, Jean, *Histoire du Mouvement Anarchiste en France (1880–1914)*, Paris, 1951.

Mayeur, J. M., *Les débuts de la Troisième République 1871–1898*, Paris, 1973.

Rebérioux, M., *La République radicale? 1898–1914*, Paris, 1975.

Seager, Frederic H., *The Boulanger Affair*, Ithaca, 1969.

Sedgwick, A., *The Ralliement in French Politics 1890–1898*, Harvard, 1965.

Sternhell, Z., *La droite révolutionnaire 1885–1914: les origines françaises du fascisme*, Paris, 1978.

Vizetelly, E. A., *Republican France, 1870–1912*, London, 1912.

Watson, D. R., *Georges Clemenceau: A Political Biography*, London, 1974.

Wilson, S., *Ideology and experience. Antisemitism in France at the time of the Dreyfus Affair*, London and Toronto, 1982.

Zola, Émile, *La vérité en marche*, Paris, 1901.

12

The Republic of the Radicals

The Waldeck-Rousseau Ministry of 1899–1902 was one of the most remarkable of the Third Republic as well on account of its composition, its duration, its achievements and the direction it gave to French politics as because of the personality of its head. In addition to a number of distinguished young Radicals, such as Delcassé at the Foreign Office and the 36-year-old Joseph Caillaux at the Ministry of Finance, it included General the Marquis de Galliffet as Minister of War and Millerand, the first Socialist to enter any European Cabinet, as Minister of Commerce. These last two appointments raised an outcry, yet both showed the boldness and wisdom of the new Prime Minister. In Galliffet, an old beau of the Second Empire, a gallant soldier and an aristocrat of independent views, who had been a friend both of Gambetta and the Prince of Wales, Waldeck-Rousseau had chosen a man whom he could expect to have the necessary prestige and courage to carry out reforms in an army still largely officered by aristocrats; in selecting Millerand he had recognized the importance of the parliamentary Socialists, invited them to become a respectable government party and shown his intention of tackling problems of social reform. Millerand's acceptance of office had, however, been made without the formal approval of his party and his *cas* was hotly disputed by his Socialist colleagues several of whom wished to exclude him for the crime of entering a 'bourgeois' Cabinet. Until 1904 he was allowed to retain his party membership, but the dispute helped to retard the union of French Socialists in a single political party which Jaurès had long been working for. This was not to be achieved until 1905, when the Guesdists and Moderates, or Reformists, at length fused in what was to be known as the Section Française de l'Internationale Ouvrière (SFIO). In other words, the French Socialist party in 1905 became a single branch of the Second International which was at this time largely dominated by German Marxists, and in doing so the moderates had to yield to the intransigence of the doctrinaires, to forgo co-operation with other parties, to submit to a discipline alien to them,[1] to refuse to take part in 'bourgeois' governments and to vote against all credits for military expenditure or colonial domination. The international character of French Socialism becomes much more marked, and with it its emphasis on the solidarity between Socialists and workers in all countries and its pacifism and opposition to what it denounces as Imperialism and Militarism. In the years after 1905 when France is adding the last territory to her colonial Empire and when the danger of war in Europe more than once seems imminent this trend of French Socialism is, as we shall see, of great importance.

The inclusion of Galliffet in the Cabinet angered the Left, the inclusion of Millerand irritated the Right as well as some of his own brethren; and when the new Government first met the Chamber its majority was so small that it looked as though its life would be a matter of weeks, if not days. In fact, however, it lasted nearly three years. This triumph of duration was largely due to the forceful personality and the tactical skill of the Prime Minister. An ardent disciple of Gambetta, who had first given him office, Waldeck-Rousseau was as silent, cold and reserved as his master had been eloquent, warm-hearted and expansive – 'imprisoned in his silence as a pike is imprisoned in aspic' was Barrès' description.[2] A Progressist, in the tradition of Gambetta, he none the less, through the circumstances in which he formed his Cabinet and by his subsequent policy, split his party and so put an end to the long period of Opportunist-Progressist ascendancy which had been virtually uninterrupted since 1879. Although he carried with him a considerable number of Progressist followers, his Cabinet was essentially dependent on the support of the Radicals, of the new Group of Radical-Socialists, often so difficult to distinguish from the Radicals except in name, and of the Socialists. Thus he prepared the way for the preponderance of the so-called Republican bloc of Left-wing groups in which the Radicals were long to be the dominant element and whose theory of political strategy was to be summed up in the phrase 'No enemies to the Left'. Under his government the country enjoyed a period of relative quiet after the turmoil of the Dreyfus Affair, the regime was consolidated anew and the international position of the country was strengthened.

The return to stability in 1899–1900 was in many ways reminiscent of the return to stability after the Boulangist crisis. Once again the firmness of a government of Republican defence disposed of real or imaginary plotters, put an end to disorder in the streets and restored public confidence. Once again a great banquet of the mayors of France demonstrated the loyalty of the people's representatives in local government; and once again a great exhibition in Paris, that of 1900, turned the attention of Frenchmen away from politics to the contemplation of the benefits of material prosperity.

In other respects, however, the consolidation of the Republic at home recalled 1879 rather than 1889. The Dreyfus Affair had shattered the Ralliement and all hopes of *entente* with the Right. As in the days of Moral Order and the crisis of 1877, the clergy and the army appeared to many Republicans to have shown themselves in their true light as impenitent adversaries of the ideal of a liberal democratic regime. They had exercised political pressure and they must be called to order. If Waldeck-Rousseau had shown any inclination to forget that it was Gambetta who had denounced clericalism as the enemy, his Radical supporters, as fanatically sectarian as ever, were at hand to remind him of the saying. Anti-clericalism was in fact the cement which bound the different elements of the Republican bloc together and so long, therefore, as the religious question was to the forefront, so long was the bloc likely to hold together. Accordingly the measures taken to curb the Church and to purge the army were, as in 1879 and afterwards, among the most significant of the acts of the new Government. Numerous changes were made in the high command of the army, and, most important of all, the power of promotion was transferred from the military commission, which had hitherto been responsible, to the Minister of War. This meant that under a politically minded Minister army rank might depend upon an officer's political views rather than on his professional competence. In fact this new power was to be flagrantly abused by General André, the man appointed by Waldeck-Rousseau to succeed Galliffet upon his resignation in 1900; André, an ardent Positivist, did not scruple to use freemasons to act as spies and draw up reports upon the political opinions of army officers. These reports, collected on a card index at the Grand Orient Lodge headquarters, were then consulted by the Minister when making promotions. The revelation of this practice by a Nationalist deputy in 1904 naturally caused a sensation and André was obliged to resign; but the knowledge that the Ministries of the Bloc Républicain had tolerated such espionage caused much bitterness both among the public and within the army itself. The Dreyfus Affair had already discredited and divided the army and encouraged the spread of pacifism and anti-militarism among the public – the practices of an André perpetuated and intensified the divisions.

In dealing with the Church the Government was, like so many earlier French Governments, mainly concerned with the religious orders, which were now officially stated to number 3216 different congregations with a total membership of nearly 200,000 in France. Waldeck-Rousseau himself had denounced them as a political danger – a rival power within the State – and in pointing to their milliard francs' worth of property he seemed deliberately to evoke memories of the *émigrés'* 'milliard' of Restoration days and to encourage the hopes of anti-clerical despoilers. In 1900 the powerful order of Assumptionists, who had shown their enterprise by organizing pilgrimages to Lourdes and elsewhere[3] and whose paper *La Croix* had been one of the most violent and influential clerical organs, was convicted of having subsidized Nationalist candidates in elections and was dissolved. More important, however, was the effect upon the orders of the law of 1901 relating to the Contract of Association. Ever since 1871 the problem of securing satisfactory legislation to permit of freedom of association had been discussed but left unsolved. No fewer than thirty bills had been brought forward and either defeated or allowed to drop. The only exception was the law sponsored by Waldeck-Rousseau in 1884 which had accorded legal freedom to professional syndicates. Now, as Prime Minister, the architect of that law, an able legist concerned with the problems of order in the State, was eager to complete his work. The bill, which he first put forward in 1899 and which, after much debate and many amendments, mainly of an anti-clerical nature, was finally passed in July 1901, was both a general statement of public law and an offensive measure against the religious orders. While it laid down freedom of association as a general principle, it restricted such freedom to native societies: associations controlled or partly composed of foreigners were excluded, and in consequence the law ruled that each congregation must apply for legal authorization or be dissolved. The Government's wish that such applications should be submitted to the Conseil d'État was overruled with the result that they were subjected not to the supposedly dispassionate scrutiny of a legal body, but to the examination of the Chamber of Deputies with its political prejudices. Furthermore, an anti-clerical deputy succeeded in tacking on to the bill a clause which had no strict relevance to the liberty of association, but was rather a refurbishing of the famous Article 7 of Jules Ferry and directed against the free or Catholic schools. Henceforward no member of any unauthorized congregation was to be permitted to teach. The bill, as it eventually passed, could justifiably be described by the anti-clerical historian, Debidour, as 'the most decisive act of anti-clerical policy since 1870'.[4]

This law on Associations had already gone further than Waldeck-Rousseau's intention and it was soon to be seen that he had launched an anti-clerical offensive which he was no longer able to control and was presently to deplore.

The revival of the clerical question had roused intense interest and feeling throughout the country and brought no less than 90 per cent of the electorate to the polls in the general elections of 1902. The result was an overwhelming victory for the Bloc Républicain, who obtained nearly 370 seats compared with the 220 which went to the Conservatives and Moderates, although in actual votes these Right-wing groups polled only

200,000 less. Waldeck-Rousseau might perhaps have been able to continue in office for a further long term had not fatigue and ill-health compelled him to retire. Possibly, too, he hesitated to face such a solidly anti-clerical rank and file, for the Radicals were now the strongest element in the bloc, and the result of the elections was universally understood to have been a vote in favour of the continuation of an anti-clerical policy which he may well have thought had now gone far enough. Unfortunately, he was himself to give it still further impetus by his recommendation of a successor. Like another able barrister, the last Prime Minister but one of the Third Republic, Paul Reynaud, Waldeck-Rousseau partly ensured the frustration of his own work by his faulty judgement of men. The appointment of André as War Minister was one serious blunder, the recommendation of Émile Combes as the next President of the Council was another.

The *petit père* Combes, as he was known to his familiars, an elderly and comparatively little known Radical Senator, had begun life as a seminarist and a professor of theology and now had all the renegade's fanatical hatred of religious orders. The victory of the bloc made it certain that the Chamber would be likely to press for a strict application of the Association Law; Combes' accession to power meant that it would be applied with rancorous severity and that there would soon be a general offensive against the Church on all fronts in order to fulfil the Prime Minister's desire for what he called the complete triumph of 'the spirit of the Revolution'. By the end of 1902 all schools (some 12,000 in number) conducted by unauthorized congregations had been closed. In the following March the Government sent to the Senate the applications for authorization of the five male orders whose existence it was still prepared to tolerate, the Trappists, the White Fathers, the African Missions, and two others, while it referred to the Chamber the remaining requests, which were all duly rejected in spite of vigorous protests from the Holy See, the clergy and numerous outside bodies. In consequence fifty-four male congregations were dissolved, comprising some 20,000 friars and monks distributed through 1500 houses in various parts of the country. In the following June eighty-one applications from female congregations were likewise rejected *en bloc*, and a year later a law was passed forbidding all congregations to give teaching of any kind. Those which had been legally recognized as teaching orders were to be compelled to give up their teaching work within ten years. The last speeches of the dying Waldeck-Rousseau were eloquent protests against the perversion of his own legislation, but they were made in vain. Combes was not to be deterred. But his victory was partial. Many secularized clergy continued to teach in Catholic schools.

The policy of Combes naturally irritated the Vatican and brought the question of separation of Church and State once more to the fore. Yet, although the demand for separation had remained an integral part of the Radical programme ever since 1869, it is possible that the Concordat of 1801 might still have been maintained for some while longer but for the personality and policy of the new Pope, Pius X. Even a Combes could see, as many an Opportunist had seen before him, that the Concordat gave the State certain powers of control over the Church which it might do well not to relinquish.

The great Leo XIII, who had once been hailed by Gambetta as a 'consecrated Opportunist', who had done his best to bring about peace between the French Catholics and the Third Republic, and who had given such a notable impulse to new movements of a Catholic Socialist character by the Encyclicals in which he declared that it was the duty of the Church to have a care for the social problem and a concern for the material as well as spiritual welfare of the working classes, had died in August 1903 at the age of ninety-three. His successor, the 69-year-old Pius X, though a man of saintly life, was far less tactful and far more limited in vision. Following the tradition of Pius IX rather than of Leo XIII, he was concerned not so much to adjust the policy and functions of the Church to the changing conditions of a new century as to defend the stronghold of faith from the subtle assaults of an individualist modern world and to stand out inflexibly for the maintenance of Papal rights and prerogatives. Thus it was that the man who promptly condemned the modernist thought of the Abbé Loisy and was presently to pass sentence upon the 'Sillon', one of the most fruitful of the endeavours of French Catholic laymen to develop a vigorous movement of Catholic Socialism and the precursor of the important political party of the Fourth Republic, the Mouvement Républicain Populaire, soon came into conflict with the French Government on other issues. Already before Leo XIII's death Combes had begun a quarrel over the interpretation of the Concordat, a sort of twentieth-century investiture dispute, in which he had claimed to nominate bishops to French sees without any previous consultation with the Papal representatives in France. This claim was resisted by the Pope, and the quarrel became more bitter when Pius X threatened to withhold canonical institution from any bishops who were appointed by the French Government without his prior approval. Still more important was the incident of March 1904 when the Pope in his character as 'Prisoner of the Vatican' sent a secret note to the Governments with whom he was in diplomatic relation protesting against a visit by President Loubet to the King of Italy in Rome. Loubet was the first head of any Catholic State to enter the Quirinal since 1870 and the Pope denounced his visit as an act 'offensive' to the Holy See whose capital city the Italian State had seized in defiance of 'all rights'.[5] The disclosure of this note by Jaurès' paper, the Socialist *Humanité*, caused acute tension

between France and the Vatican. As a result of this and of a further incident in which two French bishops, known to have Republican sympathies,
were summoned to Rome to account for alleged improprieties. Radical
and anti-clerical passions were further roused and Combes was pushed by
his followers into severing diplomatic relations with Rome and, in
November 1904, introducing a bill for the separation of Church and State.
Although he fell two months later, discredited for having applied to the
control of civil administration 'Bonapartist' methods of espionage not
unlike those practised by André in military matters, he was still able to
exert strong anti-clerical influence in the Senate, and the much more
moderate ministry under Rouvier, who succeeded him, dared not abandon the proposal for separation which had just been unanimously
endorsed by a Radical Party Congress, although the French public as a
whole was remarkably indifferent to the issue.

The new Government, however, showed its comparative lack of
enthusiasm by leaving the main work of piloting the bill through Parliament to a new deputy, a comparatively young journalist and lawyer
named Aristide Briand, who acted as *rapporteur*. Briand had begun his
career at St Nazaire as a militant Socialist, but he was, in reality, too
nonchalant to be an ardent doctrinaire and it was not long before he was to
throw off his Socialist allegiance. Now, aided by the combination of an
exceptionally musical voice and unusual expressiveness of face and
gestures, he showed extraordinary suppleness and tactical skill, fascinated
the Chamber by his eloquence and established a parliamentary reputation. The momentous law of 9 December 1905,[6] which eventually
emerged was thus largely his work. It declared that the Republic ensured
freedom of worship and guaranteed its free exercise subject to regulations
necessary for the preservation of public order. At the same time, however,
the Republic ceased to recognize or subsidize any form of worship, Roman
Catholic, Protestant or Jewish, there was an end of the *budget des cultes* –
and church revenues and endowments were to be handed over to new
associations cultuelles which were to be formed within a specified time
limit by the laity of parishes in order that religious services might be
maintained. An inventory of all Church property was meanwhile to be
made in order to facilitate the reallocation of assets.

In fact the separation of Church and State, deplored by Bodley as the
'first serious breach made in the administrative fabric constructed by
Napoleon',[7] meant the substitution of one set of legal relationships for
another, and when they saw that separation was inescapable the main
concern of French churchmen was that the financial loss involved in the
change should be as slight as possible. Unfortunately for them, however,
their material position was considerably prejudiced as a result of the

attitude of the Pope and of the absence, since the severance of diplomatic relations, of any official channel of negotiation between the French Government and the Vatican. It was in fact regrettable that relations between the French Republic and the Holy See were such that an arrangement which had worked for over a century was terminated by the unilateral act of one of the parties to the Concordat instead of by an agreement. The result was that, without waiting to consult the French episcopate, the Pope vehemently denounced the principle of separation and refused to recognize lay *associations cultuelles*. Although the taking of the inventory of Church property had led to disturbances in some parts of France, where the faithful regarded it as a sacrilegious proceeding, any hopes that the Pope may have had that there would be a revulsion of feeling in favour of the maintenance of the Concordat were doomed to disappointment by the results of the general election of 1906. This reaffirmed the supremacy of the bloc and soon led to the formation of a new Ministry in which Briand became Minister of Public Instruction and Worship and in which Clemenceau took office for the first time as Minister of the Interior. The continued refusal of the Pope to sanction the formation of the proposed *associations cultuelles* meant that there was now no legal body to which the Church's property could be assigned or its buildings transferred. In consequence, since the Church refused to comply with the terms of the law, the State sequestered its property, handing over its funds to public relief organizations and its buildings to the local municipalities. Only 'buildings needful for worship' remained for the clergy's use and even these were not legally in Church ownership.

Thus the Pope's uncompromising attitude had the extraordinary result that 'The Catholic Church was without legal status of any kind; it could hold no property; it was "literally an outlaw" '[8] existing merely upon the sufferance of the theoretically 'neutral' state. Materially it was extremely hard hit. The clergy were now dependent entirely upon the support of the faithful and many of them in poor districts were condemned to a life of great poverty. The natural consequence was that recruits fell off, the number of the clergy declined and many parishes could no longer be served. On the other hand the general quality of the priesthood, reduced though it was in numbers, was greatly improved, since in general only those who had a real vocation and were prepared to face a life of hardship and privation were now prepared to enter the ministry. In the long run, although the elimination of organized Christian influences from French life was quickened, the momentous separation of 1905 was probably beneficial to both sides. Republican Governments and Chambers no longer spent a disproportionate amount of their time in sterile quarrels with the Church, while the Church, though materially poorer and numerically weaker, now enjoyed a real freedom from State interference and in its altered condition was soon to show a new intellectual vigour and to attract into its fold some of the finest minds in France. Finally, although anti-clericalism was still to remain a force to be conjured with in France and persists until this day, the removal of the main grievances of the anti-clericals did contribute to a general appeasement once the bitterness attendant upon separation had had time to die. In so far as this happened, the work of Waldeck-Rousseau, Combes, Briand and Clemenceau during the years 1899 to 1907 was a real contribution to Republican consolidation, not merely in the sense that it helped to bring about a succession of electoral victories of the Republican bloc and to demonstrate the power-lessness of the old enemies who had played such a conspicuous part in opposition to the regime during the first thirty years of its existence, but because it removed the root cause of many of the main difficulties with which the Republic had had to contend. The new settlement was neither just nor generous, but in the end it worked better than the old.

Meanwhile, during these same years, important steps were taken to strengthen the position of France in Europe and for these she was largely indebted to another disciple of Gambetta, Théophile Delcassé, who became Foreign Minister in 1898 and retained the post through the best part of four successive Ministries, a notable example of the way in which ministerial instability and apparent fluctuations of policy might some-times be corrected by continuity of action in a particular department. Delcassé, indeed, a little dark, spectacled, buttoned-up, secretive person of unimpressive professorial appearance and enormous industry, showed remarkable pertinacity in pursuing his aims. He did his utmost to re-inforce the Franco-Russian alliance, ensuring the continued validity of the military agreement between the two powers, and in 1901 and 1902 there was a fresh exchange of visits between the Tsar and the President of the Republic. Still more important was the success he achieved in effecting a rapprochement with Italy and in bringing to an end a long period of friction with Great Britain.

Relations with Italy, strained ever since France had established her protectorate in Tunisia, had deteriorated still more since Italy's adherence to the Triple Alliance in 1882 and the denunciation in 1887 by the violently anti-French Crispi of the Franco-Italian Treaty of commerce, which led to eleven years of trade warfare more damaging to Italy than to France. In 1896, however, the Italian defeat of Adowa in Abyssinia led to the fall of Crispi and put an end for the time being to Italy's bellicose attitude. The way lay open for a revision of Italian policy, and a speedy improvement in Franco-Italian relations ensued. In that same year an agreement regulating the status of Italians in Tunisia was tantamount to a recognition by Italy of France's position in the Beylicate. Two years later, in November 1898, Delcassé was able to conclude a new commercial treaty. At Rome he was ably assisted by another of Gambetta's disciples, Camille Barrère, who remained there for more than a quarter of a century and helped him to put the relations of the two countries on a new footing of confidence and friendship. The most important immediate results were the conclusion in 1900 of a secret agreement whereby France promised Italy a free hand in Tripolitania in return for recognition of her own claims in Morocco, and the confidential assurance given by the Italian Government in 1902, when it once again renewed the Triple Alliance, that it did not consider itself bound thereby to take part in any aggression against France under any circumstances whatsoever. This *entente*, which practically invalidated the effect of the Triple Alliance in so far as Italy was a potential ally for Germany against France was more openly demonstrated by the visit of part of the Italian fleet to Toulon in 1901 and by the exchanges of visits between the King of Italy and President Loubet, which, as we have seen, had such momentous consequences for the relations of Church and State in France. The German Chancellor, Prince Bülow, who had some inkling of what was going on but could not prevent it, attempted to treat the rapprochement as an innocent flirtation: 'In a happy marriage,' he told the Reichstag, 'the husband should not be upset if his wife enjoys an innocent waltz with another man.' But, as a French historian has remarked, 'the flirtation was to develop into a liaison'.[9]

Still more important was the rapprochement with Great Britain. Ever since the end of the Restoration when France had resumed her advance as a colonial power, in spite of periods of more or less close *entente* in Europe, the traditional spirit of jealous rivalry had tended to dominate her relations with Britain overseas. In the great period of colonial expansion during the last quarter of the nineteenth century the extension of the new French overseas Empire had not been halted by the furore about Tonkin which led to the dramatic fall of Jules Ferry in 1885; and by 1894 the rulers of the Third Republic had become sufficiently conscious of their imperial responsibilities to set up a separate Ministry of Colonies. The creation of the Indo-Chinese Union in 1887 was followed in the 1890s by the conquest of Dahomey (1890), the establishment of the Ivory Coast as a separate colony (1893), the occupation of Timbuctoo (1894), and the annexation of Madagascar (1896). Throughout the world, from the fisheries of Newfoundland to the rivers of Siam and the islands of the Malayan Archipelago, French and British sailors, explorers and traders, met and competed; and although agreements such as that for the establishment of a condominium in the New Hebrides in 1887, the Constantinople Convention of 1888 neutralizing the Suez Canal, and the Convention of

French Africa

(stippled)	FRENCH AFRICA c 1875
(diagonal hatch)	Territory added by c 1900
(vertical lines)	" " by 1914
(horizontal lines)	" received under mandate, 1919
(fine diagonal)	" ceded to Germany, 1911
(cross hatch)	" " " Italy, 1919

Map 4: French Africa

1890 delimiting French and British spheres of interest in the Niger Valley brought temporary local appeasements, on the whole relations between the two countries tended to grow steadily worse. The loss of Egypt continued to rankle with the French, and rivalry in Madagascar and trouble in Siam added fresh causes of friction. Already in 1893 the British Ambassador in Paris, Lord Dufferin, had described the feeling of all classes towards Great Britain as one of 'animosity and bitter dislike'.[10] During the next five years events in Africa were to bring the two countries to the verge of hostilities. The penetration of French explorers, traders and missionaries to the heart of Africa from bases on the Senegal in the west or the Congo in the south had opened up visions of a vast French African Empire which might extend not only north and south from the Congo to Algeria, but also east and west from the Senegal to the Nile and beyond. A small but influential pressure group known as the Comité de l'Afrique Française even hoped that by gaining a strategic foothold on the Upper Nile France might force the British to evacuate Egypt. But Britain stood in the way; and when in 1898 a small French expeditionary force under Captain Marchand was encountered by Kitchener of Khartoum at Fashoda in the Sudan the British Government demanded its withdrawal.[11] Fortunately, Delcassé, like Grévy in 1887, kept his head despite popular anger and never lost sight of the fact that so long as the Germans continued to hold Strasbourg and Metz they were France's only permanent enemy. France could not engage in war against the greatest naval power in the world, and any attempt to do so for spheres of influence in a remote part of Africa could lead only to the loss of her newly won Empire. The Minister persuaded his colleagues in the Dupuy Cabinet, and Marchand was ordered to retire. A few months later a new Anglo-French Convention left the Tchad area to France and confirmed Britain's control of the Upper Nile. Thus Fashoda decided that East Africa should remain predominantly British while West Africa would continue to be predominantly French. French soldiers, obliged to abandon their efforts at eastward expansion, were to find plenty of scope for their energies during the next forty years in opening up the vast, largely desert, interior between the Niger and the Mediterranean countries and in rounding off France's African domain by the establishment of a protectorate in Morocco.

War was thus averted, but at the price of a severe blow to French prestige, and during the next few years French opinion was more than ever virulently hostile to Great Britain and showed its animosity by its open sympathies with the Boers during the Boer War of 1899–1902. Soon after Fashoda, the President of the Republic himself, Félix Faure, went so far as to tell a Russian diplomat that Great Britain, not Germany, was France's real enemy;[12] and some of the anti-British propaganda of the Boer War period was so forceful that the Germans thought it worth while to reprint it when they occupied France in 1940.[13] On their side the British did not hide their contempt and pity for a country which after so many scandals was now in the throes of the Dreyfus Affair.

But the drain of the Boer War upon British resources, the loss of prestige which it involved and the revelation of British unpopularity abroad necessitated a revision of British policy. Isolation was now becoming more dangerous than splendid, and, after negotiations for some sort of Anglo-German alliance had broken down as had efforts to reach friendly agreement with Russia, she had turned in 1902 to Russia's new enemy in the Far East and concluded an alliance with Japan. This inclined her all the more to try and compose her differences with Russia's ally France, so that she should not be faced with the hostility of the French as well as of the Triple Alliance powers. Meanwhile France on her side had for some time been preoccupied by the growing anarchy in Morocco and by the disposition of other powers to interfere in what she had long designed as her own preserve. Italy, as we have seen, already recognized her claims, but there remained Spain, Great Britain, and, last but not least, the Germany of William II, now belatedly seeking a 'place in the sun'. If Great Britain also could be induced to recognize the preponderance of French interests in Morocco, the way might lie open to a wider understanding which would be advantageous to both powers, since in Europe itself, politically and commercially, there was no real reason why they should not be friends. Thus the Moroccan question on the one hand and the German menace on the other disposed both Governments to a settlement of outstanding questions. In arriving at an *entente* both were well served by new men, France by its new ambassador in London, Paul Cambon, appointed to the Court of St James in 1898, and Great Britain by her new sovereign, Edward VII, whose genial tact and readiness to visit Paris in 1903 did much to overcome the French people's hostility to England and to prepare the way for political understanding.

In April 1904 a comprehensive agreement was signed. In return for a formal recognition of her position in Egypt Great Britain gave France a free hand in Morocco, and in an accompanying convention and declaration disputes in Newfoundland and Africa and in Siam, Madagascar and the New Hebrides were finally settled. The old colonial rivalry was brought to an end with the closing stages of the great period of expansion and as a result there came into being the *Entente Cordiale*. The relations of the two countries were revolutionized. They gradually developed the habit of co-operation: henceforward they would be more inclined to combine for the defence of their Empires, and their friendship meant a new alignment of the Great Powers. It was soon to be seen that Great Britain had definitely cast her weight into the European balance on the side of the Dual Alliance. The logical corollary was a similar agreement between Great Britain and Russia, signed in 1907, towards which French diplomacy naturally contributed. With its conclusion the Triple Alliance of Germany, Austria-Hungary and Italy was faced by a Triple *Entente* of France, Great Britain and Russia. The division of the European Great Powers into two rival and heavily armed camps was complete.

Agreements with Italy, Spain and Great Britain: all these could appear, and were hailed as 'so many "jalons" planted on the path to peace'.[14] Following soon after the Hague Peace Conference of 1899, which had been unexpectedly summoned by the Tsar to call a halt to the continuing increase in armaments, and had led to the Hague Convention for the peaceful settlement of international disputes, they might appear to suggest that world peace was more secure than at any time since Bismarck's fall and that it might be preserved for another generation. But there was one power which had not had any part in these Moroccan negotiations, and which was affronted at her exclusion and at the coldness with which Delcassé received the advances she made to France; and that power, Germany, was also the power who had been the chief obstacle to a limitation of armaments by the Hague Conference of 1899 and whose naval and commercial rivalry with Great Britain was yearly growing sharper. Irritated by a diplomatic revolution, which seemed to diminish her relative importance, but heartened by Russia's defeat at the hands of Japan in 1905 and by its revelation of Russia's military weakness, she sought to break first the Franco-Russian alliance and then the Anglo-French *entente*. Her efforts to do so and their failure were, as we shall see, to lead to growing tension. The armaments race continued and the ineptitude of German diplomacy, compared with the success of French, led Europe nearer to war because of the suspicions and fears of isolation and encirclement which resulted in the minds of Germany's rulers. For the time being, however, the conclusion and maintenance of the *Entente Cordiale* appeared to be an important new guarantee of continued European peace.

Thus in appearance the Third Republic was strengthened at home and abroad as a result of the policy of Waldeck-Rousseau and his successors. But, although in spite of the questionable practices of Combes the Radicals returned stronger than ever after the elections of 1906, the signs of strength were, as so often before, offset by signs of weakness which led shrewd observers to question the solidity of the regime and to doubt the value of France as an ally.

The bloc and the Radicals had entrenched themselves in place and power, but they had not, any more than their predecessors, succeeded in uniting all Frenchmen in allegiance to the Republic. The regime was still attacked from both flanks. On the Right, although the Monarchists of the old school had been virtually eliminated as a parliamentary force by the elections of 1902 and 1906, a new movement had come to infuse fresh vigour into Royalism and equip it with a highly developed intellectual doctrine. The group of the *Action Française*, an extreme nationalist paper founded in 1899, who announced their conversion to the cause of monarchy in 1904, never became a factor of any importance inside a parliament which they affected to despise; but by their teachings and writings, their intellectual vigour, their narrow concept of 'integral Nationalism', and their violent attacks on the Republic, their leaders, Charles Maurras, Léon Daudet, and others, were to exercise a considerable influence for the best part of forty years. On the Left, and more immediately menacing, were the Syndicates with their traditional sympathy with Anarchist theories, later reinforced by the teachings of Georges Sorel, author of a famous work called *Réflexions sur la Violence*.[15] In 1895 the formation of a Confédération Générale du Travail (CGT) or Trades Unions' Congress, followed in 1896 by that of a general 'Fédération des Bourses du Travail', under the guidance of Fernand Pelloutier, an able young consumptive, marked the development of Syndicalist organization upon a national scale; and when in 1902 the Fédération des Bourses du Travail amalgamated with the reorganized CGT a small body (in 1904 it had only 150,000 members) came into being which has ever since influenced French economic and political life. From the first there was a conflict within the CGT, just as there was in the political Socialist groups, between moderates and radicals, between those who were prepared to co-operate with the Parliamentary Socialists and those who preferred to rely solely upon direct action by economic means. At the Amiens Congress of the CGT in 1906 the revolutionary Syndicalists won a notable victory, and, in the so-called Amiens Charter, carried a resolution in which the Congress formally disowned connexion with any political doctrine and advocated the general strike as the instrument by which it hoped to achieve its ultimate aim, the expropriation of the capitalist class and the reconstruction of society on a syndicalist basis.

This resolution was the signal for industrial unrest and lengthier strikes which reached a numerical peak in 1906. The next two years were marked by strikes and disturbances in many parts of the country, strikes of electricians, of workers in the building and food industries, and of navvies in 1907 and 1908 in big towns such as Paris, Marseilles, Le Havre and Dunkirk, disturbances in 1907 among the vine-growers of the south who had lately formed a union and were suffering from a fresh depression, and last, but not least disquieting to the Government, a strike of post-office workers in 1909, followed by a call from the CGT for a great general strike. These syndicalist strikes and disturbances, which in many cases were accompanied by anti-militarist propaganda, presented a challenge to the authority of the State which Clemenceau, Prime Minister from October 1906 to July 1909, had no hesitation in accepting. In many cases troops were employed to deal with strikers; the new and illegally formed Primary Teachers' Union was refused permission to affiliate with the CGT; a number of Trade Union leaders were arrested and civil servants who struck were dismissed. Thus Clemenceau, who had so often in his early years been a destructive force, typifying the Radical distrust of strong government, now, in his 60s, experienced what it was to be defied by disruptive elements. He kept order and the general strike was a fiasco; but he split the bloc, for his policy of repression became more and more distasteful to the Parliamentary Socialists. However much they disapproved of certain aspects of the Syndicalists' theory and action, they refused to disown them by supporting the Prime Minister. Clemenceau throughout his ministry was the object of attacks by Jaurès and others, which were scarcely less bitter than those he himself had once launched against Jules Ferry. The clash of policies was accentuated by the clash of personalities, for the optimistic, warm-hearted, eloquent Jaurès, a sort of doctrinaire professorial Gambetta, was the very antithesis of the dry, sceptical, authoritative, old Jacobin fighter Clemenceau. And so in the end Clemenceau found himself in the paradoxical situation of leaning more and more on the support of his old enemies, the Progressists, and of being attacked more and more violently by his old allies, The Socialists. When his government fell, defeated, like so many French Cabinets, on a comparatively minor issue, he was succeeded by Briand, whose suppleness and talk of appeasement suggested that he might be the man to repair the breaches in the bloc. Such hopes were unfulfilled. In 1910 there was a fresh wave of strikes, notably on the railways, and Briand, who, a decade earlier had been one of the ardent Socialist advocates of the general strike, had by now, like Millerand, moved away from the Socialists, and, like Clemenceau, was to find how different social problems looked from the seat of government. He dealt no less firmly – withstood the strikers and refused to allow civil servants who had been punished to resume their posts. As a result he, too, failed to win Socialist support and lost that of many Radical-Socialists. His fall in February 1911 definitely marked the end of the bloc for the time being and opened a new period of instability. During the three years before the outbreak of the Great War of 1914 there were no less than seven Cabinets, and the fact that some of them were headed by former Progressists such as Poincaré and Barthou and that Poincaré was in 1913 elected President of the Republic showed to what an extent the bloc had for the moment disintegrated.

Thus the social problem had once again come to the fore during the years following the Dreyfus Affair; under Millerand's guidance at the Ministry of Commerce some important measures had been taken to deal with labour problems: a Direction du Travail or Labour Department had been set up under the presidency of Arthur Fontaine, one of the most remarkable of the civil servants of the regime; a Conseil Supérieur du Travail had been established on which Trade Unions were given representation and much encouragement was given to Union organization. Furthermore, in 1900, the Waldeck-Rousseau Cabinet had secured the passage of a law for the gradual reduction to ten hours of the working day of all employees in mixed establishments. But since then, although many proposals for social legislation had appeared in Ministerial programmes, scarcely any important measures of social reform had reached the statute book, apart from a law providing for old-age pensions introduced by Clemenceau and passed in April 1910, under the Briand Ministry. The dispute of Church and State had been a growing preoccupation between 1901 and 1905 and where the social question again forced itself on public attention in 1906 and afterwards it had been mostly in the ugly form of strikes, and remedies had been sought in repression rather than in legislation.

The triumph of the Dreyfusard party at the opening of the century had been accompanied by a 'great wave of democratic feeling' which had seemed to promise much in the way of achievement. But by 1911, as a Left-wing French historian has admitted, 'only bitterness was left'.[16] Parliament had seemed to spend itself in sterile disputes and intrigues.

In fact, the defects of the French parliamentary system, which we have already noted as productive of violent discontent in the 1880s and 1890s, had by now become still more deeply rooted. The legislature was still unchecked, or where controlled it was so not by the executive but by the pressure of sectional interests in the electorate. The habit of interpellation had increased; so too had the number of parliamentary standing commissions which tended more and more to arrogate to themselves a power to interfere in administration. In consequence deputies were coming to win a patronage of administrative posts, which meant that they were constantly solicited by their electors and constantly under the temptation to bestow places for political motives. Moreover, as the class of professional politicians grew, so more and more deputies were guided in their conduct by the financial need to keep their seats. Hence the increasing inclination of the nation's representatives on the eve of a general election to vote for the lavish expenditure of public funds on objects likely to win the votes of constituents, irrespective of the state of the national finances, which had in fact steadily tended to deteriorate since the turn of the century;

and hence their increasing dependence upon those local electoral committees whose interests tended, as we have seen, to be so petty.

In addition to the local committees and the standing parliamentary
commissions we must also note the emergence of another form of committee evolved by the bloc, the Délégation des Gauches. This was
composed of representatives of the four main groups of the Bloc and acted
in such constant consultation with the Government that it to some extent
dictated Government policy, especially from 1902–5 and so exercised a
new form of *pouvoir occulte*. Furthermore, the temptation, later so
notable in the Fourth Republic, for sectional groups of the community to
seek to capture the machinery of State or to exercise pressure for their own
economic or political ends was more than ever apparent. By disavowing a
Minister, the executive committee of the Radical and Radical-Socialist
groups might destroy a Cabinet, and many syndicates were so highly
disciplined as virtually to dictate the votes of their members. Thus the
highly centralized state structure, perfected by Napoleon and so carefully
and deliberately preserved by succeeding regimes, seemed to be crum-
bling away under the dissolving action of a myriad groups and committees.[17] The State had granted freedom of association, but there was
soon to come a time when certain associations seemed to be strongholds of
a new feudalism able to defy the State. Under this Republic of Committees, which in its demagogic aspect deserved the title once given it by a
clever writer of 'La République des Camarades',[18] national interests
appeared more than ever to be obscured by those of groups and
individuals. Denounced or derided by the Syndicalists and the Action
Française, disappointing the most clear-sighted and patriotic of the
Republicans, the machine of government once again seemed sadly in need
of an overhaul. No Bonaparte was at hand to recast it from the beginning;
no statesman was strong enough to impose a constitutional reform which
would strengthen the executive and limit parliamentary irresponsibility;
and so once again the politicians who sought to redress matters turned to
juggling with the electoral procedure. In 1910 Briand, in a striking
speech, had declared the need for a strong 'purifying breeze' to pass across
'all the little foul and stagnant ponds which are being formed and spreading more or less over the country'. The remedy, eagerly sponsored alike by
the Right and by the Socialists, was the introduction of proportional
representation, but in spite of a favourable vote in the Chamber in 1912
and of continuous propaganda, it was strenuously opposed by the Radicals
whose organization was largely built up on the basis of *scrutin d'arrondissement*; and it was rejected by the Senate, which had now for many
years shown itself the sort of Conservative body it was originally intended
to be – except that the order of things it conserved was fundamentally

Republican – resolutely opposing all change whether in the form of an income tax, of votes for women, or a new electoral procedure. So the elections of 1914 were once again held under the old system, and, incidentally, they led to a re-formation of the bloc. The Socialists were ready to abandon their ardour for electoral reform in order to back the Radicals upon an issue about which they felt more strongly. Events abroad and the increasing risk of war had brought the question of the army once more to the fore.

The anti-militarism, which had grown notably in the late 1880s and 1890s, partly in reaction against Boulangism, partly as the result of the unpopularity of conscription with young men of letters who wrote novels[19] throwing a somewhat lurid light upon conditions in the army, and last but not least because of the Dreyfus Affair and the development of Socialism with its internationalist pacifist teachings, came to a climax with the bill passed in 1905 by which the length of military service was reduced from three to two years and in the reduction of military expenditure and neglect of the navy. The law of 1905, which incidentally suppressed exemptions, thus making compulsory service for the first time practically as well as theoretically equal for all, had been introduced in 1901 at the time of the Franco-Italian rapprochement and became effective just after the conclusion of the Anglo-French *Entente*. Following not long after the Hague Peace Conference and upon this improvement in France's diplomatic position it might equally with the *entente* be held to be a factor for peace. But in this momentous year, the year also of the separation of Church and State and of the formation of a united French Socialist party, the international situation deteriorated sharply.

Now that France had the goodwill of Great Britain and Italy for her designs on Morocco, she was anxious to consolidate her position as quickly as possible. But Germany, sore at not having been consulted by Delcassé in spite of her treaty rights in Morocco, was unwilling to abandon her own Moroccan ambitions without a struggle, and eager to break the Anglo-French *Entente* if she could. In March 1905 the Kaiser had visited Tangier and delivered a resounding speech in which he declared that Germany regarded the future of Morocco as an international question. When Delcassé refused to agree to the subsequent German proposal for an international conference, the German Government demanded and obtained his resignation from the Rouvier Cabinet who were alarmed, knowing France's military unpreparedness, and put little trust in Delcassé's assurances of English support. This enforced resignation was a blow to French pride and prestige, but in the ensuing conference, which met at Algeciras in 1906, Germany gained little, since the majority of the Powers represented agreed that the organization of police services in Moroccan ports should devolve upon France and Spain. Thus France's dominant interest was recognized, although nominal supervision by a Dutch or Swiss Inspector-General, and the fact of the conference itself, preserved a semblance of international control, and her new duties gave her the opportunity to strengthen her foothold in Morocco. Moreover, instead of being weakened, the *Entente Cordiale* was reinforced by the crisis, since, although the British Government resolutely resisted the French suggestions that *entente* should be converted into alliance, they did agree to allow military staff conversations: even though they were in no way to bind the two Governments, this action of the British was significant.

In 1909 a change in German policy suggested that the Moroccan question need no longer give trouble, but this hope was illusory. For Germany the Bosnian crisis of that year relegated Moroccan affairs to a secondary place and the German Government agreed to the conclusion of a Franco-German convention whereby they recognized French political preponderance in Morocco in return for the grant of facilities for German nationals to co-operate with French in obtaining economic concessions. But this *détente* did not last long. When in 1911 a rebellion against the Sultan led the French to seize the opportunity of strengthening their grip on the country by sending troops to Fez and Central Morocco, delaying their promised withdrawal, Germany reacted and rightly declared that France's action was contrary to the Algeciras Act of 1906. She sent a gunboat, the *Panther*, to Agadir, nominally to protect German interests in Southern Morocco, and said that it would be withdrawn only when France offered suitable compensation: in return for formal recognition of freedom of action by France in Morocco she must receive the whole of the French Congo. For some time there was something of a war scare reminiscent of 1875 and 1887. But the French Government kept its head, and Caillaux, the new Prime Minister, aware that victory in war was far from sure, sought a pacific settlement. Moreover a clear indication by Great Britain that she thought Germany's claims excessive and would go to France's help if she were attacked, caused the German Government to think twice about imposing their demand by force. Eventually, after long and difficult negotiations, a new Franco-German Convention was signed in November 1911. Germany at last gave France a free hand in Morocco and agreed that she might set up a protectorate there. In return there was a territorial readjustment on the borders of the German Cameroons, whereby a considerable area of the French Congo passed under German rule.[20]

The Agadir crisis was important for a number of reasons. It led in March 1912 to the formal establishment of a French Protectorate in Morocco similar to those already set up in Tunis and Annam. By 1914 General Lyautey, the first Resident, had brought the country almost wholly under control and so, as someone said, 'he, a Royalist, gave an Empire to the Republic'. A new area of 440,000 km² and some 5,000,000 people was added to the vast French African domain, which was now finally rounded off eighty-four years after the conquest of Algiers. But this success had been bought at a price which was dear and in conditions which were disquieting and humiliating. Caillaux had hoped, as had Rouvier in 1905, that the opportunity of discussions with Germany might lead to a general settlement of disputed questions and open a new era in Franco-German relations, but nothing came of such hopes and he himself had to resign as a result of the disclosure that he had conducted the German negotiations largely behind the back of his own Foreign Minister, De Selves. In fact the effect of Germany's 'big stick' diplomacy was to lead a large number of Frenchmen to see that German policy was a threat alike to French security and to European peace, to induce the French Government to attempt still further to strengthen its ties with Great Britain[21] and Russia, and to encourage a campaign by the Nationalists and the Right for the reimposition of three years' military service. The laws of 1912 and 1913, by which the Austro-Hungarian and German Empires further increased the size of their armies, alarmed the French military authorities and in 1913 they sponsored a bill for the re-establishment of three years' service which became law in August of that year. But this law met with strenuous opposition from the Socialists and from some of the Radicals. Men like Jaurès held firmly to the old Radical Republican view that a truly Republican army should consist merely of 'the nation in arms' and that there should be no professional force; and believing that alliances and competition in armaments were the main causes of war they pathetically hoped that the solidarity of Socialists and workers in the two countries would lead to a Franco-German rapprochement. For them, therefore, it was important that France should take no step which might be construed as 'provocative', while Marxists and revolutionary Syndicalists like Gustave Hervé believed that there had to be a choice between war and revolution and that any measure calculated to reinforce the army must be opposed because they held it to be *ipso facto* strengthening the militarist domination of the capitalist State.

This new law was far from popular, for it increased the country's financial burden – and in the autumn the Radicals, hitherto divided on the military question, calculated that opposition to it would pay them best and made this one of the chief points of their programme. When the time came for the general elections of May 1914 their attitude was much less clear. Nevertheless their decision had enabled the bloc to be temporarily re-formed and to win a striking victory. The Socialists gained some thirty seats and the Radicals of various shades came back 260 strong. When the

Vineyards of France c 1900

Famous Vintages
{
● Red wines
○ White wines
△ Liqueurs
■ Brandy
}

By this time the vineyards had recovered from the
phylloxera and in 1896 wine production, which in
1885 had fallen to 23,223,000 hectolitres compared
with 83,662,000 in 1875, had risen to 44,656,000
hectolitres, or as much as the combined output
of Italy, Spain and Austria

Miles

0   20   40   60   80   100

Map 5: Vineyards of France c. 1900

R. Aisne
R. Oise
R. Marne
R. Meuse
R. Moselle
Reims
Epernay
PARIS
CHAMPAGNE
BURGUNDY
R. Seine
ЛÉANAIS
Auxerre
R. Yonne
R. Loire
Dijon
FRANCHE COMTÉ
NIVERNAIS
Pouilly
R. Loire
R. Cher
CÔTE D'OR
Beaune
R. Saône
MÂCONNAIS
R. Indre
Mâcon
BEAUJOLAIS
R. Rhône
Lyons
AUVERGNE
R. Dordogne
R. Allier
R. Isère
DAUPHINÉ
R. Lot
R. Durance
R. Rhône
LANGUEDOC
R. Tarn
Avignon
COMTAT
Montpellier
PROVENCE
oulouse
R. Aude
ROUSSILLON

new Chamber met it seemed certain that the law was doomed. Indeed the first Cabinet to confront the new Chamber fell that same day partly because it proposed to maintain the law. Here, however, we come to one of those rare moments when the personality of the President of the Republic was of extreme importance. The election of Poincaré, a firm, tenacious Lorrainer, as President in January 1913, reflected the nationalist desire for a strong man. He had long been preoccupied by the dangers of the international situation and was fully convinced that the three years' law was necessary for national security. In spite of the attitude of the Chamber and of Jaurès' admonition reminding him of Gambetta's warning to a former President who ventured to oppose the Lower House, that he must submit or resign, Poincaré was determined not to give way without a struggle. He chose as his next Prime Minister, Viviani, a Socialist who was ready to play for time. Then on 28 June another event occurred which saved the law. The death at Sarajevo of the heir to the throne of the Austro-Hungarian Empire by the hand of a Serbian assassin provoked a new crisis for which there was to be no solution save that of war.

For a while, however, this crisis was widely regarded as a purely Balkan affair. The general public was far more interested in a sensational trial resulting from a dramatic incident which contributed to the fall of the Doumergue Ministry on 2 June: on 16 March the wife of the Finance Minister, Caillaux, exasperated at the campaign conducted against her husband by a Right-wing paper, the *Figaro*, had waited for the Director in his office and shot him dead. Like the Choiseul-Praslin crime in 1847 and the murder of Victor Noir in 1870, Madame Caillaux's action was a prelude to a greater drama. Nor was it the last or the most important crime of its kind. On 31 July, on the very eve of the cataclysm, a half-witted fanatic, led astray by the violence of the attacks by the Nationalist Press against the 'pro-German Socialist traitor' shot Jaurès in a restaurant. The great orator's trust in the solidarity of Socialists in all lands was vain and by a strange irony the new pacifist Chamber, of which he had been one of the most notable members, spent virtually all its life wrestling with the problems of war and the defence of an invaded country.

Notes

1 The Socialists became the first party in France to have any regular standing party organization for electoral and other purposes. The results of unity and good organization were soon reflected at the polls. They obtained 59 seats in the Chamber in 1906, 76 in 1910 and 104 in 1914.
2 Barrès, *Leurs figures*, p. 185.
3 Lecanuet, E., *L'Eglise de France sous la Troisième République*, p. 361.

4 Cit. Phillips, C. S., *The Church in France, 1848–1907*, p. 263. For its text see Bodley, J. E. C., *The Church in France*, or Thomson, D., *France: Empire and Republic*.
5 Cit. Zévaès, A., *Histoire de la Troisième République, 1870–1926*, p. 448.
6 For the text, see Cahm, E., *Politics and Society in Contemporary France (1789–1971)*, pp. 633–5.
7 Bodley, op. cit., pp. 3, 114.
8 Phillips, op. cit. The law on property was often ignored.
9 Cit. Baumont, M., *L'essor industriel et l'impérialisme colonial (1878–1904)*, p. 323.
10 Cit. Langer, W. L., *The Diplomacy of Imperialism, 1890–1902*, vol. 1, p. 49.
11 For the background, see Brown, R. G., *Fashoda Reconsidered: The Impact of Domestic Politics on French Policy in Africa 1893–1898*.
12 Cit. Baumont, op. cit., p. 301.
13 E.g. *L'Assiette au beurre*, no. 119 of 1903.
14 Cit. Baumont, op.cit., p. 360.
15 But there is little echo of Sorel in working-class thought: his appeal was to the intellectuals.
16 Bourgin, G., *La Troisième République*, p. 180.
17 The Radical policy of Combes, known as 'Combisme', was described approvingly by the Radical philosopher Alain as nothing else but the continuous control of the elected by the elect. Halévy, D., *Décadence de la liberté*, p. 63n.
18 Robert de Jouvenel.
19 E.g. Peladan, J. (1886) *Curieuse*, Hermant, Abel (1887) *Le cavalier Miserey*, and Descaves, Lucien (1890) *Sous-offs*.
20 See Map 4, p. 201.
21 For instance by the naval agreement of 1912, whereby the French concentrated their main naval forces in the Mediterranean while Great Britain transferred part of her Mediterranean squadron to the North Sea. Such an arrangement gave France a strong moral claim to British support should war break out.

Bibliography

Allain, J.-C. *Agadir 1911*, Paris, 1976.
Andrew, C. M., *Théophile Delcassé and the making of the Entente Cordiale*, London, 1968.
Baumgart, W., *Imperialism: the Idea and Reality of British and French Colonial Expansion 1880–1914*, Oxford, 1982.
Becker, J.-J., *Comment les Français sont entrés dans la guerre*, Paris, 1977.
Cambon, Paul, *Correspondance, 1870–1924*, vol. 2 (1898–1911), Paris, 1940.
Chastenet, J., *La France de M. Fallières*, Paris, 1949.
Derfler, L., *Alexandre Millerand: the Socialist Years*, The Hague, 1977.
Goldberg, H., *The Life of Jean Jaurès*, Madison, 1962.
Keiger, John F. V., *France and the Origins of the First World War*, London, 1983.

Larkin, M., *Church and State after the Dreyfus Affair*, London, 1974.
Porch, D., *The March to the Marne. The French Army 1871–1914*, Cambridge, 1981.
Sorlin, P., *Waldeck-Rousseau*, Paris, 1967.
Watson, D. R., *Georges Clemenceau: A Political Biography*, London, 1974.
Weber, E., *Action Française: Royalism and Reaction in Twentieth-century France*, Stanford, 1962.

13

France in 1914

In 1815, on the morrow of the Napoleonic Wars, we paused to take a brief glance at French society. Now, in 1914, when France is once again about to enter a great European conflict, it is fitting that we should halt for a moment and consider the changes wrought in that society after nearly half a century of Republican Government.

In 1914, on the eve of the first World War, France was a land of some 39,600,000 people. Thus her population had increased by 10,000,000 in a hundred years, but she was no longer the most populous country in Europe apart from Russia. She had been outstripped by Great Britain who now had some 43,000,000 people, and, still more conspicuously by her great enemy Germany, the number of whose inhabitants had soared to 70,000,000. Moreover, the birth-rate had fallen from 26 per 1000 in the decade 1861–70 to 18.7 per 1000 in 1912.[1] This fall was, however, partly offset by a simultaneous decline in the death-rate, with the result that the figures of the total population since the turn of the century had been more or less stationary. Unfriendly critics pronounced France to be decadent and declared that the decline in her birth-rate was due to the corruption of her morals. In fact various causes had contributed to this decline. The growing standard of comfort among the bourgeoisie led to a restriction of the size of middle-class families – the bourgeois being often content with an only child. The Code Napoléon which endorsed the widespread custom of equal division of property among a man's heirs also had a limiting effect upon peasant families, since excessive sub-division meant that holdings became too small to provide a livelihood. Other subsidiary causes which may have had a restrictive effect were the growth of alcoholism among sections of the working class[2] and the relatively high price of bread under the protectionist system which sheltered French agricultural interests after 1892. In a world free from war and rumours of war such a decline and such numerical inferiority compared with Germany need not have greatly mattered. But, coupled with comparable industrial and military inferiority, in the world of 1914 they were a cause of grave anxiety.

France, as we have seen, could already by 1870 be reckoned a big industrial power. So she was still in 1914; but for her, unlike her industrialized neighbours such as Great Britain, Belgium and Germany, agriculture was still the biggest 'industry'. Just over 22 million people still lived in the country and even as late as 1939 more than 55 per cent of the population was to be found in villages or small towns of less than 4000 inhabitants.[3] In 1911 only 26 per cent lived in towns of over 20,000. There were good reasons for this approximation of France, unlike the other big industrial nations of the West, to a balanced economy. Her Governments had long looked upon the peasantry as the backbone of the country and had aimed at maintaining virtual self-sufficiency in foodstuffs; and at the same time her poverty in natural resources, especially coal, meant that she was handicapped in comparison with many of her neighbours. The new coal pits of the Nord and Pas-de-Calais, opened up at the end of Louis Philippe's reign, were hard to work and France's output in 1913, although treble that of 1869, was only 41,000,000 tons compared with the 279 million tons produced in Germany and the 292 million in Great Britain.[4] She was particularly poor in home supplies of good coking coal, and, furthermore, large parts of the country were remote from any of the coal-producing areas. Thus industrialization had proceeded less rapidly than in neighbouring countries. Big industries of course there were, as we have seen long since, and they continued to develop much as did big industries elsewhere. For instance, the formation of 'comptoirs' foreshadowed the development of the large Cartel or Trust. But the continued, if not growing, importance of luxury trades for export markets and the tendency of manufacturers in many other industries to concentrate mainly upon the requirements of the home market[5] meant that France was still predominantly a land of small industries. Although work at home had become increasingly rare, as late as 1931 no less than 60 per cent of France's industrial workers were to be found in firms which employed less than twenty persons.[6] This meant that the tradition of fine craftsmanship was still very live, that French individualism still persisted in industry, and that a vast number of employers still had direct personal relationships with their men. The possession of a balanced economy meant that the country was much less liable than many others to suffer from the fluctuations of world markets and the evils of unemployment. But it also meant that, if war were to come, France with her multitude of small factories and her relatively small number of industries equipped for rapid mass production on a big scale would be much less fitted than Great Britain or Germany to turn out the vast quantities of armaments and munitions without which it could not be waged. 'As early as 1913,' it has been said, 'the ratio of industrial potential as between Germany, England and France was computed at – Germany 3, England 2, France 1.'[7]

This, of course, did not mean that enormous strides had not been made, especially after 1896, in continuance of that industrial development, which was so notable under the Second Empire, and that most Frenchmen were not greatly affected by these further material transformations. The development of iron and steel made possible the manufacture of a host of new tools and revolutionized the building industry. By 1913 France's output of steel fell not far short of that of Great Britain and the exploitation of the Briey basin after 1892 had made her the greatest exporter of iron ore in the world. Her consumption of raw cotton had trebled and the hand-loom weavers had almost disappeared as a result of increasing mechanization. Mechanization had also transformed the silk industry and the woollen industry, now largely concentrated in Roubaix and Tourcoing, and the manufacture of artificial silk had begun in 1890. France had developed chemical industries which were themselves to transform a host of others, electricity, one of the wonders of the 1889 Exhibition, soon superseded gas as a widespread means of lighting and the electrolytic process and native supplies of bauxite made her an important producer of aluminium. But, compared with Great Britain and Germany, lack of coal and suitable raw materials put her at a disadvantage in the production of heavy chemicals, while she was slow to make use of the hydro-electric power which might be easily harnessed from her abundant mountain rivers. Although Paris had its first underground and the Paris-Lyons-Marseilles railway company began to electrify its lines in 1899, by 1914 France lagged behind Germany and Switzerland in her development of power and the great period of electrification was not to begin until after 1918. At the same time industrialization and the distribution of industrial products were further facilitated by the growing improvement of communications. By 1890 the mileage of railway track had doubled since 1870, largely by the construction of local lines at heavy loss to the State, the canal system had been standardized and extended and rivers improved to fit them for traffic. About the same time the motor car had made its appearance: by 1914 there were some 99,000 vehicles in the country, production was second only to that of the USA, and the Paris taxis could be ready to contribute to the victory of the Marne.[8] Already the long-distance cable and the telephone had conquered space, though here again France was behind Great Britain and Germany. Already aviation, the cinema and the wireless were exciting the interest of pioneers. Blériot had flown the Channel, the Lumière brothers had made the cinema a practical possibility and Branly had contributed to the development of wireless. But while these new inventions foreshadowed still more extraordinary things to come they had not yet developed sufficiently to affect the everyday life of the ordinary Frenchman.

Nevertheless, in spite of the importance of industry and the industrial worker, it is rural France which still presents, outside Paris, the most characteristic pictures of French society. Big industry was largely confined to five departments of the North, to the periphery of the Massif Central, and to a few large cities such as Paris, Lyons and Marseilles. Elsewhere agriculture in all its variety was the occupation of the majority of working Frenchmen. The structure of agricultural society had altered little during the century. The large estates reconstituted in the early part of the nineteenth century were still a feature of the landscape in certain districts, although many of them had changed hands and passed out of the possession of impoverished nobles into that of prosperous business men. The number of independent peasant proprietors and tenant farmers had tended to increase while that of the métayers and landless labourers had declined: but this had been no revolution, merely a gradual process. So, too, the configuration of holdings was little changed. France had had no enclosure movement like Great Britain and many of the peasant holdings were still widely scattered. They were also on the average, compared with British farms, exceedingly small. Out of a total of nearly 4,000,000 holdings no fewer than 2,500,000 were less than 25 acres in extent. Such small units effectively prevented the growth of anything like a rural proletariat, except in specialized occupations or areas like the big vineyards of the south, the big farms near Paris or among the foresters: but at the same time their existence and the prevalence of scattered holdings meant that farming was bound to be more conservative in character than in many other countries, since lack of capital hampered the introduction of machinery and new technique. Nevertheless, progress had been made especially after the end of the long depression of the 1870s and 1880s and the protection accorded by the high Méline tariff of 1892. Much of this was due to State encouragement. In 1879 the Government had sponsored vine defence syndicates to combat the phylloxera. After Waldeck-Rousseau's law of 1884 had permitted the formation of professional unions, agricultural syndicates, co-operatives and insurance societies had received Government encouragement. And so by 1914 ploughing with oxen, cutting corn and hay with scythes and sickles, and threshing with flails or antiquated horse machines, were much less common. Moreover, although the numbers of the rural population had begun to decline absolutely after 1875 and although the area under wheat declined steadily after 1862, the yield increased, largely owing to improvements in technique and the abandonment of fallow. Thus, although the yield per acre was less than in Great Britain, Belgium or Germany, France was still the greatest wheat-producing country in Europe outside Russia. Meanwhile the vineyards recovered so effectively from the phylloxera that by 1907 over-production and a fall in prices led to violent disorders and a swing to Socialism in the South.

The Industrial Revolution and the slow but steady fall in the agricultural population, had other important consequences. Good roads, an increasing number of railways and the telegraph, all facilitated specialization and so certain districts became famous for market and flower gardening and for dairy produce. At the same time the decline in the population meant that more land was put to pasture and there was a notable increase in the numbers of horses, cows and pigs. Nevertheless, the drift of the labourers to the towns and the not infrequent reluctance of younger sons of peasants to return to the land after doing their military service affected parts of the country in another way. Any Englishman travelling in France must have been struck by the spaciousness of a land in which the population was two and a half times less dense than in his own country. Still more must he have been surprised at the not uncommon spectacle of villages half or wholly deserted. During the 1914–18 war the American Ambassador was to record his astonishment at finding nearly all the houses of Vieux Perouges in the Auvergne in ruin 'from the combined action of time and abandonment'.[9] After the war which took such toll of peasant life the exodus to the towns was still more rapid. Yet the highly important fact that Belgians, Spaniards, Italians and even Poles came across the borders to work on the land did something to arrest the depopulation and showed that conditions of labour in France might nevertheless be more attractive than in their own countries. By 1914 there were well over 1,000,000 of these foreign workers.

France, indeed, was as a whole still a singularly rich and prosperous country in which a great number of people lived cheaply and well. The peasant was better clothed, fed, and housed, and more independent than ever before of the *curé* and the château. 'You no longer,' wrote Clapham, 'praised a man by saying he was "as good as good bread," because it no longer seemed a high compliment. You no longer talked of the "black bread of adversity", because black bread was not made in France. The most unfortunate Frenchman ate the white wheaten bread that was served to princes in the middle ages, and ate it freely. Besides his abundance of good bread, the average Frenchman, during the second half of the nineteenth century, increased his consumption of wine and potatoes by 50 per cent; his consumption of meat, beer and cider by 100 per cent; his consumption of spirits by 200 per cent; his consumption of sugar and coffee by 300 per cent.'[10] The urban wage-earner had his share in this increase as well as the peasant and the bourgeois. The standard of living had notably increased for every class, except perhaps the old aristocracy, and the general optimism and belief in indefinite material advance had been widespread, especially in the 1880s and 1890s: it is still evident to the traveller who observes the number of cafés rejoicing in such names as 'De l'Avenir' or 'Du Progrès'. This prosperity had what would seem grave defects to most European Governments forty years later. As we have seen, it probably contributed to the decline in the birth-rate. It also led to a great increase in the number of small *rentiers*. The family business was never so characteristic in France as in England, and now more than ever it was the ambition of many a small business man and prosperous *petit bourgeois* to work as hard as possible in order to cease work as soon as possible. His one aim was to retire early, acquire a small piece of land and in Candide's well-known phrase 'cultivate his garden'. Many men of under fifty might thus be found throughout France who spent their time pottering in gardens, fishing and playing bowls or busying themselves with local politics.[11]

More than ever, of course, in the France of 1914 it was the bourgeoisie who dominated the scene, ruled the world of politics, industry, letters and the arts, enjoyed the good things of life, and set the tone in dress, manners and customs for the rest of their country. Their ascendancy and the growth of communications was leading in France, as in every country, to a growing uniformity so that local customs and costumes and local traditions and dialects began to disappear. The nobility after the end of the 'République des Ducs' had more and more lost their separate political and social importance, although some of them still maintained a closed circle in the Faubourg St Germain in Paris[12] and carried on something of a country-house life in the châteaux which still remained to them. More and more, however, they tended to become merged with the bourgeoisie; many of them married into the families of industrialists and business men, and some even took to business themselves. It was the industrialists and business men who most frequently had bought their châteaux and their collections of furniture or works of art. The great banking and industrial families were still more influential than before. After the British it was the French financiers who were the bankers of the world. The amenities and pleasures provided for the wealthy increased. Yachting and racing joined hunting among their main sports, while fishing, shooting and dancing remained popular with all classes and football and cycling races aroused intense enthusiasm. The manners of the richer bourgeoisie were aped by the *petite bourgeoisie*, but the distinguishing mark between them, according to one historian, was the absence of a *salon* or drawing-room in the *petit bourgeois'* home.[13] Increasing uniformity of customs was accompanied by a much greater freedom of address and by a greater gentleness of manners, a more humanitarian outlook which coincided with a revolution in the art of medicine which did much to relieve human suffering under medical treatment. Yet amid all these changes the essential element in the social structure, the family, stood firm, and the Frenchwoman in general was so satisfied with her position in the family, which often enabled her to manage her husband's business or at least share in the direction of his work, that she showed little interest in agitating for the vote.[14]

Thus, materially and socially, the century has seen great changes especially under the Third Republic. During the forty-four years since its proclamation the Republic had indeed witnessed much besides scandals and political crises and party struggles; and, lest we should have seemed to be too much preoccupied by its political vicissitudes, we must add a word about other aspects of French destiny during that time. Most noteworthy is the wider sense of national identity. As a result of conscription and compulsory education most peasants were really becoming Frenchmen while the coming war would show that the workers, too, had been integrated into the French nation. Literacy was now widespread among the lower classes. Culture, however, remained the monopoly of the bourgeoisie. Never before had there been such a spate of journals and reviews and books. Never before had writers, artists and composers been treated with more respect. The French were singularly free from social snobbery or colour prejudice: and if there was a definite snobbery it was an intellectual one, arising from the bourgeois cult of the man of letters. For this there was good reason. Paris was as ever a centre for the practise of the arts and a market for their productions, and France of the Third Republic had continued to show that intellectual distinction in an extraordinary variety of subjects for which she had now so long been distinguished. With the death of Victor Hugo in 1885 there had disappeared the last and greatest of the Romantics. But, as we have seen, the Romantic movement had long since given way to Realism and Realism in turn had passed into the still more realistic and 'scientific' Naturalism, which had a widespread influence throughout Europe, and of which Zola was the leader among French novelists. Meanwhile Guy de Maupassant had become the acknowledged master of the short story, Daudet had created the immortal Tartarin de Tarascon, and the discovery of the Russian novel in the years following Hugo's death contributed to an interest in the new 'science' of psychology. Thus the novels of men like Barrès and Bourget marked in their turn a reaction from the Naturalist School, a reaction which was enormously strengthened in another sphere by the work of Henri Bergson, whose philosophical teaching stressed the importance of the irrational factors in the development of man. In poetry, too, moving away from Parnassianism, Verlaine, Mallarmé and the Symbolists had emphasized anew the musical quality of verse, while another novelist, Pierre Loti, appeared to escape from it by setting the scenes of most of his tales amid the exotic luxuriance of distant lands. Nationalists like Barrès, Bourget, Péguy and Maurras had been confronted by internationalists like Anatole France and Romain Rolland. Sardou had been one of the most prolific and popular writers for the theatre, in which Sarah Bernhardt was now the queen among actresses, and Rostand had produced his *Cyrano de Bergerac*.

Nor were the artists behind the men of letters. The Impressionists had continued to exercise an extraordinary influence under the lead of men such as Manet, Monet, Renoir and Degas. The great figures of Cézanne, Van Gogh and Gauguin had followed. Seurat had been the exponent of Pointillisme, and Picasso, Braque and Matisse had begun to perplex, shock or delight a wide public with their new Cubist paintings. In sculpture France had produced the greatest master of modern times in Rodin, and in music she had given birth or a home to more composers of distinction – Massenet, Saint-Saens, Bizet, César Franck, G. Fauré, Vincent D'Indy and Debussy – than perhaps at any time in her history. Furthermore, distinction in the world of creative imagination had been nearly matched in that of learning and the sciences. Taine, Renan and Fustel de Coulanges had continued their work as historians and been succeeded by men such as Sorel, Hanotaux and Lavisse. J. H. Fabre had won renown for his study of insects; Vidal de la Blache for his work as a geographer; Durkheim, Tarde and Le Bon for their studies of social psychology; and Marcel Bertrand as a geologist. Henri Poincaré had shown himself one of the foremost mathematicians of the age. Pasteur had continued his great work in microbiology and the Institut Pasteur had been founded in 1888 by international subscription in recognition of his services to mankind. Marcellin Berthelot had been the father of synthetic chemistry, and last but not least the Curies had opened up a vast new field of scientific and medical inquiry by their discovery of radium in 1898.

Thus political crises had done nothing to hinder the flowering of French inventive genius which had at many points sensationally broken with tradition. At the same time beneath the superficial instability there was the solidity given by a conservative social structure; and that solidity was strengthened by the continuance of the centralized administration and by the influence of many distinguished civil servants. It was in these years that, in addition to the institution of the secular primary school and the reforms of secondary education which, as we saw, formed such an important part of the anti-clerical offensive of the 1880s, higher education was transformed by the creation of Universities in the proper sense of the word, by the foundation of many more or less specialized schools such as the École des Sciences Politiques, and by a great improvement in the facilities for scientific study. It was in these years that the great battle between the champions of a classical and a 'modern' education began anew, until in 1902 the modernists won a notable victory when the Minister for Education decided that Latin and Greek need no longer be required for the Baccalauréat or matriculation examination. Yet on the whole France lagged behind her more industrialized neighbours in technical education. The war of 1914–18 was necessary in order to give it a development on a wide scale.

It was the civil servants and teachers who did the work in making the new educational facilities effective. It was the civil servants and soldiers who at the same time administered and consolidated the vast new Empire which had been built up by Jules Ferry and his successors, the second largest in the world. Here, too, there was a great battle waged over policy. Were the peoples of the Empire to be assimilated and to become Frenchmen just as the conquered peoples of Rome eventually became Roman citizens or were they to develop on the lines of the peoples of the British Empire towards some kind of self-government within a French Commonwealth? On the whole the assimilationist policy tended to prevail and so alongside the experiments in the government of native peoples conducted by the British Colonial Office very different experiments were being carried out by the civil servants and administrators of France.[15] But the words 'French Empire' or Lyautey's later summary of the assimilationist ideal – 'France is a nation of 100 million inhabitants' – must not blind us to the fact that this Empire was created piecemeal and contained the utmost diversity of race, religion, language, economic resources and cultural development. Nor indeed was it all subject to a single Ministry of Colonies. Protectorates like Morocco and Tunisia were the responsibility of the Ministry of Foreign Affairs while Algeria, since it was regarded as an extension of Metropolitan France, came under the Ministry of the Interior. Thus, however much uniformity might be aimed at on paper, in practice a considerable variety of treatment was inescapable.

This vast and varied Empire was a reservoir of manpower and economic resources of great potential importance: but here too the war of 1914–18 was necessary before either French Governments or French public opinion became fully alive to their value in supplementing the deficiencies of the mother country. Originally colonies, in so far as they were not acquired for purely political or strategic reasons, had been primarily regarded as useful markets for France's own products; and when the capacity to absorb French manufactures or foodstuffs fell below expectation investors and public opinion had lost interest. As we have seen, it was only in relation to the Egyptian or German problems that colonial expansion and the

development of the Empire really became matters of prime concern either
for the average politician or for the general public. Thus, since the Empire
held but a small place in the consciousness of the ordinary Frenchman in
1914 we will not attempt to examine its problems in any further detail.
The soldiers and the civil servants on the spot often did admirable work
but administration was costly and lack of interest at home often went hand
in hand with the reluctance to grant funds for development.

Here we come to a last point to be made in this brief survey. The France
of 1914 was a land of wealth and prosperity, but the French State by
comparison with the people was poor. Of old the main contact of the
people with the State had been through the person of the taxgatherer and
the State had been disliked and distrusted accordingly. Natural thrift,
individualism and distrust of the State had all combined to create a strong
public resistance to direct taxation and a strong desire to restrict State
expenditure. In fact that expenditure had increased from between 1875
and 1913 by an average sum of no less than 68,000,000 francs per annum
and in nearly a century it had risen from 864 million to what the men of
1819 would have regarded as the astronomical figure of 5,191 million.[16]
This was largely due to the great development of social services and
pension and other payments under the Third Republic. But it is arguable
that had the politicians been willing to make personal sacrifices, brave
opinion, and impose an income tax in the 1880s or 1890s instead of
waiting until 15 July 1914, France would not only have had a better system
of budgeting – already the practice of voting supplementary credits and
extraordinary expenditure apart from the Budget proper was tending to
falsify the true picture of the financial situation – but would also have
been able to spend more money on technical, scientific and colonial
development. In view of the ordeal by which she was about to be faced
such money would have been well spent, such additional contributions by
a wealthy people to the national exchequer well repaid.

And so we see France on the eve of the Great War, a rich and prosperous
people full of intellectual vigour; but a people sharply divided politically
and socially, distrustful of the State and inferior to her Eastern neighbour
in population and industrial resources and potential. If we discount the
operation of outside factors the odds must be overwhelmingly against her.

Notes

1 Seignobos, C., *Histoire sincère de la nation française*, p. 455.
2 The average consumption of alcohol was tripled between 1870 and 1914.
3 Maillaud, P., *France*, p. 17.
4 Clapham, J. H., *Economic Development of France and Germany, 1815–1914*,
   p. 234.

5 In the twenty years before the 1914–18 war French exports increased by 66 per
   cent; but those of Germany and Belgium increased by 124 per cent and 129 per
   cent respectively.
6 Maillaud, op. cit., p. 75.
7 ibid., p. 76.
8 A number of taxis were used to transport reinforcements.
9 *The War Memoirs of William Graves Sharp*, p. 147.
10 Clapham, op. cit., pp. 402–3.
11 Huddleston, Sisley, *France and the French*, p. 31. His comment on this
   tendency after 1918 also holds good of the years before 1914.
12 Reminiscent of the circle of the Listomères so well described by Balzac in *Le lys
   dans la vallée*.
13 Seignobos, op. cit., p. 467. For a fuller analysis, see Duroselle, J.-B., *La France
   et les Français 1900–1914*, ch. 1.
14 Huddleston, op. cit., p. 58. Cf. Leslie, S., *Memoir of J. E. C. Bodley*, p. 371,
   for Bodley's views on the French women.
15 The treatment of the native peoples, for instance in the Congo and Indo-
   China, has been sharply criticized by some Frenchmen for its inhumanity.
16 Marion, M., *Histoire financière de la France depuis 1715*, vol. 6, p. v ff.

Bibliography

Augé-Laribé, M., *L'évolution de la France agricole*, Paris, 1912.
Clapham, J. H., *The Economic Development of France and Germany,
1815–1914*, 4th edn, Cambridge, 1936.
Clough, Shepard B., *France: A History of National Economics 1789–1939*, New
York, 1939.
Duroselle, J.-B., *La France et les Français 1900–1914*, Paris, 1972.
Holt, Richard, *Sport and Society in Modern France*, London, 1981.
Huddleston, Sisley, *France and the French*, London, 1925.
Morazé, Charles, *La France bourgeoise, XVIIIᵉ–XXᵉ siècles*, 3rd edn, Paris, 1952.
Rebérioux, M., *La République radicale? 1898–1914*, Paris, 1975.
Seignobos, Charles, *Histoire sincère de la nation française*, 15th edn, Paris, 1933.

14

The Great War of 1914-18

On 28 June 1914 the Archduke Francis Ferdinand was assassinated. Once again, as so often in recent years, there was a strained situation in the Balkans, but not so strained as to deter Poincaré, the new President of the French Republic, with his Prime Minister, Viviani, from carrying out an engagement to visit Russia. An opportunity to reaffirm and strengthen the Russian alliance was not lightly to be discarded and on 16 July they set sail for the Baltic. On the 23rd Austria-Hungary delivered an ultimatum to Serbia and within a few days, in spite of Serbia's acceptance of all the Austrian demands, save one, the situation looked so threatening that the French Government, whose offers of mediation had proved vain, telegraphed urgently to the President and Viviani to return. On the 28th Austria-Hungary declared war on Serbia and on the following day Russia, anxious to check further Austrian aggrandisement in the Balkans and loth to stand by while fellow Slavs were crushed, ordered a partial mobilization which was converted into total mobilization on the 30th. The Russian action, unfortunately, did not lead Austria to call off hostilities. Instead it extended the area of tension. On the 31st Germany intervened with two ultimata, one demanding that Russia should immediately demobilize, the other asking for a statement from the French Government of the attitude they would adopt in case of war between Germany and Russia.

France had no intention of abandoning her Russian ally, but she was still eager to strain every nerve to avoid war. In order to show her will for peace she had withdrawn all troops to a distance of 10 km behind the Franco-German frontier, but the last chance of preventing German intervention and a general European war appeared to lie in persuading Great Britain to make a clear declaration that she would come to France's aid if she were attacked. The pressing appeals of the French Government were backed by a personal letter from President Poincaré to King George V, but in vain. British opinion was still greatly divided and by no means ready for intervention in a continental war arising out of an incident in the Balkans: the

British Government felt unable to give the assurances for which France was so anxious, and the German declaration of war on Russia on 1 August meant that a general European war was inevitable. That evening the French Government ordered a general mobilization and for the first time in history proclaimed a general state of siege throughout the country. Events now moved with extraordinary rapidity: on the 2nd German troops entered Luxembourg and demanded free passage through Belgium; and on 3 August, on the pretext that French aeroplanes had bombed Nuremberg, the German Government declared war on France. On the 4th, treating their solemn guarantee of her neutrality as a 'scrap of paper' they marched into Belgium. In face of this flagrant breach of international good faith, and of the menace to the Channel ports which it implied, the British Government could hesitate no longer. From that day all three powers of the Triple *Entente* were at war with Germany and Austria-Hungary, and on 3 September the *Entente* was converted into an Alliance by an agreement that no one of them would conclude a separate peace.

Thus for the third time within a century France was faced by a German invasion. But in contrast with 1815 and 1870 she was no longer alone and the knowledge that she had two powerful allies was a factor of immense moral and psychological importance in enabling the French people to meet the first tremendous shocks of the German onslaught with confidence and determination.

If Germany calculated that Republican France, so lately torn by dissension over the military law, so notorious for ministerial instability and seemingly so riddled by pacifism, would be an easy victim still more divided by war, she was bitterly disillusioned. The national emergency, the new aggression by the power which had seized Alsace and Lorraine in 1871 and had four times since then, in 1875, 1887, 1905 and 1911 threatened France with war again, brought all Frenchmen together. Ideological differences were temporarily sunk and the response to Poincaré's appeal for an *union sacrée* in face of the foe was immediate and moving in its sincerity. The Syndicalists and Socialists rallied to the defence of the country, and in 1915 a militant anti-Clerical like the octogenarian Émile Combes would accept a Cabinet post only if a prominent Right-Wing Catholic, Denys Cochin, were also included.[1] The Government, who had been ready to arrest a number of leading Syndicalists, pacifists, and suspected spies, named in a black list known as 'Carnet B', wisely left all Frenchmen on the list at liberty and also instructed prefects to suspend the laws against congregations. In the first seven months of the year there had been 654 strikes involving some 160,000 workers, but in the remaining five there were no more than eighteen. Workers and peasants, bourgeois and nobility, Catholics and freemasons, indeed every section of French society, with very few exceptions, did its best during these first months to place the cause of national defence before all else. In addition to the confidence derived from the fact of having allies there were other important factors to account for this unity. There were few who did not regard the territory of France as something sacred and its violation by an invader as sacrilege; and so the defence of French soil was an almost religious duty. Furthermore, French patriots could hope that the hour of *la justice immanente*, in which Gambetta had proclaimed his faith, was now at hand and that the injustice of 1871 would at last be repaired. France had never herself sought *revanche* by aggression, but now that war had been forced upon her she hoped to obtain it. Finally, just because it had been so patently forced upon her she could claim, as Poincaré did in his message of 4 August, that her cause was the cause of Right. This belief that she was fighting for justice and for the maintenance of a democratic way of life which was threatened by a militarist Imperialism, undoubtedly helped to rally the Left. It was well that this was so, for in the trials ahead France was to need every addition of strength which unity could give.

In area, population and resources the Allies had an immense superiority. Their European populations alone exceeded those of the Central Powers by more than 100 million; additional manpower and raw materials of all kinds might be drawn from their overseas dominions, which together covered a considerable part of the globe; and they had the mastery of the seas in spite of the strength of the German fleet. But men and materials were of no avail unless they were trained and adapted for military purposes. The Germans and Austrians, who had long been preparing for war, were at the outset only slightly inferior in the numbers they could put into the field and this inferiority was more than compensated by their greater weight of armament and more efficient military organization. As in 1870, Germany counted upon this, on superior mobility, and on the advantage given her by having the initiative. She confidently expected to be able to destroy the French armies within six weeks. Once France was out of the war she would be able to dispose of Russia and Great Britain at her leisure. Thus everything depended upon the power of France to withstand the initial shock.

The immediate French mobilization of some 3,700,000 men, 2,887,000 of whom were reservists,[2] took place with smoothness unknown in 1870. By the middle of August the army numbered some forty-six regular infantry and ten cavalry divisions. In addition there were twenty-five divisions in reserve. On its left flank it co-operated with the Belgian army of six divisions and the British Expeditionary Force of five divisions. Against these eighty-two infantry divisions under three different commands Germany massed nearly the whole of her forces, seventy-eight divisions under a single command.[3] The French High Command were well aware that the main German assault was likely to be in the west and that a German invasion of Belgium was probable, but they made a grave error in believing that for political reasons the Germans would not advance in Belgium beyond the Meuse. Consequently the bulk of the French forces was concentrated too far south and the Germans were able to carry out a vast sweeping movement on their right flank through Belgium and to win the so-called Battle of the Frontiers. At the end of August the French and British troops were in retreat almost all along the line. By the beginning of September most of Belgium was in German hands, the Belgian army was blockaded in Antwerp, and the army of Von Klück had swept down through Northern France, crossed the Marne at several points and penetrated almost to the gates of Paris. On 2 September, at the instance of the Commander-in-Chief and anxious not to repeat the error of 1870 and risk being blockaded in the capital, which it was agreed to defend to the last, the Government left Paris for Bordeaux. (They returned on 20 December.)

For a few agonizing days it looked as though Germany's confident expectation of a speedy decision in the west was going to be justified. But in Joffre, the massive, imperturbable French Commander-in-Chief, the German Von Moltke had found his match. At exactly the right moment when Von Klück had extended his forces too far Joffre launched a counter-offensive against the German right flank. The Battle of the Marne was a momentous victory for the Allies, and when the German troops failed to break through at Verdun, and their subsequent drive to seize the Channel Ports was frustrated at Ypres and Dixmude in November, it was clear that the enemy had been out-generalled. The superior coolness of Joffre had saved France from disaster, but unfortunately neither the French nor the British had the men or material to follow up their advantage. By the end of the year the opposing armies were interlocked in a struggle on a front which extended from the English Channel across North France to the Vosges and the Swiss frontier and which was to undergo comparatively little change of contour until the last phase, in spite of titanic efforts by both sides to break it. The 'miraculous' victory of the Marne meant that the war in the west was to be converted from a war of movement, which nearly all the prophets on both sides, soldiers, politicians and economists alike, had confidently expected to be over by Christmas 1914, into a war of trenches which was to drag on for nearly four years.[4]

The deadlock on the western front and the consequent prospect of a long struggle changed the whole perspective of the war and made it necessary for the French and other Allied Governments to adjust themselves to an entirely novel situation. In a long war their superior manpower and resources might very well be the decisive factor: and so the training and equipment of men, the provision of munitions and the maintenance of food and other essential supplies became problems of the first magnitude, while the quest for new allies and for financial aid, the enforcement of an economic blockade and attempts to create diversions in other parts of Europe became important objects of policy.

The process of adjustment was no easy one. Hitherto Governments, eager for and relying on a quick decision, had thrown most of their manpower into the forces and been content to fight on stocks of munitions and other war supplies, while in France full-scale mobilization had caused a temporary paralysis of commerce and industry and led to a sharp rise in unemployment. The problem for France was aggravated by heavy losses in men and material. The tremendous battles of the first four months had cost her 455,000 men killed or missing and another 400,000 wounded.[5] They had saddled her with nearly 900,000 refugees, including some 150,000 Belgians, some 600,000 of whom were virtually destitute and had to be given relief.[6] Furthermore, they meant that she was obliged to continue the war the poorer for the loss of ten departments which had been wholly or partly invaded. These covered no more than 11.5 per cent of French territory,[7] but they included some of the most fertile land and some of the most important industrial areas in the country. In 1913 they had produced no less than 20.4 per cent of the wheat crop, 25.52 per cent of France's oats and 49.48 per cent of her sugar-beet production.[8] They contained 16.3 per cent of her manufacturing capacity, 21.1 per cent of the labour employed in manufacturing industries and 41 per cent of the steam motive power utilized in those industries.[9] Their loss meant the loss of an important part of the metallurgical, coal-mining and textile industries vital for war production. It had to be made up by costly imports.

Thus the prospect of a long war materially modified and extended the tasks of government. As Tocqueville had written more than seventy years earlier: 'War cannot fail to add enormously to the functions of civil government; almost inevitably it concentrates in the hands of the latter the direction of the whole population and the direction of everything.'[10] So it was now; and the remarkable achievement of the Third Republic was that it was able to adapt itself to the new conditions without any fundamental change of constitution. There were many, even in France, who had doubted the capacity of the Republican regime to direct the country in time of war and the doubt had only recently again been expressed in a volume by the Socialist deputy, Marcel Sembat, to which he gave the arresting title of *Faites un Roi, sinon faites la paix*. These gloomy prophets were to be confounded. The Government, for a few months on its own responsibility and then for the remainder of the war in more or less close

Map 6: 1914: Main centres of industrial concentration

collaboration with the legislature, was able to conduct the war without any fundamental modification of the parliamentary regime of 1875.

When the Chambers met in special session in August 1914, they had authorized the Government to maintain the state of siege for the duration of hostilities, to proclaim a moratorium, to suspend the freedom of the Press, to incur certain kinds of expenditure without reference to them, and to obtain short-term loans or special advances from the Bank of France. The emergency at the end of the month and the German threat to Paris had impelled Viviani to reform his Government in accordance with the principles of *union sacrée* so as to include some of the most eminent statesmen, Briand, Delcassé, Millerand and Ribot, as well as two prominent Socialists, Marcel Sembat and the veteran Jules Guesde, and very soon afterwards, a Presidential decree terminated the parliamentary session. During the critical four months which followed the Government were forced to improvise all kinds of measures in order to meet the exigencies of war and they did so without reference to the Chambers. Their powers over the press developed into a wide censorship; they instituted summary courts martial at the front on Joffre's request; they set up all manner of new public services and by decree considerably modified existing legislation about army recruitment and freedom of trade. From 2 September to 22 December 'all powers were concentrated in the hands of the Government: it was invested, on its own authority, with a kind of dictatorship'.[11] And, such was the desire for strong government, such the continuing force of *union sacrée* that this dictatorship was accepted virtually without protest or question.

The need to improvise continued, as did legislation by decree. Gradually, under the pressure of military requirements, the State exercised increasing direction of the economic life of the country, requisitioning crops and purchasing coal supplies, fixing maximum prices and erecting a multiplicity of controls. Often these overlapped and duplicated one another, causing muddle and delay; but such defects, as we in this country knew full well, are inseparable from any improvised war-time bureaucracy; and in the France of 1914–18 controls were indispensable. Private enterprise, so highly individualist and so little organized for associative purposes, though it did much, had neither the capital nor the authority necessary for directing the French economic war effort unguided by State supervision and aid. Gradually, then, as the war proceeded, the State, without any doctrinaire intention, accustomed Frenchmen to state interference and even to the idea of nationalization. It also accustomed an increasing number to look to it for aid and benefits – pensions and relief of all kinds which had to be paid either out of charity or as incentives to fresh effort. These things were of great importance. But in the new period of war, which followed the battles of movement, the Government no longer acted wholly on their own. According to the Constitution, the Chambers were bound to reassemble in the second week in January and there is no evidence that the Government had any intention of prolonging their dictatorship beyond that date. On the contrary, they took the Chambers into partnership, allowed them to sit in permanent session, determining their own vacations, and granted Senators and deputies who were serving in the forces the right to obtain furloughs in order to take part in parliamentary business. The executive still enjoyed considerable independence; party quarrels were silenced by the *union sacrée*; deputies were loth to overturn Cabinets when the country was in danger; and unwelcome criticism could be checked by alleging reasons of military secrecy: none the less, the Chambers once again played a part in public affairs and gradually showed an increasing wish to extend their control. This reassertion of parliament's desire to check the executive and to call it to account was to have important effects upon the direction of the war.

The most urgent requirements for the continued effective prosecution of the war were, as we have seen, those of manpower and munitions. By the beginning of 1915 the supply of light artillery was nearly exhausted and there was a shortage of most kinds of munitions. The initial unemployment had been largely reduced and there was a pressing need for more skilled labour. Women did much to help fill the gap made by mobilization, and engaged in all manner of occupations usually reserved for men. They became bakers, wheelwrights, masons, gang foremen, train drivers and much else besides. But the need for skilled labour in war factories could only be met by releases of men from the army and in July arrangements were made for 500,000 men to return to industry. Eighteen months later the decline in food production also gave cause for anxiety – not only was there the loss of the north-east departments, but the mobilization of agricultural labour without reserve had meant that most of the farms of France were left to the care of old men, women and children. They made heroic efforts, but inevitably the yield of crops declined and land went out of cultivation. Hence, despite attempts to check the fall in production by the use of prisoners of war and of what little foreign and colonial labour could be obtained, another 300,000 men had to be released to work on the farms. Nevertheless, large quantities of foodstuffs still had to be imported.

As the casualties on the western front mounted, the problem of manpower became more and more acute, and in their attempt to maintain the numerical strength of the forces the army authorities had time and time again to relax their standards of physical fitness. Behind the lines man hours were saved by greater standardization, the remodelling of plant and more scientific factory organization. The conditions of some French industries were transformed by the introduction of American methods. But all these measures were merely palliatives. France could not have borne the strain of maintaining the western front and keeping up the manufacture of munitions and agricultural production had she been alone. Already, before the end of 1915, Joffre had expressed his doubts of the country's ability to endure a long war of attrition unless the Allies took a large share in operations on land. France's manpower problem was only soluble with the help of her Allies. Fortunately that help was now speedily forthcoming, and, although throughout the war the French continued to hold by far the largest section of the western front,[12] Great Britain was soon able to send large numbers of men across the Channel. By the autumn of 1915 the original divisions of Old Contemptibles had swelled into the first thirty-five of Kitchener's army; by the spring of 1916 they numbered seventy. Meanwhile the Russians had borne the brunt of the German offensive of 1915. They had been obliged to give up the whole of Poland, Galicia and Lithuania, and had suffered enormous losses of men and material. But once again the Germans failed to deliver a knock-out blow. The eastern front still remained in being to occupy a large number of divisions. Without it, it is very doubtful whether the western front could have withstood the whole weight of the enemy forces.

The problem of munitions was not solved before Parliament had displayed its concern and shown the revival of its influence upon policy. At first this influence was exerted mainly through its standing committees. In particular the Army Committees of the two Chambers were active in criticizing the conduct of the War Ministry, the alleged inefficiency in dealing with the munitions shortage, and the weakness of the civil authorities in tolerating the growth of an enormous military bureaucracy. Their attacks led in August 1915 to the resignation of Millerand, the War Minister, whose general policy had been to leave Joffre and the army authorities a very free hand. His resignation was soon followed by that of the whole Cabinet. It was succeeded by a second *union sacrée* Ministry, headed this time by Briand and including two octogenarians, Combes of anti-clerical fame and Freycinet, a historic link with the national defence of 1870.

Meanwhile the area of conflict was steadily widening. In October 1914, Turkey had joined the Central Powers, thereby barring the easiest way of communications between France and her remote Russian Ally; and British and French attempts to reopen it by seizing the Straits had met with a sanguinary check in the Dardanelles. In May 1915 Italy entered the war, selling her alliance to the Allies who had offered the highest price in the large territorial gains promised by the Secret Treaty of London of April that year; and in September Bulgaria, eager for revenge on her old enemy Serbia, cast in her lot with Germany, thereby bringing about the final collapse of the Serbs. Thus, on balance, the advantage in the other European theatres of war by the end of 1915 lay very definitely with the Central Powers. In the West, too, victory for the Allies seemed as remote as ever. Attempts to create useful diversions to relieve the Russians were of little avail, and, as the stalemate continued, so parliamentary suspicions of the wide powers and jealous independence exercised by Joffre and his subordinates tended to grow. In September the Government demanded that Joffre should release four divisions to serve as part of an Anglo-French expeditionary force to be sent under General Sarrail to Salonika in the vain hope of relieving the harassed Serbs; but Joffre protested against the new arrangements and the difficulty was solved by a decree of 2 December extending his authority to cover the new army of the Near East. From the first big clash of civil and military authority Joffre had triumphed and emerged a Generalissimo. So, too, early in 1916 Briand stood by him when Galliéni, the Minister of War, who had criticized the weakness of certain defensive positions near Verdun, was proved to have been right and submitted to his colleagues a memorandum on the 'reorganization of the High Command'. It was Galliéni and not Joffre who resigned.

It was well for France that this was so, for the calm manner in which Joffre adhered to his plans in the face of great provocation saved her from a new disaster. In February 1916 Falkenhayn, Moltke's successor as German Commander-in-Chief, launched his great offensive against the seemingly vulnerable Verdun salient, to the retention of which he rightly believed the French would attach great importance. He reckoned that the attempt to defend it against an enormous concentration of German men and armament would lead to such heavy losses – a proportion of 5 to 2 – that France would be bled white and no longer able to continue the struggle. But he, too, like Moltke, miscalculated: the French casualties were indeed heavy, 275,000, but in that remorseless six months' battle the German losses were almost as many.[13] Moreover, Joffre coolly persisted with his own plan for an offensive on the Somme, and the fact that he was able to deliver it in July, even though only on a much reduced scale, finally frustrated Falkenhayn's plan. The Germans had to divert troops to the north; on the Somme the Allied artillery was, for the first time, superior; and in the ensuing battle the enemy lost no less than 267,000 men and 6000 officers.[14] Verdun was saved and its stubborn defence for ever afterwards remained a glorious symbol of French gallantry and powers of resistance. But the Somme was costly, too, for France, and once again the Allies had failed to break through. Ever since Galliéni's resignation, criticism of the High Command had increased and Parliament now at last vigorously asserted the right of the legislature to exercise some measure of control over the executive and to curtail the liberty of the military power. By June 1916 it had established its claim to sit in Secret Committee in order to debate matters which could not safely be discussed in public, and in this Secret Committee the Government once again had to face interpellations as in pre-war days. At the same time the Army Committees obtained authorization both to inspect conditions in munition factories and arsenals in the interior and to investigate 'the preparation of means of defence and offence, whether industrial or military' in the zone of operations itself.[15] Much could be said in criticism of this parliamentary interference in military matters, but there is little doubt that its general effect was salutary. It provided a useful corrective to military complacency and helped to check the arbitrariness and inefficiency or wastefulness of military administration. It was, however, a severe blow to the Commander-in-Chief and by the end of the year, after the failure of the Somme offensive, it was clear that Joffre's position was seriously shaken. The Government decided to relieve him of his command, but mindful of the great services he had rendered they made him Marshal of France. With his removal civil authority asserted itself still more vigorously. There was no longer a unified command over all French armies, but each front had its separate Commander-in-Chief, while the general direction of the war was left to the Minister of War, who now 'unhesitatingly travelled about the front, visited the army commanders, and called for the plans of attack'.[16] In April 1917 the Minister was aided in his task by the appointment for the first time of a Chief of Staff, first of all Pétain and subsequently Foch.

Thus, largely as the result of parliamentary pressure, there had been vital changes in the High Command. Unfortunately at the same time the prolongation of the war began to impair the unity of Frenchmen. While the principle of the *union sacrée* was as yet uncontested in Parliament there were disquieting signs of a rift outside. As early as the autumn of 1914 a handful of Syndicalist leaders, including the secretary of the powerful Union des Métaux, had protested against the collaboration of the Socialist Party in the Government of National Defence. During the following two years Socialists and Syndicalists in neutral states had begun to organize propaganda denouncing the 'Imperialist' war and calling for a speedy peace without indemnities and without annexations. This propaganda gradually had some effect in the belligerent countries, all of which were by the end of 1916 beginning to experience internal difficulties. In December it was significant that nearly half the delegates at the French Socialist Party's annual congress voted in favour of resuming relations with Socialists in other (including enemy) countries, and that nearly half also opposed the continued participation of the Socialists in the Government. It was clear that the days of *union sacrée* were numbered, and in the following September the Socialists declined to take part in a new Painlevé Cabinet.

Meanwhile the military position in the west had been seriously affected by events in the east. By the autumn of 1916 most of Roumania which had joined the Allies in August had been overrun, and Russia, isolated and disorganized, was so crippled by social and political discontent, that her Allies were led to fear the outbreak of revolution and the conclusion of a separate peace. In such circumstances the tonic of success in the west was all the more desirable, but unfortunately all the more difficult to achieve.

General Nivelle, however, Joffre's successor as Commander-in-Chief on the western front, was a man of sanguine temperament. Eager to put an end to the 'war of attrition', he was wedded to the idea of a big offensive, which, in accordance with a principle adopted at one of the inter-allied military conferences now held at increasingly frequent intervals, was to be simultaneous with offensives on all fronts. But the outbreak of the threatened revolution in Russia and the overthrow of the Tsardom in March 1917 paralysed activity both on the Italian and on the eastern Russo-Roumanian front, since the Italians feared to draw upon themselves the whole weight of the Austro-Hungarian army. Moreover, a strategic withdrawal by the Germans in the sector of the German front on which Nivelle proposed to attack, further modified the chances of success. None the less, in spite of the criticisms both of several of his own subordinates and of Haig, the British Commander-in-Chief, Nivelle, strongly backed by Poincaré, persisted in carrying out his plan. The offensive launched in April, from which he had so optimistically expected a triumphant success, was a complete failure. On 15 May Nivelle, his authority gone, was relieved of his command and succeeded by Pétain, who had distinguished himself at Verdun, while Foch became Chief of Staff.

These events, the paralysis of Russia and the bitter disappointment at this fresh check in the west, coinciding as they did with abortive peace soundings and with more intensive Socialist and defeatist propaganda, had disquieting consequences in France. In May and June there were disturbances among workers in Paris and the St Etienne district and a large number of strikes, and on 20 May several regiments refused to return to the line, while two at Soissons mutinied and threatened to march on Paris. These troubles among workers and soldiers were not unconnected, but although defeatist propaganda was circulated by the Fédération des Métaux and the extremist Comité de Défense Syndicaliste, there is no evidence that they were part of an organized conspiracy. When the workers in the factory or the *poilus* home from the front saw how many behind the lines were living in comfort and making handsome profits while boasting of their patriotism, they became disillusioned and bitter. The enthusiasm of the first months had long since given way to a dogged resignation. At the front the fundamental cause of the wavering of morale was military, a revulsion not against resisting the Germans but against the seemingly endless series of useless and bloody offensives ordained by unsuccessful generals. Pétain understood and in both cases the authorities acted leniently: the Government refused to employ force against the workers and adopted a conciliatory attitude towards the Unions; in a few weeks the troubles died down: in the army about fifty only of the 554 mutineers condemned to death by court martial were executed; and Pétain soon restored discipline by wise improvements in the conditions of service – food was bettered, leave and rest periods were given more regularly and generously, and closer contact was established between officers and men. None the less, the failure of the Nivelle offensive and the unrest following upon it meant that for several months the French army was reduced to a comparatively passive role and that the British forces during that period had to bear the main brunt of operations. Moreover, the disturbances, the defeatist propaganda and the leniency of the Minister of the Interior caused disquiet in political circles. Here too, there were signs that the determination of some was beginning to waver. Men like Caillaux were ready to think of a compromise peace; and the revelations of the summer and autumn with their suggestions of treason and conspiracy led to a growing demand for stronger leadership. In July Clemenceau made a violent attack upon the Minister of the Interior, Malvy, denouncing both his weakness in dealing with the defeatist Syndicalists and his personal association with the once Anarchist editor of a suspect paper, *Le Bonnet Rouge*. As a result of this and of a Press campaign which ensued, Malvy resigned on 31 August, and his resignation was soon followed by that of the whole Ribot Cabinet which had been in office since Briand retired in March.

The next Ministry, headed by Painlevé, was weaker than any of its war-time predecessors because, as we have seen, the Socialists now definitely broke the *union sacrée* and refused their support. It was also weakened by the revelation of further instances of treachery, notably the acceptance by a dubious individual named Bolo Pasha of 10,000,000 francs from the Deutsche Bank for the purpose of buying the majority of shares in *Le Journal*. Attacked by the Socialists on the Left and by all those further to the Right who were anxious for much more forceful treatment of the defeatists, it fell in November, the only Cabinet during the war to be overthrown on an adverse vote in the Chamber. By this time the outlook at home and abroad was gloomy indeed. At home the atmosphere was poisoned by suspicion and mistrust; abroad, although the failure of the unrestricted submarine campaign launched by Germany in January had saved Great Britain from dire peril and the entry of the USA on the side of the Allies in May had opened up an immense hope, prospects had darkened with the Italian defeat at Caporetto in October and the Bolshevik Revolution in November. The Italian defeat revealed that the morale of the Italian troops had also gravely deteriorated, and necessitated the diversion of a number of French and British divisions to the new line of resistance on the Piave. The Bolshevik Revolution made the withdrawal of Russia from the war a practical certainty. When this happened Germany's war on two fronts would be at an end and she would be free to transfer almost the whole weight of her forces to the West. The first handful of American troops had landed in France in June 1917, but they had been a mere handful, and no one could say whether others would follow in sufficient force to provide the necessary reserves to meet the German offensive which must inevitably be delivered in 1918. In this grim and depressing situation a tonic was essential. Fortunately one was to hand. On 14 November the President, Poincaré, called upon Clemenceau to take over the government of France. 'So long as victory is possible,' Poincaré had written in August 1914, 'he (Clemenceau) is capable of upsetting everything! A day will perhaps come when I shall add: Now that everything seems to be lost, he alone is capable of saving everything.'[17] The day had come. In the words of Winston Churchill: 'The last desperate stroke had to be played. France had resolved to unbar the cage and let her tiger loose upon all foes, beyond the trenches or in her midst.'[18]

Clemenceau, the stormy petrel of French politics for over forty years, was now an old man of seventy-six, but he had a toughness and dynamic energy far beyond that of many who were half his age. A Jacobin Radical in the classical tradition of 1793, he had, in his paper *L'Homme Libre* which, when censorship interfered, at once reappeared as *L'Homme Enchaîné*, and as President of the Army Committee of the Senate, been an incessant gadfly since the outbreak of war, goading all, sparing none with his relentless exposures of inefficiency and ruthless demands for greater energy. Now he had but one aim – victory; and home and foreign policy alike were summed up in his famous phrase: *'Je fais la guerre!'*

The effect of Clemenceau's accession to power was immediate; a sigh of relief passed through the country and public confidence was rapidly restored. France now had the strong government which she so urgently required and the war was to end as it began under a virtual dictatorship: only Clemenceau did not silence the Chambers or abandon the appearance of co-operation with them. Some months earlier they had refused a demand by Briand for authority to take all necessary measures by decree;

but now, on 10 February 1918, they granted to Clemenceau the power to legislate by decree in all spheres of economic activity, and he induced them to abandon the Secret Committee practice which hampered the work and authority of the Government. Nor was there any revival of the *union sacrée*; the Socialists still held aloof, but they were a minority over whom at such a moment Clemenceau could ride roughshod. Such was the emergency and such the public trust in Clemenceau that he was able to impose his will upon parliament almost without question; and as his Cabinet, like Gambetta's 'Grand Ministère', was composed of much lesser men than himself, the dictatorship was virtually that of a single man. Clemenceau in himself was a Committee of Public Safety.

Waging war at home meant short shrift for those whose will to wage it had faltered. Painlevé had fallen because of the dissensions in his Cabinet. Clemenceau at once made examples. Malvy and Caillaux were arraigned before the High Court; Bolo Pasha, Mata Hari and other spies and traitors were executed; and rough justice was dealt to many lesser suspects. Many who were innocent may well have suffered, but there could be no Dreyfus Affair in time of extreme peril. Public opinion demanded strong government and this was what Clemenceau was determined to give. Reason of state and the requirements of public safety, which he had denounced so vigorously in the days of Dreyfus, were now overriding in their urgency.

Waging war against the enemy meant above all doing the utmost to hasten American aid and to secure unity of command on the decisive western front. With the approach of spring the situation became ever more critical. The Russians had concluded an armistice in December 1917; on 3 March 1918 they signed the peace of Brest-Litovsk and withdrew from the war. On 16 March Roumania capitulated and five days later the Germans launched their threatened offensive. They struck with tremendous force between Arras and La Fère at the point of junction between the British and French armies, surprised the British, routed Gough's troops, and drove a wedge between the Allied forces. The situation looked so serious that Clemenceau prepared for the necessity of moving the Government once more from Paris. But the crisis settled the question of military co-ordination. At an historic conference at Doullens on 26 March, attended by Poincaré, Clemenceau, the British War Minister, Lord Milner, and the British and French Commanders-in-Chiefs of Staff, Foch was entrusted with the task of co-ordinating the operations of the Allied armies on the western front; on 3 April he was given the strategic direction of these operations, and on the 17th he formally became 'General in Chief of the Allied Armies in France'. Unity of command was established and confidence restored. In Foch, a Pyrenean like Joffre, calm, quick and imaginative, the Allies had the man they needed. But, although a swift move by French troops filled the gap on the Somme, gruelling days were still ahead. The attack near Arras was only the beginning of the German offensive and Ludendorff was prepared to throw in his whole strength to force a decision before American soldiers could reach Europe in sufficient numbers to turn the scale. An attack on the Lys in April, held by the British at Kemmel Hill, was followed in May by the catastrophe of the Chemin-des-Dames. The French in turn were surprised and the Germans broke through to the Marne once more and penetrated as far as Château Thierry, only 50 miles from Paris. The capital was again in danger and the enemy began to bombard it at long range. Behind the lines morale began to waver anew. At once there were clamours for scapegoats and demands that Foch and Pétain should be relieved of their commands. At such a moment Clemenceau was indomitable; he refused to listen to the Deputies' demands for a public debate or a Secret Committee. The Generals had his complete confidence, and he told the Chamber that it must be patient: 'There is only one thing that matters: that is the final success, the last victory.' To get it, he was prepared, like Gambetta in 1871 and like a great Englishman later, to wage war unconquerably: 'The Germans may take Paris,' he told General Mordacq, 'but that will not prevent me from going on with the war. We will fight on the Loire, we will fight on the Garonne, we will fight even on the Pyrenees. And if at last we are driven off the Pyrenees, we will continue the war at sea.'[19]

His confidence and patience were amply justified. The Germans were held at the gates of Paris, and their last big attack in Champagne in July was a failure followed by a speedy French counter-attack which brought them to the brink of disaster and obliged them to abandon almost all the territory they had conquered since 27 May. Already, in June, American troops had distinguished themselves in the battle area between Rheims and Soissons, and in July the first independent units had been in action at Château Thierry. By 1 August no less than 1,145,000 men had been landed in France and nineteen divisions were ready to be sent to the front. Reinforcements were following at the rate of 250,000 a month. The tide had turned: the time had come, wrote Foch, 'to abandon the defensive attitude hitherto imposed by numerical inferiority and to go over to the offensive'[20] – the time to which he had looked forward from the moment when he had assumed the Supreme Command. By the beginning of September the German forces were in full retreat and the German Government and High Command had realized that all chance of winning the war had gone. In the middle of the month Austria-Hungary was suggesting peace negotiations; by the end, the Allied Army of the Near East, now under the command of General Franchet d'Espérey, had helped to bring Bulgaria to her knees, and the German Government themselves, abandoned by their allies, had decided, too, to ask for an armistice and peace. On 11 November the armistice was signed and France's long ordeal was over. Through the help of her allies, the tenacity of leaders such as Joffre and Poincaré, Clemenceau and Foch, and the gallantry and courage of the great mass of her people, soldiers and civilians, men and women alike, she had survived and emerged victorious. For four years she had sustained the greatest part of the western front; her troops had fought at the Dardanelles, in Serbia, in Italy and at Murmansk; they had conquered Togoland and helped to take the Cameroons. Her ships had guarded the Mediterranean. Her Empire had remained loyal and in it she had recruited a great reserve of manpower, 198,000 workers and 669,000 soldiers, while Lyautey had completed the pacification of Morocco and even raised troops there to fight in Europe. Her institutions had survived virtually unchanged, and shown that they were supple as well as strong. But the cost of her efforts was tremendous. She was victorious, but exhausted. One million three hundred thousand of her best men were dead and 740,000 maimed; 289,000 houses had been destroyed and 3,000,000 acres of good land rendered unfit for cultivation.[21] She was short of labour and raw materials; plant and rolling stock urgently needed renewing. The growth of public expenditure had been enormous and had had to be met by loans and the issue of paper money with a consequent rise of prices and danger of inflation. Her public debt had increased from $33\frac{1}{2}$ milliard francs in 1913 to over 219 milliard in 1919.[22] She owed 33 millard francs to foreign countries and a once favourable trade balance now showed a deficit of 21 milliards.[23] Her economy had been seriously disrupted, her society in many ways revolutionized by the incidence of State control. All the European belligerents were in a similar plight, but in the West it was France which had been the battlefield and France with her declining population was least able to support the loss of manpower. After the armistice it remained to make peace and to garner the fruits of victory; but on a sober reckoning it was to appear highly doubtful whether they could ever compensate her for the losses of war. 'My work is finished,' said Foch to Clemenceau, on 11 November when he handed him the completed document of the armistice. 'Your work is beginning.'[24] Clemenceau could be relied on to do his best, but even he could not secure a peace which fully satisfied French requirements.

Notes

1 *The War Memoirs of William Graves Sharp*, p. 43.
2 Fontaine, A., *French Industry during the War*, p. 26. The reservists were ill-trained. By the end of the war 7,935,000 men had been called up.

3 These figures are taken from Renouvin, P., *La crise européenne et la grande guerre*, pp. 187–8, 208.

4 It is only fair to recall that 'Had it not been for Russia's immediate offensive in East Prussia [in accordance with the stipulations of her military convention with France], the German invasion of France would probably have been as complete in 1914 as it was in 1940.' Namier, L. B., *Diplomatic Prelude: 1938–1939*, p. x.

5 Fontaine, A., *French industry during the War*, p. 27.

6 ibid., p. 37.

7 ibid., p. 20.

8 Augé-Laribé, M., *Agriculture and Food Supply in France during the War*, p. 55.

9 Fontaine, op. cit., p. 20.

10 Cit. Renouvin, P., *The Forms of War Government in France*, vol. 2, p. 11.

11 ibid., p. 99.

12 Fontaine, op. cit., p. 28. 'At the Armistice the Belgian army occupied 30 km of front, the British army 90 km, the American army 100 km, the French army 330 km.'

13 Renouvin, P., *La crise européenne et la grande guerre*, p. 331. Considerably higher figures are given by Falls, C., *A Hundred Years of War*, p. 184.

14 Renouvin, P., *La crise européenne et la grande guerre*, p. 338.

15 Renouvin, P., *The Forms of War Government in France*, p. 133.

16 ibid., p. 88.

17 Cit. Jackson, J. Hampden, *Clemenceau and the Third Republic*, p. 168.

18 ibid., p. 171.

19 ibid., p. 179.

20 Cit. Renouvin, P., *La crise européenne et la grande guerre*, p. 545.

21 ibid., p. 605. But Ferro, M., *The Great War 1914–1918*, says 700,000 houses were destroyed and Bernard, P., *La fin d'un monde 1914–1918*, that 388,800 men were 'mutilés'.

22 Renouvin, P., *La crise européene et la grande guerre*, p. 604.

23 The percentage ratio of imports to exports had increased from 123 in 1912 to 472 in 1918. Fontaine, op. cit., p. 18.

24 Cit. Jackson, op. cit., p. 186.

Bibliography

Augé-Laribé, M. and Pinot, P., *Agriculture and Food Supply in France during the War*, Yale, 1927.

Becker, J.-J., *Comment les Français sont entrés dans la guerre*, Paris, 1977.

Bernard, P., *La fin d'un monde 1914–1929*, Paris, 1975.

Chastenet, J., *Jours inquiets et jours sanglants, 1906–18*, Paris, 1955.

Duroselle, J.-B., *La France et les Français 1914–1920*, Paris, 1972.

Ferro, M., *The Great War 1914–1918*, London, 1973.

Fontaine, Arthur, *French Industry during the War*, Yale, 1926.

Jackson, J. Hampden, *Clemenceau and the Third Republic*, London, 1946.

Jèze, G. and Truchy, H., *The War Finance of France*, Yale, 1927.

Kemp, T., *The French Economy 1913–1939*, London, 1972.

King, Jere Clemens, *Generals and Politicians: Conflict between France's High Command, Parliament and Government, 1914–1918*, Berkeley, 1951.

Néré, J., *The Foreign Policy of France from 1914–1945*, London, 1974.

Pedroncini, G., *Les Mutineries de 1917*, Paris, 1967.

Poincaré, R., *Au service de la France: neuf années de souvenirs*, 10 vols, Paris, 1926–33.

Renouvin, P., *The Forms of War Government in France*, Yale, 1927.

Renouvin, P., *La crise européenne et la grande guerre (1904–18)*, Paris, 1924; 5th edn, (title slightly changed), 1969.

Renouvin, P., *L'armistice de Rethondes 11 Novembre 1918*, Paris, 1968.

Stevenson, D., *French War Aims against Germany 1914–1919*, Oxford, 1982.

Tanenbaum, J. K., *General Maurice Sarrail 1856–1929: The French Army and Left-Wing Politics*, Chapel Hill, NC, 1974.

Watson, D. R., *Georges Clemenceau: A Political Biography*, London, 1974.

15

From victory to the economic slump of 1929

France had been three times invaded by German troops and four times threatened with war by German Governments during the space of a century. Whereas 1870–1 had cost her less than 150,000 killed,[1] 1914–18 had meant death for 1,300,000, and the strain of the four years' war just ended had, as we have seen, been almost unbearable. Her troops had re-entered Alsace and Lorraine and no ally would deny her right to their recovery. But the achievement of *revanche* and fulfilment of *la justice immanente* still left unsolved the wider problem of Franco-German relations. Germany was defeated and for a moment torn by revolution, but her population was still far greater than that of France – where the casualties of war had led to an increase in the fall of the birth-rate – her territory was virtually untouched by the devastations of war and she retained an enormous industrial potential. What guarantee could there be that in twenty or thirty years' time, when she had recovered her strength, this great, efficient, industrious nation, with her memory of vast ambitions frustrated, would not in her turn seek *revanche* and make a fresh bid for the world domination so nearly within her grasp in 1914 and in 1918? Unless there were to be an immediate and enduring rapprochement between the two countries, a thing impossible for Frenchmen who were in a state of impassioned hatred engendered by the strain and horrors of war, the only solution could be one of force. France must have material guarantees strong enough to ensure her security and Germany must be crippled and kept down. This problem of security against a recurrence of German aggression is the central and thorniest problem of the peace negotiations between France and her Allies, and because those negotiations fail to provide a solution, it overshadows the whole of subsequent French history.

The armistice of 11 November 1918 had been greeted by most of the peoples of Europe with an immense relief and with an immense hope;

relief that the carnage was over, hope that a new device of international organization would make the repetition of such slaughter for ever impossible. Had not President Wilson in his famous message to Congress on 8 January proposed as the last of his Fourteen Points the formation of a new holy alliance of peoples, a League of Nations, whose object would be to afford 'mutual guarantees of political independence and territorial integrity to great and small states alike'?[2]

For most Frenchmen, at any rate at first, the League was, however, only alluring if it could be made to ensure security by the use of force; and when it was clear that Wilson and Lloyd George would have nothing to do with Léon Bourgeois' plan to endow the League with its own army and the power to enforce military sanctions, Clemenceau, the leader of the French delegation, lost all interest in its organization. For him it was clear that the Franco-German problem must be settled by other means and that the end of security could be achieved only by hard bargaining at the conference table. So it was that he demanded that Germany should pay the whole cost of the war, that the Saar district with its coal mines should be ceded permanently to France, and that the whole of the left bank of the Rhine should be detached from Germany, occupied permanently by the Allies, and constituted as a separate state or states. This solution of the Rhineland problem was considered by Foch to be essential for French security and his view was shared by Poincaré, a large number of politicians, and the great mass of French opinion. But British and American ideas on these questions were very different – annexations and separations of territory went clean-counter to the principle of self-determination which was so dear to President Wilson's heart and which had been newly consecrated in the Fourteen Points; while to Lloyd George an independent Rhineland spelt a new Alsace-Lorraine, and permanent occupation a commitment which no British Government could undertake. Thus it came about that Clemenceau, 'terrifying figure' though Lloyd George sometimes found him to be, was forced to compromise on every one of his main demands. By the Treaty of Versailles, signed on 28 June 1919, in the Hall of Mirrors, where Bismarck had proclaimed the German Empire, France resumed sovereignty over Alsace-Lorraine without having to hold a plebiscite, and as a result of Germany's renouncing of her colonies added almost the whole of Togoland and the Cameroons to her African Empire[3]; but instead of Germany's paying for the whole cost of the war, the Allies were to receive reparations for all damage done to civilians and their property; instead of obtaining full sovereignty over the Saar district, France had to be content with the ownership of its coal mines and with its government by a League of Nations Commission for fifteen years, at the end of which a plebiscite was to decide whether the inhabitants preferred incorporation in France or in Germany; and instead of securing the separation of the Rhineland and its permanent military occupation, she could obtain only the demilitarization of the right bank to a depth of 50 km and the military occupation of the left bank and the bridgeheads for fifteen years. Two important clauses were, however, secured by Clemenceau, stipulating that, if Germany failed to fulfil her treaty obligations or if the 'guarantees against unprovoked aggression' were not considered sufficient, the territory on the left bank might be reoccupied or its evacuation deferred.

'The guarantees against unprovoked aggression' – these were a cardinal factor in the negotiations. Wilson and Lloyd George, impressed by the strength of the French desire for security, had come forward with the offer of a joint Anglo-American undertaking to go to France's aid if on any future occasion she was again the victim of an unprovoked German attack. But it had been conditional on Clemenceau's withdrawal of his demands for a separate Rhineland and permanent military occupation. Clemenceau was obliged to choose. Before the war French statesmen had in vain sought for such an undertaking from Great Britain. Its offer now by the representative of the USA as well as of Great Britain exceeded his fondest hopes. With the automatic assistance of the two most powerful states in the world France's security might well seem assured. She accepted the offer and gave up the main French demands concerning the Rhineland; with the result that, although British and American opinion long regarded Clemenceau as the unrelenting advocate of a harsh and tyrannical peace, he was attacked by many of his countrymen for his weakness and leniency. It was only after protracted and passionate debates that the Treaty was eventually ratified by the French Parliament in October 1919. Unfortunately for France the American Congress was still more critical of it and in March 1920 the Treaty of Versailles and the League of Nations were repudiated by the American Senate. With them went the American guarantee to France and in consequence the British offer, which had been conditional upon American participation in the general scheme for international security, ceased to hold good. France had fallen between two stools. She had failed to secure the strategic frontier which her military experts regarded as indispensable and the pledges given her in return for its abandonment had not been honoured. Painfully and laboriously she had to seek for some other solution of the German problem. In the transformed and disunited Europe with which she was now confronted and in the divided state of her own public opinion this was to be no easy quest.

With the end of the war and the collapse of the Central Powers in 1918, the old European order had vanished and the balance of power, not only in Europe but also in the world, was greatly altered. A large part of the European Continent lay prostrate, disorganized by revolution and impoverished by war. On the other hand the countries of the New World had grown rich as their exports to the European belligerents had risen by leaps and bounds. Among them there towered the USA, now a creditor nation and a world power of the first magnitude, but showing by her repudiation of the Versailles Treaty and the League of Nations that she was not yet ready to accept the permanent responsibilities which her new rank implied. In Central and Eastern Europe where formerly there had been the three great Empires of Germany, Austria-Hungary and Russia, there were now, in addition to a Republican Germany and a Bolshevik Russia, no less than ten relatively small states, all more or less intensely nationalistic and jealous of each others' pretensions. Their existence was a triumph for the Wilsonian principle of self-determination, but it made the problems of European unity more complex and it left a series of weak powers on Germany's eastern border instead of two strong ones. Moreover, the task of creating a new and harmonious order on the ruins of the old was rendered infinitely more difficult by the October Revolution of 1917 and the definite triumph of Bolshevism in Russia by 1920. The spread of Communism with its call for revolution in all capitalist states had at once been recognized as a threat to the established way of life in every country west of the Pripet Marshes. This threat, as we shall see, was parried and Communism triumphed only in a single country. But its entrenchment there, in the very country which had so lately been France's ally, on whom she had long relied to maintain the balance of European power, was regarded as a standing menace to the internal order of European states and therefore a profound cause of internal disunion. So it was that, although the temporary settlement of Germany, the disappearance of Austria-Hungary and the outlawry of the Russian pariah gave France for the moment an unquestioned preponderance on the Continental mainland, the distant outlook was far less reassuring. The day might come when France would have to choose between German military and Russian social aggression. More than ever before, her politics were to become subordinated to direction by forces beyond her own frontiers.

Meanwhile her situation was none the easier for the difficulties of transition from war to peace at home. On 24 October 1919 hostilities terminated officially and measures enacted by law or decree for the duration of the war ceased to have effect. Military and economic demobilization proceeded apace and the essential but burdensomely expensive business of repairing the damage in the occupied departments was begun. Demobilization from the forces was completed within a year of the armistice; requisitioned railways were restored to their owners, but in such bad condition that they soon had to be completely reorganized; import control restrictions were removed; and almost all the war-time ministries and services, except those concerned with further employment and the recruitment of foreign labour, closed down. The recovery of Alsace and Lorraine did not wholly make up for the decline of population by 2,000,000 between 1911 and 1921 and France became increasingly dependent on foreign help for certain types of labour, especially in the mines.[4] On the other hand she gained the valuable iron ore and metallurgical works of Lorraine and the textile factories and newly-developed potash mines of Alsace. It was, as we shall see, much less difficult to integrate these assets into the French economy than to solve the psychological problems of incorporating populations whose mode of life had for nearly half a century been conditioned by a different set of laws. Materially, the general transition from war to peace was often easier than might have been expected. The unemployment feared as a result of speedy demobilization was mitigated by the need for labour for reconstructing the devastated regions and by the introduction of a shorter working day. Yet there was much social unrest and in 1919 and 1920 there were a great many strikes including an abortive general strike. Inevitably discipline in factory and workshop tended to relax after the war-time effort, and discontent was aggravated by the fact that the eight-hour day introduced in accordance with the Treaty of Versailles was too often ignored by employers, that there was a steady increase in the cost of living, which caused much hardship to those dependent on small fixed incomes, that wages failed to catch up with the increasing rise in prices, so that in 1920, if not in 1919, real wages had fallen below the 1911 level,[5] and last but not least that there was a good deal of Communist propaganda which had a disturbing effect. The most striking result of Communism was to split the ranks of the Socialists. At the Socialist Party Congress at Tours in 1920 there was a clash between the moderates, who believed in parliamentary methods, upholding the Versailles settlement and remaining loyal to the Second International, and the extremist majority who believed in the imminence of world revolution sponsored by Russia, denounced the peace as a capitalist contrivance for the maintenance of bourgeois supremacy, and voted for adherence to a new Third International whose headquarters were in Moscow. Immediately, Socialism was weakened, for the split affected both the party and the CGT. The new Communist party, founded in 1920, recruited its adherents from the dissident Socialists and took over the newspaper L'Humanité, while the CGTU (Confédération Générale du Travail Unitaire), affiliated to the Moscow Profintern, was set up as a rival to the CGT. A new disciplined party thus arose on the Left and by 1924, after being purged and 'bolshevized', it was clearly controlled by a foreign power. If we discount the political activities of Ultramontanes and religious orders this was a new and sinister development in French party politics.

In parliament, too, there was a reaction against war-time discipline, the discipline which Clemenceau had carried on beyond the armistice. But the life of the Chamber of 1914 was drawing to a close, after having already been prolonged beyond its normal term, and a general election was fixed for 1919. For a moment it seemed as though a new and invigorating spirit was going to sweep through French politics. The old method of election by *scrutin d'arrondissement*, so dear and so safe for the Radicals, was set aside in favour of a new and complicated system of proportional representation, which told heavily in favour of the most disciplined group and resulted in a sweeping majority for a new bloc called the Bloc National. This election of the so-called 'Chambre bleu horizon' was the counterpart of the Khaki election of 1918 in Great Britain. The majority of the new deputies were ex-servicemen of varying political origins who had come together, abjuring their old parties, in order to carry forward into the realm of politics the fraternity in arms acquired at the front. The new bloc was a sort of derivative of *union sacrée* which cut right across the old pre-war Bloc des Gauches because it split the Radicals. For this reason, and because it included several Royalists and many Catholics but excluded the Socialists, its character was distinctly Conservative. For the first time in the history of the Third Republic since the establishment of the Constitution of 1875 a Conservative majority had been returned to a French Chamber. In fact the nearest analogy to this first Chamber after the war of 1914–18 was the first Assembly after the war of 1870. In both cases the stress of war and anxiety about the international future had simplified the issues and so momentarily obscured the normal trend of party politics. In both cases a great many men had been elected who were newcomers to politics. Just as the return of the Royalist majority in 1871 (and also in 1815) had been a vote for peace and order, so the return of the Chambre Bleu Horizon was also a vote for peace and order – for a firm insistence on the execution of the terms of the Treaty and for order in the face of the Communist menace. But as they were absorbed into normal peace-time occupations it was soon to be seen that the 'Anciens Combattants' would lose their solidarity under the solvent influences of civilian life and the propaganda of the traditional parties, and would resume their old political habits. Meanwhile, the return of the Bloc National had appeared momentarily to unite the soundest elements in the nation in defence of its fundamental interests. The fact that the Bloc included a number of practising Catholics suggested, moreover, that the splendid record of the clergy during the war had finally disposed of the old anti-clericalism.

Almost the first important task of the new Chamber was the election of a President to succeed Poincaré, whose term was due to expire in January 1920. Two candidates were nominated, Clemenceau and Deschanel, a former Progressist whose main qualifications were his exceptional elegance and the tact with which he had frequently presided over the Chamber. The National Assembly, Nationalist though it was, rejected Clemenceau and took Deschanel. So ended the long public career of the most notable of the statesmen of the Third Republic. In accordance with custom on the election of a new President, Clemenceau, now 79 years of age, at once resigned his premiership and retired into private life. He had in the end fallen a victim to the same treatment which he had on a memorable occasion meted out to Jules Ferry – once again a Republican Assembly had treated one of her greatest men with its ancient prescription of fear and ingratitude. Only by occasional public utterances and conversation with his friends did the wonderful old man continue to show how much clearer-sighted he was than most of his contemporaries and what leadership the nation had lost during the years of doubt and hesitancy to come. France could have had no abler pilot through the shoals of European politics; and, if it is argued that at home his presidency might have provoked a constitutional crisis, the answer is that one was to come in any case. Within a few months there was yet another Presidential election. Clemenceau had advised the National Assembly in 1887 to vote for the stupidest – ironically enough when the Assembly of 1920 chose Deschanel in preference to him they voted for a man who shortly afterwards had a breakdown and had to be removed to a mental home. On the next occasion they were not afraid to vote for a strong man; they elected the man who had succeeded Clemenceau as Prime Minister, the former Socialist, Millerand, and he, like MacMahon, was to clash with the succeeding Chamber.

With the signature of the Treaty of Versailles, the election of the Chambre Bleu Horizon, the retirement of Clemenceau and the repudiation of the Treaty by the American Senate, we enter upon a new phase of French history which is marked by sharp fluctuations of domestic and foreign policy, fluctuations which correspond to growing cleavages of opinion at home.

The Chambre Bleu Horizon and Senate had rejected Clemenceau, not because of his nationalism, but because of his authoritarianism and his Jacobin anti-clericalism which still persisted. They still wanted a nationalist and a man of authority to keep order and defend French interests; in Millerand they found the person they needed both as Prime Minister and subsequently as President. He pursued a firm policy of insisting on the exact fulfilment of the Treaty and he acted vigorously in the face of threats to social order. Thus in April 1920 he replied to the German Government's unauthorized dispatch of 20,000 men to keep order in the Ruhr by the immediate occupation of Frankfurt and Darmstadt; and in January 1922 when Briand, whose reparations policy was under fire, abruptly left a conference with Lloyd George at Cannes and resigned without having been defeated in the Chamber, he took the unprecedented step of calling upon a former President of the Republic, Poincaré, to form a Ministry. This choice was largely determined by the fact that Poincaré could be relied on to take a strong line in dealing with Germany. So indeed he did; Poincaré, the sternly patriotic Lorrainer, who had presided over the destinies of the country during the Great War was also a cold clear-headed legist, and would go to the limit in exacting fulfilment of the Treaty of Versailles. Thus it was that in 1923, when Germany defaulted in the payment of reparations, he sent French troops to occupy the Ruhr, in spite of British disapproval, already manifested in 1920 on the occasion of the march into Frankfurt and Darmstadt. It was Millerand also who sought to check the spread of Bolshevism by sending a French military mission to Poland in 1920 under General Weygand. The Poles were then at war with the Russians and, although in fact Weygand's advice went largely unheeded, their victory in the Battle of Warsaw effectively stopped the Russian advance. Thus Millerand fully represented the policy of the Bloc National and indeed it was to his undoing that he identified himself with them too closely.

Gradually, as the life of the 1919 Chamber wore on, the Radicals sat more loosely to the Bloc; and eventually they left it altogether and renewed their friendship with the Socialists. So when the time came for the next general elections in 1924 they had reverted to their old attitude of 'No enemies to the Left' (with the exception now of the Communists), and with the Radical-Socialists and Socialists they formed a combination called the Cartel des Gauches which was but the old pre-war Bloc Républicain under another name. In the meantime, as peace-time habits became more general, the Radical committees and electoral machinery had regained much of their influence. Moreover, Poincaré's policy of the strong arm did not succeed: the Ruhr occupation met with passive resistance on the part of the Germans, it made an additional call upon French manpower and finance and it did not achieve its object of making Germany pay. It was therefore not hard for its opponents to declaim against 'Poincaré la guerre' and to represent the occupation as a foolhardy, costly adventure: and at a time when France was beginning to comprehend her own weariness, to know that beyond all else she desired peace without adventures and to suffer from an acute financial crisis, their attacks had considerable influence. They were also able to make much capital out of the budgetary deficit, the continued rise in prices, the depreciation of the franc and the Poincaré Government's imposition of additional taxation in order to remedy the situation. Consequently, in the 1924 elections the Cartel obtained a handsome majority in the Chamber, although its poll was not much more than in 1919. At once it sought to exploit its victory. The Socialists had long been hostile to Millerand as a deserter from their ranks; he was mistrusted on account of his authoritarian tendencies and his open advocacy of a revision of the Constitution which would increase the powers of the President of the Republic; and the whole Cartel maintained that he had, during the elections, shown his sympathies too openly with the Bloc National. They were therefore determined to have his head. One of their papers, the *Quotidien*, came out with a demand for 'all the places and at once'; and this meant that they claimed even the Presidency of the Republic. So there arose a first-class constitutional crisis which recalled both 1887 and 1877; 1887, because when Millerand sought to form a Ministry from among the majority in the new Chamber he was unable to do so since the potential Prime Ministers went on strike and refused to serve him; 1877, because he then abandoned the attempt, formed a minority Cabinet, and like MacMahon, attempted to induce the Senate to concur in a dissolution of the Chamber. The Senate refused and Millerand had no alternative but to resign. But the Senate had still some care for the balance of power in the State. If the Cartel then proceeded to procure the election of one of their own nominees from the Chamber, the President of the Republic would become a mere creature of the legislature. The Senate therefore put up its own President, Doumergue, against the President of the Chamber, Painlevé, and secured his election by a large majority. A Radical Government was at once formed by Edouard Herriot, the Mayor of Lyons, with Socialist support. The general outline of French political groupings resumed its 'normal' pre-war aspect, and the resemblance was strengthened by the fact that the Radicals once again stirred up the issue of Church and State.

This advent of the Cartel to power led to notable changes in policy at home and abroad. The new Government made haste to terminate the unpopular Ruhr occupation and to accept the revised scale of reparation payments proposed by the so-called Dawes Plan. The German policy of the Bloc National might well be held to have failed. So far from making Germany pay it had only embittered her, involving France in financial loss and estranging her from Great Britain, which thought that France was abusing her position as the dominant state on the Continent and tended in consequence to back the weaker Germany in the interests of the balance of power. The Herriot Government sought to achieve the main end of security by conciliation instead of by force. It agreed to the admission of Germany to the League of Nations, it renewed diplomatic relations with Russia and sought to revive the *entente* with Great Britain. Its predecessors had aimed at security, first by obtaining a new form of guarantee from Great Britain once the old one had been nullified by the American repudiation, and secondly, by the conclusion of alliances with some of the new states in Eastern Europe whose very existence was so largely dependent upon the maintenance of the Versailles settlement. It was in pursuance of this policy that in 1921 they had entered into a formal alliance with Poland, which was accompanied by a military convention and the grant of a loan to enable Poland to purchase French supplies; that in 1924 this was followed by a Treaty with Czechoslovakia; and that closer political and economic relations had been developed with the two other members of the so-called Little *Entente*, Roumania and Yugoslavia. They had not, however, been successful in obtaining a new guarantee from Great Britain, which took the view that France's security was adequately assured by the League of Nations Covenant with its guarantee and sanctions clauses, and which insisted on linking any specific proposal with the settlement of a number of outstanding European problems. Thus frustrated, they had turned to the League itself, there seeking to extract security concessions from Great Britain by blocking the progress of the disarmament talks, by which the British Government set great store, and to strengthen the League Covenant which they regarded as full of loopholes. But although they had been able to block disarmament, they had made little headway with security. Draft Treaties of Mutual Assistance and Geneva Protocols alike were wrecked by the reluctance of successive British Governments to take on any new commitment. By 1925, however, since the advent of the Cartel, much closer relations had been established with Great Britain and something of the spirit of the old Entente had returned – thenceforward until the end of the Republic it was notable that relations between the two countries were much easier when a Government of the Left was in power in France. This was perfectly understandable: the Left were more conciliatory in their approach to the German problem, more genuinely inspired with belief in the Wilsonian ideals, which after all had so much in common with the great Liberal tradition of the French Revolution, and in consequence wholehearted supporters of the League of Nations; on the other hand the Right were those whose thought was more strongly coloured by the violent 'integral Nationalism' preached by the 'Action Française' – as far back as Fashoda and the Boer War it had been this Right who had been the most vociferous in their hostility to the British Empire. It was the Right, too, who had adopted an intransigent attitude towards Germany which the British found exceedingly difficult to understand or appreciate, and who distrusted the League of Nations as a mere 'talking shop'. So now it was a Government of the Left which came nearer than any Government of the Bloc National to achieving through friendship with Great Britain the guarantees it so persistently sought.

The Locarno Agreements of October 1925 appeared to be a great triumph for Briand, now Foreign Minister in the second Cartel Government, and for Austen Chamberlain, the British Foreign Secretary. They comprised a series of agreements whereby Great Britain, France, Italy, Belgium and Germany mutually guaranteed Germany's western frontiers. In this way France at last secured a British undertaking of support against any unprovoked attack and Germany formally recognized the permanence of the frontier arrangements made at Versailles. This seemed to mean that she had effectively been brought back into the European States system and to open up the prospect of a new and more cordial phase in Franco-German relations. Gradually, it appeared, the unity of Europe was being reforged by amicable agreement on the basis of existing treaties, and Locarno gave rise to a wave of optimism and confidence. Moreover, its maintenance was so important that Briand, the man of Locarno, throughout the vicissitudes of home politics was to remain at the Quai d'Orsay for nearly seven years – the longest tenure of the Foreign Office in the history of the Third Republic.

Thus the foreign policy of the Cartel Governments achieved some notable success, but at home they were much less happy in their handling of affairs, and their domestic policy was to bring them to confusion long before the term of the Chamber of 1924 expired. They were soon confronted by trouble in Alsace and Lorraine, revolt in Syria, and a serious financial crisis.

The trouble in Alsace and Lorraine was largely of their own making. The war, with its need for *union sacrée*, and the conciliatory attitude of both Church and Governments during the decade 1914–24, had allayed much of the old bitterness arising out of the Separation of Church and State. Many of the dissolved religious orders had been allowed to return. Priests and Catholic laymen had given magnificent service in the field of battle. The Pope had in 1923 permitted the formation of diocesan associations to take the place of the *associations cultuelles* originally envisaged in the Separation law,[6] and diplomatic relations with the Vatican had been re-established. But Herriot and the Radicals still retained much of their old sectarianism, and, thinking perhaps that there was still nothing like a display of anti-clericalism for binding the groups of a Left-wing Cartel more closely together, they lost no time in opening an offensive against the Church, threatening to apply the Laws against the Congregations in all their strictness and to recall the French Embassy from the Vatican. These threats were mainly harmful in that they diverted attention from more important issues; but there were more serious consequences when Herriot proposed to extend all the anti-clerical legislation passed between 1871 and 1914 to the recovered provinces, and when his successor did away with the High Commissioner's Office, substituting a Directorate-General with its headquarters in Paris. In Alsace and Lorraine the Concordat of 1801 still remained in force, slightly modified by arrangements made during the German occupation. The population contained a large number of devout practising Catholics who in German days had had close association with the powerful German Catholic Centre Party. Already the business of reincorporating the two provinces had occasioned friction and misunderstanding between French officials and the local populations and this now came to a head, especially in Alsace. The protests were so widespread that Herriot was unable to impose his policy, but the very fact that he had intended to introduce it left a legacy of unrest and disaffection which was to afford an opportunity for the growth of home rule or autonomist movements, and subsequently for the development of a German 'Fifth Column'.

In Syria, too, anti-clericalism worked harm as the tactless conduct of the new High Commissioner, General Sarrail, perhaps appointed because of his anti-clerical sympathies, led in 1925 to a violent rising throughout the south of the country which it took several months and cost many lives to suppress. But the main source of the trouble which brought the Cartel to grief was not anti-clericalism but finance. Finance, which before the war had interested few but the experts, was now a matter of growing public concern. The continued rise in prices, the over-valuation of the franc, lavish expenditure and the flight of capital abroad called for firm remedies, but the doctors of the Cartel were divided – the Radicals attempting to eke out their existence by a series of expedients such as short-term loans from banks; the Socialists calling for drastic measures such as a capital levy and a compulsory consolidation of Treasury bonds, which alarmed the financial interests of the country and only increased instability. From April 1925 to July 1926 there was a series of crises owing to the inability of the Chamber to come out firmly in favour of a decided policy because of the risk of splitting the Cartel. Ministry followed Ministry and plan upon plan was put forward in vain. At length in July 1926 when the franc had fallen from 70 francs to the pound in May 1924, when the Cartel came into office, to 250 and the French Treasury was almost empty, the Radicals came to a decision. Fundamentally, in spite of the mystique of Leftism which served them so well at election times, they were Conservative in their instincts and had many ties with the financial world. They rejected the Socialist prescriptions and rallied round Poincaré and orthodox finance. Once again the former President of the Republic was called in to govern with a strong hand; and because of his prestige, because his Republicanism was irreproachable, and because he was able to form a government of Union Nationale, public confidence was very quickly restored. Indeed the Chamber itself went so far as to grant to him what it had refused to Briand and Caillaux six months earlier, namely the power to take all necessary measures for ending the financial crisis by decree-laws. Such power had never been granted in peace-time before – only once in 1918, as we have seen,[7] in the darkest hours of the war, had similar authority been granted to Clemenceau. This abdication by the legislature, conscience-smitten at the results of its own incompetence, was a significant event. Poincaré used his dictatorial powers sparingly, but their very existence afforded a precedent which might be revolutionary in its consequences.

For nearly three years, thanks to Poincaré's restoration of confidence and to his policy of strict economy and cheap money, the country enjoyed a period of relative calm and prosperity. The process of reconstruction had been completed, and French export trade had notably expanded both as a result of this and of the devaluation of the franc. At home Poincaré stabilized the franc at a fifth of its pre-war value, set up a sinking fund, concluded a number of commercial agreements stabilizing tariffs, and began the construction of a great defensive line near the eastern frontier known as the Maginot Line. Abroad, the completion of Germany's disarmament in accordance with the Versailles Treaty, the preparations for a conference on general disarmament, the Kellogg Pact outlawing war, the formation of the International Steel Cartel by producers of Germany, France, Belgium, Luxembourg and the Saar, the conclusion of treaties of alliance with Roumania (June 1927) and Yugoslavia (March 1927), all seemed to strengthen France's position and to renew or perpetuate the greater confidence in European stability which had been engendered by Locarno; and in 1929 Briand was even to go so far as to expound to the League Assembly a somewhat Utopian scheme of European Union. At home, too, the return to the traditional electoral machinery of *scrutin d'arrondissement* (a proposal backed by both the main parties, Radicals and Socialists, in the late Cartel) for the elections of 1928 emphasized the orthodoxy of the new dispensation, which a French historian has compared to 'the Conservative Republic dreamt of by Thiers, realized for a moment in the time of Méline and broken by the Dreyfus Affair'.[8] But, underlying the so-called Union Nationale, there were deep clefts, and an economic blizzard was soon to blow, causing financial distress and political unrest in every country in the world.

The Union Nationale was far from being an *union sacrée*; in spite of its name it was primarily an alliance of groups of the centre, the first to govern since Thiers' day.[9] Moreover, the crisis of 1925–6 and the break-up of the Cartel had caused much bitterness on the Left. Never before had the Left groups been faced by a financial crisis of such magnitude and they attributed their failure and Poincaré's success in settling it to the hidden power of financial interests. They were easily led to believe that reforms had been blocked by the so-called 'Mur d'argent' erected by the bankers and industrialists, and that these men would continue to oppose any and every measure which would tend to a redistribution of wealth. And since the financial crisis had paralysed government, and orthodox finance meant retrenchment, it was easy to argue that the 'Mur d'argent' was opposed to all kinds of social reform. Thus the events of 1924-8 widened the age-long gulf between different groups of Frenchmen on the social question, and in 1928 shattered the Union Nationale, for although the elections of that year had been an undoubted triumph for Poincaré, in November at the Radical Party Congress the militant members on the Left wing of the party took advantage of an imprudently 'clerical' measure of the Prime Minister to declare against its continued participation in the Government. By associating themselves with the Union Nationale the Radicals had, as we have seen, joined a movement which was essentially one of social and economic conservation. Once the immediate aims were achieved the old tendency of the party to regard itself as a revolutionary party of movement which must have no enemies or as few enemies as possible to the Left reasserted itself. The support of the Socialists for *scrutin d'arrondissement* brought the Socialists and Radicals together again and the departure of the Radicals from the Poincaré Government in November foreshadowed the re-formation of the Cartel. There was the same swing back to coalition of these two parties as in the years before the war. The Radicals as the centre party are constantly torn between opposing forces and the course of French parliamentary history is governed by the fluctuations of their alliances. Unfortunately for France, the opposing forces on the two flanks, under the impact of economic crises and of new developments abroad will tend to become more and more violently antagonistic. France is torn between them with such tension that in the end she is wellnigh in a state of veiled civil war. For if the Left was embittered, the Right had never disarmed. Always anti-democratic and anti-parliamentary in its tendencies, much attracted, indeed, by the rise of Italian Fascism, it had violently attacked the Cartel Governments on all aspects of their policy. In particular, it had denounced the Locarno Agreements for the position of equality they gave to Germany and for their omission to guarantee Poland's western frontier, and it pursued Briand with unrelenting hostility until his death. Although it had been thrown into disarray in 1926 by the Papal condemnation of the Action Française, whose political doctrines were wholly amoral, the return of economic instability and of threats to security from abroad soon gave it a fresh opportunity to exert its influence. In November 1929 the slump in the

USA led to an economic and financial crisis of the first magnitude. On 30 June 1930, the last French troops left the Rhineland and two months later 107 National-Socialist Deputies were elected to the German Reichstag. Storm clouds were gathering which threatened both Briand's Locarno settlement and Poincaré's restoration of French prosperity. And in July 1929 Poincaré had to retire from the Premiership on account of ill-health while Briand, tired and ageing, would not long remain to face the tempest. In the lean years ahead the guidance of French destinies was to fall into the hands of younger and lesser men.

Meanwhile the war and the monetary crises which followed had increased the sense of insecurity, impoverishing the man who depended on dividends or a pension and rendering the producer, notably the peasant, more independent. 'The collapse of the franc,' it has been said, 'after over one hundred years of stability, was utterly demoralizing in a society whose greatest economic virtue was thrift!'[10] 'Never,' wrote the French historian, Seignobos, 'not even during the French Revolution, had the State dealt such a blow to private property; stabilisation reduced the value of investments by four-fifths while death duties ate into inheritances.'[11] In consequence the tendency to social levelling continued; while the growing uniformity of dress and manners was accelerated by American production methods, mass entertainment, and inventions such as the wireless and cinema. In sport France now for the first time began to make a mark with champions such as Suzanne Lenglen and Borotra in lawn tennis and Carpentier in boxing. To science she still made distinguished contributions, particularly in the realm of physics with the work of Jean Perrin, Paul Langevin, and those eminent brothers, the Duc de Broglie and Prince Louis de Broglie. Intellectually, however, the war in many ways acted as a disruptive agent, and this was especially noticeable in French literature. Already the philosophy of Bergson with its exaltation of intuition had exercised a profound effect upon novelists like Proust, most of whose work was first published after 1919. Already Gide, who was the most influential literary figure of the 1920s, had derived much of his inspiration from the amoralism of the German Nietzsche. Such philosophies, together with the growing interest in psychology, had encouraged escapist cults of sensation and extreme artistic and literary movements like that of the Surrealists with their enthronement of the unconscious. The war, with its bloodshed and destruction of much of the old European order, had further contributed to undermine traditional human values and to drain much of the post-war literature of ethical or national content. There was still an abundance of artistic talent; the sense of form remained strong and was conspicuously displayed in French films or in the work of writers such as Mauriac and Giraudoux, but in the realm of ideas there was what a French author has called a 'fever of intellectual denationalization'.[12] Such a phenomenon was by no means peculiar to France at this time, but in a society where the national traditions had been so deep-rooted, and part of which was so highly intellectual, the disarray caused by the jettisoning of old values and by the restless search for new ones outside the French traditions may well have had a deeper and ultimately more damaging effect than elsewhere. When we come in the next chapter to look upon a picture of growing darkness it will be wise to bear in mind the importance of this moral and intellectual disorder as a possible element in the tragedy of 1940.

Notes

1 Clough, Shepard, B., *France, a History of National Economics*, p. 203.
2 For the text of the Fourteen Points of the League of Nations Covenant see Butterfield, H., *Select Documents of European History, 1715–1920*, p. 194ff.
3 See Map 4, p. 201. Strictly they were mandated to France by the League.
4 By 1931 there were no less than 1,600,000 foreign wage earners in France, including 287,000 Poles, 194,000 Spaniards, 156,000 Belgians, and 475,000 Italians. I am indebted for these figures to the Research Department of Chatham House.
5 The real wages of workers in industry and agriculture were, with few exceptions, higher in 1921 than in 1911, but the delay in adjusting remuneration to the increasing price rise brought them below the 1911 level in 1920. The net salaries of Government employees, except those in the lowest categories, were considerably lower than in 1911. Fontaine, A., *French Industry during the War*, p. 69.
6 See pp. 197–8 above.
7 See p. 242 above.
8 Madaule, J., *Histoire de France*, vol. 2, p. 348.
9 Seignobos, C., *Études de politique et d'histoire*, p. 311.
10 Landes, David S., in Earle, E. M., *Modern France, Problems of the Third and Fourth Republics*, p. 339.
11 *Histoire sincère de la nation française*, pp. 488–9. By 'investments' he must have meant to imply fixed-interest securities.
12 Maillaud, P., *France*, p. 96.

Bibliography

Albrecht-Carrié, R., *France, Europe and the Two World Wars*, New York, 1968.
Bernard, P., *La fin d'un monde 1914–1929*, Paris, 1975.
Bury, J. P. T., *France: The Insecure Peace*, London, 1972.
Chastenet, J., *Les années d'illusion 1918–1931*, Paris, 1960.
Fauvet, J., *Histoire du parti communiste français 1917–1939*, Paris, 1964.

Howard, J. E., *Parliament and Foreign Policy in France*, London, 1948.

Jordan, W. M., *Great Britain, France and the German Problem, 1918–39*, Oxford University Press, 1943.

Joseph-Barthélemy, *Le Gouvernement de la France*, Paris, 1939.

Kemp, T., *The French Economy 1913–1939*, London, 1972.

Middleton, W. L., *The French Political System*, London, 1932.

Néré, J., *The Foreign Policy of France from 1914 to 1945*, London, 1974.

Pickles, Dorothy M., *The French Political Scene*, London, 1938.

Sauvy, A., *Histoire économique de la France entre les deux guerres, 1918–1931*, Paris, 1967

Siegfried, A., *Tableau des partis en France*, Paris, 1930. (Translated into English under the title of *France, A Study in Nationality*, Yale, 1930.)

Wolfers, A., *Britain and France Between Two Wars*, New York, 1940.

16

Catastrophe

The economic crisis was more damaging to the more highly industrialized nations than to France. She was much less dependent than the United Kingdom or Germany upon foreign trade and it was not until 1931 that she seriously began to feel the pinch. By then successive currency depreciations abroad had eliminated the competitive advantage hitherto enjoyed by French exports, and these were further hampered by the trade barriers which foreign countries began to erect. At first, therefore, the most alarming consequences of the crisis for France lay in its political effects in Europe and above all in Germany. There the depression assumed disastrous proportions, and by 1932 the number of unemployed, which in France never exceeded *c.* 1,400,000, had risen to 4,000,000. Germany was no longer able to meet her obligations and in 1932 reparations were virtually abrogated by the Lausanne Conference, which reduced the amount due from 38 milliard francs to three milliards, payable in thirty-seven years after a three years' moratorium. The crisis played directly into the hands of the growing National Socialist party which had laid responsibility for it at the door of the Treaty of Versailles and of the weak Weimar Republic and preached a militant Nationalism. By 1932 the National Socialist leader had polled no less than 13,000,000 votes in the German presidential election. His party appeared to be not only the party of German rearmament but also that of German *revanche*.

But it was just at this time that the question of disarmament came to the fore. In 1932 the long-prepared Conference forgathered, and France found herself confronted by a formidable dilemma. On the one hand Germany had been declared to have completed her obligations under the Treaty of Versailles and once this declaration had been made the other signatories were formally bound by the same Treaty to disarm themselves, while if they failed to do so, but still wished to treat Germany as an equal, there could be no reason for not allowing her to rearm up to their limit. On the other hand Germany's industrial potential and her manpower were far greater than France's, and if the National Socialist party came into power what guarantee could there be that it would observe any limit or submit to international control? Once again France sought to link the question of disarmament to that of security and once again put forward a plan for the creation of an international force and for strengthening the political authority of the League of Nations, but it was coldly received by Great Britain, who still looked askance at all proposals to turn the League into a sort of super-state. Before the Conference entered on its next phase critical elections had taken place in both Germany and France.

In France there were two elections, the general elections to the Chamber and an unexpected election to the Presidency of the Republic, since Paul Doumer, who had been elected in preference to Briand in May 1931 – yet one more example of a vote for the lesser man – was assassinated by a Russian *émigré* named Gorguloff between the first and second ballot. The first ballot had shown a majority in favour of the reformed Cartel or Union des Gauches, but it was the old Chamber which joined with the Senate in electing the President and their choice fell, as on many occasions before, upon the President of the Senate, a moderate named Albert Lebrun. The second ballot reinforced the first; the Cartel returned triumphant to the Chamber and Herriot became Prime Minister for the second time, once again forming a Radical Ministry which was supported by the Socialists, but did not include any of their representatives. It was 1924 over again; only the Cartel did not now claim 'all the places' and were content to leave Lebrun in the Élysée. It remained to be seen whether in this new European situation this new Government of the Left would embark upon such a reversal of politics as had marked the administrations of 1924–6.

In Germany parliamentary elections were held in July and here they took an opposite course. The flow of the tide towards the extremes of National Socialism on the one hand and Communism on the other hand had continued: but the National Socialists were in the ascendancy; they won 230 seats and became the largest party in the Reichstag. Six months later President Hindenburg appointed Adolf Hitler Chancellor of the German Reich. The problem of disarmament was going to be still more difficult and by now the economic crisis was beginning to hit the French economy.

Once again, indeed, it was the misfortune of the Cartel to be confronted by acute financial difficulties and once again they were unable to resolve them because of the disagreement of Radicals and Socialists concerning the remedies to be adopted. Once again this inability meant the lack of a stable majority and a succession of ministerial crises. In December 1932 Herriot fell because of his wish to honour France's war debts to the USA, whereas a majority held that war debts were linked to reparations and that, as it was due to American insistence that Germany had been granted a moratorium on the payment of reparations, France had no obligation to pay the USA so long as she received nothing from Germany. Between December 1932 and February 1934 no fewer than four Cabinets, those of Paul-Boncour, Daladier, Albert Sarraut and Chautemps, had followed one another in rapid succession without being able to impose a strong policy leading to financial recovery. Half-way through the life of the second Cartel Chamber it was once again high time for the Left parties to admit their impotence and call a Poincaré not only to rescue the finances but also to regenerate the regime and to mobilize all the energies of the nation before it was too late. But there was no Poincaré at hand, and it was necessary for an insurrection to add political to economic crisis and expose more clearly the depths to which the Republic had sunk, before a new saviour could be brought to power.

Once again the old symptoms of disease, already visible in the days of Gambetta and Ferry and of Panama and the Dreyfus Affair, had manifested themselves – mediocrity of the deputies, *esprit de clocher*, parliamentary corruption, multiplication of groups, ministerial instability, paralysis of legislation. Reform of all kinds, social, constitutional, financial, was blocked by the conservatism of deputies and senators who had vested interests in the maintenance of a regime which gave the Chambers virtual dictatorship, and who flattered themselves that because they were elected by the nation they were necessarily also the elect of the nation. At the same time the situation of France in the world was rapidly deteriorating. Her birth-rate continued to decline and her security was increasingly imperilled. The failure of the League of Nations to deal with the Manchurian crisis in 1931–2, and the failure of Tardieu and Herriot to reinforce the League by investing it with military powers, had shown that it was but a broken reed. The abortive Four Power pact to which Ramsay MacDonald had induced France to adhere in 1933 had alarmed her Eastern allies and had led Poland to conclude a pact of non-aggression and friendship with Germany in 1934, while the economic crisis had further weakened France's ties with the Little *Entente* powers since she was no longer able to give them financial aid. Finally, Germany's abrupt decision to leave the Disarmament Conference and the League of Nations in October 1933 emphasized the menace of militant National Socialism and its contempt for the European order established at Versailles. Once again, as in Boulanger's days, public opinion, especially in Paris where a powerful section of the press had long been anti-parliamentary in tone, became more and more impatient with a regime so seemingly ineffective; and the growing hostility manifested itself in the reviving strength of the Action Française and in the formation of new Leagues, of which the most notable was the association of ex-servicemen known as the Croix de Feu led by Colonel de La Rocque.

When the Stavisky scandal of 1933 followed those of Hanau in 1928 and Oustric in 1930, both of which involved more or less prominent politicians, and when it was widely believed that the 'suicide' of the financial adventurer Stavisky had been 'arranged' by the police with the connivance of the Prime Minister, Chautemps, in order to prevent him from making revelations of parliamentary corruption on a scale reminiscent of Panama,[1] indignation came to a head. There were street demonstrations in Paris on 12, 22 and 27 January 1934, when Chautemps resigned. His successor, Daladier, attempted to form an above-party coalition, but met with passive hostility from the Right. To secure his majority, he dismissed Chiappe, the Prefect of the Paris Police, who was detested by the Socialists for his Right-wing leanings. The Prefect's dismissal prompted the large-scale demonstrations of 6 February which were arranged by the Leagues and their allies in Parliament and the Municipal Council of Paris. The demonstrators converged on the Place de la Concorde, where they attempted to break through the police cordon guarding the Chamber of Deputies. Thereupon the police opened fire. Fourteen rioters were killed and over 600 injured. Many people, including the Socialist leader, Léon Blum, thought that these riots indicated a definite plot on the part of the Right to overthrow the Republic. The whole truth will probably never be known, but the aims of most of the demonstrators were almost certainly more limited. The most they could have hoped for was Daladier's resignation and his replacement by a man who could be relied on not to treat with the Socialists. Had not Daladier taken precautions and had the Chamber not been guarded, there might well have been a repetition of the scenes of February 1848 and September 1870. As it was, the *journée* of 6 February 1934, was the first occasion since 1848 on which blood had been shed in the streets of Paris in a manifestation which seemed to menace the existence of the regime.

The casualties naturally exasperated the demonstrators and heightened the tension. Rioting continued, there were threats of more serious trouble, and counter demonstrations by the Left culminated on the 12th in French Labour's first successful general strike. Meanwhile, notwithstanding the fact that at the very moment when the crowds were massed in the Place de la Concorde he had been given a vote of confidence, Daladier, who spoke little and bore a slight resemblance to Napoleon, thereby conveying the illusion that he was a strong man, resigned. Thus the executive abdicated and still further betrayed its weakness. For the first time in the history of the Third Republic a government which enjoyed parliamentary support had yielded to pressure from outside parliament. The President of the

Republic had to look outside the ranks of the parliamentarians who had so ignominiously fumbled with the governmental machine during the past four years. Once again, a former President of the Republic was summoned to save the situation. Millerand's successor, the elderly and genial Doumergue, like Cincinnatus from his plough, was called from his rural retreat near Toulouse and hastened to Paris to become Prime Minister and form a new Government of National Union, which included members of all parties except the Socialists and Communists. Louis Barthou, one of the Progressist 'boys' of the 1890s, became Minister of Foreign Affairs, Tardieu and Herriot Ministers of State, and Marshal Pétain, one of the heroes of the 1914–18 war, accepted the Ministry of War. The effect on the public was immediate. Disturbances ceased, confidence was restored and the Chamber, thoroughly scared by the danger through which it had passed, once again invested the Government with power to legislate by decree. Henceforward it shows itself more and more disposed to abdicate part of its functions in this way, thereby singularly perverting the character of parliamentary democracy.

But although Doumergue's Government, the ninety-sixth of the Third Republic, sought to restore the financial situation and, as we shall see, improve France's diplomatic position, it failed to dissolve the armed leagues, reduce the cost of living or effect any constitutional reform. More than ever a revision of the constitution, such as Millerand and many others had advocated, seemed indispensable if the old diseases were not once again to cripple the body politic as soon as parliament resumed full sovereignty. Revision had been the insistent cry of the Boulangists and the Ligue des Patriotes nearly half a century earlier; revision was undoubtedly one of the main desires of many of the demonstrators of 6 February 1934, but the Republic was incapable of reform of this kind and even the very modest proposals put forward by Doumergue for strengthening the executive were blocked, mainly by the opposition of the Radicals, who had such strong vested interests in the *status quo*. On 7 November the Doumergue Cabinet fell. In spite of the shock of 6 February the parliamentary regime was to stumble along as before, unreformed, but tempered now by increasing recourse to the device of legislation by decree, a device which really concealed a greater menace to parliamentary sovereignty than any which was likely to arise from a moderate measure of constitutional reform.

The other limiting feature about the Doumergue Cabinet of 'Union Nationale' was that it was by no means a Cabinet of *union sacrée*. Socialists and Communists were both excluded and began to draw together in opposition to the Government and to its financial deflationary policy, which was both ineffective and soon very unpopular. Hitherto, ever since the split in the Socialist ranks in 1920, the main characteristic of the relations between the two chief working-class parties had been their bitter antagonism. Their new alliance, confirmed by an agreement of 1935 and their participation in the so-called Rassemblement Populaire of the same year, was a momentous event which was to lead to an amalgamation of the dissident CGTU with the CGT, to be decisive for the result of the general elections of 1936, and to thrust the social problem once more into the forefront of French politics, already troubled by so many other issues. The deflationary policy failed to stimulate a rise in production and soon disquieted the Radicals, who hastened to dissociate themselves from the Union Nationale and to return to the application of their old principle of 'No enemies to the Left'. Hence, with the formation in 1936 of the Front Populaire, there came into being a new bloc of the Left-wing parties, a new Cartel des Gauches, but vitally different from the Cartels of 1924 and 1932, in that it now for the first time included the Communists. Moreover, the strength of the Communists' appeal to the electorate in May 1936 had been much reinforced by developments abroad. Before we consider the programme of the Front Populaire and the reasons for its electoral triumph we must glance at the evolution of French policy and the growth of international tension since 6 February 1934.

Louis Barthou, Foreign Minister in the Doumergue Cabinet, an energetic and cultivated man of the older Republican school, lost no time in attempting to strengthen France's weakening security by reinforcing her eastern alliance system and by seeking to negotiate a sort of Eastern Locarno which would give the Versailles frontiers in Eastern Europe, including Germany's eastern frontier, the same sort of guarantees as those devised for Germany's western frontier in 1925. He visited Warsaw, Prague, Bucharest and Belgrade, and, in order to compensate for Poland's new leanings towards Germany and to extend the area of eastern security, brought Russia into the negotiations and obtained her admission into the League of Nations a year after Germany had left it. As part of the general plan France was ready to guarantee Russia's western frontier in exchange for a Russian guarantee of the Franco-German frontier. But Germany's reply to Barthou's invitation to take part in the negotiations was a virtual refusal, and Poland's was so hedged about with conditions and counter-suggestions that the general scheme came to nothing. None the less, it had had the most important results. Russia's emergence from her long isolation and her consent to join the League showed that Stalin, too, was seriously disturbed by Hitler's advent to power in Germany. It held out a prospect of immense importance for French security and foreshadowed a renewal of the classic Franco-Russian Alliance of 1894–1918, for, although the general Eastern Locarno came to nothing, two of the powers concerned in the negotiations with France, Russia and Czechoslovakia, had been favourable to Barthou's proposals and were ready to do their part. The momentous result was the signature, in May 1935, of the Franco-Russian Pact of mutual assistance, and of a similar Russo-Czech Pact dependent for its operation upon French intervention should aggression occur.

But by then, owing to the inadequacy of French police precautions, Barthou was no longer alive to make the most of this new orientation. In October 1934, in the very course of strengthening French bonds with Yugoslavia and welcoming her sovereign to French soil, he was assassinated at Marseilles and the King fell with him. At a critical moment in European history Yugoslavia lost a strong king and had to substitute a weak Regency; and in the same hour France lost a vigorous French Foreign Minister, one who had never played such a commanding role as Briand, Poincaré or Millerand, but who was the last notable figure of the generation which made its political début before 1900. His successor was a very different person. Doumergue now entrusted the direction of foreign policy to a dark Auvergnat named Pierre Laval, a man of obscure origin who, like Briand, had begun his career as a Socialist agitator on the extreme Left but had gradually moved farther to the Right until he was now a moderate with Right-wing sympathies. It was he who signed the Franco-Russian Pact, visited Moscow immediately afterwards and obtained from Stalin a declaration in praise of France's rearmament plan – for two months earlier, on 16 March, Hitler's reintroduction of compulsory military service in Germany had effectively put an end to any further serious projects of disarmament under the auspices of the League of Nations. Thus far Laval continued Barthou's policy, but he was also concerned to conjure the growing German menace by other means and showed no haste to ratify the Franco-Russian Pact. Above all he was anxious to improve relations with Italy.

Ever since Versailles Italy had shown her discontent with a peace settlement which had failed, she considered, to do justice to her legitimate territorial aspirations. She was thus what, in the parlance of the 1930s, was called a 'have-not' power, anxious for a revision of the peace treaties. Moreover, since 1922 she had overthrown democratic government and established Fascism. In spite of the fact that in July 1934, when the Nazis had attempted a Putsch in Vienna, Mussolini had massed troops on the Brenner Pass, there was still a grave risk that sooner or later ideological sympathies and a common desire for treaty revision would force Germany and Italy into one another's arms. Meanwhile Franco-Italian relations had been distinctly strained in the 'twenties and there was still room for their improvement. Thus it was that already, in January 1935, Laval had visited

Rome and sought, like Delcassé and Barrère forty years earlier, a settlement of outstanding questions and a new *entente*. The Rome agreements of that month brought the two powers closer together than at any time since 1919, and for a while there was much talk of a Latin Bloc, which, in French Catholic and Conservative circles at least, was regarded as a potential bulwark against Bolshevism as much as against Nazism. The two powers undertook to co-operate for the maintenance of Austrian independence – the Nazi Putsch, if successful, would have meant the immediate annexation or Anschluss of Austria to the German Reich – and of friendly relations with the Danubian states for whose favour they had been hitherto competitors. They agreed upon a new status for Italians in Tunisia and upon a small rectification of the frontiers of Libya and Somaliland in Italy's favour. But this agreement was reached only at a price, and Laval's willingness to pay it was to land him in a grave dilemma. He agreed that Italy should have a free hand in Abyssinia. In other words, she should be free to carve out for herself the colonial empire in East Africa which she had failed to found under Crispi in the 1890s. The move was in the best tradition of pre-war Bismarckian diplomacy. Even as Bismarck had sought to avert the danger of French *revanche* by encouraging France to go to Tunis and Egypt, so Laval sought to divert 'have-not' Italy from her grievances in Europe and to reduce the risks of a German-Italian alliance by encouraging her to go to Abyssinia. But 1935 was very different from 1878 or from 1904, the year of the Anglo-French *Entente* which had given France herself a free hand in Morocco. Abyssinia, like Italy and France, was now a member of the League of Nations in which France had played a dominant role and whose Covenant she had sworn to observe. If collective security throughout the League of Nations was to mean anything at all, it meant that, if Italy attacked Abyssinia and Abyssinia appealed to the League, France must go to Abyssinia's aid and enforce sanctions against the aggressor. If she refused to do so and clung to her new friendship with Italy, she would be turning her back on the whole of her post-war policy which had been directed to the achievement of collective security through the League as well as to the conclusion of alliances with Germany's neighbours; she would wreck the newly concluded Franco-Russian Pact, estrange Great Britain, perhaps irremediably, and find herself either in complete isolation or forced back upon a rapprochement with Nazi Germany, no comfortable bedfellow.

There is little doubt that Laval hoped that he might not be faced with a direct choice: after all, in September 1931, the League had failed to impose sanctions against Japan when she seized Manchuria, and the preservation of the newly-formed Stresa front of Great Britain, France, and Italy in Europe might seem to be of much more importance in restraining

Germany and keeping the peace of the world than an Italian 'colonial' escapade in Abyssinia. Unfortunately for him, however, the Italian attack on Abyssinia, when it came in September 1935, caused such strong public resentment in Great Britain that the British Government, whom France had so long vainly sought to convert to a strengthening of the League Covenant, now for the first time since the League came into being, took a 'strong' view of that Covenant. But Great Britain could not act effectively without France, and so there was still a chance for a *modus vivendi* which would save the face of Great Britain and the League without mortally offending Italy. But, unfortunately for Anglo-French relations, details of the Hoare-Laval negotiations to this end leaked into the French press, and their premature disclosure roused such a storm of protest in Great Britain that Sir Samuel Hoare, the British Foreign Secretary, was compelled to resign. Laval, by now Premier as well as Foreign Minister, was reluctantly forced to make the choice he sought to evade, and France joined Great Britain, albeit very half-heartedly, in applying economic sanctions to the power with whom she had so lately acted in concert.

The consequences of the Abyssinian affair were indeed serious for France and for Europe. The half-hearted application of sanctions did nothing to prevent the Italian conquest of Abyssinia but merely further discredited the League of Nations and proved the ineffectiveness of collective security. On the other hand, the fact that France applied sanctions at all alienated her from Italy and precipitated the Italian rapprochement with Germany which the Rome Agreements had been designed by the French to prevent. Worse still, the Hoare-Laval crisis, following close upon an Anglo-German naval agreement concluded without French approval, made many Frenchmen, particularly of the Right, see in Great Britain the enemy who had undermined France's position in Europe by forcing her to choose between Italy and the League. There was a wave of Anglophobia among the Nationalists of the Right, which was so violent as almost to recall the passions of the Boer War, while on the other side of the Channel Englishmen were aggrieved that the uncooperative attitude of France had allowed Italy to snap her fingers at the cherished League. In the winter of 1935–6 Anglo-French relations were more strained than at any time since Poincaré's occupation of the Ruhr, if not since the foundation of the Entente Cordiale in 1904. The consequences of this tension were soon to be seen in that part of Europe which most nearly affected France's vital security. On 7 March 1936, using as a pretext the French Chamber's vote in January in favour of the ratification of the Franco-Russian Pact, Germany, without any previous notice, proceeded to the military reoccupation of the Rhineland. This action was an undoubted breach of the Locarno Agreements of 1925, but it could be questioned whether it was a flagrant breach requiring immediate British aid to France and Belgium. It was a test case of Hitler's ability to break international agreements with impunity, and the time and the ground were well chosen. Not only were Anglo-French relations strained, but British public opinion, which had never understood the French anxiety about the Rhineland, and which was unfamiliar with the texts of the Locarno agreements, as of most treaties, tended to regard Germany's action as no more than an assertion of reasonable rights over part of her own territory and was by no means disposed to take a firm line. In these circumstances, faced at home by a wave of pacifism and the hesitations of their General Staff, the French Government – an ephemeral Cabinet headed by the Radical, Albert Sarraut – also hesitated, and finally contented themselves with a protest. Thereby they missed their greatest opportunity of checking the victorious tide of National Socialism before it overflowed the German borders. All the evidence subsequently disclosed goes to suggest that Hitler's army was still too weak to resist a French advance in force, and that, had a Poincaré been in power, France might have administered a rebuff such as would seriously have weakened the Nazi movement. Instead the prestige of the Nazi regime was enhanced and the Germans were able to entrench themselves in the Rhineland, build the great defensive Siegfried Line and prepare fresh attacks upon existing treaties. Otherwise, the main consequence of their breach of Locarno was to bring the two main western signatories together again. Although Great Britain was not ready to act in March 1936 the British Government promptly reaffirmed their recognition of the validity of the Locarno Agreements, and, in return for a reciprocal assurance from France, offered to initiate staff talks in order to consider ways of concerting military action should unprovoked aggression compel either power to fulfil its obligations. France readily responded and in December 1936, the French Foreign Minister told the Chamber that all French forces would at once go to the aid of Great Britain were she the victim of an unprovoked attack. Henceforward, in view of the growing power of Germany and the estrangement of Italy, France had no alternative but to follow the lead of Great Britain in her attempts to preserve European peace. It was the easier for her to do so since she now once again had a Government of the Left.

There were many reasons, old and new, which explained this new success of the Left at the polls. Once again the mystical charm of carrying on the movement of the Great Revolution by casting a vote on the Left had exercised its traditional attraction. Once again, as in 1889 or 1902, the men of the Left had successfully posed as the defenders of Republican liberties, not this time against Royalism or clericalism but against the menace of growing Fascist tendencies among elements of the Right with their semi-military Leagues such as the Croix de Feu and the more sinister Hooded Men, or Cagoulards, and their avowed sympathies for Fascist Italy at the time of the Abyssinian crisis. Anti-Fascism took the place of anti-clericalism as the cementing force in the new Bloc. But more important still were the widespread economic discontent and the hopes of remedying it held out by the economic and social programme of the Popular Front. Since 1931 France's economic situation had been steadily deteriorating under the impact of the world slump. Whereas in most other countries the bottom of the depression had been reached by 1933, in France the bulk and value of foreign trade, whose recovery was hampered by price disparities, continued to fall in spite of some measure of success eventually achieved in lowering production costs by a deflationary policy. The luxury trades were hard hit, the tourist traffic fell off sharply because France's adherence to the gold standard made her one of the dearest countries in Europe, the tonnage of her mercantile marine and the value of her income from freights declined, and by the beginning of 1936 there were 500,000 unemployed in receipt of relief and many others out of work.

All this had coincided with a sharp fall in agricultural prices in 1932 and a new bitterness and unrest amongst the agricultural community. The threat of devaluation had encouraged speculation and involved a loss of gold from the Bank of France, and the subsequent insistence on a deflationary policy with its accompanying economies, cuts in staff and reduction of salaries, had been extremely unpopular with many of the workers and also with many *petits bourgeois* and others dependent on fixed incomes. Accordingly, many of the votes cast for the Front Populaire had been votes for the abandonment of deflation and for increases in wages. Finally, the victory of the Front marked an upsurging of all the forces which had so long and so vainly called for social reform. The brief movement of idealism and aspiration towards social collaboration, by which the relations of employers and employed and Government and unions had been characterized on the morrow of the armistice, had quickly been dissipated, and they had swung back to their pre-war condition of tension and distrust. Individual employers, in a spirit of benevolent paternalism, might treat their workers admirably, providing them with garden cities, dispensaries, family allowances, and insurance schemes, but the majority looked on the eight-hour day with disapproval and were reluctant to adjust the wages of their men to meet the rises in living costs. Attempts to force an improvement in conditions by wide-spread strikes in 1919 and 1920 had failed and the following fifteen years had been on the whole a period of 'social stability and working-class apathy'.[2] The Cartel Governments of 1924 and 1932, submerged by other problems, had not added any important measure of social reform to the

statute book; and a bill in favour of compulsory holidays with pay for
workers in industry and commerce, which was voted by the Chamber in
1931 and might have had an important psychological effect had it
immediately become law, had been turned down by the Senate. Since
1919 almost the only important pieces of social legislation were comprised
in two laws of 1928 and 1930 providing for a system of compulsory
insurance and in a further law of 1932 instituting a general system of
family allowances. Thus the Front Populaire, with its slogan of 'Bread,
Peace and Liberty' and its programme for the nationalization of key
industries and improvement of working-class conditions, seemed to offer
to a vast number of Frenchmen, to many of the bourgeoisie and peasants
– the most striking Communist successes were in farming districts – as
well as the workers, the one solution of their material difficulties, the one
hope of relief from hardship, discontent and years of struggle. For this
reason alone its victory was of considerable significance.[3]

The new coalition was in many ways similar to the Cartels of 1924 and
1932, but there was an important difference in the balance of forces within
it. For the first time it was the Socialists and not the Radicals who were the
largest single party; while further still to the Left, Communist representation had increased from ten to seventy-two. This striking Communist
success was not due merely to social discontent. The Franco-Russian Pact
and Stalin's declaration approving the French decision to rearm had been
of real importance, both because they gave the Communist party in France
a new respectability and because they led it to one of those abrupt reversals
of policy which were such conspicuous features of the history of Communist groups all over the world. The French Communists, hitherto anti-
democratic, contemptuous of the Republic and violent opponents of
rearmament, now came forward as champions of democracy and Republican liberty, claimed to be legitimate heirs of the French Revolution, sang
the 'Marseillaise' and were among the foremost to urge the acceleration of
national defence; while in their hatred of the extremists of the Right they
even declared themselves ready to co-operate with Catholics in order to
combat the menace of Fascism. This volte-face certainly did much to
account for their success at the polls. Furthermore, their success emphasized the growing tendency for France, like Germany earlier in the 1930s,
to be torn between two extremes which were international in their connections; while the preponderance of the Socialists clearly indicated that the
long ascendancy of the Radicals was drawing to an end. As the largest
single party, after the elections of 1924 and 1932, had been the Radicals, it
was they who had formed the Government: but now the rise of massive
groups to their Left forced them more obviously into the position of being
the Conservatives that they really were; and the Socialist predominance

meant that the first Front Populaire Government was headed by Léon Blum, the first Socialist to be a French Prime Minister. Nevertheless the Radicals were still a very important element; the new Government was not exclusively Socialist, but a Socialist-Radical combination. The Communists gave it their support but declined to take part in the Cabinet, thus enjoying 'the advantages of electoral victory without its responsibilities'.[4] The application of Socialist legislation would be possible only in so far as it was tolerable to the Radical Ministers.

In a speech to the Socialist Congress immediately after the elections Léon Blum described the Front Populaire as 'not merely a combination of parties, but a powerful mass movement'.[5] And such indeed it appeared to be when, without waiting for the formation of the new Government or for instructions from their Unions, the workers in the aeronautical industries, the nationalization of which had been demanded in the electoral programme of the Front Populaire, downed tools; and when their example was followed in a host of other industries, especially in the region of Paris. There was a great wave of spontaneous stay-in strikes by workers who were flushed with electoral victory and thought that they were masters at last. 'The people' as in 1848 and 1871, believing themselves in control got out of control; and although the strikes were singularly free of violence either towards individuals or towards machinery, the forces of order and many of the bourgeoisie, as in 1848 and 1871, took instant alarm.

This time their alarm was all the greater and more comprehensible because they now saw France threatened with social disorder and anarchy at the very moment when the international situation was growing more menacing. Just as the workers saw the hand of the foreigner behind the Fascist formations of the Right, so the bourgeoisie saw the hand of the foreigner behind the strikes which interrupted the rearmament programme. Discounting the Communists' new-founded patriotism, they suspected the influence of Russia and the deliberate fomenting of social revolution. Thus the advent of the Front Populaire, instead of inaugurating a new period in which long-needed social reforms would bridge the gulf between classes in France and by reinforcing political with social democracy, create a new unity among the French people, only increased their divisions, confirmed the fears and suspicions of Right and Left and accelerated the drift towards extremes. Significantly enough it was in the very month in which the first Blum Government took office, in June 1936, that a new anti-Communist group, the Parti Populaire Français was founded by an ex-Communist deputy named Jacques Doriot. Within a year it claimed to have 200,000 members. Significantly enough, too, the fact that the new Prime Minister was a Jew gave a new impetus to the growing anti-semitism of the Right. Anti-semitism, so rampant at the time of the Dreyfus Affair, had greatly decreased by the time of the Great War, and in the 1920s it had been confined mainly to the comparatively small circles influenced by such papers as the *Action Française* and the more scurrilous *Gringoire*. But since 1933 it had grown considerably as a result of the influx of several thousand German and Austrian Jewish refugees. Now that Blum was Prime Minister there were many on the Right who talked, in language strangely like that of the German National Socialists, of the menace to French society from Jewish Bolshevism.

For many of its most naïve and enthusiastic supporters the advent of the Front Populaire had seemed to herald the millennium. But little more than a year after it took office the Blum Government fell and gave place to a Ministry in which a much more cautious Radical policy prevailed. In fact, the Front Populaire went the way of the Cartels before it. It, too, came to grief on finance. Its social policy was costly; the outbreak of further strikes meant the continuance of the fall in exports; taxation did not produce a return sufficient to balance the budget; and, in spite of the Government's emphasis on peace, the grave international situation compelled it to shoulder the financial burden of a growing armament programme. This did not in any way mean that it had achieved nothing. It had not reformed the Constitution of 1875 – that was not one of its aims – nor had it radically altered the social and economic structure of the country, for, as Blum explained, its aim had been 'to administer the bourgeois State', 'to put into effect the Popular Front programme, not to transform the social system'.[6] It had, however, given the Bank of France a more democratic constitution in which the State had more effective control, and it had provided for the progressive nationalization of the armament industries. Furthermore, the so-called Matignon agreements, concluded under Government auspices by the CGT and representatives of industrial employers on the morrow of the formation of the Blum Cabinet, together with subsequent legislation in 1936 had amounted virtually to a French 'New Deal' and had much improved working-class conditions. Wages were raised by an average 12 per cent; every worker was to have a fortnight's holiday with pay each year and an Under-Secretary was appointed especially to provide amenities for his leisure hours; conditions of work were to be regulated for each industry and each economic region by collective contracts between representatives of employers and employed; workers' delegates were to be elected in all factories employing more than ten people; the normal working week was reduced to forty hours; labour disputes were to be submitted to conciliation and compulsory arbitration without prejudice to the right to strike, a procedure which was subsequently to be given juridical form in 1938.

All these measures represented great gains from the workers' point of view; but their application inevitably took time, and the adjustment of industry to the new conditions involved much bitterness and friction which showed itself in the continuation of strikes throughout 1936 and 1937. Much more immediately effective in producing appeasement was the Government's success in adjusting the level of agricultural prices; and in particular the stabilization of wheat prices through a newly created National Wheat Board. But the general economic results of the Government's legislation were disappointing: unemployment was only slightly reduced; production did not increase, and would probably have shown a decline but for the rearmament programme and the temporary stimulus provided by devaluation of the franc in September 1936. By February 1937, after the initial measures had been carried through and under the menace of growing financial difficulties, the parties in the Popular Front could no longer agree upon further reforms and Blum was obliged to call a halt. Once again, as in 1926 and 1932, there was a conflict between those Socialists who wished to continue a thorough-going policy of structural change and the basically conservative Radicals who feared social disorder and favoured more limited remedies. The substitution in June 1937 of a Government headed by Chautemps for that of Blum meant that the Radicals had won: and although Radical-Socialist co-operation continued uneasily for some months to come there was little further reform of great significance. Once again Governments were preoccupied by growing financial difficulties and, still more important, by the progressive deterioration of the international situation; and when in 1938 the second Blum Cabinet was replaced by a new Union Nationale Ministry it was clear that the Front Populaire had finally broken down. More than ever France required national unity under a strong leader. But she now had no Poincaré or Clemenceau, nor even a Doumergue: but only a mediocre Radical named Daladier.

In many ways France had been behind other countries in social legislation and the conditions in which she allowed her people to live and work. Reforms were long overdue and the Front Populaire had done much to remove the grounds for reproaching France with social backwardness. The bitter irony of the situation was, however, that, as we have seen, the Front Populaire came to power in circumstances which intensified instead of lessening the hostilities among Frenchmen and that its reforms, which inevitably tended to reduce production, came at the very moment when increased output was vital. In consequence, the last Governments of the Third Republic were more than ever paralysed and unable to respond with decision to the series of crises provoked by German initiative; and each crisis served only to emphasize the division and confusion of French opinion.

This the first Blum Government had discovered very soon after its accession to power. In July 1936 an insurrection of the Spanish Right against the Republican Government in Spain, which in its composition closely resembled the French Front Populaire, roused passionate partisan feeling in France. Spanish affairs, as we have seen,[7] had often in the past led to French intervention, and now the militants and Left wing of the Front Populaire put strong pressure on Blum to go to the aid of the Frente Popular. Not only did they urge this in the interests of Republican and Socialist solidarity but also of French security, for it was soon clear that the rebels in Spain were being aided by Germany and Italy, who in November proclaimed their alliance in the so-called Rome-Berlin Axis. But the Right and the Catholics in France were equally strongly in favour of General Franco, the rebel leader, while the British Government were far from enthusiastic about supporting the Spanish Government. With a divided nation behind him, a lukewarm Britain on his flank, and a hostile Germany and Italy in his rear, Blum had to content himself with non-intervention and a joint Anglo-French patrol of the Mediterranean, where submarines of unknown nationality became a menace to neutral and Spanish Republican shipping. When the protracted civil war ended it was the Axis protégé who emerged victorious. In 1939, as in 1870, Germany had skilfully arranged that her intended victim should seem to be menaced on the Pyrenees as well as on the Rhine. Meanwhile, however, the Communists and Left wing of the Front Populaire long continued to hope for a reversal of the non-intervention policy; and their agitation on behalf of the Spanish Republicans, and the fact that many of them served as volunteers with the Republican forces, made it all the easier for the Right in France to denounce the Front Populaire as the party that wished to land the country in war.

Here, we must note a strange reversal of roles. From the days of Boulanger, it will be remembered, it had been the Right who had supplanted the Left as the militant patriots and Nationalists; it was they who had been most eager for *revanche*, most jealous in upholding French prestige abroad, most strongly in favour of a hard peace and most critical of any relaxation of the stipulations of the Treaty of Versailles. But with the Abyssinian crisis of 1935, eager to avoid war with Italy at all costs, they reverted to the attitude which had characterized them during the first seventy years of our period and once again became the party of peace. This attitude was perfectly intelligible: the last thing the French people as a whole desired was to be involved in another great war such as that of 1914–18; collective security had broken down; the eastern system of alliances had been weakened; Russia was remote, suspect to the Right on ideological grounds and militarily a doubtful quantity; Great Britain, which had not even enforced conscription, could not be expected to give France much help of immediate value on land; and France was sadly

conscious of her numerical inferiority and the backwardness of her rearmament programme compared with that of Germany. If, in addition, she
was deeply divided on social and other questions and war and defeat were
likely, as in so many countries in 1918, to bring social revolution in their
train, what wonder that the Right should regard the preservation of peace
as the highest French interest? Unfortunately their obsession with the
Communist menace was to lead them beyond this view to the view that
peace and an accommodation with Germany were desirable at any price.[8]
Their sense of values became distorted and they failed to see that a peace
bought at the cost of submitting to intimidation and dishonouring
pledges could lead only to servitude and be no true peace at all.

This inability of divided France to take a lead and react vigorously to the
attacks on the European order established at Versailles now made by the
revisionist powers was still more evident in 1938. The international situation progressively deteriorated. In November 1937, the Axis was
extended from Rome and Berlin to Tokyo, and, by veiling their territorial
ambitions with the cloud of the Anti-Komintern Pact, Germany, Italy and
Japan cast fresh dust in the eyes of Conservatives, many of whom were led
to believe that these three states were indeed the bulwark of European
civilization against a real Communist menace. A few months later, after
Eden's resignation from the Chamberlain Cabinet had shown that the
forces which favoured appeasement of the Axis Powers were still in the
ascendant in Great Britain, the Germans marched into Austria and
imposed Anschluss by annexation. The forcible overthrow of the Versailles
territorial settlement had begun and France and Great Britain could do no
more than protest. It was not long before the next victim was singled out
for attack. In the summer Germany began her war of nerves against
Czechoslovakia, unleashing the Sudeten Germans of Bohemia to claim
incorporation with the Reich. Here was yet one more critical test for
France. If Czechoslovakia yielded it would mean the distintegration of the
Czechoslovak state, menaced at the same time by Polish and Hungarian
claims on the northern and southern borders: and with Czechoslovakia the
whole alliance system built by France with such care, but already gravely
weakened in spite of the Blum Government's attempts to strengthen it,
would be in danger of falling to the ground. If, on the other hand,
Czechoslovakia refused to yield and was attacked by Germany, France was
bound by treaty to go to her aid. The war she was so anxious to avoid
would be inevitable. In this crisis there were many on the Right in France
who sought to argue that the French undertaking to Czechoslovakia was
no longer binding since the Locarno system had broken down.[9] Paralysed
by the divisions of French opinion, incapable of giving a firm lead, the
weak Government of Daladier neglected Russia and left the initiative to

Great Britain, who had no obligations to Czechoslovakia, to try and find a compromise solution which would appease Hitler, preserve the Czechoslovak state and save Europe from war. After an acute crisis in September 1938 the compromise was discovered at Munich where Chamberlain and Daladier, ignoring Russia's interests in Eastern Europe, met Hitler and Mussolini and sacrificed Czechoslovakia on the altar of a highly precarious peace. The Czechoslovak state was maintained, but shorn of territory in such a way that it became strategically defenceless. The Franco-Russian Pact had failed to operate and the eastern alliance system had broken down. Peace had been preserved, but France's prestige had immeasurably declined and her relative position in Europe had been weakened still further.

If there were any in France, as well as in England, who were naïve enough to believe that Munich meant peace in their time they were speedily disillusioned. On 15 March 1939 Hitler overthrew the Munich settlement and marched into Prague. No one in either country could any longer believe in the effectiveness of a policy of appeasement. It was clear to the dullest that Germany now aimed at nothing less than the domination of the Continent. Great Britain at once reacted vigorously, giving a guarantee to Poland and undertakings to assist Roumania and Greece, should their independence be threatened. Once again the French Government followed the British lead. They reaffirmed the Franco-Polish alliance, they gave similar undertakings to Roumania and Greece and signed a pact of mutual assistance with Turkey. But the British and French attempts to bring Russia into their new combined front against aggression were doomed to failure. On 23 August 1939, while their representatives were still in Moscow attempting to negotiate a military agreement, they and the whole world were confounded by the news that Ribbentrop, the Nazi Foreign Minister, had also been there and had signed a pact of non-aggression and friendship with Stalin. The Western Powers had bought time independently of Russia at Munich: now Russia paid for the same commodity independently of them at Moscow. The way was free for the next German offensive which followed at once in a series of demands upon Poland. This time there was to be no second Munich. All attempts at conciliation broke down. Germany invaded Poland on 1 September, and on 3 September 1939, Great Britain and France declared war on Germany. But it was significant of the change in the positions of the two countries since 1914 that the British declaration preceded that of France by six hours.

Thus all the efforts of France since 1918 to build up such a system of security as would make a renewal of German aggression for ever impossible had come to naught. Once again, as in 1914, because of the aggression of a

Germanic power in Eastern Europe she was at war with her traditional foe, and once again Great Britain was her chief ally in the west. But in the east instead of Russia she had only Poland as an ally,[10] and Poland was overrun and crushed in two months. Whereas, from 1914 to 1917 at least, Germany had been weakened by the necessity of fighting on two fronts, she was now very quickly at liberty to throw the whole weight of her forces against the west. Unless the Allies could upset her plans she would be free to choose her own moment and exert her utmost strength to force an immediate decision. The danger which threatened France after the outbreak of war in 1939 was still more terrible than that of August and September 1914. In the face of that earlier peril she had sunk her internal differences and achieved the impressive moral and political unity of *union sacrée*; then she had had the leadership of a Poincaré and a Joffre, and had worked the 'miracle' of the Marne. Now, however, she was still morally and politically divided and had only a Lebrun, a Daladier and a Gamelin, no miracle workers, but men of stature much too small for so great an emergency. The story of 1939–40 was to be tragically different from that of 1914.

Initially all seemed to go well. The army was mobilized without a hitch, and there was an appearance of political unity when the emergency war credits were voted by all parties including the Communists and when the Communist deputies went off to join their regiments. But the Russo-German Pact and the consequent Russian invasion of Eastern Poland on the one hand, and the absence of any serious hostilities in the west on the other, soon had a disintegrating effect. It is arguable that a real revival of French unity could have been achieved only under the stimulus of a violent German attack on the western front immediately after the declaration of war. Then, so long as the defence held, it is probable that the desire to defend the sacred soil of France would have outweighed every other consideration. But no such attack came, even after Poland had been crushed; there was not even any aerial bombardment and the French general staff had made a serious psychological error in not attempting to create a diversion while Poland was still resisting. To the Polish débâcle there succeeded the long winter months of the 'phoney' war.

Such a period of expectancy would in any case have been sorely trying to the morale of a nation so impetuous as the French. In the conditions of 1939–40 it was most damaging. The Russo-German Pact and Russian invasion of Poland had led in September to the dissolution of the French Communist Party and to the eventual unseating and trial of many Communist deputies and Senators. These high-handed measures were justified on the grounds that the Communists were agents of a foreign power in league with France's enemy. But the party, well equipped for clandestine activity, continued its propaganda which was now directed against the Government as 'Fascist' and the war as an 'Imperialist' war with which the French soldier should have nothing to do. Thus during the months of inaction there were, as in 1917, insidious attempts by the extreme Left to undermine the morale of the troops and the workers. At the same time, and still more disquieting because of its political influence, there grew up a peace party headed by men of the Right such as Laval who asked what point there was in beginning a war in the west, now that the war in the east was over, and suggested that peace, if necessary at the price of some concessions, a new Munich, would be preferable to defeat and the loss of many lives.[11] Thus the German subtlety in abstaining from war in the west for so many months reaped rich dividends in France. Moreover, Russia's attack on Finland at the end of November and Finland's heroic resistance still further confused the issue. For many, both in England and France, not content with being at war with Germany, were eager to go crusading against Russia, and, had Finland been more easy of access, it is probable that an Anglo-French expeditionary force would have been sent to her aid. Incidentally this diversion and the failure of the Allies to take the initiative in the west led to increasing criticism of Daladier in France and of Chamberlain in England. On 20 March Daladier resigned, and in May, after the collapse of the Allies' attempt to save Norway, Chamberlain made way for Churchill.

In France the peace party had worked against Daladier and hoped to supplant him, but the President of the Republic called upon Paul Reynaud to form a Ministry. That choice meant that war would be waged with greater determination, although it was disquietingly significant that in its first meeting with the Chamber the new Cabinet only obtained an effective majority of one. It also meant that the alliance with Great Britain would become still closer. Already on 12 December 1939, an agreement between the French and British treasuries had provided for a striking measure of financial co-operation. The two Governments had also agreed in principle that both their armies should be under a single commander, the French Generalissimo, General Gamelin. Now on the morrow of the formation of the Reynaud Cabinet they united in a solemn declaration not to negotiate or conclude an armistice or treaty of peace except by mutual agreement, and undertook to maintain community of action in all spheres for as long as might be necessary after the conclusion of peace. Hitler's hopes of shattering the unity of the Allies without a blow were vain when Churchill and Reynaud were in power. He could not afford to wait indefinitely and on 10 May launched the great land offensive in the west for which the world had so long been waiting.

In many ways, in spite of the moral and political disunity by which she was weakened, France had learnt the lessons of the last war and was therefore more quickly prepared for the emergency of 1939-40. The material welfare of the troops was better provided for; there was less dislocation because the distribution of manpower was better adjusted between the needs of the army and of the war industries; and power to legislate by decree, once again granted by a Chamber which had agreed to prolong its own life by two years as early as 21 March 1939, gave the Government greater freedom of action. But there was one field in which she had learnt nothing or learnt wrong and in which she proved incapable of learning even from the Polish campaign of 1939. It was France's crowning disaster that her generals as well as her politicians were inferior to their task. They had prepared for another war of trenches; they had become obsessed by the defensive mentality of the Maginot Line and ignored the fact that it was the offensive war of movement which had won the final victory even in 1918. They had devoted enormous sums to the construction of the Maginot Line, but had not carried it along the Belgian frontier to the sea,[12] above all they had neglected the air and, deaf to the warnings of men like Reynaud and De Gaulle, who had urged that the victory in modern war would go to the most highly mobile mechanized army, had subordinated their considerable new armoured forces to the requirements of the infantry and of defence.[13] Thus they had failed in their first duty of being imaginative and keeping abreast with the technical developments of modern war. When to this were added grave errors of judgement in meeting the German attack the results were fatal.

On 10 May the Germans launched their offensive through Holland and Belgium. It looked like a repetition of 1914. Then Joffre had concentrated his forces too far south and had not been prepared for the vast German enveloping movement in the north-east: now the French High Command hurried troops to parry the enveloping movement and were caught off their guard at the pivotal point where the Maginot Line came to an end. It was here, near Sedan, so full of memories of an earlier débâcle, that the Germans broke through in force with seven Panzer divisions: and, once they had broken through, their crushing superiority in air power and their superior use of armoured vehicles were decisive. They had almost unlimited freedom of movement. The Dutch had already given in on 15 May and the Belgians were to capitulate a fortnight later, on the 28th. Meanwhile the French High Command had made a fatal mistake in not ordering the immediate withdrawal from Belgium of the French and British armies of the north as soon as it knew of the German break-through. This meant that forty British and French divisions were caught by a vast encircling movement and that when they failed to break through the German ring they had no choice but to evacuate by sea from Dunkirk in order to escape annihilation. The 'miracle of the Marne' in 1914 had been a victory. Dunkirk, too, was a 'miracle', but it was still part of a great defeat. Already on the morrow of the Norwegian catastrophe Reynaud had broadened his Cabinet by including two new Ministers of the Right. Now he replaced the Commander-in-Chief, Gamelin, by Weygand, Foch's Chief of Staff in the last war, who had recently distinguished himself in pacifying Syria, and brought Pétain into his Cabinet as Vice-President. But it was too late and these were old men, tired and disillusioned, Weygand seventy-three and Pétain eighty-four. It was a thousand fresh planes and tanks and a supply of young generals with a fresh outlook that France required, and the tanks and planes did not exist. Already by the end of May Weygand had made up his mind that the defeat was irretrievable. By the end of the Dunkirk evacuation France had lost two-fifths of her effectives and eight-tenths of her material.[14] The British losses in material were almost as heavy.

The defeat of the French forces was a military defeat, the victory of the power which had an overwhelming superiority in men and materials and knew how to use them with ruthless efficiency. The demoralization caused in the French army by the 'phoney war' and by the insidious propaganda of Communist and fifth columnists weighed little against the gallantry once again displayed by the ordinary French soldier in Norway, Belgium and France. But such gallantry was powerless against such odds and the battle was lost often before it could be said to have been joined. A heavy weight of responsibility lies indeed upon the French General Staff of the late 1920s and 1930s.

France had suffered great military disasters before, but she had not given in. In 1870 she had witnessed Sedan and Metz but had gone on waging war to the knife, even after the capitulation of her main regular armies. Again, in 1914, she had survived the Battle of the Frontiers and in 1918 the Chemin des Dames, and wrested victory from defeat. But in 1940 she would no longer be true to herself. It was now, after the military defeat, that the demoralizing forces which we have seen at work during the 'phoney war' were to exert their influence to the country's dishonour and the ruin of the Third Republic. It was now that France needed a Gambetta or a Clemenceau and failed to find one. It was during the critical twelve days after Dunkirk that the fateful battle was fought on the home front between the men who were eager to continue the fight and those who thought only of abandonment, of obtaining power for themselves and of overthrowing the regime. On 5 June Paul Reynaud once again remodelled his Cabinet and thereby showed his poor judgement of men. For, apart from De Gaulle whom he made Under-Secretary for War, the other new Ministers were all weak men who would soon show their readiness to desert the sinking ship of state. Furthermore, like Boulanger,

Reynaud was at certain moments of crisis to be fatally influenced by his mistress, who was never far away during these last days of his Premiership.

For the time being, however, he appeared indomitable. In a telegram to President Roosevelt on 10 June he declared that the Government would withdraw to one of the French provinces – he had for some time had this idea of creating a redoubt in Brittany – and that if they were driven from the national territory they would continue the struggle in North Africa or, if need be, in one of France's American possessions. On that same day the Government left Paris, which was hourly threatened by the advancing Germans, and set out like the Government of August 1914 for Bordeaux. On that day, too, France's plight was made even worse by the decision of the 'jackal dictator', Mussolini, to stab her in the back. Italy came in on the side of her Axis partner and declared war on France and Great Britain. Two days later, in a dramatic council of war at Cangey near Tours, Weygand declared that further resistance was impossible. Pétain agreed, but the majority of the other Ministers still refused to share his view that France should ask for an armistice. In the next three days, however, the arguments of Weygand and Pétain gained ground. A Clemenceau would at once have replaced the defeatist generals and silenced the defeatist Ministers or excluded them from his Cabinet, but Reynaud, in spite of the advice of men like Campinchi and Louis Marin, hesitated to do so. The hesitation was fatal. By the 16th the Germans had entered Paris and the Government had reached Bordeaux; Reynaud had failed to persuade Weygand that the proper course of action was to follow the Dutch example, allowing the army to cease fire in France without any formal capitulation while the Government and what men and material could be saved continued the struggle from North Africa; he had failed to make good use of the support of the Presidents of the Chamber and Senate; he had failed to dismiss Weygand and dominate his Cabinet and the result was that the peace party within it now gained the upper hand. The dramatic British offer of a Franco-British Union was turned down. Reynaud had allowed his authority to be gradually undermined and that evening he resigned. The appointment of the vain and aged fatalist, Marshal Pétain, as his successor, made an armistice inevitable and spelt the doom of the Third Republic. It meant the triumph of Laval and of the party who hated Great Britain, who were convinced that she, in turn, would speedily succumb, and were eager to make terms with Germany, reverse the old alliance system, erect an authoritarian regime and earn for France a comfortable place in the new European order. It also meant the breach of the Solemn Declaration of 28 March, for France was bound to go on fighting unless she was formally relieved from her engagements by Great Britain; and the British Government, although on the 16th they had reluctantly agreed that France should inquire about armistice terms, had made it a *sine qua non* of their agreement that the French fleet should be sent for safe keeping to British ports while any armistice negotiations were in progress. Of this categoric condition the Pétain Government took no account. Furthermore, they refused to preserve their own freedom by moving the Government to North Africa, in spite of the representations of the Presidents of the Senate and Chamber and of the President of the Republic himself. Pétain, urged on by Laval, clung fatalistically to the notion that it was honourable for him and the Government to share the lot of their compatriots in metropolitan France and that France's interests could not be defended if she were abandoned. The brave men like Mandel, Minister of the Interior in the Reynaud Government, and various deputies and others, who, notwithstanding, set out for Morocco and attempted to raise the standard of resistance there, were arrested and in consequence some of them eventually met their death.

And so it was that on 22 June 1940, the representatives of the Pétain Government signed the most humiliating armistice in French history. France was to be cut in two; the northern and western half, including Paris and all the Atlantic coast-line, being occupied by the Germans, and only the southern departments being left in nominal independence to the Pétain Government which established its headquarters at Vichy; the fleet was to be demobilized and disarmed; and one million four hundred thousand men were to remain prisoners in German hands.[15] Two days later an armistice followed with Italy. In their brief campaign in the Alps French troops had more than held their own, and only a small area of French territory was to be occupied by Italian troops under the armistice terms. Germany had won the victory; it was only natural that she should seize the lion's share of the spoils.

The Third Republic did not long survive these humiliations. On 10 July the Senate and Chamber met together at Vichy as a National Assembly and by 569 votes to eighty passed a new Constitutional Law giving 'full powers to the Government of the Republic to promulgate in one or more Acts, by the authority and under the signature of Marshal Pétain, the new constitution of the French State'. On the following day Pétain issued the first of his constitutional acts under that law. Thereby he abrogated the Law of 1875 defining the functions of the President of the Republic, assumed the functions of 'Head of the French State' and arrogated to himself all the effective power. The Constitutional Law had been signed by the President of the Republic, Lebrun, who had been re-elected in 1939, and, although he never formally resigned, that signature and the vote of parliament meant that the President of the Republic, and the Chamber of 1936 – the Front Populaire Chamber, whose election had aroused such extravagant hopes, together had virtually abdicated and voted and signed away the Third Republic.

Thus the regime born of defeat in 1870 succumbed in the catastrophe of 1940. It had never fully succeeded in reconciling the opposing forces born of the Revolution of 1789 or in solving the social problems created by the Industrial Revolution, and because of these failures it was in its last years the less able to put up an effective resistance to the disruptive pressure of alien ideologies. It had been weakened at the outset by the constitutional crisis of 1877, which had destroyed the internal balance of power and brought about an unhealthy preponderance of the legislature: and last but not least the country over which it presided, had never completely recovered from the strain of the First World War with all that that entailed. Yet, for all its defects, it had probably given a majority of Frenchmen as much government as they wanted and the sort of government they could best tolerate for a long period of years. It had lasted more than three times as long as any other regime since 1789 and the star of France, although dimmed and tarnished, was not wholly extinct. Already on 18 June from London General de Gaulle had issued his rousing call to all Free Frenchmen to rally round him. It was one of the many tragedies of those tragic weeks that by the end of that June so very few Frenchmen were free.

Notes

1 In fact it was a smaller affair and the main victims of Stavisky's frauds were insurance companies cf. Werth, A., *France in Ferment*, p. 62.

2 Laroque, Pierre, *Les rapports entre patrons et ouvriers*, p. 303. Goguel, F., *La politique des partis sous la IIIe République*, vol. 1, p. 354.

3 It is to be noted that the Right still remained a considerable force. 'The decrease in their voting strength was only 124,409 votes from 1928 to 1932, and 178,419 from 1932 to 1936,' when they still polled about 43 per cent of the total votes. Cf. Micaud, Charles A., *The French Right and Nazi Germany*, p. 12n.

4 Joll, James, 'The Making of the Popular Front' *The Decline of the Third Republic* (St Anthony's Papers, No. 5), p. 65.

5 Cit. Pickles, D. M., *The French Political Scene*, p. 134; for text of the Front Populaire programme see Thomson, D., *Democracy in France*, 4th edn, pp. 317ff.

6 Pickles, op. cit., p. 130.

7 See comment above, pp. 28–9, 56, 62–3.

8 Ever since 1871 there had always been Frenchmen – Gambetta, Ferry, Rouvier and Caillaux are notable examples – who had asked themselves whether it was not fatal for both countries that France and Germany should for ever remain

irreconcilable foes and who at one time or another believed that reconciliation was possible. But hitherto such men had been mostly of the Left.

9 E.g. the article entitled 'Conscience angoissée' in *Le Temps* of 12 April 1938, by Joseph-Barthélemy.

10 It is noteworthy that Poland never received from France a tithe of the military aid which France received from Russia in 1914, nor even a tithe of what she 'had been led to expect or at least to hope for'. B. H. Sumner review of Namier, L. B., *Diplomatic Prelude in International Affairs*, July 1948.

11 It may be noted here that there had been a striking growth of intellectual pessimism in the 1930s and that writers such as Sartre and Anouilh had already begun to expound their doctrines of futility.

12 One reason alleged was fear of offending the Belgian Government. But as P. Maillaud pointed out: 'As Belgium never agreed to co-ordinate her own strategy with that of the French, save at the last minute, it is difficult to see how the Belgian Government could have taken exception to elementary measures of self-defence', *France*, p. 105; cf. Churchill, W., *The Second World War*, vol. 1, p. 373.

13 It is now generally agreed that the French had approximately the same quantity of mechanized vehicles as the Germans in May 1940: but their mobility was inferior and they were hopelessly dispersed.

14 Kammerer, A., *La vérité sur l'armistice*, p. 61.

15 Maillaud, op. cit., p. 77; for the text cf. Thomson, op. cit., 2nd edn, pp. 279ff, or his *France: Empire and Republic*, pp. 357–64.

Bibliography

Azéma, J.-P., *De Munich à la libération 1938–1944*, Paris, 1979.

Bloc, March, *Strange Defeat*, Oxford, 1949.

Chapman, G., *Why France Collapsed*, London, 1968.

Colton, J., *Léon Blum: Humanist in Politics*, New York, 1966.

Dubief, H., *Le déclin de la Troisième République 1929–1938*, Paris, 1976.

Duroselle, J.-B., *La décadence 1932–1939*, Paris, 1979.

Fauvet, J., *Histoire du parti communiste français, 1917–1939*, Paris, 1964.

Joll, James (ed.), *The Decline of the Third Republic* (St Antony's Papers, No. 5), London, 1959.

Jordan, W. M., *Great Britain, France and the German Problem, 1918–39*, Oxford, 1943.

Larmour, Peter, J., *The French Radical Party in the 1930s*, Stanford, 1964.

Micaud, Charles A., *The French Right and Nazi Germany, 1933–9*, Durham, NC, 1943.

Namier, L. B., *Diplomatic Prelude, 1938–1939*, London, 1948.

Namier, L. B., *Europe in Decay, 1936–1940*, London, 1950.

Néré, J., *The Foreign Policy of France from 1914 to 1945*, London, 1974.

Osgood, S. M. (ed.), *The Fall of France 1940*, 2nd edn, Lexington, 1972.

Warner, G., *Pierre Laval and the Eclipse of France*, London, 1968.

Werth, Alexander, *The Twilight of France 1933–40*, London, 1942.

APPENDIX 1

Genealogical Tree of the Houses of Bourbon and Bourbon-Orléans

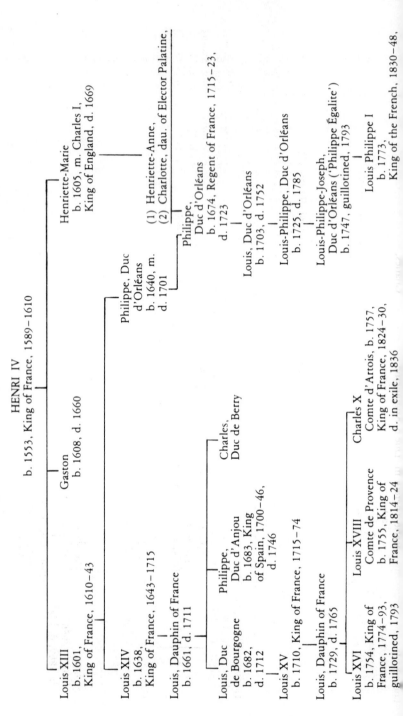

Louis XVI

Charlotte
b. 1778,
d. 1851

Marie Thérèse b. 1775, d. 1844

Duc de Berry,
b. 1778, m. Caroline, dau.
of Francis I of Naples,
assassinated, 1820

Antoine
Philippe,
Duc de
Montpensier
b. 1824,
d. 1890

('the prisoner in
the Temple'),
b. 1785, d. 1795

Henri Charles, Comte
de Chambord ('Henri V'),
b. 1820, m. Marie-Louise, dau.
of Francis IV, Duke of Modena,
d. in exile 1883

Henri
Eugène,
Duc
d'Aumale
b. 1822,
d. 1897

Louise Marie Thérèse
m. 1845, Charles III,
Duke of Parma

Louis
Ferdinand,
Prince de
Joinville
b. 1818,
d. 1900

Louis,
Duc de
Nemours
b. 1814,
d. 1896

Clementine
b. 1817,
m. Prince
Augustus
of Saxe-
Coburg-
Gotha

Ferdinand
b. 1861
Prince of
Bulgaria,
1887

Marie
b. 1813,
m. 1837,
Duke of
Wurtemburg,
d. 1839

Louise
b. 1812,
m. 1832,
Leopold I,
King of the
Belgians,
d. 1850

Robert, Duc de Chartres
b. 1840, d. 1910

Ferdinand-Philippe,
Duc d'Orléans
b. 1810, d. 1842

Jean,
Duc de Guise
b. 1874, d. 1940

Louis Philippe,
Comte de Paris
b. 1838,
d. in exile, 1894

Henri, Comte de Paris
(the present Pretender)
b. 1908

Philippe,
Duc d'Orléans
b. 1869, d. 1926

APPENDIX 2

The Presidents of the Third Republic

1 ADOLPHE THIERS: Appointed Chief of the Executive Power, 17 February 1871. Given title of President of the French Republic by Law of 31 August 1871. Resigned 24 May 1873.
2 MARSHAL MACMAHON: Elected, 24 May 1873. Resigned January, 1879.

Elected at Versailles in accordance with the constitutional laws of 1875

3 JULES GRÉVY: 30 January 1879. Completed his term. Re-elected 28 December 1885. Resigned 2 December 1887.
4 SADI CARNOT: 3 December 1887. Assassinated 24 June 1894.
5 JEAN-PAUL CASIMIR-PÉRIER: 27 June 1894. Resigned 15 January 1895.
6 FÉLIX FAURE: 17 January 1895. Died 16 February 1899.
7 ÉMILE LOUBET: 18 February 1899. Completed his term.
8 ARMAND FALLIÈRES: 17 January 1906. Completed his term.
9 RAYMOND POINCARÉ: 17 January 1913. Completed his term.
10 PAUL DESCHANEL: 17 January 1920. Resigned 17 September 1920.
11 ALEXANDRE MILLERAND: 23 September 1920. Resigned 11 June 1924.
12 GASTON DOUMERGUE: 13 June 1924. Completed his term.
13 PAUL DOUMER: 31 May 1931. Assassinated 7 May 1932.
14 ALBERT LEBRUN: 10 May 1932. Completed his term. Re-elected 5 April 1939.

APPENDIX 3

The Charter of 1814*

AFTER a lengthy preamble the Charter follows thus:
'À ces causes,
Nous avons volontairement et par le libre exercice de notre autorité royale, accordé et accordons . . . tant pour nous que pour nos successeurs et à jamais . . . la Charte constitutionnelle qui suit.

Droit public des Français

1 Les Français sont égaux devant la loi, quels que soient d'ailleurs leurs titres et leurs rangs.

2 Ils contribuent indistinctement, dans la proportion de leur fortune, aux charges de l'État.

3 Ils sont tous également admissibles aux emplois civils et militaires.

4 Leur liberté individuelle est également garantie, personne ne pouvant être poursuivi ni arrêté que dans les cas prévus par la loi, et dans la forme qu'elle prescrit.

5 Chacun professe sa religion avec une égale liberté, et obtient pour son culte la même protection.

6 Cependant la religion catholique, apostolique et romaine, est la religion de l'État.

7 Les ministres de la religion catholique, apostolique et romaine, et ceux des autres cultes chrétiens reçoivent seuls des traitements du Trésor royal.

8 Les Français ont le droit de publier et de faire imprimer leurs opinions en se conformant aux lois qui doivent réprimer les abus de cette liberté.

9 Toutes les propriétés sont inviolables, sans aucune exception de celles qu'on appelle nationales, la loi ne mettant aucune différence entre elles.

* Following Cahen et Mathiez I have omitted six relatively unimportant Articles, namely nos 26, 30, 31, 39, 45 and 73.

10   L'État peut exiger le sacrifice d'une propriété pour cause d'intérêt public légalement constaté, mais avec une indemnité préalable.

11   Toutes les recherches des opinions et votes émis jusqu' à la Restauration sont interdites. Le même oubli est commandé aux tribunaux et aux citoyens.

12   La conscription est abolie. Le mode de recrutement de l'armée de terre et de mer est determiné par une loi.

Formes du gouvernement du Roi

13   La personne du Roi est inviolable et sacrée. Ses ministres sont responsables. Au Roi seul appartient la puissance exécutive.

14   Le Roi est le chef suprême de l'État, commande les forces de terre et de mer, déclare la guerre, fait les traités de paix, d'alliance et de commerce, nomme à tous les emplois d'administration publique, et fait les règlements et ordonnances nécessaires pour l'exécution des lois et la sûreté de l'État.

15   La puissance législative s'exerce collectivement par le Roi, la Chambre des pairs, et la Chambre des députés des départements.

16   Le Roi propose la loi.

17   La proposition de loi est portée, au gré du Roi, à la Chambre des pairs ou à celle des députés, excepté la loi de l'impôt qui doit être adressée d'abord à la Chambre des députés.

18   Toute loi doit être discutée et votée librement par la majorité de chacune des deux Chambres.

19   Les Chambres ont la faculté de supplier le Roi de proposer une loi sur quelque objet que ce soit et d'indiquer ce qui leur paraît convenable que la loi contienne.

20   Cette demande pourra être faite par chacune des deux Chambres, mais après avoir été discutée en comité secret; elle ne sera envoyée à l'autre Chambre qu'après un délai de dix jours.

21   Si la proposition est adoptée par l'autre Chambre, elle sera mise sous les yeux du Roi; si elle est rejetée, elle ne pourra être représentée dans la même session.

22   Le Roi seul sanctionne et promulgue les lois.

23   La liste civile est fixée, pour toute la durée du règne, par la première législature assemblée depuis l'avènement du Roi.

De la Chambre des pairs

24   La Chambre des pairs est une portion essentielle de la puissance législative.

25   Elle est convoquée par le Roi en même temps que la Chambre des députés. . . .

27   La nomination des pairs de France appartient au Roi. Leur nombre est illimité. Il peut en varier les dignités, les nommer à vie ou les rendre héréditaires selon sa volonté.

28   Les pairs ont entrée dans la Chambre à vingt-cinq ans, et voix délibérative à trente ans seulement.

29   La Chambre des pairs est présidée par le chancelier de France et, en son absence, par un pair nommé par le Roi.

32   Toutes les délibérations de la Chambre des pairs sont secrètes.

33   La Chambre des pairs connaît des crimes de haute trahison et des attentats à sûreté de l'État qui seront définis par la loi.

34   Aucun pair ne peut être arrêté que de l'autorité de la Chambre, et jugé que par elle en matière criminelle.

De la Chambre des députés des départements

35   La Chambre des députés sera composée des députés élus par les collèges électoraux, dont l'organisation sera déterminée par des lois.

36   Chaque département aura le même nombre de députés qu'il aura eu jusqu' à présent.

37   Les députés seront élus pour cinq ans, et de manière que la Chambre soit renouvelable par cinquième.

38   Aucun député ne peut être admis dans la Chambre s'il n'est âgé de quarante ans et s'il ne paie une contribution directe de 1,000 francs.

40   Les électeurs qui concourent à la nomination des députés ne peuvent avoir droit de suffrage s'ils ne payent une contribution directe de 300 francs, et s'ils ont moins de trente ans.

41   Les présidents des collèges électoraux seront nommés par le Roi et de droit membres du collège.

42   La moitié au moins des députés sera choisie parmi des éligibles qui ont leur domicile politique dans le département.

43   Le président de la Chambre des députés est nommé par le Roi sur une liste de cinq membres présentée par la Chambre.

44   Les séances de la Chambre sont publiques, mais la demande de cinq membres suffit pour qu'elle se forme en comité secret.

46   Aucun amendement ne peut être fait à une loi s'il n'a été proposé ou consenti par le Roi, et s'il n'a été renvoyé ou discuté dans les bureaux.

47   La Chambre des députés reçoit toutes les propositions d'impôts; ce n'est qu'après que ces propositions ont été admises qu'elles peuvent être portées à la Chambre des pairs.

48   Aucun impôt ne peut être établi ni perçu s'il n'a été consenti par les deux Chambres et sanctionné par le Roi.

49   L'impôt foncier n'est consenti que pour un an. Les impositions indirectes peuvent l'être pour plusieurs années.

50   Le Roi convoque, chaque année, les deux Chambres; il les proroge, et peut dissoudre celle des députés des départements; mais, dans ce cas, il doit en convoquer une nouvelle dans le délai de trois mois.

51   Aucune contrainte par corps ne peut être exercée contre un membre de la Chambre durant la session, et dans les six semaines qui l'auront précédée ou suivie.

52   Aucun membre de la Chambre ne peut pendant la durée de la session être poursuivi ni arrêté en matière criminelle, sauf le cas de flagrant délit, qu'après que la Chambre a permis sa poursuite.

53   Toute pétition à l'une ou à l'autre Chambre ne peut être faite ou présentée que par écrit. La loi interdit d'en apporter en personne à la barre.

Des ministres

54   Les ministres peuvent être membres de la Chambre des pairs ou de la Chambre des députés. Ils ont en outre leur entrée dans l'une ou l'autre Chambre, et doivent être entendus quand ils le demandent.

55   La Chambre des députés a le droit d'accuser les ministres, et de les traduire devant la Chambre des pairs, qui seule a celui de les juger.

56   Il ne peuvent être accusés que pour fait de trahison ou de concussion. Des lois particulières spécifieront cette nature de délits et en détermineront la poursuite.

De l'ordre judiciaire

57   Toute justice émane du Roi. Elle s'administre en son nom par des juges qu'il nomme et qu'il institue.

58   Les juges nommés par le Roi sont inamovibles.

59   Les cours et tribunaux ordinaires actuellement existants sont maintenus. Il n'y sera rien changé qu'en vertu d'une loi.

60   L'institution actuelle des juges de commerce est conservée.

61   La justice de paix est également conservée. Les juges de paix, quoique nommés par le Roi, ne sont point inamovibles.

62   Nul ne pourra être distrait de ses juges naturels.

63   Il ne pourra en conséquence être créé de commissions et Tribunaux extraordinaires. Ne sont pas comprises sous cette dénomination les juridictions prevôtales si leur établissement est jugé nécessaire.

64   Les débats seront publics en matière criminelle, à moins que cette publicité ne soit dangereuse pour l'ordre et les moeurs; et, dans ce cas, le tribunal le déclare par un jugement.

65   L'institution des jurés est conservée. Les changements qu'une plus longue expérience ferait juger nécessaires ne peuvent être effectués que par une loi.

66   La peine de la confiscation des biens est abolie et ne pourra pas être rétablie.

67   Le Roi a droit de faire grâce et celui de commuer les peines.

68   Le Code civil et les lois actuellement existants qui ne sont pas contraires à la présente Charte restent en vigueur jusqu'à ce qu'il y soit légalement dérogé.

Droits particuliers garantis par l'État

69   Les militaires en activité de service, les officiers et soldats en retraite, les veuves, les officiers et soldats pensionnés conserveront leurs grades, honneurs et pensions.

70   La dette publique est garantie. Toute espèce d'engagement pris par l'État envers ses créanciers est inviolable.

71   La noblesse ancienne reprend ses titres. La nouvelle conserve les siens. Le Roi fait des nobles à volonté, mais il ne leur accorde que des rangs et des honneurs, sans aucune exemption des charges et devoirs de la société.

72   La Légion d'honneur est maintenue. Le Roi détermine les règlements intérieurs et la décoration.

74   Le Roi et ses successeurs jureront dans la solennité de leur sacre d'observer fidèlement la présente Charte constitutionnelle.

Donné à Paris, l'an de grace 1814 et de notre règne le dix-neuvième.

Signé: LOUIS.

Et plus bas, le ministre secrétaire d'État de l'intérieur, signé: Abbé De Montesquiou. Visa: le chancelier de France, signé: Dambray.

APPENDIX 4

The Declaration of the Chamber of Deputies and the clauses of the Constitutional Charter of 1830 which modified the Charter of 1814

1   Déclaration de la Chambre des Députés du 7 Août 1830.

La Chambre des Députés, prenant en considération l'impérieuse nécessité qui résulte des événements des 26, 27, 28, 29 juillet dernier et jours suivants, et de la situation générale où la France s'est trouvée placée à la suite de la violation de la Charte constitutionnelle; considérant en outre, que, par suite de cette violation et de la résistance héroique des citoyens de Paris, S. M. Charles X, S. A. R. Louis-Antoine, Dauphin, et tous les membres de la branche aînée de la maison royale, sortent en ce moment du territoire français – Déclare que le trône est vacant en fait et en droit, et qu'il est indispensable d'y pourvoir. Déclare secondement que, selon le voeu et dans l'intérêt du peuple français, le préambule de la Charte Constitutionnelle est supprimé, comme blessant la dignité nationale, en paraissant octroyer aux Français des droits qui leur appartiennent essentiellement et que les articles suivants de la même charte doivent être supprimés ou modifiés de la manière qui va être indiquée.

Moyennant l'acceptation de ces dispositions et propositions, la Chambre des députés déclare enfin que l'intérêt universel et pressant du peuple français appelle au trône S. A. R. Louis-Philippe d'Orléans, Duc d'Orléans, Lieutenant général du royaume, et ses descendants à perpétuité, de mâle en mâle, par ordre de primogéniture, et à l'exclusion perpétuelle des femmes et de leur descendance. En conséquence, S. A. R. Louis-Philippe d'Orléans, Duc d'Orléans, Lieutenant général du royaume, sera invité à accepter et à jurer les clauses et engagements ci-dessus énoncés, l'observation de la Charte constitutionnelle et des modifications indiquées, et, après l'avoir fait devant les Chambres assemblées, prendre le titre de Roi des Français.

2   Charte Constitutionnelle de 1830.

Louis-Philippe, etc.

Nous avons ordonné et ordonnons que la Charte constitutionnelle de 1814, telle qu'elle a été amendée par les deux Chambres le 7 août et acceptée par nous le 9, sera de nouveau publiée dans les termes suivants. *

ART. 6(7)   Les ministres de la religion catholique, apostolique et romaine, professée par la majorité des Français, et ceux des autres cultes chrétiens recoivent des traitements du trésor public.

7(8)   Les Français ont le droit de publier et de faire imprimer leurs opinions en se conformant aux lois. La censure ne pourra jamais être rétablie.

Formes du gouvernement du roi

13(14)   Le roi est le chef suprême de l'État; il commande les forces de terre et de mer, déclare la guerre, fait les traités de paix, d'alliance et de commerce, nomme à tous les emplois d'administration publique et fait les règlements et ordonnances nécessaires pour l'exécution des lois, sans pouvoir jamais ni suspendre les lois ellesmêmes, ni dispenser de leur exécution.

Toutefois aucune troupe étrangère ne pourra être admise au service de l'État qu'en vertu d'une loi.

15(16)   La proposition des lois appartient au Roi, à la Chambre des pairs et à la Chambre des députés. Néanmoins toute loi d'impôt doit être d'abord votée par la Chambre des députés.

17(21)   Si une proposition de loi a été rejetée par l'un des trois pouvoirs, elle ne pourra être représentée dans la même session.

De la Chambre des pairs

22(26)   Toute assemblée de la Chambre des pairs qui serait tenue hors du temps et la session de la Chambre des députés est illicite et nulle de plein droit, sauf le seul cas où elle est réunie comme cour de justice, et alors elle ne peut exercer que des fonctions judiciaires.

27(32)   Les séances de la Chambre des pairs sont publiques, comme celles de la Chambre des députés.

* Only the articles which were modified are here printed. Where they are different the numbers of the corresponding articles in the Charter of 1814 are indicated in brackets.

De la Chambre des députés

31(37)   Les députés sont élus pour cinq ans.

32(38)   Aucun député ne peut être admis dans la Chambre s'il n'est âgé de trente ans et s'il ne réunit les autres conditions déterminées par la loi.

34(40)   Nul n'est électeur s'il a moins de vingt-cinq ans, et s'il ne réunit les autres conditions déterminées par la loi.

35(41)   Les présidents des collèges électoraux sont nommés par les électeurs.

37(43)   Le président de la Chambre des députés est élu par elle à l'ouverture de chaque session.

Des ministres

L'ancien article 56 est supprimé.

De l'ordre judiciaire

54(63)   Il ne pourra en conséquence être créé de commissions et de tribunaux extraordinaires, à quelque titre et sous quelque dénomination que ce puisse être.

Droits particuliers

64(73)   Suppression des mots et des règlements.

65(74)   Le Roi et ses successeurs jureront à leur avènement, en présence des Chambres réunies, d'observer fidèlement la Charte constitutionnelle.

66(new)   La présente Charte et tous les droits qu'elle consacre demeurent confiés au patriotisme et au courage de gardes nationales et de tous les citoyens français.

67(new)   La France reprend ses couleurs. A l'avenir, il ne sera plus porté d'autre cocarde que la cocarde tricolore.

Dispositions particulières

68   Toutes les nominations et créations nouvelles de pairs faites sous le règne du roi Charles X sont déclarées nulles et non avenues.

69   Il sera pourvu successivement par des lois séparées et dans le plus court délai possible aux objets qui suivent.

   1   L'application du jury aux délits de la presse et aux délits politiques.

2   La responsabilité des ministres et des autres agents du pouvoir.

3   La réélection des députés promus à des fonctions publiques salariées.

4   Le vote annuel du contingent de l'armée.

5   L'organisation de la garde nationale avec intervention des gardes nationaux dans le choix de leurs officiers.

6   Des dispositions qui assurent d'une manière légale l'état des officiers de tout grade de terre et de mer.

7   Des institutions départementales et municipales fondées sur un système électif.

8   L'instruction publique et la liberté de l'enseignement.

9   L'abolition du double vote et la fraction des conditions électorales d'éligibilité.

Fait au Palais-Royal, à Paris, le 14e jour du mois d'août l'an 1830.
Signé: LOUIS-PHILIPPE.

APPENDIX 5

The Constitution of
4 November 1848*

Au nom du peuple français

L'Assemblée nationale a adopté, et le Président de l'Assemblée nationale promulgue la Constitution dont la teneur suit.

Préambule

En présence de Dieu et au nom du Peuple français, l'Assemblée nationale proclame:

I   La France s'est constituée en République. En adoptant cette forme définitive de gouvernement, elle s'est proposé pour but de marcher plus librement dans la voie du progrès et de la civilisation, d'assurer une répartition de plus en plus équitable des charges et des avantages de la société, d'augmenter l'aisance de chacun par la réduction graduée des dépenses publiques et des impôts, et de faire parvenir tous les citoyens, sans nouvelle commotion, par l'action successive et constante des institutions et des lois, à un degré toujours plus élevé de moralité, de lumières et de bien-être.

II   La République française est démocratique, une et indivisible.

III   Elle reconnaît des droits et des devoirs antérieurs et supérieurs aux lois positives.

IV   Elle a pour principes la Liberté, l'Égalité et la Fraternité.
Elle a pour bases la Famille, le Travail, la Propriété, l'Ordre public.

V   Elle respecte les nationalités étrangères comme elle entend faire respecter la sienne, n'entreprend aucune guerre dans des vues de conquête, et n'emploie jamais ses forces contre la liberté d'aucun peuple.

VI   Des devoirs réciproques obligent les citoyens envers la République, et la République envers les citoyens.

* Following Cahen et Mathiez I have omitted fifteen relatively unimportant articles.

VII   Les citoyens doivent aimer la Patrie, servir la République, la défendre au prix de leur vie, participer aux charges de l'État en proportion de leur fortune; ils doivent s'assurer, par le travail, des moyens d'existence, et, par la prévoyance, des ressources pour l'avenir; ils doivent concourir au bien-être commun en s'entr'aidant fraternellement les uns les autres et à l'ordre général en observant les lois morales et les lois écrites qui régissent la société, la famille et l'individu.

VIII   La République doit protéger le citoyen dans sa personne, sa famille, sa religion, sa propriété, son travail, et mettre à la portée de chacun l'instruction indispensable à tous les hommes; elle doit, par une assistance fraternelle, assurer l'existence des citoyens nécessiteux, soit en leur procurant du travail dans les limites de ses ressources, soit en donnant, à défaut de la famille, des secours à ceux qui sont hors d'état de travailler. En vue de l'accomplissement de tous ces devoirs, et pour la garantie de tous ces droits, l'Assemblée nationale fidèle aux traditions des grandes Assemblées qui ont inauguré la Révolution française décrète, ainsi qu'il suit, la Constitution de la République.

Constitution

CHAPITRE I

DE LA SOUVERAINETÉ

1   La souveraineté réside dans l'universalité des citoyens français. Elle est inaliénable et imprescriptible. Aucun individu, aucune fraction du peuple ne peut s'en attribuer l'exercice.

CHAPITRE II

DROITS DES CITOYENS GARANTIS PAR LA CONSTITUTION

2   Nul ne peut être arrêté ou détenu que suivant les prescriptions de la loi.

3   La demeure de toute personne habitant le territoire français est inviolable; il n'est permis d'y pénétrer que selon les formes et dans les cas prévus par la loi.

4   Nul ne sera distrait de ses juges naturels. Il ne pourra être créé de commissions et de tribunaux extraordinaires, à quelque titre et sous quelque dénomination que ce soit.

5   La peine de mort est abolie en matière politique.

6   L'esclavage ne peut exister sur aucune terre française.

7   Chacun professe librement sa religion et reçoit de l'État pour

l'exercice de son culte, une égale protection. Les ministres, soit des cultes actuellement reconnus par la loi, soit de ceux qui seraient reconnus à l'avenir, ont le droit de recevoir un traitement de l'État.

8   Les citoyens ont le droit de s'associer, de s'assembler paisiblement et sans armes, de pétitionner, de manifester leurs pensées par la voie de la presse ou autrement. L'exercice de ces droits n'a pour limite que les droits ou la liberté d'autrui et la sécurité publique. La presse ne peut, en aucun cas, être soumise à la censure.

9   L'enseignement est libre. La Liberté d'enseignement s'exerce selon les conditions de capacité et de moralité déterminées par les lois, et sous la surveillance de l'État. Cette surveillance s'étend à tous les établissements d'éducation et d'enseignement sans aucune exception.

10   Tous les citoyens sont également admissibles à tous les emplois publics, sans autre motif de préférence que leur mérite, et suivant les conditions qui seront fixées par les lois. Sont abolis à toujours tout titre nobiliaire, toute distinction de naissance, de classe ou de caste.

11   Toutes les propriétés sont inviolables. Néanmoins l'État peut exiger le sacrifice d'une propriété pour cause d'utilité publique légalement constatée, et moyennant une juste et préalable indemnité.

12   La confiscation des biens ne pourra jamais être rétablie.

13   La Constitution garantit aux citoyens la liberté du travail et de l'industrie. La société favorise et encourage le développement du travail par l'enseignement primaire gratuit, l'éducation professionnelle, l'égalité de rapports entre le patron et l'ouvrier, les institutions de prévoyance et de crédit, les institutions agricoles, les associations volontaires, et l'établissement, par l'État, les départements et les communes, de travaux publics propres à employer les bras inoccupés; elle fournit l'assistance aux enfants abandonnés, aux infirmes et aux vieillards sans ressources, et que leurs familles ne peuvent secourir.

14   La dette publique est garantie. Toute espèce d'engagement pris par l'État avec ses créanciers est inviolable.

15   Tout impôt est établi pour l'utilité commune. Chacun y contribue en proportion de ses facultés et de sa fortune.

16   Aucun impôt ne peut être établi ni perçu qu'en vertu d'une loi.

17   L'impôt direct n'est consenti que pour un an. Les impôts indirects peuvent être consentis pour plusieurs années.

CHAPITRE III

DES POUVOIRS PUBLICS

18   Tous les pouvoirs publics, quels qu'ils soient, émanent du peuple. Ils ne peuvent être délégués héréditairement.

19   La séparation des pouvoirs est la première condition d'un gouvernement libre.

CHAPITRE IV

DU POUVOIR LÉGISLATIF

20   Le Peuple français délègue le pouvoir législatif à une assemblée unique.

21   Le nombre total des représentants du peuple sera de 750, y compris les représentants de l'Algérie et des colonies françaises.

22   Ce nombre s'élèvera à 900 pour les assemblées qui seront appelées à reviser la Constitution.

23   L'élection a pour base la population.

24   Le suffrage est direct et universel. Le scrutin est secret.

25   Sont électeurs, sans condition de cens, tous les Français âgés de vingt-un ans, et jouissant de leurs droits civils et politiques.

26   Sont éligibles, sans condition de domicile, tous les électeurs âgés de vingt-cinq ans.

27   La loi électorale déterminera les causes qui peuvent priver les citoyens français du droit d'élire et d'être élu. . . .

28   Toute fonction publique rétribuée est incompatible avec le mandat de représentant du peuple. Aucun membre de l'Assemblée nationale ne peut, pendant la durée de la législature, être nommé ou promu à des fonctions publiques salariées dont les titulaires sont choisis à volonté par le Pouvoir exécutif. Les exceptions aux dispositions des deux paragraphes précédents seront déterminées par la loi électorale organique.

29   Les dispositions de l'article précédent ne sont pas applicables aux assemblées élues pour la revision de la Constitution.

30   L'élection des représentants se fera par département, et au scrutin de liste. Les électeurs voteront au chef-lieu du canton; néanmoins, en raison des circonstances locales, le canton pourra être divisé en plusieurs circonscriptions, dans la forme et aux conditions qui seront déterminées par la loi électorale.

31   L'Assemblée nationale est élue pour trois ans, et se renouvelle intégralement. La nouvelle Assemblée est convoquée de plein droit pour le lendemain du jour où finit le mandat de l'Assemblée précédente.

32   Elle est permanente. Néanmoins, elle peut s'ajourner à un terme qu'elle fixe. Pendant la durée de la prorogation, une commission composée des membres du bureau et de vingt-cinq représentants nommés par l'Assemblée au scrutin secret et à la majorité absolue a aussi le droit de la convoquer en cas d'urgence. Le Président de la République a aussi le droit

de convoquer l'Assemblée. L'Assemblée nationale détermine le lieu de ses séances. Elle fixe l'importance des forces militaires établies pour sa sûreté, et elle en dispose.

33   Les représentants sont toujours rééligibles.

34   Les membres de l'Assemblée nationale sont les représentants, non du département qui les nomme, mais de la France entière.

35   Ils ne peuvent recevoir de mandat impératif.

36   Les représentants du peuple sont inviolables. Ils ne pourront être recherchés, accusés, ni jugés, en aucun temps pour les opinions qu'ils auront émises dans le sein de l'Assemblée nationale.

37   Ils ne peuvent être arrêtés en matière criminelle, sauf le cas de flagrant délit, ni poursuivis qu'après que l'Assemblée a permis la poursuite. En cas d'arrestation pour flagrant délit, il en sera immédiatement référé à l'Assemblée, qui autorisera ou refusera la continuation des poursuites. . . .

38   Chaque représentant du peuple reçoit une indemnité à laquelle il ne peut renoncer.

39   Les séances de l'Assemblée sont publiques. Néanmoins, l'Assemblée peut se former en comité secret, sur la demande du nombre de représentants fixé par le règlement. Chaque représentant a le droit d'initiative parlementaire. . . .

40   La présence de la moitié plus un des membres de l'Assemblée est nécessaire pour la validité du vote des lois.

41   Aucun projet de loi, sauf les cas d'urgence, ne sera voté définitivement qu'après trois délibérations, à des intervalles qui ne peuvent être moindres de cinq jours. . . .

CHAPITRE V

DU POUVOIR EXÉCUTIF

43   Le peuple français délègue le pouvoir exécutif à un citoyen qui reçoit le titre dé Président de la République. . . .

45   Le Président de la République est élu pour quatre ans et n'est rééligible qu'après un intervalle de quatre années. Ne peuvent non plus être réélus après lui, dans le même intervalle, ni le vice-président, ni aucun des parents ou alliés du Président jusqu'au 6e degré inclusivement.

46   Le Président est nommé, au scrutin secret et à la majorité absolue des votants, par le suffrage direct de tous les électeurs des départements français et de l'Algérie.

47   Les procès-verbaux des opérations électorales sont transmis immédiatement à l'Assemblée nationale qui statue sans délai sur la

validité de l'élection et proclame le Président de la République. Si aucun candidat n'a obtenu plus de la moitié des suffrages exprimés, et au moins deux millions de voix, ou si les conditions exigées par l'article 44 ne sont pas remplies, l'Assemblée nationale élit le Président de la République, à la majorité absolue et au scrutin secret, parmi les cinq candidats éligibles qui ont obtenu le plus de voix.

48   Avant d'entrer en fonctions, le Président de la République prête au sein de l'Assemblée nationale le serment dont la teneur suit: EN PRÉSENCE DE DIEU ET DEVANT LE PEUPLE FRANÇAIS, REPRÉSENTÉ PAR L'ASSEMBLÉE NATIONALE JE JURE DE RESTER FIDÈLE À LA RÉPUBLIQUE DÉMOCRATIQUE, UNE ET INDIVISIBLE, ET DE REMPLIR TOUS LES DEVOIRS QUE M'IMPOSE LA CONSTITUTION.

49   Il a le droit de faire présenter des projets de loi à l'Assemblée nationale par les ministres. Il surveille et assure l'exécution des lois.

50   Il dispose de la force armée, sans pouvoir jamais la commander en personne.

51   Il ne peut céder aucune portion du territoire, ni dissoudre ni proroger l'Assemblée nationale, ni suspendre, en aucune manière, l'empire de la Constitution et des lois.

52   Il présente, chaque année, par un message, à l'Assemblée nationale, l'exposé de l'état général des affaires de la République.

53   Il négocie et ratifie les traités. Aucun traité n'est définitif qu'après avoir été approuvé par l'Assemblée nationale.

54   Il veille à la défense de l'État, mais il ne peut entreprendre aucune guerre sans le consentement de l'Assemblée nationale.

55   Il a le droit de faire grâce, mais il ne peut exercer ce droit qu'après avoir pris l'avis du Conseil d'État. Les amnisties ne peuvent être accordées que par une loi. Le Président de la République, les ministres, ainsi que toutes les autres personnes condamnées par la Haute-Cour de justice, ne peuvent être graciés que par l'Assemblée nationale.

56   Le Président de la République promulgue les lois au nom du Peuple français. . . .

58   . . . Le Président de la République peut, par un message motivé, demander une nouvelle délibération. L'Assemblée délibère, sa résolution devient définitive, elle est transmise au Président de la République . . .

62   Il (le Président) est logé aux frais de la République et reçoit un traitement de 600,000 francs par an

63   Il réside au lieu où siège l'Assemblée nationale, et ne peut sortir du territoire continental de la République sans y être autorisé par une loi.

64   Le Président de la République nomme et révoque les ministres. Il nomme et révoque, en conseil des ministres, les agents diplomatiques, les

commandants en chef des armées de terre et de mer, les préfets, le commandant supérieur des gardes nationaux de la Seine.

. . . Il nomme et révoque, sur la proposition du ministre compétent, dans les conditions réglementaires déterminées par la loi, les agents secondaires du gouvernement.

65 Il a le droit de suspendre pour un terme qui ne pourra pas excéder trois mois les agents du pouvoir exécutif élus par les citoyens, il ne peut les révoquer que de l'avis du Conseil d'État. . . .

66 Le nombre des ministres et leurs attributions sont fixés par le pouvoir législatif.

67 Les actes du Président de la République, autres que ceux par lesquels il nomme et révoque les ministres, n'ont d'effet que s'ils sont contre-signés par un ministre.

68 Le Président de la République, les ministres, les agents et dépositaires de l'autorité publique, sont responsables, chacun en ce qui le concerne, de tous les actes du Gouvernement et de l'administration. Toute mesure par laquelle le Président de la République dissout l'Assemblée nationale, la proroge ou met obstacle à l'exercice de son mandat, est un crime de haute trahison. Par ce seul fait, le Président est déchu de ses fonctions; les citoyens sont tenus de lui refuser obéissance; le pouvoir exécutif passe de plein droit a l'Assemblée nationale. Les juges de la Haute Cour de justice se réunissent immédiatement à peine de forfaiture: ils convoquent les jurés dans le lieu qu'ils désignent, pour procéder au jugement du Président et de ses complices; ils nomment eux-mêmes les magistrats chargés de remplir les fonctions de ministère public. Une loi déterminera les autres cas de responsabilité, ainsi que les formes et les conditions de la poursuite.

69 Les ministres ont entrée dans le sein de l'Assemblée nationale; ils sont entendus toutes les fois qu'ils le demandent, et peuvent se faire assister par des commissaires nommés par un décret du Président de la République.

70 Il y a un Vice-Président de la République nommé par l'Assemblée nationale, sur la présentation de trois candidats faite par le Président dans le mois qui suit son élection. Le Vice-Président prête la même serment que le Président. Le Vice-Président ne pourra être choisi parmi les parents ou alliés du Président jusqu'au 6e degré inclusivement. En cas d'empêchement du Président, le Vice-Président le remplace. Si la présidence devient vacante par décès, démission du Président, ou autrement, il est procédé, dans le mois, a l'élection d'un Président.

CHAPITRE VI
DU CONSEIL D'ÉTAT

71 Il y aura un Conseil d'État, dont le Vice-Président de la République sera de droit président.

72   Les membres de ce conseil sont nommés pour six ans par l'Assemblée nationale. Ils sont renouvelés par moitié, dans les deux premiers mois de chaque législature, au scrutin secret et à la majorité absolue. Ils sont indéfiniment rééligibles.

73   Ceux des membres du Conseil d'État qui auront été pris dans le sein de l'Assemblée nationale seront immédiatement remplacés comme représentants du peuple.

74   Les membres du Conseil d'État ne peuvent être révoqués que par l'Assemblée et sur la proposition du Président de la République.

75   Le Conseil d'État est consulté sur les projets de loi du Gouvernement qui, d'après la loi, devront être soumis à son examen préalable, et sur les projets d'initiative parlementaire que l'Assemblée lui aura renvoyés. Il prépare les règlements d'administration publique; il fait seul ceux de ces règlements à l'égard desquels l'Assemblée nationale lui a donné une délégation spéciale. Il exerce à l'égard des administrations publiques tous les pouvoirs de surveillance et de contrôle qui lui sont déférés par la loi. . . .

CHAPITRE VII

DE L'ADMINISTRATION INTÉRIEURE

76   La division du territoire en départements, arrondissements, cantons et communes, est maintenue. Les circonsciptions actuelles ne pourront être changées que par la loi.

77   Il y a: 1e dans chaque département une administration composée d'un préfet, d'un conseil général, d'un conseil de préfecture; 2e dans chaque arrondissement, un sous-préfet; 3e dans chaque canton, un conseil cantonal; 4e dans chaque commune, une administration composée d'un maire, d'adjoints et d'un conseil municipal.

79   Les conseils généraux et les conseils municipaux sont élus par le suffrage direct de tous les citoyens domiciliés dans le département et dans la commune. Chaque canton élit un membre du Conseil général. Une loi spéciale réglera le mode d'élection dans le département de la Seine, dans la ville de Paris et dans les villes de plus de 200.000 âmes.

80   Les Conseils généraux, cantonaux et municipaux peuvent être dissous par le Président de la République, de l'avis du Conseil d'État.

CHAPITRE VIII

DU POUVOIR JUDICIAIRE

81   La justice est rendue gratuitement au nom du Peuple français. Les débats sont publics, à moins que la publicité ne soit dangéreuse pour

l'ordre ou les moeurs; et, dans ce cas, le tribunal le déclare par un jugement.

82   Le jury continuera d'être appliqué en matière criminelle.

83   La connaissance de tous les délits politiques et de tous les délits
commis par la voie de la presse appartient exclusivement au jury. Les lois
organiques détermineront la compétence en matière de délits d'injures et
de diffamation contre les particuliers.

84   Le jury statue seul sur les dommages-intérêts réclamés pour faits
ou délits de presse.

85   Les juges de paix et leurs suppléants, les juges de première
instance et d'appel, les membres de la Cour de cassation et de la Cour des
comptes, sont nommés par le Président de la République, d'après un
ordre de candidature ou d'après des conditions qui seront réglées par les
lois organiques.

86   Les magistrats du ministère sont nommés par le Président de la
République.

87   Les juges de première instance et d'appel, les membres de la Cour
de cassation et de la Cour des comptes sont nommés à vie. Ils ne peuvent
être révoqués ou suspendus que par un jugement, ni mis à la retraite que
pour les causes et dans les formes déterminées par les lois.

88   Les conseils de guerre et de revision des armées de terre et de mer,
les tribunaux maritimes, les tribunaux de commerce, les prud'hommes et
autres tribunaux spéciaux, conservent leur organisation et leurs attributions actuelles jusqu'à ce qu'il y ait été dérogé par une loi.

89   Les conflits d'attributions entre l'autorité administrative et
l'autorité judiciaire seront réglés par un tribunal spécial de membres de la
Cour de cassation et de conseillers d'État, désignés tous les trois ans en
nombre égal par leur corps respectif. Ce tribunal sera présidé par le
ministre de la justice.

91   Une Haute Cour de justice juge, sans appel ni recours en cassation
les accusations portées par l'Assemblée nationale contre le Président de la
République, ou les ministres. Elle juge également toutes personnes
prévenues de crimes, attentats ou complots contre la sûreté intérieure ou
extérieure de l'État, que l'Assemblée nationale aura renvoyées devant
elle. . . .

92   La Haute Cour est composée de 5 juges et de 36 jurés. Chaque
année, dans les quinze premiers jours du mois de novembre, la Cour de
cassation nomme, parmi ses membres, au scrutin secret et à la majorité
absolue, les juges de la Haute Cour au nombre de 5 et 2 suppléants. Les 5
juges appelés à siéger font choix de leur président. Les magistrats remplis-
sant les fonctions du ministère public sont désignés par le Président de la
République, et, en cas d'accusation du Président ou des ministres, par

l'Assemblée nationale. Les jurés au nombre de 36 et 4 jurés suppléants sont pris parmi les membres des Conseils généraux des départements. Les représentants du peuple n'en peuvent faire partie. . . .

96　L'accusé et le ministère public exercent le droit de récusation comme en matière ordinaire.

97　La déclaration du jury portant que l'accusé est coupable ne peut être rendue qu'à la majorité des deux tiers des voix.

98　Dans tous les cas de responsabilité des ministres, l'Assemblée nationale peut, selon les circonstances, renvoyer le ministre inculpé, soit devant la Haute Cour de justice, soit devant les tribunaux ordinaires, pour les réparations civiles.

99　L'Assemblée nationale et le Président de la République peuvent, dans tous les cas, déférer l'examen des actes de tout fonctionnaire, autre que le Président de la République, au Conseil d'État, dont le rapport est rendu public.

100　Le Président de la République n'est justiciable que de la Haute Cour de justice. Il ne peut, á l'exception du cas prévu par l'article 68, être poursuivi que sur l'accusation portée par l'Assemblée nationale, et pour crimes et délits qui seront déterminés par la loi.

CHAPITRE IX

DE LA FORCE PUBLIQUE

101　La force publique est instituée pour défendre l'État contre les ennemis du dehors, et pour assurer au dedans le maintien de l'ordre et l'exécution des lois. Elle se compose de la garde nationale et de l'armée de terre et de mer.

102　Tout Français, sauf les exceptions fixées par la loi, doit le service militaire et celui de la garde nationale. La faculté pour chaque citoyen de se libérer du service militaire personnel sera réglée par la loi du recrutement.

103　L'organisation de la garde nationale et la constitution de l'armée seront reglées par la loi.

104　La force publique est essentiellement obéissante. Nul corps armé ne peut délibérer.

105　La force publique, employée pour maintenir l'ordre à l'intérieur, n'agit que sur la réquisition des autorités constituées, suivant les règles déterminées par le Pouvoir législatif.

106　Une loi déterminera les cas dans lesquels l'état de siège pourra être déclaré, et réglera les formes et les effets de cette mesure.

107   Aucune troupe étrangère ne peut être introduite sur le territoire français sans le consentement préalable de l'Assemblée nationale.

CHAPITRE X

DISPOSITIONS PARTICULIÉRES

108   La Légion d'honneur est maintenue et ses statuts seront revisés et mis en harmonie avec la Constitution.

CHAPITRE XI

DE LA REVISION DE LA CONSTITUTION

111   Lorsque, dans la dernière année d'une législature, l'Assemblée nationale aura émis le voeu que la Constitution soit modifiée en tout ou en partie, il sera procédé à cette revision de la manière suivante: Le voeu exprimé par l'Assemblée ne sera converti en résolution définitive qu'après trois déliberations consécutives, prises chacune à un mois d'intervalle, et aux trois quarts des suffrages exprimés. Le nombre des votants devra être de 500 au moins. L'assemblée de revision ne sera convoquée que pour trois mois; elle ne devra s'occuper que de la revision pour laquelle elle aura été convoquée. . . .

CHAPITRE XII

DISPOSITIONS TRANSITOIRES

112   Les dispositions des Codes, lois et règlements existants, qui ne sont pas contraires à la présente Constitution restent en vigueur jusqu'à ce qu'il y soit légalement dérogé. . . .

113   Il sera procédé à la première élection du Président de la République, conformément à loi spéciale rendue par L'Assemblée nationale, le 28 octobre 1848.

APPENDIX 6

The Constitution of 1852

1   Constitution Faite en Vertu des Pouvoirs délégués par le Peuple
Français à Louis-Napoléon Bonaparte par le Vote des 20 et 21 Decembre
1851.

14–22 juin 1852.

TITRE I

ARTICLE PREMIER. – La Constitution reconnâit, confirme et
garantit les grands principes proclamés en 1789 et qui sont la base du droit
public des Français.

TITRE II

FORME DU GOUVERNEMENT DE LA RÉPUBLIQUE

2   Le gouvernement de la République française est confié pour dix ans
au prince Louis-Napoléon Bonaparte, président actuel de la République.

3   Le Président de la République gouverne au moyen des ministres,
du Conseil d'État, du Sénat et du Corps législatif.

4   La puissance législative, s'exerce collectivement par le Président de
la République, le Sénat et le Corps législatif.

TITRE III

DU PRÉSIDENT DE LA RÉPUBLIQUE

5   Le Président de la République est responsable devant le peuple
français, auquel il a toujours le droit de faire appel.

6   Le Président de la République est le chef de l'État. Il commande les

forces de terre et de mer, déclare la guerre, fait les traités de paix, d'alliance et de commerce, nomme à tous les emplois, fait les règlements et décrets nécessaires pour l'exécution des lois.

7   La justice se rend en son nom.

8   Il a seul l'initiative des lois.

9   Il a le droit de faire grâce.

10   Il sanctionne et promulgue les lois et les sénatus-consultes.

11   Il présente, tous les ans, au Sénat et au Corps législatif, par un message, l'état des affaires de la République.

12   Il a le droit de déclarer l'état de siège dans un ou plusieurs départements, sauf à en référer au Sénat dans le plus bref délai.

Les conséquences de l'état de siège sont réglées par la loi.

13   Les ministres ne dépendent que du chef de l'État; ils ne sont responsables que, chacun en ce qui le concerne, des actes du gouvernement; il n'y a point de solidarité entre eux; ils ne peuvent être mis en accusation que par le Sénat.

14   Les ministres, les membres du Sénat, du Corps législatif et du Conseil d'État, les officiers de terre et de mer, les magistrats et les fonctionnaires publics prêtent le serment ainsi conçu: *je jure obéissance à la Constitution et fidélité au Président.*

15   Un sénatus-consulte fixe la somme allouée annuellement au Président de la République pour toute la durée de ses fonctions.

16   Si le Président de la République meurt avant l'expiration de son mandat, le Sénat convoque la nation pour procéder à une nouvelle élection.

17   Le chef d'État a le droit, par un acte secret et déposé aux archives du Sénat, de désigner le nom du citoyen qu'il recommande, dans l'intérêt de la France, à la confiance du peuple et à ses suffrages.

18   Jusqu'à l'élection du nouveau Président de la République, le président du Sénat gouverne avec le concours des ministres en fonctions, qui se forment en conseil de gouvernement, et délibèrent à la majorité des voix.

TITRE IV

DU SÉNAT

19   Le nombre des sénateurs ne pourra excéder cent cinquante; il est fixé, pour la première année, à quatre-vingts.

20   Le Sénat se compose: 1° des cardinaux, des maréchaux, des amiraux; 2° des citoyens que le Président de la République juge convenable d'élever à la dignité de sénateur.

21   Les sénateurs sont inamovibles et à vie.

22   Les fonctions de sénateur sont gratuites; néanmoins le Président de la République pourra accorder à des sénateurs, en raison des services rendus et de leur position de fortune, une dotation personnelle, qui ne pourra excéder trente mille francs par an.

23   Le président et les vice-présidents du Sénat sont nommés par le Président de la République et choisis parmi les sénateurs. Ils sont nommés pour un an. Le traitement du président du Sénat est fixé par un décret.

24   Le Président de la République convoque et proroge le Sénat. Il fixe la durée de ses sessions par un décret. Les séances du Sénat ne sont pas publiques.

25   Le Sénat est le gardien du pacte fondamental et des libertés publiques. Aucune loi ne peut être promulguée avant de lui avoir été soumise.

26   Le Sénat s'oppose à la promulgation: 1^0 des lois qui seraient contraires ou qui porteraient atteinte à la Constitution, à la religion, à la morale, à la liberté des cultes, à la liberté individuelle, à l'égalité des citoyens devant la loi, à l'inviolabilité de la propriété et au principe de l'inamovibilité de la magistrature; 2^0 de celles qui pourraient compromettre la défense du territoire.

27   Le Sénat règle par un sénatus-consulte: 1^0 la Constitution des colonies et de l'Algérie; 2^0 tout ce qui n'a été prévu par la Constitution et qui est nécessaire à sa marche; 3^0 le sens des articles de la Constitution qui donne lieu à différentes interprétations.

28   Ces sénatus-consultes seront soumis à la sanction du Président de la République et promulgués par lui.

29   Le Sénat maintient ou annule tous les actes qui sont déférés comme inconstitutionnels par le gouvernement ou dénoncés pour la même cause par les pétitions des citoyens.

30   Le Sénat peut, dans un rapport addressé au Président de la République, poser les bases des projets de lois d'un grand intérêt national.

31   Il peut également proposer des modifications à la Constitution. Si la proposition est adoptée par le pouvoir exécutif, il y est statué par un sénatus-consulte.

32   Néanmoins, sera soumise au suffrage universel toute modification aux bases fondamentales de la Constitution, telles qu'elles ont été posées dans la proclamation du 2 décembre et adoptées par le peuple français.

33   En cas de dissolution du Corps législatif et jusqu'à une nouvelle convocation, le Sénat, sur la proposition du Président de la République, pourvoit par des mesures d'urgence à tout ce qui est nécessaire à la marche du gouvernement.

DU CORPS LÉGISLATIF

34   L'élection a pour base la population.

35   Il y aura un député au Corps législatif à raison de 35,000 électeurs.

36   Les députés sont élus par le suffrage universel, sans scrutin de liste.

37   Ils ne reçoivent aucun traitement.

38   Ils sont nommés pour six ans.

39   Le Corps législatif discute et vote les projets de loi et l'impôt.

40   Tout amendement adopté par la commission chargée d'examiner un projet de loi sera renvoyé sans discussion au Conseil d'État par le président du Corps législatif. Si l'amendement n'est pas adopté par le Conseil d'État, il ne pourra pas être soumis à la délibération du Corps législatif.

41   Les sessions ordinaires du Corps législatif durent trois mois; ses séances sont publiques, mais la demande de cinq membres suffit pour qu'il se forme en comité secret.

42   Le compte-rendu des séances du Corps législatif par les journaux ou tout autre moyen de publication ne consistera que dans la reproduction du procès-verbal dressé, à l'issue de chaque séance, par les soins du président du Corps législatif.

43   Le Président et les vice-présidents du Corps législatif sont nommés par le Président de la République pour un an. Ils sont choisis parmi les députés. Le traitement du président du Corps législatif est fixé par un décret.

44   Les ministres ne peuvent être membres du Corps législatif.

45   Le droit de pétition s'exerce auprès du Sénat. Aucune pétition ne peut être addressée au Corps législatif.

46   Le Président de la République convoque, ajourne, proroge et dissout le Corps législatif. En cas de dissolution le Président de la République doit en convoquer un nouveau dans le délai de six mois.

DU CONSEIL D'ÉTAT

47   Le nombre des conseillers d'État en service ordinaire est de quarante à cinquante.

48   Les conseillers d'État sont nommés par le Président de la République et révocables par lui.

49 Le Conseil d'État est présidé par le Président de la République et, en son absence, par la personne qu'il désigne comme vice-président du Conseil d'État.

50 Le Conseil d'État est chargé, sous la direction du Président de la République, de rédiger les projets de loi et les règlements d'administration publique et de résoudre les difficultés qui s'élèvent en matière d'administration.

51 Il soutient, au nom du gouvernement, la discussion des projets de lois devant le Sénat et le Corps législatif. Les conseillers d'État chargés de porter la parole au nom du gouvernement sont désignés par le Président de la République.

52 Le traitement de chaque conseiller d'État est de 25.000 francs.

53 Les ministres ont rang, séance et voix délibérative au Conseil d'État.

TITRE VII

DE LA HAUTE COUR DE JUSTICE

54 Une Haute Cour de justice juge, sans appel ni recours en cassation, toutes personnes qui auront été renvoyées devant elle comme prévenues de crimes, attentats ou complots contre le Président de la République et contre la sûreté intérieure ou extérieure de l'État. Elle ne peut être saisie qu'en vertu d'un décret du Président de la République.

55 Un sénatus-consulte déterminera l'organisation de cette Haute Cour.

TITRE VIII

DISPOSITIONS GÉNÉRALES ET TRANSITOIRES

56 Les dispositions des codes, lois et règlements existants, qui ne sont pas contraires à la présente constitution, restent en vigueur jusqu'à ce qu'il y soit légalement dérogé.

57 Une loi déterminera l'organisation muncipale. Les maires seront nommés par le pouvoir exécutif et pourront être pris hors du Conseil municipal.

58 La présente constitution sera en vigueur à dater du jour où les grands corps de l'État qu'elle organise seront constitués. Les décrets rendus par le Président de la République, à partir du 2 décembre jusqu'à cette époque, auront force de loi.

APPENDIX 7

The 'Constitution' of 1875

I LOI CONSTITUTIONNELLE SUR LES RAPPORTS DES POUVOIRS PUBLICS

16–18 juillet 1875

1   Le Sénat et la Chambre des députés se réunissent chaque année, le second mardi de janvier, à moins d'une convocation antérieure faite par le Président de la République. Les deux Chambres doivent être réunies en session cinq mois au moins chaque année. La session de l'une commence et finit en même temps que celle de l'autre.

Le dimanche qui suivra la rentrée, des prières publiques seront addressées a Dieu dans les églises et dans les temples pour appeler son secours sur les travaux des Assemblées.

2   Le Président de la République prononce la clôture de la session. Il a le droit de convoquer extraordinairement les Chambres. Il devra les convoquer si la demande en est faite, dans l'intervalle des sessions, par la majorité absolue des membres composant chaque Chambre. Le Président peut ajourner les Chambres. Toutefois, l'ajournement ne peut excéder le terme d'un mois ni avoir lieux plus de deux fois dans la même session.

3   Un mois au moins avant le terme légal des pouvoirs du Président de la République, les Chambres devront être réunies en Assemblée nationale pour procéder à l'élection du nouveau Président. A défaut de convocation, cette réunion aurait lieu de plein droit le quinzième jour avant l'expiration de ces pouvoirs. En cas de décès ou de démission du President de la République, les deux Chambres se réunissent immédiatement et de plein droit.

Dans le cas où, par application de l'article 5 de la loi du 25 février 1875, la Chambre des députés se trouverait dissoute au moment où la présidence de la République deviendrait vacante, les collèges électoraux seraient aussitôt convoqués, et le Sénat se réunirait de plein droit.

4   Toute assemblée de l'une des deux Chambres qui serait tenue hors

du temps de la session commune est illicite et nulle de plein droit, sauf le cas prévu par l'article précédent et celui où le Sénat est réuni comme cour de justice; et, dans ce dernier cas, il ne peut exercer que des fonctions judiciaires.

5   Les séances du Sénat et celles de la Chambre des députés sont publiques. Néanmoins, chaque Chambre peut se former en comité secret, sur la demande d'un certain nombre de ses membres, fixé par le règlement. Elle décide ensuite, à la majorité absolue, si la séance doit être reprise en public sur le même sujet.

6   Le Président de la République communique avec les Chambres par des messages qui sont lus à la tribune par un ministre. Les ministres ont leur entrée dans les deux Chambres et doivent être entendus quand ils le demandent. Ils peuvent se faire assister par des commissaires désignés, pour la discussion d'un projet de loi déterminé, par décret du Président de la République.

7   Le Président de la République promulgue les lois dans le mois qui suit la transmission au gouvernement de la loi définitivement adoptée. Il doit promulger dans les trois jours les lois dont la promulgation, par un vote exprès dans l'une et l'autre Chambre, aura été declarée urgente. Dans le délai fixé pour la promulgation, le Président de la République peut, par un message motivé, demander aux deux Chambres une nouvelle délibération qui ne peut être refusée.

8   Le Président de la République négocie et ratifie les traités. Il en donne connaissance aux Chambres aussitôt que l'intérêt et la sûreté de l'État le permettent. Les traités de paix, de commerce, les traités qui engagent les finances de l'État, ceux qui sont relatifs à l'état des personnes et au droit de propriété des Français à l'étranger, ne sont définitifs qu'après avoir été votés par les deux Chambres. Nulle cession, nul échange, nulle adjonction de territoire ne peut avoir lieu qu'en vertu d'une loi.

9   Le Président de la République ne peut déclarer la guerre sans l'assentiment préalable des deux Chambres.

10   Chacune des Chambres est juge de l'éligibilité de ses membres et de la régularité de leur élection; elle peut seule recevoir leur démission.

11   Le bureau de chacune des deux Chambres est élu chaque année pour la durée de la session et pour toute session extraordinaire qui aurait lieu avant la session ordinaire de l'année suivante. Lorsque les deux Chambres se réunissent en Assemblée nationale, leur bureau se compose du président, vice-président et secrétaires du Sénat.

12   Le Président de la République ne peut être mis en accusation que par la Chambre des députés et ne peut être jugé que par le Sénat. Les ministres peuvent être mis en accusation par la Chambre des députés pour

crimes commis dans l'exercice de leurs fonctions. En ce cas ils sont jugés par le Sénat.

Le Sénat peut être constitué en cour de justice par un décret du Président de la République, rendu en conseil des ministres, pour juger toute personne prévenue d'attentat commis contre la sûreté de l'État.

Si l'instruction est commencée par la justice ordinaire, le décret de convocation du Sénat peut être rendu jusqu'à l'arrêt de renvoi. Une loi déterminera le mode de procéder pour l'accusation, l'instruction et le jugement.

13 Aucun membre de l'une ou l'autre Chambre ne peut être poursuivi ou recherché à l'occasion des opinions ou votes émis par lui dans l'exercice de ses fonctions.

14 Aucun membre de l'une ou l'autre Chambre ne peut, pendant la durée de la session, être poursuivi ou arrêté en matière criminelle ou correctionnelle qu'avec l'autorisation de la Chambre dont il fait partie, sauf le cas de flagrant délit. La détention ou la poursuite d'un membre de l'une ou de l'autre Chambre est suspendue pendant la session et pour toute sa durée, si la Chambre le requiert.

II LOI RELATIVE À L'ORGANISATION DES POUVOIRS PUBLICS

25–28 février 1875

1 Le pouvoir législatif s'exerce par deux assemblées, la Chambre des députés et le Sénat. La Chambre des députés est nommée par le suffrage universel, dans des conditions déterminées par la loi électorale. La composition, le mode de nomination et les attributions du Sénat seront réglés par une loi spéciale.

2 Le Président de la République est élu à la majorité absolue des suffrages par le Sénat et par la Chambre des députés réunis en assemblée nationale. Il est nommé pour sept ans. Il est rééligible.

3 Le Président de la République a l'initiative des lois, concurremment avec les membres des deux Chambres. Il promulgue les lois lorsqu'elles ont été votées par les deux Chambres; il en surveille et en assure l'exécution. Il a le droit de faire grâce; les amnisties ne peuvent être accordées que par une loi. Il dispose de la force armée. Il nomme à tous les emplois civils et militaires. Il préside aux solennités nationales. Les envoyés et les ambassadeurs des puissances étrangères sont accrédités auprès de lui.

Chacun des actes du Président de la République doit être contresigné par un ministre.

4   Au fur et à mesure des vacances qui se produiront à partir de la promulgation de la présente loi, le Président de la République nomme, en conseil des ministres, les conseillers d'État en service ordinaire. Les conseillers d'État ainsi nommés ne pourront être révoqués que par décret rendu en conseil des ministres. Les conseillers d'État nommés en vertu de la loi du 24 mai 1872 ne pourront, jusqu'à l'expiration de leurs pouvoirs, être révoqués que dans la forme déterminée par cette loi. Après la séparation de l'Assemblée nationale, la révocation ne pourra être prononcée que par une résolution du Sénat.

5   Le Président de la République peut, sur l'avis conforme du Sénat, dissoudre la Chambre des députés avant l'expiration légale de son mandat. En ce cas, les collèges électoraux sont convoqués pour de nouvelles élections dans le délai de trois mois.

6   Les ministres sont solidairement responsables devant les Chambres de la politique générale du gouvernement et individuellement de leurs actes personnels. Le Président de la République n'est responsable que dans le cas de haute trahison.

7   En cas de vacance par décès ou pour toute autre cause, les deux Chambres réunies procèdent immédiatement à l'élection d'un nouveau président. Dans l'intervalle, le conseil des ministres est investi du pouvoir exécutif.

8   Les Chambres auront le droit, par délibérations séparées, prises dans chacune à la majorité absolue des voix, soit spontanément, soit sur la demande du Président de la République, de déclarer qu'il y a lieu de reviser les lois constitutionnelles. Après que chacune des deux Chambres aura pris cette résolution, elles se réuniront en Assemblée nationale pour procéder à la revision. Les délibérations portant revision des lois constitutionnelles, en tout ou en partie, devront être prises à la majorité absolue des membres composant l'Assemblée nationale. Toutefois, pendant la durée des pouvoirs conférés par la loi du 20 novembre 1873 à M. le maréchal de Mac-Mahon, cette revision ne peut avoir lieu que sur la proposition du Président de la République.

9   Le siège du pouvoir exécutif et des deux Chambres est à Versailles.

III   LOI RELATIVE À L'ORGANISATION DU SÉNAT

24-28 février 1875

1   Le Sénat se compose de 300 membres: 225 élus par les départements et les colonies et 75 élus par l'Assemblée nationale.

2   Les départements de la Seine et du Nord éliront chacun 5 sénateurs Les départements de la Seine-Inférieure, Pas-de-Calais, Gironde, Rhône,

Finistère, Côtes-du-Nord, chacun 4 sénateurs. La Loire-Inférieure, Saône et Loire, Ille-et-Vilaine, Seine-et-Oise, Isère, Puy-de-Dôme, Somme, Bouches-du-Rhône, Aisne, Loire, Manche, Maine-et-Loire, Morbihan, Dordogne, Haute-Garonne, Charente-Inférieure, Calvados, Sarthe, Hérault, Basses-Pyrénées, Gard, Aveyron, Vendée, Orne, Oise, Vosges, Allier, chacun 3 sénateurs. Tous les autres départements chacun 2 sénateurs. Le territoire de Belfort, les trois départements de l'Algérie, les quatre colonies de la Martinique, de la Guadeloupe, de la Réunion et des Indes françaises éliront chacun un sénateur.

3   Nul ne peut être sénateur s'il n'est Français, âgé de quarante ans au moins et s'il ne jouit de ses droits civils et politiques.

4   Les sénateurs des départements et des colonies sont élus à la majorité absolue et, quand il y a lieu, au scrutin de liste, par un collège réuni au chef-lieu du département ou de la colonie et composé: 1^0 des députés; 2^0 des conseillers généraux; 3^0 des conseillers d'arrondissement; 4^0 des délégués élus, un par chaque conseil municipal, parmi les électeurs de la commune.

Dans l'Inde française, les membres du conseil colonial ou des conseils locaux sont substitués aux conseillers généraux, aux conseillers d'arrondissement etaux délégués des conseils municipaux. Ils votent au chef-lieu de chaque établissement.

5   Les sénateurs, nommés par l'Assemblée, sont élus au scrutin de liste à la majorité absolue des suffrages.

6   Les sénateurs des départements et des colonies sont élus pour neuf années et renouvelables par tiers, tous les trois ans.

Au début de la première session, les départements seront divisés en trois séries contenant chacune un égal nombre de sénateurs. Il sera procédé, par la voie du tirage au sort, à la désignation des séries qui devront être renouvelées a l'expiration de la première et de la deuxième periode triennale.

7   Les sénateurs élus par l'Assemblée sont inamovibles. En cas de vacance par décès, démission ou toute autre cause, il sera, dans les deux mois, pourvu au remplacement par le Sénat lui-même.

8   Le Sénat a, concurremment avec la Chambre des députés, l'initiative et la confection des lois. Toutefois, les lois de finances doivent être, en premier lieu, présentées à la Chambre des députés et votées par elle.

9   Le Sénat peut être constitué en Cour de justice pour juger, soit le Président de la République, soit les ministres et pour connaître des attentats commis contre la sûreté de l'État.

10   Il sera procédé à l'élection du Sénat, un mois avant l'époque fixée par l'Assemblée nationale pour sa séparation. Le Sénat entrera en

fonctions et se constituera le jour même où l'Assemblée nationale se séparera.

11   La présente loi ne pourra être promulguée qu'après le vote définitif de la loi sur les pouvoirs publics.

Index